THE TRUTH OF CHRISTIAN GNOSIS

The Truth of
Christian Gnosis

JEAN BORELLA

Translated by G. John Champoux

Angelico Press

Originally published in French as
Problèmes de gnose
Copyright © L'Harmattan, 2007
5–7, rue de l'Ecole polytechnique; 75005 Paris

First published in the USA
by Angelico Press 2023
Copyright © Angelico Press 2023

All rights reserved:
No part of this book may be reproduced or transmitted,
in any form or by any means, without permission

For information, address:
Angelico Press, Ltd.
169 Monitor St.
Brooklyn, NY 11222
www.angelicopress.com

ppr 978-1-62138-937-8
cloth 978-1-62138-938-5

Book and cover design
by Michael Schrauzer

CONTENTS

PREFACE xi

FIRST PART
General Problems of Gnosis 1

CHAPTER 1
Christian Gnosis and Antichristian Gnosis 3
Position of the Problem—3; Gnosis and Gnosticism—6; Modern Gnosticism—13

CHAPTER 2
The Scriptural Origins of Gnosis 19

CHAPTER 3
Truly Named Gnosis 33
"Gnosis" and "Gnosticism" in the Early Centuries—34; Criteriology—41; Theology—49; Gnosis Consummated—56

SECOND PART
Gnostics of the 19th and 20th Centuries 63

CHAPTER 4
Hegel, or the Transformation of Gnosis into Logic 65
Genuine Gnosis and Apparent Gnosis—65; Hegelian Pseudo-Gnosis—69; Alienation of Religious Consciousness and Cultural History—74; The Sophistry of Becoming—77; The Failure of the Symbol According to Hegel—85; Conclusion: The Confinement of the Sacred—94

CHAPTER 5
Ruyerian Gnosis, A Religion of the Scientific Age 105
The History of a Title—107; The Nature of the Ruyerian Project—110; Comtian Synthesis and Ruyerian Synthesis—112; From the God of Life to the God of the Cosmos—116; Semantic Participation, the Key to Ruyerian Gnosis—118; Eleusinian Initiation—121; Ruyerian Gnosis: A "Cosmologism"?—123

CHAPTER 6
Gnosis and Gnosticism in René Guénon 134
Encounter with the Neo-Gnostics—137; Gnosis: Sacred Intellectuality—152; Gnosis and the Possibles—158; Appendix I—205; Appendix II—207

CHAPTER 7
Christian Dogma and Schuonian Gnosis 210
Introduction—210; On the Nature of Dogma—223; Some Points of Dogmatic History—239; The Dogmatic Cavern of Gnosis—245; Conclusion—256

THIRD PART
Concerning Christian Gnosis According to its Essence 259

CHAPTER 8
Memoir on Gnosis 261
History of an Encounter—261; Latins Have Ignored the Term "Gnosis"—263; "Gnose" is Absent From French Dictionaries Before 1840—266; Until the Nineteenth Century, "Gnosis" was Catholic—268; The Scriptural Dignity of Gnosis—271; From Pagan Gnosis to Judeo-Christian Gnosis—274; Three Reasons to be Silent—279; Gnoses and Gnosticism—283

CHAPTER 9
Concerning the Concept of Gnosis According to its Formal Unity 290

CHAPTER 10
How Gnosis Arrives at Knowledge 305

CHAPTER 11
Gnosis Lost or Agnostic Knowledge 313

CHAPTER 12
The Art of Gnosis is Taught by Transcendence 317

CHAPTER 13
Gnosis is also an Objectively Stateable Knowledge 324

CHAPTER 14
How Gnosis Changes into Gnosticism   335

CHAPTER 15
Death and Resurrection of the Gnostic Intellect   346

CHAPTER 16
A Last Glance at the Guénonian-Schuonian Gnosis...   353

CHAPTER 17
...And at Some Others   364

GENERAL CONCLUSION
Hymn to Holy Gnosis   376

SCRIPTURE INDEX   381

INDEX OF NAMES   383

"Raised up by Christ himself, true gnosis is a communion of love with Him, which bears Christian life towards its ultimate degree, that of contemplation. On the path of a progressive configuration with the divine nature..."

Benedict XVI,
audience of Wednesday April 18, 2007

PREFACE

FOR SEVERAL YEARS, PIERRE-MARIE SIGAUD had expressed the wish to bring together in one volume the articles I had published on gnosis. The task seemed easy enough in principle, but proved more difficult than expected. In twenty-five years of readings and reflection, my thinking had become more precise, even transformed. So I could not just reproduce the texts from previous studies, even rid of their faults or factual errors. They had also to be adjusted to the present state of my thinking.[1] Furthermore, never having wanted to do the work of a historian, but of a philosopher, I was led either to add to my studies critical examinations unwarranted by circumstances at the time of their initial publication, or to flesh out what had previously only been sketched. Finally, a more general problem was posed. True to my philosophical intent, I could not be satisfied with criticizing, but had also to explain the conception of gnosis justifying these criticisms. But the philosopher does not proceed only *in the abstract*. Being master of neither things nor words, he must educate himself in the school of history. His concept of gnosis cannot be a purely ideal construction. It can only consist in a certain way of looking at this reality, to which the name of gnosis is commonly given. No doubt one will be thereby led, like St. Paul, to distinguish a "truly-named gnosis" from a "falsely-named gnosis"—and in many respects this distinction will be seen as the recurring theme of the present book.

---

[1] Six chapters of this book reprint four already published articles and two as yet unpublished texts. Chapter 1 appeared in *La Pensée Catholique*, num. 193, July–August 1981. Chapter 2 is a reprint of the second part of the study published in *Dossier H: René Guénon*, L'Âge d'Homme, 1984. Chapter 3 appeared in the review *Krisis*, num. 3, September 1989, and num. 4, December 1989. Chapter 4, drawn from our doctoral thesis, was written in 1981. Chapter 5, with the exception of its last part, appeared in *Raymond Ruyer. De la science à la théologie*, edited by Louis Vax and Jean-Jacques Wunenburger, Éditions Kimé, 1995. Chapter 6, with the exception of its last part, is a reprint of the first and third parts of the study published in *Dossier H: René Guénon*. Chapter 7 was written, with the exception of its introduction, in 1974. The rest of the book was written between June 2004 and February 2007.

However, this view of gnosis has no other purpose than to shed light on what we consider orthodox gnosis—to shed light on it, not fabricate it. This requires in turn that we are able to designate those historical forms in which orthodox gnosis has been realized—so that we can refer to a tradition of gnosis. In addition, we must likewise be able to identify the historical forms (whether ancient or current) of falsely-named gnosis.

But that is not all. For whether orthodox or falsely-named, these forms are in some respects always forms of gnosis, which implies that one can identify a general concept of gnosis that may be more or less ascertained in all forms, whether upright or deviated. By degrees, it is the whole history of religions that must be called upon, and all branches of human knowledge that must be consulted, if we would attempt to answer the following questions: historically, is gnosis as defined according to its general concept a universal religious phenomenon? What are its causes? To account for it, do we have to turn to physiology, psychology, sociology, ethnology, the science of religions and philosophy?

An example will help us grasp the difficulties of an undertaking involving a wide variety of possible fields and scientific disciplines. We can ask ourselves (and we mention this hypothesis never to return to it) if adherence to the path of gnosis is not related to the predominance in the gnostic of a melancholic temperament (*melancholia* = black bile). Henri-Charles Puech, Hans Jonas, and Pierre Hadot, among other scholars, have stressed that the basic feeling of being a *stranger* to the world was to be met with in the gnostic. The world of bodily things, like that of human beings as a whole, seemed to him ugly and of a rightly painful coarseness. The oceanic presence of this feeling was, in his eyes, a sign that his being was the bearer of a divine (in Hinduism one would say "avataric") element that suffers from its exile in the created, but that is also the proof of one's election. The gnostic is thus obsessed with the ineradicable conviction of his salvation: he is by nature one of the elect. Conversely, how can this same gnostic explain how the good God could have projected the saving spark of Whom he is the bearer, a spark of such a noble origin, into such an evil world? He must admit that this world is not His work but that of a demiurge who perverted the cosmogonic plan of the supreme and good God.

The theme of melancholy obviously goes beyond that of gnosis and vice versa. This theme, presented for the first time (?) in a text attributed to Aristotle (Problem XXX, 1), but probably due to his disciple Theophrastus,[2] has pervaded European culture and is linked to the planetary signature of Saturn—as the 1964 literary event, *Saturn and Melancholy: Studies in the History of Natural Philosophy, Religion, and Art*,[3] has shown. Today, however, it does not seem impossible to reconcile the two themes.

Being little inclined by nature to melancholic pessimism, which I had deemed a literary pose and sign of narcissism, I have somewhat underestimated for quite a while the strength and depth this could reach in some people, as well as its factual importance. The progress of my readings and labor of reflection led me to take this pessimism into account as soon as I could see its presence in avowed gnostics of our time (among other amazing similarities). Thus, according to René Guénon, "the true reason" for Dante's quasi-ontological sadness, Dante who is reputed to have "never smiled...was that he had 'redescended from Heaven,'" and not that he returned from Hell,[4] which does not make him an incarnation divine in the sense of Christ, but a being who, having realized his identity with the divine Principle, descends by sacrificial compassion into the manifested world—making him akin to a *Bodhisattva*. Here we are surely in diametric opposition to the Valentinian gnostic who to the contrary only aspires to leave the exile of this world to join his true homeland, that of his divine nature. And yet when it comes to psychological concomitances, the presence of the melancholic humor in both cases—and the

---

2 This text has been translated into French (with adjacent Greek) by Jackie Pigeaud, published by Rivages-poche / Petite Bibliothèque: *Aristote, L'Homme de génie et la Mélancholie*, 1988.
3 By Raymond Klibansky, in collaboration with Erwin Panofsky and Fritz Saxl (London-New York: Basic Books, 1964).
4 *Initiation and Spiritual Realization* (Ghent, NY: Sophia Perennis, 2001), 178, n 15.

CONCERNING CHRISTIAN GNOSIS ACCORDING TO ITS ESSENCE

almost identical spiritual justification given for it—establish a true kinship between them. After all, is not the gnostic, he too, an avataric (pneumatic) substance lost in the sense world and in a world that he, unlike the *Bodhisattva*, did not choose? Likewise, we will grant their full significance to the declarations of Frithjof Schuon, decidedly a gnostic, who made explicit in our presence that in his youth he was subject to a serious melancholy that could have led him to suicide, and that he considered an effect of his pneumatic nature. And we could certainly mention many other such figures.

It is however all too obvious that the Saturnian theme, as broad as it is, does not bring together all aspects of gnosis, and not even the entirety of what is called Gnosticism. In many ways, Teilhard de Chardin and Raymond Ruyer are irrefutably gnostics, although not melancholics. As relevant as they are, the analyses of Jonas, Hadot, or Puech are concerned with real but relatively accidental aspects of gnosis. Physiology, psychology, sociology, and the science of religions shed light on the accompaniments of gnosis, and their elucidations are most valuable: they are irreplaceable. What remains is that the essence of gnosis, and thus also the genesis of its deviations as well, can only be sought through a meditation on the cognitive process itself. If there is a secret to true gnosis, it is in the truth of gnosis (that is, of knowledge) that we have a chance of finding it, or at least of gaining a presentiment of it.

Such is the path we have tried to follow. To write a book that would have embraced all forms of gnosis and all the problems it poses far exceeds our competence, and would have led to interminable analyses. Either we would have to give up writing the desired book, or run the risk of being at once very incomplete and very ambitious, since we aimed at recovering nothing less than the essence of gnosis: not only to describe the general shape of *homo gnosticus* as he presents himself throughout history, but also to gain access to gnosis in itself—in its pure 'idea'—and see why it is achieved precisely in the Christian way.

But before starting out in pursuit of this essence (this being the subject of the last part of this book) we have to first learn about its existence, an indispensable condition for any philosophical process. Thus we have first to describe gnosis as revealed to us by the history of religions in the complex interlacing of problems posed to the Gnostics themselves, to the Great Church, to the Fathers and the Doctors, and also to historians. That, however, is not enough to induct us into the genuine search for the essence, for there the problematic of gnosis was apprehended almost entirely in the religious context of its historical manifestations. For the Christian philosopher to become informed about a truly metaphysical dimension of gnosis, he must also (and this is the second part of the book) present the figures of some modern gnostics foreign to the Christian religion, even by virtue of belonging to a heretical sect, or in any case without ties to a particular revelation. We had to present each of their doctrines with all due attention and necessary rigor because here the idea of gnosis is manifested in itself (and no longer as a function of a religious belief), and is developed in these doctrines to its most extreme consequences.

That is the plan behind the arrangement of this book's contents. The unity of the work imposed modifications in the re-employment of previously written texts. Without wanting to over-multiply references and thereby oblige the reader to interrupt the course of his reading, we have nonetheless let a few repetitions remain—for it is sometimes not useless to bring back to one's attention questions already set forth in a slightly different light. After all, the very nature of our approach has forced us to do this: in many respects a meditation is a recovery and a rumination; this is what is called "the patience of the concept."

Nancy, February 8, 2007

FIRST PART

General Problems of Gnosis

CHAPTER 1

Christian Gnosis and Antichristian Gnosis

Gnosis has had a bad press in Christianity. Instinctively, it is reputed to be the worst enemy of true religion. It is somewhat paradoxical, then, to speak of a Christian gnosis, which is just what I would like to respond to in the following reflections. At a time when the current of ideas sometimes seems to be making a return to a pagan and anti-Christian gnosticism, it is perhaps not useless to show that a true Christian gnosis does exist, a gnosis more profound and more radical than the one some are attempting to resurrect.

POSITION OF THE PROBLEM

In general, religious and philosophical doctrines can be defined, on the one hand, *historically* (who was it that professed them? when did they live? was the name given to them a fitting one? &c.), and on the other *speculatively* (what were the doctrines involved? their contents?) These various demands are not easily satisfied in the case of what one has agreed to call gnosis. The object of my study is inseparable from the various perspectives by which it has been viewed. The history of gnosis (and gnosticism) is the history of its historiography. Until quite recently in fact this cosmological-religious conglomeration was known only through the refutations of its Christian (and Neoplatonist) adversaries. "Heresiologists" are the ones chiefly involved, that is, those Christian writers (Irenaeus, Justin, Hippolytus, &c.) who around the second and third centuries combated gnosticism in works of sometimes vast proportions, works that included lengthy citations from the adversaries being refuted. These citations, studied by historians from the sixteenth to the twentieth centuries, form the greater part of our documentation.

But then, in 1945, a Gnostic library dating most likely from the fourth century after Christ was discovered near Nag Hammadi in Upper Egypt. With respect to gnosis, it was the most important discovery in the history of Christianity. This library included thirty volumes (under the form of *codices* or notebooks) comprised of texts and text fragments either straightforwardly gnostic or utilized by the gnostic community. The problems raised by these texts are far from resolved. Moreover, it does not even seem that the historical knowledge of gnosticism, in becoming more extensive, has become any clearer. What, then, are the theses raised by this religious movement whose historical and geographical importance should not be exaggerated? (Here I will chiefly follow H. C. Peuch and Jean Doresse.)

Historians first saw in Gnosticism a purely Christian heresy. And since, as Tertullian declares, heresy comes after orthodoxy, gnosticism can only be posterior to the formation of Christian doctrine, or at the very least almost contemporary. Therefore it would date from the first and second centuries. However, historians have not agreed on the meaning of this heresy. For some (principally Harnack) gnosticism is a "radical and premature Hellenization" of a religion of Eastern origin, a Hellenization in connection with which the Church will succeed with more moderation and less haste to become Christianity as we know it. For the others (especially for the German Bousset) gnosticism would have been, to the contrary, an attempt to make a religion regress towards an Eastern source, a religion that quite as a natural matter of course would have assumed a Greek form.

A second stage in the historiography of gnosticism was reached when, as a result of the just-mentioned Bousset's works, it became clear that there were around the Mediterranian basin, prior to Christianity, currents and religious groups that, by several of their features, belong to what historians of Christianity rightly term gnosticism. These currents, such as Jewish apocalyptic (studied by Cardinal Daniélou) in the first century before Christ, or the traditions of Hermeticism (studied by Father Festugière), and groups such as the Zoroastrians or Mandeans (the "gnostics"), are encountered in numerous cultural spheres: Palestine, Egypt, Syria, Iran, &c. Christianity in its beginnings had known these movements and could have received contributions from some of their doctrines. In this respect, it is therefore possible to speak broadly of a non-Christian gnosticism. What remains to ask is how, in fact, did gnosticism properly speaking, as clearly identified by historiography, nevertheless manifest itself as a specifically Christian phenomenon, so intimately mingled with Christianity that one at times hesitates about whether or not a particular doctrine is heretical?

This is why we would now like to propose a third hypothesis about the origins of Christian gnosticism. This hypothesis is not the consequence of an historical examination of the problem's data. Had we been tempted to give a verdict in the name of history and to take part in the debates of scholars, the reading of their works would have been enough to convince us that, in this matter, the sole proof we could contribute was proof of our incompetence.[1] Our hypothesis is of the philosophical order and rests on a certain idea of Christianity in which we see a "gnostic religion." We will clarify what is meant by this, but for the moment want to stress in what way this hypothesis answers major questions posed by gnosticism. If one admits—and how can one deny it?—that there was a "pre-Christian gnosis" (so named analogically since its representatives have not used the term to identify themselves) and that this "gnosis" has played a role in the formation of Christian gnosticism (without being its origin), would this not be because, coming into contact with Christian revelation, it would have somehow recognized it as the bearer of something which felt so familiar? And yet this "something" offered itself with an incomparable spiritual force,

---

[1] Simone Pétrement's book, *Le Dieu séparé. Les origines du gnosticisme* (Paris: Cerf, 1984), provides a good idea of the problems raised by specialists: all the texts and all the problematics are examined and discussed. But, although we accept her main thesis—historically identifiable gnosticism is Christian—we do not share her decisions at every point, and we reject her exegetical biases. Moreover, we do not see why the concept of "gnosticism," a creation of modern historiography designating a properly Christian heresy, might not be extended, broadly, to prechristian religious currents exhibiting certain affinities with this gnosticism.

a potency, a youthfulness: nothing in the Asiatic religions was as extraordinary, as radiant, as solar as the figure of Jesus Christ. What an irresistible attraction must this figure have exerted on the fervor which, in these religions, animated the most "mystical" groups! Hence their desire to become associated with it and to be nourished by it. In short, the Christic revelation came to arouse and awaken in such pre-Christian gnostics what there was of the most profound, offering an authentic fulfillment. Thus is explained how gnosticism is at once specifically Christian and yet, through some of its elements, seems to harken back to non-Christian forms of religious feeling. To become convinced of this it is obviously necessary to strive, beyond the texts and scholarship, to take into account the lived reality of things and events—which is first formed, not by (necessary) historiographic abstractions, but by person-to-person encounters. And so, in a certain manner, we are approaching the problem here in reverse order. In posing the question of gnosticism's origins, one is generally asking oneself: what relationship does Christianity have with certain pre-Christian religious movements? We ask: what relationship might these religious movements have had with nascent Christianity? What were they feeling when they became cognizant of this faith?

GNOSIS AND GNOSTICISM

A dual task is now imposed on our thesis: to show just how Christianity actually realizes the truth of gnosis, and also to identify the error of gnosticism and specify the deviation it caused true gnosis to undergo. However, the preliminary question of the terminological justification for the words "gnosis" and "gnosticism" comes first.

It might be asked: why call Christianity a gnosis, since this term implies so many doubtful matters and unacceptable theories? I will reply first that I am making a distinction between gnosis, a transliteration of the Greek *gnosis* (by which the interior and saving knowledge of God should be understood), and gnosticism, which designates a historically-fixed systematizing of this knowledge in such a way that gnosis is found reduced to some of its constituent elements. In this sense, every gnosticism is a heresy, since a heresy consists in *choosing* (*haïrésis* = choice) from within the bosom of the total truth a few elements of this truth that are then formed into a totality to which all else is reduced.

Next, notice that in its previously defined meaning the term *gnosis* rightly belongs to Christianity, since it was used in this sense for the first time by St. Paul.[2] And likewise, with St. Paul we find the first denunciation of gnosticism, that is to say "pseudo-gnosis" (1 Tim. 6:20). But although St. Paul is the greatest authority we can call upon, he is not alone. In his *Adversus Haereses*, St. Irenaeus of Lyon does not denounce gnosis, but—as the original title of his book declares, a title which Eusebius of Caesaria, St John of Damascus and others have preserved for us—a "gnosis falsely so called" (*Elenkos kai anatrope tes pseudonymou gnoseos*). Clement of Alexandria as well, although combating gnosticism, proposes to teach us "true gnosis"—the one coming from Christ through apostolic tradition, the one which the study of Scripture and the sacramental life actualizes within us. In the same way the great Origen speaks of this "gnosis of God" that few possess and by which Moses penetrated into the divine Darkness.[3] Such historical grounds justify speaking of a Christian gnosis.

But after the name we must now consider the thing itself. In what way then is Christian revelation a gnosis? If gnosis and gnosticism are identical, then my thesis is untenable, for Christian truth is not, *a priori*, reserved for a secret elite, although, as many of the parables teach, everyone does not have the same understanding and does not fathom alike the deepest meanings. But if it is true that by gnosis we should understand an interior and saving knowledge of God, then it is quite difficult to deny that such a definition may be applied preeminently to Christ's own message. That "eternal life" is a gnosis is just what Christ himself affirms in the gospel according to John: "This is eternal life, that they know thee

---

2 Cf. Dom Jacques Dupont, *Gnôsis. La connaissance religieuse dans les Epîtres de saint Paul* (Louvain: Gabalda, 1949).
3 *Contra Celsum*, VI, 17.

the only true God, and Jesus Christ whom thou hast sent" (17:3). Thus knowledge of God is *life*, and even eternal life. Now, eternal life is precisely the salvation Jesus Christ has come to bring us, since He saves us from sin and death. Also, according to certain exegetes (C. H. Dodd in particular), was not the fourth gospel essentially written to prove that true gnosis is faith in Jesus Christ and in the saving power of His Name (John 20:31)?

But this knowledge is not only saving, it is also interior. It is so first with respect to Judaism. In fact, according to the medieval adage, *Doctrina Christi revelat quod Moysi velat*: Christianity is the revelation of the interior mystery of Judaism. Somehow it is the disclosure in broad daylight of the Mosaic religion's "esoterism," of what was "most secret" in it.[4] It is likewise so in itself: for the six hundred thirty-two prescriptions of the Jewish law Jesus Christ substitutes the love of God and neighbor. The multitude of extremely complex ritual obligations are replaced by faith in Christ and participation in the sevenfold sacraments. Even the law of the Sabbath can be transgressed if the good of man requires it. What matters is the "religion of the heart," the one concerned with a being's interiority, for "the kingdom of God is within you." It is not an exterior worship reduced to its own exteriority that pleases God, but, in the psalmist's words, the "sacrifice of a broken spirit" (Psalm 50:17), a sacrifice realized by the death of Christ. Also, it is the pure heart which will see God.

The wondrous novelty of this spiritual way appears even more clearly if compared with the idea a Greek or Roman had of religion. According to Varro, as we know, religion was of

---

4 The "discipline of the arcane," the obligation to keep certain teachings secret, existed in the Church at least until the fifth century. Is it not known (an astonishing thing which should give us food for thought) that at the time of St Ambrose and according to the very recommendation of the saintly bishop, it was forbidden to put into writing the Apostles' Creed, which was therefore transmitted only orally and could not be recited in front of the profane? (*Explanatio Symboli*, num. 9; Sources chrétiennes, num. 25 *bis*, 57–9.) But today we are hardly aware of the truly prodigious character of the teachings it reveals. We deal with the question of the discipline of the arcane in *Christ the Original Mystery: Esoterism and the Mystical Way*, trans. G. J. Champoux (Hillsdale, NY: Angelico, 2018), 296–393.

three kinds: mythological for the poets, physical (or natural) for the philosophers, civil (or political) for the populace of the cities. What then was the degree of religious awareness of a Greek participating in the Panathenaean processions? The degree of faith of a poet embellishing complaisantly on the adventures of the gods and goddesses? How right Plato was to condemn this literary impiety and this wholly exterior worship! But what unknown God can one adore "with all of one's soul"?

Compared to all of these religious forms, Christ's teaching appeared as a message of interiority. And here we have it: "The hour is coming when neither on this mountain nor in Jerusalem will you worship the Father.... But the hour is coming, and now is, when the true worshipers will worship the Father in spirit and truth, for such the Father seeks to worship him" (John 4:22-3). But the Christian rites themselves, Baptism and the Eucharist foremost, seem to recapture, in order to assume and perfect it, what was most authentically religious in pagan Hellenism—i.e., the mystery cults. Was not Baptism called "initiation" and "illumination"? Is Baptism not a truly initiatic rite that transforms the soul and confers upon it the grace of Christic gnosis? And the Eucharistic rite, by having us participate in the sacrificial banquet of the divine Body of Christ, does it not communicate in the *mysterium fidei* a most intimate knowledge—that of God's very Being? Let us go even further. Does not the unveiling of God-the-Trinity realize a veritable initiation into the very interiority of the divine Being, which suddenly displays to the eyes of faith the super-intelligible mystery of its own Heart? Is it not as if here is the revelation of the unspeakable secret of Abrahamic and philosophic monotheism (which somehow bursts forth "from within"): God ceasing to be this unique, transcendent and impenetrable point in order to enable us to contemplate the infinity which resides within Him?

This is precisely the authentic interiority of Christian gnosis that makes manifest the error and falsity of non-Christian gnosticism. For gnosticism, by virtue of its partial and garbled vision, could only conceive of an interiority that excluded exteriority, whereas Christian gnosis reveals its truth, its "understanding" in this: that Christ has not come to abolish the law but fulfill it, not to refute exteriority and condemn it, but to assume it and save it. This is why gnosticism is necessarily dualistic. And every dualism constitutes a "metaphysical heresy" (just as every monism does). We could say that gnosticism is on the one hand an "anti-creationist angelism," and on the other a "Christological docetism."

Anti-creationist angelism is clearly seen in reading the texts of Marcionite and Valentinian gnosticism, for example. The corporeal world is wicked. It can then only be the work of a wicked demiurge, identified by Marcion as the God of Genesis. The serpent teaching Eve to disobey the wicked demiurge constitutes a first attempt to amend the evil caused by YHWH-*Elohim*. Thus the Greek idea of a cosmos, that is, the idea of an orderly world the order and harmony of which make everything beautiful (an idea to which Plotinus will return in his fight against gnosticism) — this idea is entirely abandoned. Creation of itself is consigned to destruction and death. The flesh is impure. Matter is unworthy of the transcendence of the true God, who is a pure spirit. The true pneumatic should live like an angel. Clearly, we recognize here the themes that will be taken up later by the Cathar movement, whose doctrine was a death-threat to all of society.

But according to this heresy the true God intervened to save the pure from the flesh by sending an almost divine being, a heavenly Power, who came to make access possible to the higher world of spiritual realities of which the lower world is only a counterfeit. However, when this Power is identified with Jesus Christ, his descent here-below is not interpreted as an incarnation. It is only in appearance that Christ possesses a body and suffers his Passion (this is precisely what is called the docetist heresy, from the Greek *dokeo*: "to seem," "to appear"). "For them the Savior appears in his fullness only incorporeally, after the Resurrection."[5]

---

5 Jean Doresse, *La Gnose*, in *Histoire des religions* (Paris: Pléïade, 1972), tome II, 395.

Christian Gnosis and Antichristian Gnosis

The denial of the incarnation, then, is incidental to a denial of creation, and both are pronounced in the name of divine transcendence. That is, supreme reality is too high and too sublime to tolerate the lowliness of the corporeal world, and therefore *a fortiori* too lowly for a being emanating from the higher world to be able to really assume such conditions. If now, leaving aside the descriptions of the theses of historical gnosticism, we judge them from the metaphysical point of view—that is, if we take them seriously and stop seeing them as a cultural oddity—this is what we will say: anti-creationist angelism and its corollary, Christological docetism, far from reducing or erasing the impurity, the taint, the opaqueness of matter, only reinforce it. The act by which dualist gnosticism proceeds to the rejection of a matter reputedly evil, by the selfsame stroke constitutes this matter as a reality antinomic to the luminous Principle, thereby elevating it to the dignity of being its contrary, and definitively identifying it with its tenebrous dimension.

Let us recall our definition of gnosis: an interior and saving knowledge. Henceforth, precisely for want of a real understanding of salvation and interiority, it is clear that gnosticism cannot pretend to such a knowledge. As for salvation, we clearly understand that the wiping away of the taint it envisages, the purification it proposes, are wholly *negative*. In the same way, interiority, such as gnosticism conceives of it, is only the exclusion of all exteriority, and therefore a negative and formal interiority. By denying all divine immanence, all presence of the Uncreated Light at the heart of the most opaque darkness, gnosticism even makes the least liberation impossible. Indeed, it makes of a creation emptied of all glory an insurmountable obstacle, an eternal hell.

True interiority, to the contrary, should assume exteriority. Certainly, it should surpass it by drawing it into glory—but by transfiguring it and therefore also perfecting it. This axiom says it all: only the more can truly do the least. Only God, the Absolute and the Infinite, "can do" the relative and the finite, which is to say God can not only create them (this is obvious) but can grasp and truly embrace the finite, integrally realize the nature of the finite, going right to the end of the finite, truly exhausting it—and this is much less recognized. In other words the finite, the worldly, the exterior, or the flesh cannot by itself go to the end of itself. It cannot realize by itself the truth of its nature, its relativity and contingency. The finite is truly *finished* only in the bosom of the Infinite. The Light shines *in* the darkness and the darkness comprehends it not. The Light is therefore immanent to the darkness. Moreover, it is by this very immanence that darkness realizes the truth of its nature. But Light is incomprehensible to darkness, since, to the contrary, it is in truth the Light that comprehends darkness—which is to say envelops it and knows it. For not only does the darkness not comprehend Light, it does not even comprehend itself.

Thus, true interiority should not leave exteriority outside of itself, and this is precisely what is realized in the sacrificial Incarnation of Jesus Christ. Christ has been made sin, says St Paul. This extraordinary saying reveals the metaphysical inconsistency of gnosticism by realizing the true "gnosis" of creation. For in being made sin Christ "knows" (existentially) the true nature of post-Edenic creation. Christ goes right to the end of our world's finiteness, this end being his death on the Cross. By "perfecting" the finiteness of the created, by realizing its crucifying and mortal contradiction, he also reveals its connecting-point, a cordial and transcendent knot. He surpasses and traverses the exteriority of the created by leading it back to its original center—out of which are thrust, and back to which converge, the arms of the Cross. Then there appears the positive interiority of the true gnosis of the Father, who is Christ Himself, since the Son is the eternal knowledge the Father has of his own Divine Essence. Thus Christ on the Cross is the revelation of an assumptive and transforming interiority—a revelation—for Christ is held upright in his agony before the world. And in his death, in this Good and Holy Friday that is true gnosis, the divine interiority opens wide: Christ, who is the very interiority of the knowledge of the Father, is transpierced and opened by the centurion's lance, and blood and water stream forth. This is the very interiority of God that is shed without and that communicates to all things the virtue and quality of gnostic interiority. In a cosmic baptism, all creation is bathed in Christ's death and blood. It is gnosis of the Father that has thus been poured forth and communicated.

MODERN GNOSTICISM

We may only speak of a modern gnosticism, I think, in a sense very different from that of ancient gnosticism. The gnosticism of the Christian heresiologists is deeply religious, that is, it intends to connect with God through a knowledge that is not only purified of all corporeal elements (this is its interiority) but still enables someone to really escape, in his very being, from this corporeal world (this is its saving character). Modern gnosticism is not religious. It is even anti-religious, and in any case anti-Christian. How then is it still justifiable to speak of gnosis in this connection? We will have to concede—without it being possible to do otherwise than rest content with a level of extreme generality—that this involves doctrines which deem science to be the true religion, not in the manner of the nineteenth century scientism that thought science should *eliminate* religion, but in the manner of people convinced that science should *replace* religion by assuming all its functions. Obviously, this implies a transformation of scientific knowledge. Scientific knowledge can be a gnosis only if it ceases being subject to the rationalist dualism of subject (spiritual) and object (material), in favor of becoming a participative knowledge of a *universe-man continuum*, a continuum indwelt under various forms by a Spirit merged with Nature. Matter is spirit upside down and inside out. Neognosis is the "revelation" of this reversal, and effects a kind of speculative or theoretical "salvation" by putting things back in place. Such at least is the purest type of this modern gnosticism as found in Ruyer. For others, this is much more a question of a declared and basically anti-Christian attitude than of a developed and articulated doctrine. Gnosticism becomes, then, a kind of adoration of the physical world in which one invests those affective values ordinarily elicited by religion, but amputated of all reference to God, whereas Ruyerist gnosticism is deist in a declared and explicit way. However that may be, it seems evident that this modern gnosticism realizes the demands of gnosis no more than ancient gnosticism does. And this is what I would like to show quite briefly. Nonetheless, although it usurps and travesties the true sense of gnosis, it is in a way somehow the inverse of Hellenic gnosticism. In the name of divine transcendence the latter denied God's immanence to the world. The former, to the contrary, in the name of immanence—and even of a pantheist identification of the Spirit with matter (as with Jean E. Charon, for example)—rejects all transcendence and all "historical" intervention of the transcendent in the world of man. We have described the first denial as a misunderstanding of the sacrificial Incarnation; the second we would describe as a misunderstanding of the Easter Resurrection.

If there is in fact a resurrection of the flesh, this is because the divine principle, which is immanent to the world in the very substance of matter, by virtue of its own transcendence cannot but tear the physical body out of the cosmic order to which it clings in order to manifest the very transcendence of the flesh when truly indwelt by the Spirit. What this modern gnosis lacks is both the distinction of the degrees of reality and the perfection deriving from it. The Spirit dwells in the world, but the world is less real and less perfect than the Spirit. At the very least there is a degree of the world—precisely the one we are experiencing—whose imperfection crushes us and leads to death. Who can deny it? The truth of the Spirit's presence in the world demands, under pain of being only a formula of purely theoretical expediency, that the world's very reality *gives proof* of this presence. And how could it, unless by a transfiguration in which the spiritual and *glorious* nature of the flesh itself finally appears? This operative and saving gnosis of the world is just what Christ's Resurrection realizes. This is what puts things back in place, just as Ruyer wanted. This is what obliges us to look at the created through new eyes. This is what topples our vision of the cosmos.

We will get a clear idea of this if only we consider the role played by our bodies as the instruments of our presence in the world. It is in fact through the body that we are present in a world of bodies. But this presence, of which we believe ourselves to be the masters since it is somehow identified with us, is in reality a *passive* and *involuntary* presence. It was Merleau-Ponty who showed in *The Phenomenology of Perception* that to see an object is "to be able to make a tour of it." And how is it possible to make a tour of it if not because the object imparts itself indefinitely and inexhaustibly to the surveying gaze, because it can do nothing but offer itself to our gaze, but be seen. To *be* seen, and to be corporeally present, is all one. My corporeal presence is my visibility, but my visibility is not my own. Rather, it belongs to every gaze, unbeknownst to me and without being able to do anything about it — an ignorance and impotence inherent to the very essence of my visibility. Thus, no one is master of his corporeal presence — and even more, to be corporeally present is not to be master of this presence.

What happens then, to the contrary, in the Resurrection of Christ? What happens is that the resurrected Body is as if a witness, a living proof, a saving irruption of the glorious nature of the created within the bosom of its dark and opaque modality: Christ's body is still the instrument of presence in the world of bodies, but by a total change it is no longer of the essence of this presence to be passive and involuntary. The soul that inhabits this instrument is entirely master of it and makes use of it at will. Christ can actualize the corporeal mode of His presence according to His own decision and as He judges good. The relationship He entertains with the corporeal *medium* of His presence has been completely transformed: a presence active to the world because a presence really in act. All the relationships uniting this corporeal *medium* with the rest of the bodies, that is, with the entire world and with the conditions that define it, all these relationships have been changed. Christ *is no longer seen, he causes himself to be seen.* This is exactly what the gospels teach, and which so many modern exegetes are incapable of understanding. Christ glorious is not "above" the world of the senses, except in a symbolic sense. Simply put, he is no longer *subject* to the conditions of this corporeal world. His bodily presentification becomes then a simple prolongation of its spiritual reality entirely dependent upon this reality (whereas in the state of fallen nature, it is the person's spiritual reality that is extrinsically dependent upon its bodily presence)—a presentification that the spiritual person may or may not effectuate, as freely as human thought can, in its ordinary state, produce or not produce such or such a concept or feeling. Whoever stops to consider this doctrine of the reversal in the relationship of the person to his corporeal *medium*, and the consequences that this entails, will take into account the remarkable light it casts on the significance of Christ's post-paschal appearances according to the gospels.

From this point of view, and without elaborating on the cosmological implications apt for clarifying to a certain extent the "how" of this reversal, we understand that Christ's Resurrection presents itself as the sacrament of the transfiguration of the cosmos, that is, the sacrament in which the cosmos is restored to its true nature. Ruyer was quite right in saying that our ordinary experience of the world is that of a world inside out, that the "place" of the world is by nature semantic and intelligible, and that only the semantic consistency of the world accounts for its "non-pulverization." But this inverted and inverting experience of ours remains. This is also a reality, a fact, whereas the rectified vision, the ortho-theory of the world, is nothing but a discourse, words on paper, ideas in my head. Surely, this is not nothing. It is even all that we are capable of for the moment. But it is not an experience, not a true gnosis in the sense that we have constantly given this term. And of course, with respect to Christ's Resurrection, we are in the same situation: an affirmation by the Scriptures that we welcome into our minds. With two differences however: it does not involve the proclamation of a theory, but of a testimony; and this testimony deals with an unheard-of reality that the apostles have *experienced*. And what they testify to is having had, indirectly, in the person of Christ, the experience of the glorious nature of creation, whereas modern neo-gnosis excludes precisely the very possibility of such an experience and thus remains simply a theoretical (or speculative) knowledge of what it nevertheless affirms to be the true nature of cosmic reality. And even more, the apostles and all true Christians affirm that all children of God are called to participate in the prototypical Resurrection of Christ, that the Resurrection will become the direct and personal experience of each.

As we see, faced with ancient as well as modern gnosticism, Christianity alone goes right to the end of the demands of gnosis. It truly realizes all the consequences, before which the most well-known speculative audacities fall back (as with the gnosticism of Hegel, who, writing a life of Jesus, ended it with the crucifixion). Christian theologians themselves, however, hesitate to ratify this term of "gnosis" when applied to Christianity. Can we so name what has a share in the soul's sanctification and its posthumous destiny? Again, does this involve a knowing in the sense that this word might have for us? Here-below, are we not limited on the one hand to faith, and on the other to reason laboring over the data of faith? Probably. And yet it seems that to want to define theological work as a work of pure natural reason (in such a way that, as an extreme case, an atheist could be a theologian, provided he speculatively welcomes—that is, by way of hypotheses—the data of faith), one would be unable to avoid a certain rationalism, that either leads theology to dessication, to theology as a gratuitous exercise, or exposes it to a pure and simple rejection in the name of the concrete, the existential, the pastoral, and "commitment." This is, in any case, an altogether real possibility, as the present crisis in theological wisdom seems to tragically and undeniably bear out. By maintaining to the contrary that theology should be mystical, not in the sense wherein a theologian should know what is properly called mystical states, but in the sense wherein he retains a lively awareness of how the light of the intellect is, according to the word of St Thomas Aquinas, "almost derived from God." This is a doctrine of knowledge in the light of the Word that forms the basis for Augustinian and Dionysian theology. And let no one be deceived: awareness of the almost divine nature of human intellection actualized beneath the light radiating from the object of faith—which is itself an objective concretion of the Word—this awareness is not nothing. To the contrary, it communicates to theological knowledge a vibration and a perfume that tear it away from the ordinary exercise of thought and prevent it from getting caught in the snares of its formulations. In the very act of knowing, such an intellect rightly tastes already something of the Holy Spirit. And that is gnosis.

CHAPTER 2

The Scriptural Origins of Gnosis

W E DO NOT INTEND TO DEAL WITH the history of gnosticism as an expert. This field (by far exceeding our competence) is so vast and complex that an entire volume would not suffice. Besides, good treatments of this difficult subject already exist.[1] We only wish to mention some facts about the genesis of this phenomenon to enable us to account for, as much as possible, the hypothesis outlined in the previous chapter.

---

[1] To our knowledge, the best remains the one given by H. C. Puech in 1934: "Où en est le problème du gnosticisme?" reprinted in *En quête de la gnose*, Gallimard, 1978, tome I, 143–83. For an overview on the doctrines of gnosis and their history, the account by Jean Doresse entitled "Gnose," in *Histoire des Religions*, tome 2, in the *Encyclopédie de la Pléiade* (op. cit.), 361–429, succeeds as a *tour de force* by being both clear and complete. Provocative insights are to be found in Mircea Eliade, *Histoire des croyances et des idées religieuses*, tome 2 (Paris: Payot, 1978), 345–76. Simone Pétrement has devoted a chapter to the "Problème du gnosticisme" in *Le dualisme chez Platon, les gnostiques et les manichéens* (1974, reprint 1982 [Paris: Ed. Gerard Montfort]), 129–59, in addition to her already mentioned survey: *Le Dieu séparé*, the introduction to which, "Le problème du gnosticisme" (9–45), is especially important. The reference manual for a scientific introduction to the question was published by Michel Tardieu and Jean-Daniel Dubois: *Introduction à la littérature gnostique, tome I—Collections retrouvées avant 1945* (Paris: Cerf, 1986); this work includes: a history of the word, a review of the tools of the craft (texts, translations, languages, &c.) and specialist notes on all the text collections known prior to the discoveries of the Nag Hammadi manuscripts. The classic work of H. Leisegang, *Die Gnosis* (1924) is very useful, as well as *La Gnose éternelle* by the Dominicans H. Cornelis and A. Léonard (Paris: Arthème Fayard, 1959). *Cahiers Évangile* has published a supplement to Cahier 58 devoted to Nag Hammadi—*Évangile selon Thomas. Textes gnostiques*, presented by R. Kuntzmann and J. D. Dubois, which offers excerpts from all the texts of Nag Hammadi and the *Gospel according to Thomas* in its entirety (Paris: Cerf, 1987). Gedaliahu Guy Stroumsa, in *Savoir et Salut* (Paris: Cerf, 1992), has collected the very learned articles he has written on little known aspects—Judeo-Christian in particular—of gnosticism. Lastly, Prof. Wouter J. Hanegraaf, of Amsterdam University, in collaboration with Antoine Faivre, Roelof van den Broek and Jean-Pierre Brach, has published in 2006 a *Dictionary of Gnosis and Western Esoterism* (Leiden & Boston: Brill) which is, although otherwise exceeding the scope of gnosis as defined, a major reference work.

GENERAL PROBLEMS OF GNOSIS

The first point to stress is that the history of gnosticism is inseparable from its historiography, which is actually rather recent. The oldest works (Massuet, Le Nourry, Le Nain de Tillemont, Mosheim, &c.) are not prior to the seventeenth century. Moreover, they deal with the thing itself, not the French term, which only dates from 1828 (the English term dates back to 1664). In fact, we have to wait for the works of the great German historian Adolf von Harnack (1851–1930) for what constitutes a truly historical science of gnosticism. From that moment the most eminent scholars have been fascinated with this question, which became a major problem for the history of religions. In 1945 this interest surged with one of the most extraordinary discoveries of Christian archaeology, that of a library at Nag Hammadi (Khenoboskian) in Upper Egypt.[2] From an unearthed jar buried in the sand, thirteen volumes in the form of a *codex* (i.e. assembled manuscripts and not rolls or *volumen*[3]) were discovered, "bringing together in total, according to the most recent evaluations, fifty-three documents, the majority gnostic,"[4] which from then on allowed direct access to the texts. Actually, until then all that was known about those called "gnostics" was limited to quotations and summaries made by heresiologists (chiefly St. Irenaeus and St. Hippolytus), or to some fragments of rough interpretation.[5] The question of gnosticism had to be, for all that, either definitively clarified or fundamentally transformed.

---

2 The other discovery, curiously enough made about the same time, is that of the Dead Sea scrolls.
3 The substitution of *codex* for *volumen* transpired during the time of Augustus.
4 H. C. Puech, *En quête de la gnose* (Paris: Gallimard, 1978), tome I, xi; a veritable "curse," in the words of H. Jonas (*The Gnostic Religion*, 3rd ed. [Boston: Beacon Press, 2001], 290), weighs heavily on this find: rivalries, jealousies, disagreements among specialists, &c., have delayed its publication. A facsimile edition was only completed in 1976. The texts are now available in *The Nag Hammadi Scriptures: The Revised and Updated Translation of Sacred Gnostic Texts* by M. W. Meyer and J. M. Robinson (New York: HarperCollins, 1990).
5 Let us add, among others, a treatise, the *Pistis Sophia* (in Coptic), dating from perhaps the beginning of the fourth century, but which furnishes an already altered state of Gnostic doctrines (H. Jonas, *The Gnostic Religion*, 40). The French translation of this text by E. Amelineau in 1894 has been republished in 1975 by Archè, Milan (an antiquated introduction falsely attributes this text to Valentinus).

What, then, is this all about? Frankly, it is impossible to answer this question. It could be done if there truly existed schools of thought giving themselves the title of gnostic and characterized by a well-defined body of doctrine. There is nothing of the sort. The term "gnosticism" is of recent coinage and does not appear before the beginning of the nineteenth century. The term "gnostic" (*gnostikos*), a Greek adjective signifying, in the ordinary sense, "one who knows," a "savant," is only very rarely used to technically characterize a philosophico-religious movement: the Ophites alone, among all of the gnostic sects, have been designated in this way. This is why one can conclude: "In primitive Christianity there is no trace of 'Gnosticism,' in the sense of a vast historical category, and the modern use of 'Gnostic' and 'Gnosticism,' designating a religious movement at once ample and poorly defined, is totally unknown in the first Christian period."[6] Certainly, when historians apply this religious category to a particular doctrine, it is not absolutely unreasonable: common religious elements and themes are to be rediscovered here and there, the two most constant of which appear to be the condemnation of the Old Testament and its God, on the one hand, and, on the other, the condemnation of the sensible world. However, the use made of this category necessarily depends upon the idea they have formed of it, which is to say basically upon the conception of gnosis itself and upon what they can understand about it. To the extent that gnosis likewise connotes ideas of mysterious and salvific knowledge, having been communicated only to a certain few under the veil of symbols, putting into play an extremely complex cosmology and anthropology, and only realized through a kind of dramatic theo-cosmology—to this extent the concept of gnosis is quite broad. Historians will then be justified in discovering it in quite unexpected domains.

And yet is it possible to find a fixed and incontestable landmark? Could *the* word *gnosis* provide it?

In Greek, this term signifies knowledge. But it is rarely employed alone, and nearly always requires a complementary

---

[6] R. P. Casey, "The Study of Gnosticism," in *The Journal of Theological Studies* 36 (1935): 55.

noun (knowledge *of* something), whereas *episteme* (knowledge, science) can be employed absolutely. This is why we will grant, along with Bultmann, that *gnosis* signifies not knowledge as result, but rather the act of knowing.[7] Moreover, contrary to what some uninformed people assert, it is not the only noun the Greek language has at its disposal to express the same idea. Plato and Aristotle also use, in proximate senses, besides *episteme* (and the verbs *epistasthai* or *eidenai*), *dianoia*, *dianoesis* (and *dianoeisthai*), *gnome*, *logos*, *mathema*, *mathesis* (and *manthanei*), *noesis* and *noein*, *noerna*, *nous*, *phronesis*, *sophia*, *sunesis*, &c. Besides this ordinary use of the term, can one speak, as Bultmann does,[8] of a "gnostic" usage in which it would be employed absolutely in the sense of "pre-eminent knowledge," i.e., "knowledge of God"? The examples provided by "pagan" literature are hardly convincing.

This is no longer the case with the sapiential literature of the Old Testament in its Greek version (the "Septuagint"). Here for the first time, in an incontestable fashion, the verb *ginosko*, used to translate the Hebrew *yd* (equally but more rarely rendered by *eidenai* and *epistasthai*), and the noun *gnosis* acquire "a much more accentuated religious and moral significance, in the sense of a revealed knowledge whose author is God or *Sophia*."[9] In this way the Bible speaks of God as the "God of gnosis" (1 Sam. 2:3). Why did Alexandrian Judaism choose this term (and not *episteme* for example) to express the idea of a sacred and unitive knowledge in which the entire being participates? Must we see in this the influence of a mystical (or mysterial) Hellenism that would have already utilized the term in this sense? For reasons of principle—and not only for always contestable factual reasons—we do not believe so: it is inadmissible that a religion can be subjected to such an alteration in what is essential to it, namely the unique and mysterious relationship established between the human being and God in an incomparable act, to which it specifically gives the name "knowledge." Rather the reverse is true: it is Jewish tradition that confers upon the

---

7 Cf. the *ginosko* entry in *Theologisches Wörterbuch zum Neuen Testament*, Gerhard Kittel et al. (Stuttgart: Verlag W. Kolhammer, 1966), tome I, 688–715.
8 *Op. cit.*, 692–693, which refers in particular to Plato, *Republic*, VI, 508e.
9 Bultmann, op. cit., 699.

Greek word its full religious significance.[10] And if *gnosis* was the term chosen *in order to* express this act of "knowledge," this is precisely because it was of a neutral significance; while a term like *episteme*, with a very precise philosophic sense, would not have lent itself to such a process. We in no way deny the existence of a religious Hellenism or an Egyptian tradition, since these are the two sources historians have wished to ascribe to the biblical *gnosis*. Quite the contrary, the existence of such sacred phenomena are obvious. But, as we have underscored in another work,[11] it would be good if historians stopped thinking with the single concept of "influence" that leads them without fail to the concept of "sources." There is perhaps no academic field in which such research is more futile than that of gnosis and gnosticism. From one tradition to another there can be influence, borrowing and transference with peripheral elements, but not with what these traditions hold as essential, at the very least while they are still living.

However, in abiding by the texts (particularly in the book of Proverbs, where *gnosis* is most often employed), we are not yet dealing with gnosis in its ordinarily understood sense, that is, in the sense of a purely inner and deifying knowledge and no longer just an *act*, but also a *state* that God alone can confer on a pneumatized intellect,[12] and that can be called the "charism of gnosis." Not that the thing itself does not exist in the Old Testament, but there the term gnosis does not assume such a significance.[13] It is necessary then to await the New Testament, particularly 1 and 2 Corinthians, Colossians, and 1 Timothy, to see the word *gnosis* appear and be employed in the sense

---

10 This is the conclusion advanced by Dom Jacques Dupont after a lengthy analysis of the texts and hypotheses, in his work *Gnôsis. La connaissance religieuse dans les épîtres de saint Paul* (Paris: Gabalda, 1949), 357–65.
11 *Histoire et théorie du symbole* (Lausanne: L'Âge d'Homme, 2004), 34, n 23.
12 We have laid out the Christian doctrine of the pneumatization of the intellect in our book *Love and Truth, The Christian Path of Charity*, trans. G. J. Champoux (Brooklyn NY: Angelico, 2020), 130, 163–66, 292, 401, 411, 415–20, 426, 430, 433.
13 Is this likewise the case for pre-Christian Alexandrian Judaism? The question would require a special study. But, in any case, the texts remaining are almost always posterior to the New Testament, and Philo of Alexandria, who is its contemporary, seldom uses *gnosis* and, as a good Platonist, prefers *episteme* or *theoria* to it (Dupont, op. cit., 361).

just defined above. That the decision to so designate the state of spiritual knowledge finds its origin in the Septuagint is obvious, and there is no need to appeal to Hellenistic culture. But that this is the teaching of Jesus Christ and the revelation of the divine *Logos* within Him, which had rendered possible this state of gnosis in the souls of those who have believed, this is also no less incontestable. In its essence, Christianity is wholly a message of gnosis: to "know... and adore God in spirit and in truth" (John 4:22–24), and no longer only through sensible or ritual forms. Or rather: to be united to Jesus Christ, who is Himself the gnosis of the Father, and who in Himself transcends the created world as well as religious obligations. Certainly the word is of Helleno-Biblical origin. But the thing itself, the inner and salvific knowledge, the charism of gnosis by which faith attains its deifying perfection—that is quite simply and fundamentally *Christian*. It is this kerygma of love of and transforming union with God that Jesus has come to reveal, and it is enough to read the Gospel for this to be recognized. Faced with the ritualism of the Pharisees, Christ, the incarnate gnosis of the Father, comes to reopen the "narrow door" of spiritual inwardness. How else would it be possible for the Apostles, St. Paul, and the first Christians to live their most profound commitment "in Christ"?[14]

This is why one encounters no documentary evidence, despite the research (and sometimes assertions) of eminent historians,[15] for the existence of a "gnosis" so named previous to the New Testament. True, out of the 29 New Testament occurences of *gnosis*, all do not designate a *spiritual state*. They do however have a religious sense each time (except for 1 Peter 3:7), and if the "gnostic" sense is above all Pauline,[16] it appears to

---

14 We are returning here, with a more developed historical foundation, to our thesis proposed in the previous chapter.
15 This is especially the case with Reitzenstein and Bultmann.
16 *Gnosis* occurs twice in St. Luke, once in St. Peter, and 26 times in St. Paul. A certain evolution of the terminology of gnosis, from one epistle to another, has been ascertained. St. Paul moreover also employs *epignosis*. On all of this, see E. Prucker, *Gnôsis Théou: Untersuchungen zur Bedeutung eines religiösen Begriffs beim Apostel Paulus und bei seiner Umwelt*, Cassiciacum, IV (Wurzburg: Rita-Verlag, 1937), and the summary of it given by Dom J. Dupont, op. cit., 48–49.

The Scriptural Origins of Gnosis

be equally present in St. Luke when Christ declares: "Woe to you, Doctors of the Law, because you have taken away the key of gnosis, you yourselves not having entered in, and those who would enter you have chased them away" (11:52), above all if one admits that the true key is gnosis itself, which in reality is identified with the "Kingdom of Heaven," as the parallel passage in St. Matthew (16:19) proves. If there had existed a "gnosis" (so named), it therefore appears certain that it had been Christian at first and, even more, "Christic." One has to be really blind to the "phenomenon" of Christ not to notice the prodigious spiritual effect he must have produced upon those who were his witnesses (an effect which, two thousand years later, has still not been exhausted). How can we doubt for a single moment that this Jesus Christ, who was "more than a prophet," communicated to those whom He would meet and who would welcome His words a gnosis, a state of inner and deifying knowledge incommensurate with anything experienced by them until then? It is this spiritual state that St. Paul designates with the name *gnosis*, and in which he sees the perfection of faith.[17] It is this that we discover in the writings of Pauline inspiration, like the Epistle of Barnabas—sometimes numbered among the New Testament texts—whose author declares that, if he writes to his interlocutors who already abound in faith, this is "so that, along with the faith that you *possess*, you may have perfect gnosis."[18] This is also why St. Paul can say, with some lines intervening (1 Cor. 8:1–7): "We all have gnosis" and "all do not have gnosis," according to whether it is simple theoretical knowledge which is, as such, an "ignorant" knowledge, full of itself, or else an actual realization of its transcendent and divine nature, which shelters it from all "external" attack (learned ignorance).

There remains to be asked why St. Paul is, as it were, the only New Testament writer to speak of *gnosis*, and why St. John

---

17 As is proven by a certain number of passages: Rom. 15:13–14, Eph. 1:15–18, 3:16–19 (we have commented upon this text in *Love and Truth*, 241–48), Col. 1:14, &c. All these texts give gnosis pre-eminence over faith. But other texts also give first place to charity. There is no contradiction: there is no knowledge without love, and no love that is not, in its essence, knowledge.

18 I, 5. cf. *Les ecrits des Peres apostoliques* (Paris: Cerf, 1963), 242.

GENERAL PROBLEMS OF GNOSIS

is totally unaware of this term,[19] although one may with good reason consider him the most "gnostic" writer of the New Testament. Surely the response will be that we need to see here a proof of the influence of the Septuagint Bible which, as we have seen, is the first to confer an essentially religious connotation upon this term. A man as versed in rabbinical science as Paul was must have been especially sensitive to this influence. Certainly more than a St. John, whose knowledge has its source in the direct vision of Gnosis incarnate, Jesus Christ, and who, in expressing himself, essentially uses lofty traditional symbols rather than concepts.[20]

However, St. Paul's particular situation would not be enough to explain the quasi-absence of gnosis in the Gospels. We believe that another, more profound and less circumstantial reason must be added here. This is that, among the founding authorities recognized by Christian dogmatics, St. Paul occupies an altogether curious place. He is certainly a major authority, one of the "pillars of the Church," a custodian of the authentic message, and yet he has never "known Christ in the flesh"![21] Every Christian is obliged to believe that the totality of Revelation has been given in Jesus Christ, and that the Apostles are its authorized custodians only because they have received it. Given the supernatural character of this Revelation, it necessarily comes from the outside: *fides ex auditu*, says St. Paul. In relation to this Revelation (written or oral) that alone is authoritative, there can be only private revelations (stripped of the authority *of faith*) or theological commentaries explaining revealed data. That St. Paul, like any other Christian, has *received* a teaching from the Apostles, this is incontestable. However, among all those sharing in this situation, he is the only one whose word has the value of revelation. This is because, in addition, he has received a revelation directly from the Lord

---

19 There is moreover, in the Johannine writings, no noun for designating knowledge. In return, it is with him that the most numerous instances of *ginosko* and *oida* (*eidenai* in the infinitive) occur. We always rely on data furnished by the *Concordance de la Bible, Nouveau Testament* (Paris: Cerf and D. D. B., 1970).
20 Let us be clear: we accept, for all practical purposes, as a certainty the traditional identification of the author of the fourth gospel with St. John the apostle.
21 Cf. 1 Corinthians 15:8.

himself (1 Cor. 11:23). It confirms or completes the apostolic tradition, but the mode of its communication can be only interior.[22] Christian dogmatics admits then that there may be at least *one* revelation not coming uniquely from the "historical" Christ, but also from the inner Son whom God, St. Paul tells us, has revealed "within me" (Gal. 1:16). In other words, it admits that there can be a "spiritual experience" equal to revelation, a mode of knowledge through which the pneumatized intellect participates in the knowledge that God grasps of himself in his Word. True, for St. Paul this experience assumes an exceptional character—it is willed by God as a doctrinal norm and reference of the Christian faith, *yet without forming a "second revelation."* And yet the very existence of such a mode of knowledge proves that the Christian religion does not *a priori* dismiss it. Indeed, it is to this mode of knowledge, which realizes the perfection of faith, that St. Paul gives the name gnosis. This knowledge obviously does not exhibit in every "gnostic" the degree it does in St. Paul, nor above all does it possess his privilege as objective norm for a traditional collectivity (which makes Paul a "pillar of the Church"), but it remains a possibility in principle. This is why it is so important for Christianity to count St. Paul—he who "did not know Christ according to the flesh"—specifically among the pillars of the Church.[23]

However, St. Paul's gnosis should not be considered solely under its charismatic and inner aspect. This is surely the most profound and *decisive* dimension, but not the unique one. As its name indicates, Pauline *"gnosis"* is also a knowing in the primary sense of the term, which therefore implies a properly intellectual activity, potentially capable of being formulated and expressed in a clear and precise way. From this point of view, St. Paul opposes glossolalia, an indistinct and inarticulate

---

22 "For I declare to you, brothers, the gospel which I have preached to you has nothing from man; for it is not from a man that I have received or learned it, but by a revelation of Jesus Christ," Gal. 1:12.
23 Assuredly, the privilege of having received a revelation from the *glorified* Christ, through the *communication* of the Holy Spirit, is not peculiar to St. Paul: all the apostles have benefited from this, since revelation is closed only at the death of the last of them. But what remains is that St. Paul did not know Christ "historically."

"speaking in tongues," to "speaking in gnosis," which uses the meaningful articulations of language to transmit a knowledge, a doctrine, and, as a consequence, for the "building up" of the community (1 Cor. 14:6–19). Gnosis is at once ineffable and interior, a spiritual state, but also objective and able to be formulated, a doctrinal *corpus*. It is thus transmissible and can be the object of a *tradition*. Let us go further. The specificity of gnosis resides exactly in the conjunction of these two aspects. True gnosis is not an abstract theory, a futile conceptuality illusorily contenting itself with its own formulations, or a confused mysticism all too easily lapsing into the incommunicable. In this light, one understands the importance with which this term could not fail to be clothed in the eyes of the first Christians and, later, of the first Church Fathers. Something of the irreplaceable and the infinitely precious would be formulated with it: the affirmation of a kind of "internal verification" of the outwardly revealed and believed doctrine, the possibility for theology[24] to be something other than a simple rational exercise, to accede to an intellective and delightful experience of dogmatic truth — in short, to a *sacred intellectuality*. Such are the reasons inducing the early Fathers to make use of this term, even though they had other words at their disposal for expressing the idea of knowledge.

This is the case, in the highest degree, with St. Clement of Alexandria, the (so named) greatest doctor of Christian gnosis, who presents it at once as a secret tradition taught by Christ to a few apostles,[25] as consisting in the interpretation of the Scriptures and the fathoming of dogmas,[26] and finally as the perfection of the spiritual life and the fulfillment of the grace of the Eucharist.[27] This is also the case with Origen, who however, in *Contra Celsus*, also uses such terms as *dogma*, *didaskalia*, *episteme*, *logos*, *sophia*, *theologia*, &c., but who maintains the use of "gnosis"

---

24 This word only acquired its current sense later (after the thirteenth century). Originally, for Christians, it designated sacred writers (St. John, for example), or even the pure contemplative.
25 *Hypotyposes*, fragment 13.
26 *Stromateis* VII, 57, 3.
27 *Strom.*, V, 66, 1–5: "For gnosis of the divine substance is the eating and drinking of the divine Logos."

The Scriptural Origins of Gnosis

and "gnostic," even while combating a heretical gnosticism, he who has stated that "Christians have no fear of employing the same vocabulary as the Gnostics."[28] We see the same attitude in St. Irenaeus of Lyons, whose *Against the Heresies* combats the "gnosis with a false name" in order to establish "true gnosis," and likewise in St. Dionysius the Areopagite or St. Gregory of Nyssa. Thus there has incontestably existed an authentically Christian gnosis.[29] And surely it was a great misfortune for the West that the Latin language included no equivalent term for translating *gnosis*, for neither *agnitio* or *cognitio*, nor *scientia* or *doctrina* had received from their biblical, and afterwards Pauline, usage the sacred significance of the Greek word.[30] This semantic inferiority obviously must have favored the appearance and development of a theological rationalism, leading necessarily to the anti-intellectual reactions of existential theology and, ultimately, to the disappearance of the *doctrina sacra*.

But, after the biblical and Paulino-Patristic use of the word *gnosis*, we must come to its heretical use, since it is this that has given birth to what is called "Gnosticism." This use already appears in St. Paul when he denounces the "gnosis with a false name" (1 Tim. 6:21). Likewise in St. John, whose insistence on defining the divine "knowing" (*ginoskein*), can be understood as a warning against a falsification of Christic gnosis. However, in the current state of our documentation, it is impossible to affirm, at the time of the New Testament, the existence of a clearly defined and organized gnosticism. As underscored on many occasions,[31] tendencies, gnosticizing germs are involved

---

28 Marguerite Harl, *Origène et la fonction révélatrice du Verbe incarné* (Paris: Seuil, 1958), 419.
29 Louis Bouyer, "Gnôsis. Le sens orthodoxe de l'expression jusqu'aux Pères alexandrins," published in the *Journal of Theological Studies*, N. S. 4 (1953): 188–203.
30 Sometimes one finds moreover a pure and simple transposition of the Greek into Latin—thus, in the Latin version of the *Adversus Haereses* of St. Irenaeus (I, 29, 3)—though the term is generally translated as *agnitio* and more rarely as *scientia*. Let us point out that the Latin translators of the Jewish Neo-Platonic poet Ibn Gabirol have rendered the Hebrew *yediah* as *sapientia*, which would be, in fact, the most appropriate, to the extent that it expresses the unity of knowledge and wisdom.
31 Simone Pétrement, "Sur le problème du gnosticisme," *Revue de Métaphysique et de Morale*, num. 2 (1980): 152; *cf. Le Dieu séparé*, 23.

here, not an avowed and fully formed heresy. Let us not seek to make texts say what they do not say. And besides, the matter is self-evident.

The extraordinary gnostic power of the Word's manifestation in Jesus Christ could not but engender excess in some minds. Thus the charismatic complexity of the gnostic experience must have developed along with a solidification in the denial of a "Christ according to the flesh" (and, with this, corporeal creation), to the extent that gnosis is imagined as a grace of knowledge experienced in the soul's interiority. Whoever says knowledge says, in fact, degrees of knowledge, and whoever says grace given says giver: the degrees of gnosis therefore require a hierarchy of givers, hence the multiplication of divine intermediaries and the indefinite complication of angelology and cosmo-theology. On the other hand, the dramatic over-accentuation of spiritual interiority, which gives prominence to the esoterizing elitism of the sects, leads to the rejection of the Word-made-flesh and, as a consequence, to "miscosmism" and scorn for the Creator, the evil God, reduced to his demiurgic function.

Now, Christic gnosis is specifically characterized by its unity and simplicity. Divine intermediaries are reduced to the unicity of the Word-made-flesh (St. John), the Mediator between God and men (St. Paul). With respect to pre-Christian doctrines pertaining to "universal gnosis"—whether Jewish, Hellenistic, Egyptian or, possibly, Near Eastern—this is a great novelty. Christ is Himself the gnosis of God, and this gnosis, having taken a human body, is manifested to all men, in this way realizing a dazzling, metaphysical short-circuit. All degrees of knowledge, and therefore realities (the multiplicity of aeons), are synthetically "recapitulated" in Christ,[32] who thus offers a direct way to the gnosis of God. On the other hand, although the gnostic experience necessarily remains something inner and therefore esoteric, since it is the work of the Holy Spirit, yet it is immediately offered to everyone.

---

[32] Re-capitulation = *ana-kephalaiosis*, cf. Eph. 1:10. This term also signifies: to lead back to the head, to the Principle, and this is the true sense of "recapitulation" (*caput* = head).

The Scriptural Origins of Gnosis

By these two characteristics, Christic gnosis effects a kind of anticipated restoration of the Golden Age and the Edenic state. But this is precisely what extreme gnostics cannot accept. In a certain way, what has impressed and converted them is the new and irresistible energy of the Christic manifestation: it is conveyed visibly by the power of the Spirit. But they live this novelty out of ancient patterns: they want to put the new wine into old wineskins. Through its message of pure interiority, this new energy, to which they could not remain insensible, awakened the echo of ancient doctrines, which either they had known directly because they were initiated into them and had come from them, or, having only heard of them, were led by their conversion to Christianity to rediscover and become more and more interested in them. Such is, we think, the probable origin of what is rightly called gnosticism today, the historical existence of which is attested to, about the second century, in the writings of St. Clement of Alexandria, St. Irenaeus of Lyons, and St. Hippolytus of Rome. We see here something like a phenomenon of a revival of ancient and varied doctrines under the overwhelming and revelatory effect of the Christic manifestation, in which is to be heard an irresistible appeal to spiritual interiority; for this is the most central significance of the message of Jesus, the Word Incarnate. This appeal, which resounded in every ear with such urgent and obvious accents, came into consonance with many esoteric traditions, more or less somnolent, decadent, or sclerotic. The light of the Word suddenly illuminated them, raising them from obscurity, restoring to memory their living significance that had appeared to be irremediably lost. Refusing, then, to be grafted onto the trunk of the Christic olive tree and to be borne by the true root of gnosis, they wanted to do the opposite, to graft the Christic branch onto the trunk of ancient traditions, so as only to profit from its vitality and revitalize their ancient traditions.[33]

---

[33] We are commenting freely here on Rom. 11:17–24. St. Paul's paradox, which reverses the normal process of grafting, has been pointed out. But this is because the supernatural order is, in certain respects, against the grain of the natural order. Christ is the true tree, the cultivated olive, with respect to

Our explanation should not claim perfect certainty, but it at least has the merit of probability. Besides, it accords with the fact that, on the one hand, gnosticism is a Christian heresy, and on the other, that one recognizes in it doctrinal fragments of every provenance, often pre-Christian in origin. Finally, it rests essentially upon taking the powerfully gnostic character of the Christic manifestation into account, which seems hardly taken into consideration up until now.

As one sees, the stakes for this redoubtable question are not slight, and this is why we had to expand upon its history. It is highly significant that gnosticism was the first Christian heresy and that, in a certain way, the entire history of the West has been changed by it. For heretical gnosticism, although almost completely disappearing in the fifth or sixth century, has at least succeeded in one thing: it has discredited the New Testament word *gnosis* and, by this very fact, has made suspect the mere idea of a *sacred intellectuality*.

---

which all previous traditions, pagan or even Jewish, are wild olives. We can only transplant ourselves into Him. By the very fact of the appearance of the Christic tradition, all other traditions, even the most ancient, are as if thrown off-center and uprooted. This is what St. Paul means.

CHAPTER 3

Truly Named Gnosis

THE USE I HAVE MADE OF THE TERM "GNOSIS" in *La charité profanée*[1] unleashed an actual tempest in some circles. Accustomed to reading the term *gnosis* in the Greek Fathers, I had no idea its use would cause such violent reactions, especially from ecclesiastical writers—I had forgotten that it was still held in such ill repute. Frankly, I thought that I had forestalled these criticisms, both by showing, with the help of historical argument, that the word *gnosis* was scriptural in origin and therefore basically Christian, and by maintaining that there is no real difference between true gnosis and the content of the Christian faith. Despite all of this, some are of the opinion that I have played fast and loose with the heretical deviations of gnosticism and that, if gnosis is nothing but faith, we should stop using such an ambiguous term, a term that gives rise to confusion and misunderstanding, when there is a clear and unequivocal one.

Although not irrelevant, these objections seem to undermine my general thesis: namely, the legitimate existence of a way of gnosis (in the proper sense of the term) within the bosom of Christianity. To avoid misunderstandings, however, we need to take them into account as much as possible, although some criticism stems from a malice impervious to all reasoning.

My intention is then to clarify the distinction between true and false gnosis and provide an objective criterion enabling us to discriminate, *de jure* and not simply *de facto*, between one and the other. For it is not solely by the will of ecclesial practices that a particular usage is declared deviant and another not: it is at first in the name of the intrinsic truth of gnosis. However, before proposing such a criterion, it will be advantageous to ever so briefly prolong the short historical account

---

[1] Bouère, France: Dominique Martin Morin, 1979; *Amour et Vérité* (Paris: L'Harmattan, 2011) is the retitled and revised edition of this work.

of the previous chapter and cast a glance over the practices of the early centuries.

"GNOSIS" AND "GNOSTICISM" IN THE EARLY CENTURIES
Gnosis Is Primarily Jewish and Principally Christian

My starting point is the one I have already recalled and explained: gnosticism is a specifically Christian heresy—and the first of all the others—because it is within the bosom of Christianity, and chiefly with St. Paul, that the word *gnosis* was used to specifically designate the inner and saving knowledge of the divine mysteries. Surely, here Christianity is heir to the Greek-language Jewish tradition (both scriptural and liturgical), since it is this tradition that inaugurated the religious use of *gnosis* to translate the Hebrew *yd*. But ultimately, as the texts show, it is the Christian New Testament and apostolic writings that elaborate a complete doctrine of gnosis, conferring on the term its loftiest meaning, since these are the texts that provide the most numerous and most significant occurrences of this term.

One can go even further and maintain that the term "gnostic," as applied by heresiologists to the doctrines that they combat, often has only a polemical value and corresponds to no title recognized by the heretics themselves. At least this is the case, with some rare exceptions, during the first two or three centuries, for afterward the sects more readily claimed as their own a title upon which their struggle with the Great Church had conferred some prestige. But many doctrines qualified as "gnostic" remain, and yet have no precise connection with any particular gnosticism and are quite ill-defined.

Not only is this remark valid for the ancient adversaries of the gnostic heresies, it can also be applied to the modern proponents of these same heresies. But before these proponents excitedly throw themselves at the famous "Gospel according to Thomas" discovered at Nag Hammadi in Egypt, as if we were being confronted with certain teachings of Christ predating the supposed falsification to which St. Paul and the official Church had subjected it, they should first ask themselves not only if it is possible to establish the antiquity of these writings

Truly Named Gnosis

but also whether or not we are dealing with a Gnostic Gospel. On this subject, a recent work devoted to the best known of these lately discovered manuscripts concludes: "This collection of the 'words of Jesus' is, under the form presented, brazenly apocryphal in its artificial composition and its fictitious attribution to Thomas, who in reality played only an episodic role.... Likewise we need to recognize... that the writing is discrete about gnosis as codified by the major sects."[2]

Is the title "Gnostic" purely extrinsic then? Do the heresiologists, careless about details, so name all heresies that, having no bearing on a specific point of Catholic dogma, can only be designated either by the name of their founders, or by a more general term marking an equally general corruption of faith?

Some Heretics Have Claimed For Themselves the "Gnostic" Title

As contestable as they may seem to the eyes of modern historians, the heresiological categories of early church writers are not in reality uniformly devoid of precision. Several among the greatest of these authors sometimes distinguish between self- and hetero-designations.

At the beginning of his major work *Against the Heresies* (circa 180), St. Irenaeus of Lyon forewarns us that those whom he is to combat, and whom he often calls "gnostics," call themselves "disciples of Valentinus."[3] And although he deems these gnostics as the ancestors of the Valentinians, he does not formally identify the two.[4] Conversely, he expressly underscores that

---

2 Jean Doresse, *L'Evangile de saint Thomas* (Paris: Rocher, 1988), 71, 222. Following Doresse, however, let us mention that some of the elements making up this false Gospel might originate in traditions predating the establishment of the canonical Gospels (69-70). As for the words of Christ unknown to canonical or parallel literature (whether apocryphal or ecclesiastical) disclosed by the pseudo-Thomas, they number about 40 of the 114 *logia* (according to Henri Puech, *En quête de la gnose* [Paris: Gallimard, 1978], 2:51-2). On the other hand, its "false" quality is in no way prejudicial to the theological and spiritual value of a text that, to the contrary, surely presents a very ancient interpretation of Christianity, an interpretation that is "excessively subtle in its concepts, very exacting... in its ideals, and in an odd way anticipates some of the most beautiful flights of the mystical Latin Middle Ages" (Doresse, *L'Evangile de Saint Thomas*, 73).
3 Preface, 2; Fr. trans. Adelin Rousseau (Paris: Cerf, 1984), 28.
4 Ibid., I, 29, 1 and note 1, 121.

Carpocrates and the Carpocratians, about whom he is speaking, "confer on themselves the title of gnostics."[5]

Likewise Clement of Alexandria, who is not a heresiologist in the proper sense of the term,[6] points out on several occasions that he knew a particular group or individuals claiming the title of gnostic for themselves. This is the case, he informs us, of the disciples of a certain Prodicos (known only through Clement) who "call themselves gnostics."[7] He gives the same indication for the Carpocratians—which confirms the declaration of St. Irenaeus.[8] Lastly, the same remark is made about another group (also disciples of Prodicos?) and about which Clement declares: "I know that I have met with one heresy, the promoter of which states that we should fight against voluptuousness: according to this noble gnostic (for he himself also claimed to be a gnostic!), we should enter the field of voluptuousness itself to wage a feigned war."[9] A generation after Clement, Origen likewise recognized that "*certain (heretics) proclaim themselves gnostics in the same way that Epicureans style themselves philosophers.*"[10]

We will cite again the case of St. Epiphanius, who died at the beginning of the fifth century. This bishop of Salamis was endowed with a vast erudition (he knew five languages, Syriac, Coptic, and Hebrew among them), but was known neither for his broad-mindedness nor for his insight—he was essentially a battler. As an heresiologist he depends in part

---

5   Ibid., I, 25, 6, 116.
6   The *Stromateis* contain many accounts of heresies and heresiarchs, whether known elsewhere or not, but these accounts are not the main object. This aspect of the Clementine writings has been hardly studied.
7   *Strom.*, III, 30, 1; likewise: I, 69 and VII, 41; &c.
8   *Strom.*, III, 5, 1; cf. A. Méhat, *Études sur les Stromates* (Paris: Seuil, 1966), 402-3. Irenaeus and Clement agree in seeing the Carpocratians as "licentious gnostics," but the former presents them as Christianized Jews, the latter as Platonists. Irenaeus was born around 125 and probably died at the beginning of the third century. He was an Easterner who, at Smyrna, had been the disciple of St. Polycarp, himself a disciple of St. John. Clement was born about 150 (in Athens) and died about 215. His surname is of Latin origin. Before his baptism he was certainly initiated into the Eleusinian mysteries, about which he and he alone betrays "rare and precious information" (Méhat, op. cit., 43).
9   *Strom.* II, 117, 5-6; Méhat, 403, n 41.
10 *Contra Celsus*, V, 61. The passage in italics is from Celsus.

Truly Named Gnosis

upon the *Against the Heresies* of St. Irenaeus, the first book of which he transcribed. But he also had a direct knowledge of certain heretical groups and their literature. This is why it is so much more significant to see him occasionally object to the title "gnostic": "The Valesians," he says, "are not gnostics."[11]

We will return in a moment to Epiphanius, but for now we must come to the point of this brief inquiry. Are the cited texts[12] proof enough that one or several sects qualifying themselves as gnostic have indeed existed? The answer is not obvious, and perhaps the question is badly posed.

In other words, a certain heresiological "attitude" should be revised, an attitude that pertains more to our contemporaries than to the ancients. Let us leave aside the historians (Harnack, Bousset, Leisegang, Puech, Pétrement, Quispel, &c.) whose interests are, in principle, purely scientific. Rather let us consider the theologians, the church writers, the polemicists, in short all those for whom the idea of heresy is more meaningful. Like it or not, they are the ones who have imposed their own categories on the historians, because, in characterizing a religious movement as a heresy by definition, they have made it an object of study for the historians.

That this heresy is called "gnosticism" is not a historical fact, but a contrivance or by-product of the study of the ancient heresiologists by modern authors. That there was *a single* possibly complex movement, with enough unanimity, however, to be subsumed under a single concept, a movement brought together under a single label ("gnosticism"), so that in every instance it would be legitimate (and easier) to substitute the label for the thing itself to indicate what was being implied— this was something totally unknown to medieval doctors and theologians. What is more, and despite appearances, it was in fact unheard-of in Christian antiquity. To this we will add, for the sake of the most implacable foes of gnosis: neither is there any written trace in the official texts of the Church's

---

11 *Panarion*, LVIII, 1, 3. The *Panarion* ("medicine chest" in Greek) is usually cited under the name *Haereses* (Heresies). The Valesians were a sect of eunuchs.
12 Cf. the dossier in Tardieu and Dubois, *Introduction à la littérature gnostique*, 26–29.

magisterium of the condemnation of a heresy named "gnosis" or "Gnosticism."

However, from the extreme theological right to the extreme theological left (for once united), everyone concurs in denouncing what appears to both sides as the worst corruption of the faith and the greatest danger it has ever or may ever run: "eternal gnosis."[13] For gnosis *is* eternal. It is always reborn from its ashes and therefore must always and everywhere be suspect. In this hunt for gnostics, the fiercest and proudest ultra-traditionalists lend a hand—without difficulty, without revulsion—to the most radical and ecstatic revolutionaries, neither of whom seem at all surprised by such a pairing.

What the Term *Gnostic* Really Means

And yet, we will be told, have you not yourself admitted that this label was claimed by at least some of the heretics? Yes, but the entire question is precisely here: because we are by no means convinced that this claim holds the value and meaning of an *heresiological category*—at least in the beginning—either in the mouths of the heresiarchs or their disciples, or beneath the pens of the heresiologists. The literature on this subject is immense, and we are by no means an expert on it. However, I do not think that any of these alleged references to the term *gnostic* can show that it has an identifiable heresiological value.

How could it be otherwise, since early Christian tradition made good use of the term *gnosis*? Why were the heresiologists always careful to denounce any abuse of the word *gnosis* by heretics, and why, without further concern, did they acquiesce when the enemies of the church qualified themselves as "gnostics"? St. Paul is the first to expose the fraud of "pseudo-gnosis," inviting Timothy to flee "the contradictions of what is falsely called gnosis," *antitheses tes pseudonymou gnoseos* (1 Tim. 6:20).

---

13 This is the title of an already indicated work that H. Cornélis and A. Léonard published in Arthéme Fayard's collection, "Je sais—Je crois" (num. 146). This well-documented and balanced work in no way exhibits the attitude alluded to here. But this title is also that of the July–September 1983 issue (num. 53) of the review *Question de* devoted to gnosis, and edited by Emile Gillabert, head of a violently anti-Catholic "gnostic" school whose so-called "scientific" theses seem to be rather questionable; cf. *infra*, chap. 17, 365.

Truly Named Gnosis

This can indeed be translated, as in *The Jerusalem Bible*: "the objections of a pseudo-science,"[14] but the modern reader will no longer understand why St. Irenaeus thought it necessary to return to this expression in the title of his greatest work, and burden it with a long explanation, for nothing is more banal in today's language than the term science. But why does St. Paul feel the need to defend the very word *gnosis*? Why does he speak of a "falsely named" knowledge and not just of a true or false knowledge? His formula can mean only one thing: true knowledge is also *the* knowledge par excellence, that unique knowledge which, for this reason alone, must have reserved for it the term *gnosis*; and this is also why, despite certain well-founded objections, we deem it necessary to preserve this term.

Thus we see that gnosis is an immense and sacrosanct reality, a profound and mysterious reality, spoken about by the Christians among themselves without need of further explanation, *both* because each one concurs in seeing here a designation for the inward and intimate "knowledge" of God, for the effective and heartfelt awareness of the Spirit infusing itself into the soul of the believer through the grace of Jesus Christ (in short, the realization of faith), *and* precisely because such knowledge, at least in its essence, is unutterable, transcending every word, distinction, and formal awareness that we can have of it. This is why St. Paul not only specifies that "not all possess this gnosis" (1 Cor. 8:7), but also that a poorly understood gnosis makes one proud: "Gnosis puffs up, but charity builds up. If any one imagines that he knows something, he does not yet know as he ought to know" (1 Cor. 8:2–3). This means that true gnosis does not pose as knowledge that one could speak about and be dazzled with, but that it is in some manner "unknown" to itself.

St. Clement of Alexandria, that preeminent doctor of Christian gnosis who unveils this mystery as much as possible without betraying its explicit contents, puts forward no other doctrine. Fénelon, in the seventeenth century, was able to draw a collection of texts from Clement's multifaceted work,

---

14 Trans. note: Although not as glaring, the English version of *The Jerusalem Bible* likewise "waters down" this passage by rendering it as "the antagonistic beliefs of the 'knowledge' which is not knowledge at all."

entitling it *Le gnostique*;[15] and rightly so, since for Clement this term designates the perfect Christian, the one who has arrived at the goal of a perfect knowledge of Christ. From Clement, and through Origen, the tradition of this term has been bequeathed to the spiritual theology of Greek Christianity from Evagrius of Pontus to St. Symeon the New Theologian.

Now, the doctrine of St. Clement seems to lead us to an important discovery, one, strange to say, that has gone unperceived. It consists of only a few words: *the term gnostic does not designate one's belonging to a sect or religious school; it designates a spiritual state*, and quite precisely the spiritual state of one who has attained the goal of the Christian way, and therefore that of the "knowledge" of Christ, insofar as it is possible to attain it here below. It is the loftiest state: "The gnostic is consequently divine, and already holy, God-bearing, and God-borne."[16] And again, the Word "impresses on the gnostic the seal of the perfect contemplation, according to his own image; so that there is now a third divine image,"[17] so that the gnostic's very body becomes spiritual.[18]

Basically, the solution seems to correspond to the one given for the Rosicrucians by Réné Guénon, a term which, according to him, should not be applied to an initiatic organization but to those who have been reintegrated into the primordial state, a state symbolized by the rose at the center of the cross.[19] And although formed independently, my conclusion can only be confirmed by such a comparison.

A comparison with such terms as *Yogi* or *Sufi* is even more justified, since the gnostic of St. Clement has in fact surpassed the state of primordial man (or the adamic state) to attain the

---

15 This manuscript, discovered in the library of Saint-Suplice in 1927, was edited by the Rev. Dudon for Beauchesne in 1930. A new edition would be desirable. The review *La Place Royale* (num. 37 [October, 1996]: 48–102) has republished Fénelon's text, but without Dudon's introduction and notes. Cf. *infra* chap. 8, 268–69.
16 *Strom.*, VII, 13, 82.
17 *Strom.*, VII, 3, 16. Surely the first two images are those of the Word and his humanity.
18 *Strom.*, VII, 14; we are following Fénelon, op. cit., 216–18.
19 *Perspectives on Initiation*, trans. H. D. Fohr (Ghent, NY: Sophia Perennis, 2004), 242–48.

Christic or "monadic" state, the state of deified man.[20] One can moreover gauge the transcendence of the gnostic state when St. Clement declares that "the gnostic *has created himself*,"[21] that is, through love the gnostic unites himself to God's act of love creating him.[22] Such is the reason why Christian heresiologists inveighed with mockery and scorn against the sacrilegious pretense of those who adorned themselves with the title of "gnostic." Reread the texts cited from Irenaeus or Clement, and you will see that their writings by no means imply a set categorization. But neither is one implied by those who designate themselves as such: in doing this, they are by no means indicating their affiliation with a group so named, a group that has left no historical trace, but are arrogating to themselves a spiritual state.

Now, that this pretentious as well as ridiculous claim might have ended up by taking on the sense of a label, a label for designating heretical groups in a convenient, expeditious, and yet extremely vague manner, seems most probable, since this corresponds to a common outcome in such matters, examples of which are to be met with in all other cultures. Thus a Muslim holy man has said: "in the beginning Sufism was a reality without name, today it is a name without reality."

CRITERIOLOGY
The Decisive Proof of True Gnosis

Many difficulties are resolved by our thesis. In particular it answers objections raised against the authenticity of the pastoral epistles (1 and 2 Timothy and Titus), which are said to combat a gnosticism quite posterior to the time of St. Paul.[23]

---

20 *Love and Truth*, trans. G. J. Champoux (New York: Angelico, 2020), 406–9.
21 *Strom.* VII, 13, 3.
22 For a non-pantheistic interpretation of this "self-creation," cf. *The Sense of the Supernatural*, trans. G. J. Champoux (Edinburgh: T & T Clark, 1998), chap. 12; also, Father A. D. Sertillanges O. P., *L'idée de création et ses retentissements en philosophie* (Paris: Aubier, 1945), 59.
23 A thesis upheld by Simone Pétrement (*Le Dieu séparé*, 20, n 22): "the pastoral letters probably date from the end of the first century or the beginning of the second," that is "from the very period when the distinction between Creator and true God clearly made its appearance." This thesis, less in vogue today, was refuted in a rigorous manner by Philippe Rolland:

What St. Paul fought against is not gnosticism properly so-called—actually non-existent during his time—but the excesses and deviations of a Jewish esoterism, likewise present in judaizing Christian milieux, or having come from elsewhere, in particular from Zoroastrianism and a degenerating Egyptian tradition. In their analyses of the facts, historians are in a general way purely and simply unaware of the fact that every religion almost always includes a more or less secret or discrete "esoteric" dimension, but also more or less aberrant and syncretist deviations from this orthodox esoterism.[24] Judaism is not exempt from this constant law, nor Christianity in its trend toward organization fostered by St. Paul.[25] A secret or discrete teaching is not a game of "hide-and-seek" according to a futilely elitist strategy. But, on the one hand, one should not cast pearls before swine (Matt. 7:6); and, on the other, there are several degrees of comprehension: the secret of secrets is inexpressible, and in Greek "esoteric" simply means "more interior." The existence of a deviated esoterism proves the need for and the danger of forgetting caution. To go inward is to go toward the Spirit; doing this, we pierce through the forms and, at least in certain respects, inwardly surpass them. This means: to know that there is a "beyond" of forms "in spirit and in truth" (John 4:23), and therefore also to know that form as such cannot bestow everything. The usefulness of sacred and ritual forms is in their visibility: this visibility is given to everyone and rivets the gaze of saving faith, thus diverting it from being scattered by multiplicity. Of itself, it determines a pure and an impure, and poses the inevitable alternative of good and evil to human freedom. This is why the esoteric ability to surpass forms cannot but appear, *outwardly,* as a surpassing

---

La mode "pseudo" en exégèse. Le triomphe du modernisme depuis vingt ans (Éditions de Paris, 2002), 100-34.

24 Sister Jeanne d'Arc distinguishes three levels of teaching. "Jesus did not uniformly dispense a uniform teaching... To the crowds, he spoke in parables, but to his disciples, he explained everything (Mark 4:34).... There was a teaching reserved... for the Twelve.... But he goes further with some from among them (Peter, James and John)." Introduction to the *Évangile de Jean* (Paris: Les Belles Lettres, 1990), v.

25 The question of esoterism in Christianity is dealt with especially in my *Christ the Original Mystery.*

of this crucifying duality, and, therefore as the right to escape from its jurisdiction: to the pure, all things are pure.

Do not be misled: it is exactly *here* that the initiatic test, the touchstone of the true gnostic, is situated. To whomsoever judges by appearances, gnosis seems to provide a *legitimate* and metaphysically based means of freeing oneself from the duality of good and evil. And so, by a classic inversion, it is this very freedom that becomes the criterion for gnosis—as if there could be an outward sign for gnosis!

By the very fact that it is pure and inward, gnosis eludes all notice, and therefore exposes any who unduly lay claim to it to the most redoubtable of spiritual dangers, to the most diabolic of illusions—that is, the belief that one has realized unity on the very plane of duality. To the contrary, the true gnostic knows there is no surpassing of this crucifying duality other than the path of crucifixion: such is the gnosis of Christ. But this does not obviate the existence of outwardly clever yet inwardly foolish men, for whom the encounter with gnosis is a source of pretension, pride, and immorality.

This is why it is not surprising that St. Paul's most important debates over gnosis relate specifically to a question of ritual purity or impurity: can a Christian eat the idolothytes, that is, the flesh of animals sacrificed to the pagan gods? "Now concerning food offered to idols, we know that all of us possess gnosis," he declares (1 Cor. 8:1); in other words: we have all received this spiritual doctrine that enables us to escape the consequences engendered by a transgression of taboos, because, once established on the spiritual (pneumatic) plane, we are raised above the psycho-corporeal plane where these consequences unfold. Thus, as he had declared previously: "all things are lawful for me" (1 Cor. 6:12) for "the pneumatic man judges all things, but is himself to be judged by no one" (1 Cor. 2:15); and "do you not know that we are to judge angels?" (1 Cor. 6:3) But the "freedom of the gnostic," the *exousia* (power) spoken of by St. Paul, through which he has power over everything,[26]

---

26 This major theme of 1 Corinthians, which St. Paul formulates with surprising boldness, has given rise to much controversy. All we can do is refer the reader to J. Dupont, *Gnôsis*, 265–377.

should not be subjected, in order to be proven, to a kind of universal obligation to transgress: "all things are lawful to me," or more exactly, "all things are under my power, but I will not be enslaved of anything" (1 Cor. 6:12). And this is why, being "free from all," St. Paul the gnostic, in the name of charity, makes himself a slave to all: "to the Jews I became as a Jew... to those under the law I became as one under the law... to those outside the law I became as one outside the law... to the weak I became weak... I have become all things to all men" (1 Cor. 9:19-23).

The Subversion of Gnosis and the Mystery of Iniquity

These remarks suffice to show why, to the contrary, many of those who "know themselves to be gnostics," those who claim to have access to a gnosis "beyond good and evil," are also those who sometimes give themselves up to the most ignoble and bestial practices. Here we rediscover a well-known modern current which, in the line of the tiresome Marquis de Sade, leads to the glorification of a violence destructive to all of *nature*—in reality a revolt against the gift of Creation—and to that *accursed share* of which Georges Bataille sought to be the "prophet."

In the eighteenth chapter of his *Panarion*, entitled "The Gnostics," St. Epiphanius relates a few of these practices, during the course of which veritable parodies of the Eucharist are enacted.

Men and women, after copulating, gather the sperm produced and consume it saying: "The Body of Christ." In the same way, when the occasion arises, the menstrual blood is collected and consumed by all: "And, they say, this is the Blood of Christ." But there is worse. If, in the course of these communal copulations, a woman becomes pregnant, then, once the fetus takes on a visible shape, they tear it from the womb and cast it into a mortar where it is ground with a pestle. To "prevent nausea," honey, pepper, and other spices are added to this mincemeat. Each one takes a small portion and, by means of this human flesh, communally celebrate *divine* worship.[27]

---

27 St. Epiphanius, *Adversus Haereses*, lib. I, tome II. *Haereses* XXVI, c. IV and V; P.G., tome XLI, col. 338-39. My translation summarizes the diffuse and complicated text of Epiphanius.

Here we touch on the very depths of horror. But should we believe what we are told by Epiphanius? We do not know.[28] However, even if we were to think this a case of "ordinary" licentiousness—the existence of which is uncontested—we find ourselves in the presence of a gnosis perverted by a complete lack of understanding, like that gnosis already denounced by St. Paul. For by no means is this a question of a *moral* fault, the result of a culpable abandon to the deviated instincts of our nature, but of a *spiritual* and metaphysical fault, by which one intends to prove to oneself and to others that one is truly free of all duality and every distinction, even of that distinction between sacrilege and the sacred. Now we see that we are also at the source of what should be called, in Guénon's vocabulary, the "Christian counter-initiation." And this should not surprise us, for *corruptio optimi pessima*; if gnosis is the perfection (*teleiosis*) of the Christian spiritual way, its corruption is the worst of counterfeits.

Several pages after having reported this example of "eucharistic cannibalism" (according to Michel Tardieu), St. Epiphanius makes note of a Gnostic work entitled *Genna Marias* (= *The Lineage of Mary*) in Greek: "Among other abhorrent discourses," this apocryphal work claims that Zechariah was killed in the Temple and explains why: "According to this writing," Epiphanius tells us, "Zechariah, having come to the temple to proceed with an incensing, beheld a man with the face of an ass standing in the Holy of Holies; and, as he wanted to warn the Jews by crying out: "Woe to you! What are you worshiping?" the one who had appeared to him inside the Temple deprived him of the use of speech. Some days later, having recovered his speech, he revealed this secret to the Jews: this is why they killed him… They add that this is why the legislature ordained that the high priest shake bells each time he fulfilled his function, so their tinkling would warn the one whom they worshipped there to cover himself and no one would be surprised by the obscene face of this specter."[29]

---

28 Some recent experts and researchers, such as Michel Tardieu, seem to credit the possibility of this account.
29 *Adversus Haereses*, lib. I, tome II, XXVI, XII; P. G., t. XLI, col. 349-51.

Here we see the ass-headed god appear in a treatise stemming from Gnostic literature. But this is not its first appearance. Flavius Josephus informs us that this strange calumny is to be met with in the writings of Apion, a grammarian of Alexandria in the first century of our era: "Apion has the effrontery to assert that the Jews kept an ass's head [in their holy place], worshipping that animal... made of gold and worth a high price."[30] Tacitus, in his *Histories* (1.5, 3, 4), takes note of this same gossip and, like Apion, attributes onolatry to the Jews.

About the same time, Christians fell victim in their turn to this accusation, sometimes at the hands of the Jews themselves. In his *Apologeticus* in defense of the Christians against the gentiles (197), Tertullian, after having mentioned the calumnies of Tacitus, reports that at Rome one of those men hired to fight with the beasts had "exhibited a picture with this inscription: God of the Christians, born of an ass (*onochoetes*).[31] He had the ears of an ass, was hoofed in one foot, carried a book, and wore a toga."[32] In another treatise, *To the Nations* (circa 200), Tertullian reports the same incident and comments: "The crowd believed it on the word of the infamous Jew? Why not? It is an opportunity to spread base lies against us. Thus, in all the city, they speak only of the god *onochoites*."[33]

To grasp the true significance of the onocephalic god, we need to recall first that this figure is of Egyptian origin: in fact it is one of the animal forms assumed by the god Set, "Osiris's brother and murderer, to whom the Greeks gave the name of Typhon."[34] Under the form of an ass, Set represents one of the

---

30 *Against Apion*, Bk. II, 7; Josephus: *The Life, Against Apion*, trans. H. St. J. Thackeray (Loeb Classical Library; Cambridge, MA: Harvard University Press, 1926), 325.
31 The exact form of this Greek word is *onokoites*; the term is disputed, but its meaning is clear: it involves the result of a copulation of an ass with a woman.
32 *The Ante-Nicene Fathers*, ed. Roberts and Donaldson, vol. 3, trans. S. Thelwall (Buffalo, NY: Christian Literature Publishing Company, 1885), 86.
33 I, 14; P. L., t. I, col. 651. According to Dom Henri Leclerq, a comparison needs to be made between this text and a passage from *Metamorphosis* (I, 14), where Apuleius speaks of a woman enamored of an ass who is most certainly a Christian: "she was initiated into a sacrilegious religion, she believed in a single God," etc.; *Dictionnaire d'archéologie et de liturgie*, vol. 1, col. 2042.
34 Guénon, *Symbols of Sacred Science*, trans. H. D. Fohr (Hillsdale, NY: Sophia Perennis, 2001), 134–35. The Seth-Typhon identification is late (Plutarch, *On*

most redoubtable entities to be encountered by the dead in the course of their journey beyond the grave. Also, notes Guénon: "one of the darkest aspects of the 'typhonian' mysteries was the cult of the 'god with the ass's head,' to which, as is known, the first Christians were sometimes falsely accused of belonging."[35]

Actually, as Guénon explains, what we have here is the "historical" origin of Satanism and of the counter-initiation, in other words of all that which, in revolt against the divine order, undertakes to use the power inherent in sacred forms contrary to their true sense, an inverted parody that takes the infranatural for the supernatural. Such an "inside out" use presupposes the loss of the sense of the supernatural,[36] and therefore a certain degeneration of the sacred forms where such an inversion first occurs; and, once actualized, such an inferior and rightly infernal possibility will obviously attempt to seize all religious forms, even in the full strength of their orthodoxy. Under the circumstances, Guénon links this origin to the disappearance of Atlantis—the inheritor of which the Egyptian tradition was in part—and to the symbolic data provided by the sixth chapter of Genesis.[37]

Isis and Osiris). Notice, however, that the god Set in reality bears a name of Semitic origin and hence manifests the penetration of Asiatic elements into Egypt: the Egyptian texts of the Eighteenth Dynasty (fifteenth to sixteenth centuries BC) present these invaders out of Asia as the "worshipers of Set" (André Caquot, "Les Sémites occidentaux," in *Histoire des Religions*, Pléiade, vol. I, 317). Set corresponds to Baal. Thus, fifteen hundred years before our era, the Egyptians were already accusing the Semites of "devil-worship."

35 Ibid., 138. Celsus, the Greek intellectual refuted by Origen in his *Contra Celsum*, evokes "the mysteries of Typhon, Horus and Osiris in Egypt" (*Contra Celsum*, VI, 42; Sources Chrétiennes, 147, 281), as the origin of the Judeo-Christian Satan. On this subject it would be better to pass over in silence the book by Jean Robin, *Seth, le Dieu maudit* (Paris: Trédaniel, 1986), which proposes, while making use of Guénonian doctrine (!), the rehabilitation of this infernal entity. Among other lies, the author, to support his thesis, cites the names of Flavius Josephus and Tertullian "who qualify the God of the Christians as *onokoites* (lying with an ass)" (page 69). Our own citations show the real value of a method that would have an author say the exact opposite of what he did say. Let us recall that the most ancient anti-Christian depiction of the ass-headed God is a graffito of the third century, the "Palatine crucifix," discovered at Rome in 1859 in the pages' chamber of the imperial palace: this caricature represents an onocephalic man on a cross worshiped by a person standing.

36 Cf. our book *The Sense of the Supernatural*.

37 *The Reign of Quantity and the Signs or the Times* (Ghent, NY: Sophia Perennis, 1995), 222–24.

This chapter recounts how certain angels coveted the "daughters of men" and united with them. Now there is, in fact, one text among others of the Hermetic tradition that relates this mysterious event to Set-Typhon. We hear Isis the prophetess reveal to her son Horus that "as (he) was leaving to do battle against Typhon ... one of the angels that reside in the first heaven, having seen her, wanted to have intercourse with her."[38] Clearly, this symbolically indicates a descent of energy from the spiritual to the psychic level, a fall from the heavenly into the earthly, a profanatory intermingling of the two.[39] And, in the Bible, this event has a direct connection with the Flood which, according to Guénon, corresponds to the disappearance of Atlantis.[40]

From all this data we can clearly see that certain so-called gnostic schools derive from an obviously Satanic and counter-initiatory current. This corroborates the invective found in the *Corpus Hermeticum* against the dualist sects, sects qualified as being "sons of Typhon."[41] And here we return to St. Paul's warnings against a pseudo-gnosis, the true origin of "gnosticism," "which was never a pure esoterism, but, to the contrary, the product of a certain confusion between esoterism and exoterism, hence its heretical character."[42]

Thus, in some respects, the attacks against gnosis made by some of the most "intransigent" circles of present-day Catholicism are justified; provided however that we observe two rules—which, for want of competence and objectivity, are almost never respected: one, that one does not rank, under the name of gnosticism, doctrines often unrelated to the previously mentioned *religious* deviations; and two, that one clearly emphasize, in agreement with scientific data, that this pseudo-gnostic

---

38 Opuscule of Isis to Horus, 1; trans. A. J. Festugière, *La révélation d'Hermès Trismégiste* (Louvain, Belgium: Gabalda, 1944), 2:256–7.
39 In the *Book of Henoch* (an Old Testament apocrypha accepted by the Ethiopian Church), which relates the same episode (VI–VIII), it is said that this event occurred "in the time of Yered" (VI, 6), a term that is etymologically tied to the verb *yarad*, "to descend." Cf. *La Bible. Ecrits intertestamentaires* (Pléiade, 1987), 476, n 6.
40 *Traditional Forms and Cosmic Cycles*, trans. H. D. Fohr (Hillsdale, NY: Sophia Perennis, 2001), 25.
41 J. Doresse, "L'hermétisme égyptianisant," *Histoire des religions*, tome II (Paris: Gallimard, 1972), 474.
42 Guénon, *Comptes rendus* (Paris: Éd. Traditionnelles, 1986), 205.

perversion is basically anti-gnostic. The first point poses the question of *doctrinal* gnosis in general. The second leads us to respond to this situation.

THEOLOGY
Doctrinal Gnosis or the Gnostic Dimension of the Act of Faith

As I mentioned, the enemies of gnosis are recruited from the Christians "of tradition," as well as from the Christians "of progress." In their condemnations, both sides tend to see it everywhere, and so rank very different systems of thought beneath the selfsame heading.

In a recent work devoted to the relationship between gnosis and ecumenism, Valentinus, Basilides, Descartes, Hegel, and so forth, are lumped together. In their (scientific) *Introduction à la littérature gnostique*, Tardieu and Dubois identify, among the various meanings of "gnostic," an "esoteric" one, associated with the names of Massignon, Corbin, Scholem, Ruyer, and so forth, and, of course, all the figures and streams of "Occult Philosophy" that Antoine Faivre calls "Hermetism" (alchemists, Rosicrucians, theosophists, and so forth).

We cannot pretend to settle so complex a question in a few lines, a question involving various authors whose works are sometimes quite extensive. However, one remark should cast some light into this realm where it touches on the essence of Christian gnosis. Simone Pétrement has observed that, among the gnostics, gnosis "is not knowledge in general," but a "*religious* knowledge, based on a *revelation*."[43] And this is incontestably true for the literature of "gnosticism." That some, like Gillabert and his disciples, make use of this gnosticism, or that some see in it the worst of Christian heresies, matters little: both recognize in it something sacred and "religious" bound up with the revelation of Christ. The texts prove it. If we leave aside the orgiastic and "Typhonian" counter-gnosis, for which there is scant documentation, the main body of writings speak only of the most lofty metaphysical, mystical, and symbolic questions in the language of religion.

---

43 *Le Dieu séparé*, 21.

GENERAL PROBLEMS OF GNOSIS

Under such conditions, how are we to link this gnosticism to the doctrine of someone like Raymond Ruyer who, in his famous work, *La gnose de Princeton*, explicitly foreswears any reference to Jesus Christ, all religious revelation, and all belief in the immortality of the soul?[44] Analogous remarks could be made with respect to Hegel, whose doctrine is often qualified as a gnosis that, although finding religion unobjectionable, nevertheless claims to surpass it, placing philosophy above revelation and explicitly stressing the impotence of Jacob Boehme's gnosis to rise to the full possession of self, to the pure transparency of the concept.[45]

Should these designations be rejected, then, in the name of historical rigor; and should we consider Ruyer and others, like Raymond Abellio, deceived in making them their own? Clearly, many feel that they are not altogether deceived, and may even be right.

This is in fact because neither the speculative vision of Ruyer's cosmologism, Hegel's idealism, or Abellio's dynamics, are by nature simply "scientific" or philosophical in the Kantian sense of the term, that is, reflexive and abstract. Without doubt they object to the idea of a revelation, or at least they proceed by methodologically placing it in parentheses, but this is not the way that someone like Descartes or Pasteur have set aside questions derived from faith. Far from separating science and religion, reason and revelation, intellect and faith, Hegel and Ruyer, with quite different styles of approach (Ruyer did not care much for Hegel) intend to clear the way for "scientific" knowledge that is also, and by itself, a quasi-mystical participation in the being of things. One has only to reread Hegel's

---

44 Paris: Arthème Fayard, 1974, 17 fn. 1 in particular, and 264–92. At this point we should mention that there never was a "Princeton gnosis," unless as an effect induced by the book itself. In reality, the ideas expounded in the book are the work of Ruyer, who had already expressed them in several previous works, for example, in his essay *Néo-finalisme* (Paris: PUF, 1952). Disappointed by the paltry success of his theses—which represent however the cosmology of modern science—he decided to fictitiously attribute them to a mysterious group of American neo-gnostics. We will return to this point in chap. 5.
45 *Encyclopedia of the Philosophical Sciences in Basic Outline, Part 1: Science of Logic*, trans. & ed. K. Brinkmann & D. O. Dahlstrom (Cambridge: Cambridge University Press, 2010), 18–19.

Truly Named Gnosis

enthusiastic commentaries on the *Bhagavad Gita* or the poems of Jallaludin Rumi (even though he indicates that this only has to do with an "exoteric exposition"),[46] and one will understand why the perfect realization of the philosophical goal might seem to be, as Hegel says, pantheistic to the ignorant.

But, in reality, "the esoteric study of God and identity, as of cogitations and notions, is philosophy itself."[47] Similarly, for Ruyer (who has written at least two books on God),[48] the ambition to be the "theologian" of modern science is incontestable, and the theme of ontological participation (to *be* is to participate in the God-Universe) underlies his entire thought.[49]

One may, and even should, reject Hegel's as well as Ruyer's "gnosis"; the first because it is only an immanentist panlogism, a pseudo-gnosis, the second because it is a gnosis amputated from its supernatural and rightly spiritual dimension.[50] But for all that, it does not seem possible to reject the *need for gnosis* as such, seeing that the root of every intellective aspiration is recognized therein. For it is just this that is at work here. In its excesses, limitations, or even deviations, Hegelianism, like Ruyerism or Spinozism, betrays a demand native to the human intellect that is the sense and expectation of true being, the sense of the absolutely real within us. This is an unassailable fact. Man is essentially and first of all an intellectual being, a knowing being, even though this knowing may be of the most humble sensory kind; as loudly and keenly as desire might speak within him, it speaks to someone who hears and recognizes it, someone for whom it makes sense or is repudiated. Man is never a desiring

---

46 *Hegel's Philosophy of Mind*, trans. W. Wallace (Oxford: Clarendon Press, 1894), § 573, 186, 189–91 for the Eastern texts.
47 Ibid., § 573, 196.
48 *Dieu des religions—Dieu de la science* (Paris: Flammarion, 1970); *L'embryogenèse du monde et le Dieu inconnu* (unpublished). *Neofinalism*, trans. A. Edlebi (Minneapolis: University of Minnesota, 2016) and *La genèse des formes vivantes* (Paris: Flammarion, 1958) are also, in some respects, books on God.
49 Cf. *La gnose de Princeton*, 70–71, 73 and, above all, 130: "Gnosis consists in wanting to have both participables and participation enter into science, just as into religious philosophy, through the front door.... It consists in showing that science reveals participation, but only by seeing its reverse side."
50 Cf. *infra*, chap. 4: "Hegel or the Transformation of Gnosis into Logic," and chap. 5: "Ruyerian Gnosis, Religion of the Scientific Age."

machine. But neither is he a believing machine, a "religious automaton" invested with some wholly external revelation or salvation completely incongruous to his nature. He also needs to recognize the Divine Word—it needs to make sense to him and, in return, he needs to recognize himself in it. In other words, and according to Frithjof Schuon's remarkable formula, we have to admit that the intellect is "naturally supernatural" or supernaturally natural.[51] For Revelation (by definition supernatural) to be welcomed into a believer's intellect, this intellect needs to have "natural"[52] forms of intelligibility at its disposal, forms capable of receiving it and in terms of which it will be interpreted. By understanding revelation, the intellect understands itself as well; it cannot but be "itself as well." And, if this self-understanding is not an idealist reduction of what is revealed to the *a priori* conditions for knowledge of the human subject, this is because these intelligible forms are naturally ordered to metaphysical and supernatural realities.

And here we are struck by the need for a "gnostic moment" in the act of faith. Seen as an ordered and coherent whole, those intelligible forms prerequisite to the reception of the Divine Word are, in themselves, a metaphysical doctrine. A mode of intellective receptivity suitable for revelation, this doctrine, insofar as taught and communicated with the help of language, can only be the object of a semi-natural act of *knowledge* denoted by the term *gnosis* in its literal meaning. This gnostic moment is, therefore, necessarily speculative.

And this is why it is impossible, even with good intentions, to make of the word *gnosis* a simple substitute for the word *faith*. Rather, it corresponds to that prior moment, speculative

---

51 Cf. for example *Light on the Ancient Worlds*, 2nd ed., trans. Lord Northbourne (Bloomington, IN: World Wisdom Books, 1984), 64; and *Survey of Metaphysics and Esoterism*, trans. G. Polit (Bloomington, IN: World Wisdom Books, 1984), 124.
52 We have put "natural" in quotation marks because these forms are such only with respect to revelation; they are in fact conveyed by culture (first by language) and therefore *learned* in some respects. Nevertheless we must presuppose, in the final analysis, some *innate* intelligible forms, since man is not a cultural automaton either: what culture teaches should also be received and therefore understood out of those *possibilities native* to the human spirit, which might be called a "primary cultural competence." One cannot learn *everything*, but clearly it is already necessary to "know" something.

in nature and therefore autonomous in some respects, in the course of which the intellect is informed of the metaphysical categories suitable for the reception of a faith both formed and purified by them. This doctrine can be learned and therefore enunciated with words, but obviously at very unequal levels: from the elementary catechism to Meister Eckhart, and passing through St. Augustine and St. Thomas Aquinas, the various "metaphysics of welcome" are variously emphasized. To recognize in them those gnostic moments that they really are, we must stop seeing them as simple exercises of natural reason; we must see them as actualizations of those theomorphic possibilities implied by man's creation "in the image of God," an image that original sin has erased from our intellect. This has to do, then, with an intrinsically sacred or naturally supernatural intellectuality; it involves those *logoi spermatikoi*, those Forms of the Divine Word sown in every intellect (the light of the Word "enlightens *every* man ... coming into this world" [John 1:9]), and is therefore a kind of inward and congenital revelation through those intellective icons—the metaphysical Ideas—immanent to the soul. This doctrinal gnosis, by whose light the theomorphic possibilities of the intellect are illuminated and actualized, is the "Adamic science." It is the metaphysical tradition transmitted from age to age, diversified and debased at Babel, restored or adapted by divine or angelic intervention according to the different humanities (a tradition that esoteric Platonism taught orally).[53] It is also the *unwritten* doctrine taught by the New Adam to his Apostles and those disciples capable of receiving it; capable—that is to say, firstly, endowed with nobility and virtue, and thus preserved from "licentious gnosis," and secondly, endowed with humility and the sense of the sacred, and thus preserved from that speculative lack of awareness that makes us forget the urgency of salvation for the illusory self-sufficiency of mind-games.[54] And, as we learn from

---

53 Cf. the very important work by Marie-Dominique Richard, *L'enseignement oral de Platon. Une nouvelle interprétation de Platon* (Paris: Cerf, 1986).
54 St. Clement explains that the mysteries of gnosis cannot be given to all, "so that they might not receive harm in consequence of taking in another sense the things declared for salvation by the Holy Spirit" (*Strom*. VI, 15).

St. Clement, such is the Gnostic tradition (*gnostike paradosis*): "If we give the name wisdom both to Christ himself and to his working through the prophets, by means of which it is possible to be instructed in the gnostic tradition, just as he himself at his coming taught the holy Apostles, then gnosis will be a kind of wisdom; indeed, it is a knowledge and a firm and sure comprehension of present, future, and past realities, transmitted and revealed by the Son of God. Consequently, if contemplation is the goal pursued by the wise man, anyone who still devotes himself to philosophy [who devotes himself to *philo-sophia*, the love of wisdom], no matter how much he presses on towards divine knowledge, will not attain it unless the prophetic word is explained by instruction[55] [= doctrinal gnosis affords an understanding of the Word of God], an instruction through which he learns the realities that are, will be, and have been, by also learning how they are, will be, and were. And this gnosis has come down to our own day, having been handed down in succession to a few from the Apostles in unwritten form."[56] Peter, James, John, and Paul are the first keepers of the gnostic tradition;[57] it is to them, specifies a Clementine text preserved by Eusebius, that "the Lord after his resurrection imparted gnosis... and they imparted it to the rest of the apostles, and the rest of the apostles to the seventy, of whom Barnabas was one."[58]

Clement does not divulge the content of this gnostic tradition. Cardinal Daniélou's thesis, which identifies it with Jewish apocalyptic and with the knowledge of posthumous states,[59] seems too fixated on the historical dimension. True, this apocalyptic, bound up with a meditation on the first three chapters of Genesis, involves a cosmology, and even a

---

[55] Cf. 2 Peter 1:19.
[56] *Strom.*, VI, 7; according to the (modified) translation of Cardinal Daniélou, "Les traditions secrètes des apôtres," in *Eranos Jahrbuch* (1962), 201.
[57] *Strom.*, I, 11, 3.
[58] *Hypotyposes*, fragment 13; Eusebius, *Ecclesiastical History*, II, 1, 4. Fragment 13 obviously does not mention St. Paul, who was not yet a disciple at the Resurrection and who would therefore receive gnosis only later.
[59] "Les traditions secrètes des apôtres," op. cit., 199–215; *Gospel Message and Hellenistic Culture*, trans. J. A. Baker (London: Darton, Longman & Todd, 1973), 445–58.

Truly Named Gnosis

metaphysics, which gnosis specifically takes as an object of formulation, but it is not only that. We should also see here a speculative dimension subjacent to Christian dogmatics, a dogmatics that is summarized by the *Apostles Creed*, incontestably a document of apostolic origin, even though (in its transmitted form) it is later since, up until the fourth century, it was taught in secret and orally.[60] Briefly stated, this involves, on the one hand, the most universal doctrinal principles with the help of which Revelation could be imparted, and on the other, those more particular thematic forms entrusted to the orthodox memory and understanding of the Christic mysteries (essentially the Trinity and the Incarnation), in the absence of which even the New Testament is unintelligible.[61]

As you see, we are not reluctant to formulate an *a priori* theory of doctrinal gnosis or to demonstrate the intrinsic need for it—a method decried by historians. It should be obvious that, from the written documents alone, no amount of historical investigation will ever reconstruct a satisfactory idea of gnosis, for gnosis is ungraspable from without. In fact, historians use their own concepts (borrowed from the surrounding ideologies) to explain matters, naively imagining them adequate for comprehending realities no longer understood by the modern world. We repeat, doctrinal gnosis rests upon an awareness of the intrinsically sacred character of metaphysical and theological intellectuality. *Intellectuality*: it is simply the natural activity of an intellect working according to its own needs. *Sacred*: it grasps its own contents as a grace of the Word radiating within it.

Doctrinal gnosis relies, then, on a "gnostic awareness" of the intellective act, on a sacred aesthetics of the intellect for which metaphysical Ideas are divine works of art, the icons of the

---

60 This is what St. Ambrose declares, *Explanatio*, num. 9; S. C., 25 bis, 57-59.
61 Thus understood, gnosis is nothing but that identification (and not identity in the strict sense) established by St. Augustine between philosophy and religion: it is necessary "to avoid those who are neither philosophers in religion, nor religious in philosophy" (*De vera religione*, VII, 12); cf. A. Mandouze, *Saint Augustine—L'aventure de la raison et de la grâce* (Etudes augustiniennes, 1968), 499-508. John Scotus radicalizes this by declaring: "True philosophy is true religion, and true religion is true philosophy" (*De divina praedestinatione*, I, 1). We will return to and explain these themes in the last part of this book.

Word that the Holy Spirit writes within our souls. To be sure, this gnostic awareness of the doctrinal act might seem to be, from without, a rationalizing of Revelation or, conversely, a religious mythification of philosophy: hence the two divergent lines of interpretation—the hellenization of Christianity and the christianization of Hellenism—along which historians of gnosis and gnosticism are divided. And the risk is certainly no less great for Christian gnosticism: either, by pride, to reduce Revelation to some mental form, thus lapsing into sterile intellectualism; or, by dogmatic passion and lack of intelligence, to idolize the form to the detriment of its contents, thus lapsing into a blind literalism.

This is why doctrinal gnosis should not be the whole of gnosis. It is, as we have explained, ordered to the reception of Revelation; it is, as we have said, a metaphysics of welcome. This means that it is only completed by the reception of the Word Incarnate: the gnostic's first fruits of the act of faith assume their full meaning only in faith itself.[62] And, to conclude, we will now say something about them.

GNOSIS CONSUMMATED

The just-mentioned doctrine seems to find a scriptural basis in the prologue to the Gospel of John. Just as the reception of faith requires an initiation (the gnostic nature of which is not obvious to everyone), that is, the teaching of a metaphysical science without which the Revelation received would not be fully understood,[63] so John begins by declaring the metaphysics

---

[62] We can see why true gnosis should not consist chiefly in complex speculations about the sacred sciences: the science of cycles, numerology, astrology, gematria, angelosophy, and so forth. All his life St. Paul fought the hegemony of this inferior but proliferative gnosis: a cosmological gnosis bound up with the esoteric knowledge of the "elements of the world" (Col. 2:8) and even with the manipulation of demonic principles, psychic in nature, which rule them: principalities, powers, dominations, names, and so forth (Eph. 1:21). Not because he is ignorant of this gnosis, but because the essential is elsewhere, in "Jesus Christ crucified" (1 Cor. 2:2). We should not, however, end up with a rejection of all gnosis, but, to the contrary, with the unique primacy of Christian gnosis.
[63] As natural (and even as banal) as this principle might be, it has been ignored or objected to by modern preaching (Catholic or Protestant), which claims to stand by the kerygmatic nakedness of the Christic *fact*. One forgets

of the Divine Word, the Eternal Gnosis of the Father, and is most careful to point out that it is this Word that imparts to every human intellect (and not just the believer's) its capacity for cognitive illumination. Only after this does he reveal that the Word "came to his own," "became flesh," and "dwelt among us," that "we have *beheld* his glory," and finally that he is named Jesus Christ, the "exegete of the Father" (John 1:18). Taught in this way is the order needed to accomplish the act of faith, as well as the need for a gnostic initiation and the true nature of this preparatory gnosis that is the light emanating from the Word. In fact, it is "in thy light (that) we see light" (Psalm 35:9), and by it alone do we see the "glory" of Jesus Christ (John 1:14).

However, when, thanks to the light of gnosis, we see the Light-made-flesh and are confronted by the radiant glory of the Word Incarnate, confronted by the One "which we have seen with our eyes... and touched with our hands" (1 John 1), the initial and initiating light is obliterated by its very transparency, the presence of the Divine Object blinds every other knowledge, and gnostic awareness must, in some manner, renounce itself. Thus, out of the recognition of God-made-object—the visible image of the invisible God—gnosis is made man, "full of grace and truth."

Some have maintained at times that Christianity does not include a way of pure gnosis, as exemplified in some other cultures such as in Hinduism, Taoism, or Islam. Although quite true in certain respects, this betrays a superficial view of things in two ways: first, they do not know that, in reality, the elaboration of an orthodox gnosis was specifically the work of Christianity (from St. Paul to St. Clement of Alexandria); next, they do not understand that Christianity, being the religion of Christ, is by that very fact the religion of Gnosis Incarnate, since the Word is the Gnosis of the Father. Now this Gnosis Incarnate is also the preeminent spiritual way: "I

---

then that the Incarnation required the immaculate receptacle of the Virgin Mary, who is thus the prototype of the intellect purified and informed by gnosis: Mary "kept all these things in her heart" (Luke 2:51). The modes of metaphysical teaching vary: human transmission, but also direct—whether explicit or implicit—communication by the Holy Spirit.

am the Way, the Truth and the Life." It being absolute, this affirmation necessarily includes an unconditional guarantee, and in particular it guarantees that Christianity offers the highest spiritual possibilities, but obviously according to the nature of its economy: since the Word Incarnate concentrates all Truth and Grace within himself, outside of him we cannot find that which must be sought within him.

And so, what is meant by *pure* gnosis? Would its purity perchance exclude love? Such ignorance of spiritual realities! Is not the sun of gnosis that illuminates the gaze of the Maharshi radiant with love? What strange gnostics are those who dread the loss of *their* gnosis in the ocean of Divine Love! And, still more, all the Masters have taught what the prologue of St. John teaches. Here is what Shankara declares in his famous poem *Atmabodha* (Self-Knowledge): "Thanks to repeated exercises, gnosis (*jnana*) purifies the living soul, tarnished by ignorance, of its dualities; having done so, gnosis itself must disappear, like nut powder once the water is purified."[64]

By renouncing itself, gnosis somehow enters into the obscurity of faith, into that darkness where, as St. John says, the light shines. Only by this renunciation and by this "passion" can its very nature be transformed, become what it is by being converted into and united with its Object. This gnostic ordeal, this "lesson of the Darkness" wherein the spirit, like Moses, ascends the holy mountain of Sinai, the "mountain of theognosy,"[65] is that very ascent rejected by philosophism from

---

[64] Stanza 5; we quote from the beautiful translation made by François Chenique for the French School of Yoga (replacing "knowledge" with "gnosis"). Even today the *Atmabodba* is one of the basic treatises used in the formation of students in the schools of *Vedanta*. Nut powder (*kataka*) is used to rid water of its impurities.

[65] According to a symbolism developed, for example, by St. Gregory of Nyssa in *The Life of Moses* (II, 152) (New York: Paulist Press, 1978), 91. The ascent, in darkness, of the mountain of theognosy is likewise taught by Plato in the symbol of the cave, according to an interpretation that we can only outline here. The "shadow theater" situated inside the cave represents speculative gnosis, the knowledge *here below* of the metaphysical doctrine of the Ideas of the ontological Good. Ascent up the slope and access to daylight symbolize "practical" gnosis, effective realization. But the latter is at first a blinding, for the "true Light" dazzles the eye of the spirit accustomed to the light reflected in the mental mirror (*The Republic* VII, 514a–517a). This theognosic darkness does not seem

Hegel to Heidegger, namely *the absorption of knowledge into its own transcendent contents*. And, for want of seeing the need for this intellective transformation, modern philosophy has, at best, sworn itself to the sterility of indefinite analysis, at worst, to the decomposition of its rotting corpse. All too few are, alas, ready to understand this.

Returning now to the Gospel, we realize that it is teaching the same truth under the figure of St. John the Baptist. Why in this prologue—the charter of Christian metaphysics—does St. John feel the need to mention the Forerunner, the one who "was not the true light," thus inserting an historical contingency into an atemporal panorama?[66] *Fuit homo, Egeneto anthropos*, literally means "Arrived (a) man." This is as if to say: a human being (*anthropos*), and not just someone of masculine gender (*aner*), when he appears, testifying to the light. And how can we in fact speak of the *"true* light" before its direct manifestation, unless from its precursive reflection in the theomorphic man? St. John the Baptist symbolizes man as such and therefore doctrinal and preparatory gnosis: that which, already by its very existence, testifies to the existence of the Light; that which, on the other hand, actuated or revealed by Divine Grace (this *anthropos* is *apestalmenos*, he is "sent" from God), purifies the eye of the soul and prepares it for the reception of the true Light.

But, as we have said, the function of doctrinal gnosis is not only purification, but also recognition; for one only knows that which one recognizes, that which makes sense to us, that which, under the impact of a real encounter, awakens an unknown knowledge within us. And it is in fact the Baptist, the Dispenser of the lustral water of knowledge, who recognizes Christ, names him, and publicly designates him for the first time in the history of humanity: "Behold, the Lamb of God."

---

unconnected to the "Night" of St. John of the Cross. The opposition of Latin spirituality, centered on the night in Gethsemane, to the Greek, centered on the light of Tabor, does not seem *basically* true. Besides, the gnostic night does not exclude serenity. Cf. *Penser l'analogie* (Geneva: Ad Solem, 2000), chap. 13.

66 The rupture (in both meaning and style) is such that many exegetes see in this verse a later addition (Boismard, *Le prologue de Jean* [Paris: Cerf, 1953], 9-40), according to a procedure both well-known and fatal to all spiritual penetration into Scripture.

Now, the gnostic function of the Baptist stems not only from an analogy that might be regarded as a little too facile. It is also suggested more explicitly in the Gospel of St. Luke, and perhaps this will shed some light on the episode from the "Gnostic" book, *The Lineage of Mary*, translated above. Why link the name of Zechariah and the miraculous circumstances surrounding the annunciation of the birth of John, his son, to the satanic calumny involving the "onocephalic God" and to the supposed murder of Zechariah by the Jews? To answer this question, read the famous "Canticle" prophetically chanted by the father at the Baptist's birth in St. Luke: "And you, child, will be called the prophet of the Most High; for you will go before the Lord to prepare his ways, to give *gnosis* of salvation to his people in the forgiveness of their sins" (Luke 1:76–77). Along with the reference to the "key of gnosis" (Luke 11:52), these are the only occurrences of the term in the Gospels. The "child," then, gives this gnosis of salvation, and the "child" is that which is the most original and seems to be that which is smallest in man, like "Hop-o'-my-thumb," that is to say like the intellect which, through the dark forest of the world, goes "before the Lord," bringing a saving knowledge, the prophetic gnosis of the "Most High," in other words: the metaphysics of Transcendence.

But when the "Most High" descends "most low," when El-Elyon becomes Emmanu-El, "God with us," God immanent, a "horizontal" reversal is also produced: what was "before" [*devant* = in front of, spatial priority—Trans.] goes "behind"; what was "before" [*avant* = temporal priority—Trans.] changes to "after"; and what was a light (of knowledge) becomes darkness (of faith), because the reflected light is darkness with respect to the true light. And this is precisely what the Baptist declares in St. John's Gospel: "He who comes *after* me ranks *before* [*avant*] me" (John 1:15). The gnostic intellect is not the bridegroom of the human soul, only the friend of the divine Bridegroom: the one "who stands [near him] and hears him, rejoices greatly at the bridegroom's voice; therefore this joy of [his] is now full." But "he must increase [and] I must decrease" (John 3:29–30). Christ himself, in St. Matthew, gives the key

Truly Named Gnosis

to this analogical reversal that is as if the "signature" of the Forerunner: "Among those born of women there has risen no one greater than John the Baptist; yet he who is least in the kingdom of heaven is greater than he" (John 11:11). This means, among other things, that the least loftiness of a being in the reality of the Kingdom is greater than the greatest loftiness in the order of human consciousness.

The Baptist's exploit thus seals the destiny of Christian gnosis. It is an exploit in which gnosis must come to its final condition—a death-dealing sacrifice. As obvious as its prophetic nature might be, the metaphysical intellect remains however—insofar as simply human—a prisoner of Herodian thinking, that is, of the adulterous thinking of the world, of that which subjects the power of control and of the will to worldly desires, to the attraction of the cosmic dance, to the *samsaric* Salome. The severed head of the Forerunner "realizes" the truth of a "partial gnosis," the one that St. Paul says is ours *now* (1 Cor. 13:12), for "from him who has not, even what he has will be taken away" (Matt. 25:29). By losing its "head," this Johannine gnosis enters into the mystery of infinite ignorance. Created being, that which is not-God, becomes identified with its own ontological ignorance,[67] just like that pure gnostic, St. Dionysius the Areopagite, who in his martyrdom underwent that sacrificial beheading which actualizes the perfect consummation of knowledge.

This consummation of partial gnosis, which becomes an unknowing, conditions the realization of integral gnosis. The latter, as St. Paul teaches (1 Cor. 13:13), consists in knowing as we are known, which means that God's knowledge of the human creature is the rule and model of that knowledge which the creature has of God. This formula, one of the most profound bestowed on us from the universe of gnostic literature, not only postulates the analogical reciprocity of Divine Gnosis and human gnosis; it also basically implies their essential identity. Once stripped of all particular knowledge and plunged into infinite ignorance, the intellect reaches a state of perfect

---

67 Cf. "Infinite Ignorance," in *Love and Truth*, 421-23.

nakedness and pure transparency. Having thus become what it is in its depths, there is no longer anything within it to oppose its complete investment by Divine Gnosis. God knows himself within this intellect and *as* this intellect, which is therefore only one with the Immaculate Conception that God has of himself. This is why Mary is the sole key to this mystery of supreme gnosis.

SECOND PART

Gnostics of the 19th and 20th Centuries

NOTE: The history of gnostic currents in Europe in the nineteenth and twentieth centuries is yet to be achieved. The following studies in no way relate to such an enterprise. Other authors should have been included, starting with Franz von Baader, who himself reclaimed "Christian gnosis," or Schelling and German romanticism in general. Furthermore, a history requires something other than a series of prosopographies: it must mark growth, lineage, and splinterings. Nothing of all that will be found here; it would have led to the writing of an entirely different book. We present only four thinkers who, in various ways, illustrate four possible developments of gnosis, depending on the nature of their respective intentions: philosophical with Hegel, scientific with Ruyer, oriental and non-dualist with Guénon, aesthetic and mystical with Schuon. Surely the four authors we are to discuss were following, at the start, an authentic demand of gnosis, that is, the demand for a knowledge that aims at truly uniting knowing subject and known object. But they did not think they could meet this demand, the first two by denying the sacred dimension of gnosis, the last two by identifying it with the very act of the intellect.

CHAPTER 4

Hegel, or the Transformation of Gnosis into Logic

GENUINE GNOSIS AND APPARENT GNOSIS

In its most general significance, Hegel's philosophy can be seen as an artificial gnosis that results in unmitigated rationalism and dialectical sophistry.

The idea of gnosis, understood in its true sense, which must obviously be distinguished from gnosticism,[1] is the idea of a metaphysical and saving knowledge, that is, a knowledge aimed at accounting for its object by leading it back to its essence and which enables the knowing subject to gain access by this very means to its own unifying essence. If there is salvation by knowledge, this is because there is first a loss by ignorance, and because this ignorance is in some way identical to the very being of the cognitive subject. In other words, this subject's existence in its fallen state is an "ignorance" that can be erased only on condition that this existence agrees to be radically transformed—i.e., to erase, to renounce itself. This erasure, this extinction of the existence that is "ignorance," will be effected by the active realization of perfect ignorance, "infinite ignorance,"[2] when the cognitive subject knows strictly nothing any more, and poses the question: "*Eli, Eli, lamma sabacthani,*" "my God, my God, why have you forsaken me?" Only in this way can human intelligence "know" [*connaître*], that is, give birth [*naître*] to a consciousness of its participative immanence in Absolute Knowledge—in other words, realize that total Knowledge can

---

[1] Participants in an international symposium (Messina, 1966) on the origins of gnosticism proposed to clearly demarcate the meanings of the terms gnosis and gnosticism: "Gnosticism" means "a certain group of systems that everyone agrees to so designate." On the contrary, "gnosis" means "knowledge of the divine mysteries reserved for an elite" (*Origini dello gnosticismo*, xxiii; M. Eliade, *Histoire des croyances et des idées religieuses*, tome II [Paris: Payot, 1978], 498).
[2] The expression is found in Evagrius of Pontus (*On Prayer*, 117); cf. *Love and Truth*, 421–23.

be, by grace, only that which Totality apprehends of Itself, even in the knowing subject. Everything is thus "achieved" from all eternity; and yet at the same time, as the slightest experience is enough to prove, everything is to be achieved. The cognitive subject is actually immersed in the infinite light of the eternal Logos. Any intellectual act "intelligizes" from Knowledge eternally in act, from Divine Thought itself, and at the same time is ignorant of its true essence and actualizes itself only through a long process of abstraction from the sensory world and from discursive thinking.[3] It follows that in its most profound reality gnosis is ineffable because it is beyond the grasp of discourse, which by no means signifies that it lacks rigor or logic, but only that no discourse can claim to verify its logic, which would mean that language is the universal intelligible referent, while it is quite obvious that the only intelligible referent is the *Logos* itself. And this is why the teaching of gnosis basically consists of few words. Certainly, as ineffable as it may be in its essence, gnosis is humanly communicable only with words and symbols, which is moreover the case for all human teaching. But doctrinal formulations can only be extremely simple, commensurate with their Object, whose complexity—real from a certain vantage point—defies in other respects any analytical description and thus rejoins perfect simplicity. This is what Plato claims, stating that "there is no danger of

---

[3] To understand is to embrace, and therefore to surpass or overflow—since intelligence includes everything (a priori and in itself), since man is, as Ruyer says, "a universal reader," since intelligence goes beyond everything, in other words since it is, in its pure essence, participation in the infinite Intelligence of God. But cognitive being is finite, contingent, relative. This is why the "absolute surplus" that is intelligence in itself is translated into and expressed in terms of the cognitive subject's existential finitude through the abstractive distance that separates all thought from its object, and through speculation about being: (conceptual) thinking can think everything because it is nothing of that which it thinks about; the gnostic and deified intellect can know everything, because, being "more than being," it is able to be all that is. The passive indeterminacy of conceptual thinking is just the reverse reflection of the Intellect's active superdetermination, and finds its raison d'être in this. And, just as it is through the mediation of the sign that the abstractive distance of the cognitive subject and the world is manifested, likewise it is through the mediation of the symbolic sign that human intelligence reaches the truth of its divine enlightenment. cf. *Histoire et théorie du symbole*, 129–33.

anyone forgetting [these truths], once his mind grasps [them], since [they are] contained in the very briefest statements";[4] this is what emerges from the declarations of St. Clement of Alexandria on the gnostic tradition revealed by Christ to Peter, James, John, and Paul;[5] this is what is shown by the example of Lao-Tzu, who summarizes all gnosis in the *Tao Te Ching*'s[6] first chapter, of Shankara, who expresses this entire doctrine in the few stanzas of the *Atmabodha* (Knowledge of the Self),[7] of Ibn'Arabî, or one of his disciples, who writes the brief *Treatise on Unity*.[8] These examples bear witness however in favor of an indirect verification of gnosis, by the consequences that the gnostic draws from them in practice and that could be defined as a deep respect for traditional orthodoxy: the true gnostic never enters into any real contradiction with the formulations of a religious doctrine, even if some of their expressions — as was the case with Meister Eckhart — might seem exoterically in conflict with this or that dogma, and because gnosis cannot but underscore, when it manifests itself and as if in spite of itself, the inevitable limitations of traditional formulations. But even so, Eckhart bowed to his condemnation, not out of indifference and a desire for tranquility but by a deep and transcendent acceptance of the apparent contradictions of the "letter." True gnosis is not an attempt at universal conciliation, it is a silent consent to all otherness and all finitudes, because it *cannot do otherwise*, and because the magnitude of its vision surpasses and is free of all opposition. This silent consent is analogous, in essence, to God's creative consent by which absolute and

---

4 Letter VII, 344e; *The Collected Dialogues of Plato*, ed. E. Hamilton & H. Cairns (Princeton NJ: Princeton University Press, 1961), 1592.
5 *Strom*. I, 11, 3; "Gnosis is therefore," concludes A. Méhat, "at least from a certain vantage point, a doctrine communicable by teaching.... This tradition is supported by a framework similar to that which at the same time defined the heritage of philosophers: some major theses reduced to formulas, to 'dogmas'." *Études sur les Stromates de Clément d'Alexandrie*, 425.
6 One of the best French translations is by Claude Larre, S. J. (Paris: Desclée de Brouwer, 1977).
7 *Hymnes et chants védantiques*, translated from Sanskrit with introduction and notes by René Allar (Paris: Éditions Orientales, 1977), 57–66.
8 *Know Yourself, An explanation of the oneness of being*, said to be by Ibn Arabi, trans. C. Twinch (Northleach Cheltenham, UK: Beshara, 2011).

infinite reality sets free the possibilities of relative and limited creatures and, by its very absoluteness and infinitude, gives them space so that they can exist as such: everything is possible within the Unlimited, even the contradictory possibility of indefinite limitation. This doctrine we like to summarize with the following axiom: only the Most "can do" the least.

These brief remarks will suffice to indicate all that separates true gnosis from the brilliant caricature of it provided by Hegel. And this is what explains its success, not to say its triumph, with the intellectual public: Hegel offers, or rather seems to offer, the possibility of a total knowledge more "intelligent" than all those that came before, but which—O exquisite surprise!—remains entirely human and rational.[9] Not only does this "total knowledge" never clash with philosophical conventions[10]—modern philosophers have hardly grown accustomed to the recognized gnoses, such as those reaching the West from neoplatonism which so easily spill over into mystical extravagances—but it even strengthens and justifies these conventions in a definitive and unsurpassable manner. The pre-Hegelian gnoses are all more or less of a sacred nature; the knowledge about which they speak passes through a breaking away from the shadows of the Cave, inner renunciation, possibly the contingency of a revealed tradition, prayer and concentration, and the practice of charity. But here, with Hegel, we have a doctrine that proposes to understand everything and to say everything without philosophical intelligence being compelled to leave its reading nook: what a windfall! Reality in its entirety is brought

---

9 "His influence during the nineteenth century was unequaled, in Germany as well as abroad" (A. Koyré, *Études d'histoire de la pensée philosophique* [Paris: Gallimard, 1971], 147).

10 Philosophical conventions may all be reduced to a firm resolve to speak only in the name of common sense, each thinker claiming to believe it entirely possible to adhere to it, that is to say: 1) people who philosophize obey only the obvious or the most universal logical constraint, so that they mysteriously elude their own culture's determinations; 2) the individual person is no less mysteriously despoiled by the philosopher, who can thus discourse without fearing the surreptitious interventions of his own idiosyncrasies. To tell the truth, no one is quite fooled, but the main thing is to act "as if," not to openly break with this convention (although some scandals are allowed—Nietzsche for example—as long as they go in a "good direction," namely, atheism, irreligion, blasphemy).

to us on printed paper, in a discourse, without us having to go out of ourselves, to quit the field of ordinary mental activity for one knows not what metaphysical intuition!

Until Hegel's time all attempts at total knowledge had ultimately taken refuge under the veil of symbols, and even within the ineffable. But one philosopher assigns himself the task of thinking about everything with the clear light of the concept, and seems to achieve it thanks to the prodigious speculative energy with which he is endowed. There we have the wherewithal to captivate more than one mind, even those baffled by a particularly obscure language. To manage to persuade yourself and your readers that Absolute Knowledge is within the reach of human intelligence, that the philosophical discourse one is reading is, at the same time, the actual realization of it—this is surely a somewhat surprising pretention for the proprieties of common sense, but a pretention to which one ends up succumbing when we realize that, after all, Absolute Knowledge is nothing but the indefinite development of reason.[11]

HEGELIAN PSEUDO-GNOSIS

We are, for our part, convinced that such is indeed the meaning of the Hegelian endeavor. As for the clear light of the concept, the historians themselves agree: "The ineffable and the inexpressible had for him [Hegel]—and according to him—no kind of value. What he valued above all else was clarity, 'the clear concept that leaves nothing undisclosed,' and that expresses what there is of the most profound in man, his 'very nature' which is thinking and which is spirit."[12] So this does not, then, involve the Cartesian clarity and distinction of ideas that cast into the unsayable everything obscure and

---

11 Hegel—and Kojève has strongly emphasized this—presents himself as a Christian (or post-Christian) philosopher, because in the Christian religious community, not only does the infinite become finite (Incarnation), but the god-man even disappears as a lone, tangible being: the finite becomes infinite. However the religious community only "represents," and does not understand, this unity of absolute Knowledge of self. "This knowledge of the community is the text for which Hegelian philosophy claims to be an authentic translation into the language of *concept* and no longer of *representation*." J. Hyppolite, *Genèse et structure de la "Phénoménologie de l'esprit" de Hegel* (Paris: Aubier, 1946), 541.
12 Koyré, op. cit., 223, citing K. Rosenkranz, *Das Leben Hegels*, 544.

confused in anything, but rather the systematic will to say everything, to think everything, to translate everything into concepts and words. This will would have no other proof than its own realization, that is to say the Hegelian discourse itself in its full deployment. In this way does Hegelian philosophy (that is, Hegelian discourse) actually attain absolute Truth, since it is to itself its own verification. That is why it is, or so it would seem, somewhat correct to designate itself as ultimate Knowledge. Introducing the *Science of Logic*, Hegel writes that "an altogether new concept of scientific procedure is at work here." This new concept consists in an inner reflection on the content of the mind in its very movement of knowledge: "It can only be the nature of the content which is responsible for movement in scientific knowledge, for it is this content's own reflection that first posits and generates what that content is." Now, this "movement, which is thus the immanent development of concept, is the absolute method of the concept, *the method of absolute knowledge*[13] and at the same time the immanent soul of the content."[14]

On the other hand, it is not just theoretical considerations that incline one to see a gnosis in Hegelianism. There are also historical considerations. Numerous indeed are the specialists who perceive in the current of Eckhartian mysticism and Boehmian theosophy one of the sources of the Hegelian endeavor. Actually, the testimonies are not absolutely consistent. G. Lukács asserts that Hegel read Eckhart in his youth.[15] This is also the opinion of Ernst Bloch, who sees in Hegelian doctrine a retrieval of the deepest and most "revolutionary" trends in Meister Eckhart.[16] Bloch even attributes an Eckhartian influence to certain assertions in Hegel's early writings on the

---

13 Trans.—In Di Giovanni's English translation, this last phrase is rendered equivalently: "the absolute method of cognition."
14 *The Science of Logic*, trans. G. Di Giovanni, preface to the first edition (Cambridge: Cambridge University Press, 2010), 9-10 (our emphasis).
15 *Le jeune Hegel*, French translation from German by G. Haarscher and R. Legros (Paris: Gallimard, 1981), tome I, 83.
16 *Sujet. Objet. Éclaircissements sur Hegel*, French translation from German by Maurice de Gandillac (Paris: Gallimard, 1977), 78. But he recognizes that Hegel almost never cites him, no more than he cites Nicholas of Cusa.

Hegel, or the Transformation of Gnosis into Logic

need to reverse the process of religious alienation and "vindicate...the human ownership of treasures formerly squandered on heaven."[17] But, if one is to believe the testimony of Franz von Baader, he was the one who, "one day in 1824," acquainted Hegel with the writings of the Dominican master, "whom he knew only by name until then. He was so enthused," continues Baader, "that I heard him give a whole lecture on Meister Eckhart the other day, and he finished with these words: That is exactly what we want, that is the whole of our ideas."[18] In 1824, Hegel was in full possession of his system. Eckhart can represent for him only a fortunate encounter and a confirmation (against a background of misinterpretation), the one expressed in this passage from the *Lectures on the Philosophy of Religion*: "The older theologians had the most thorough grasp of this divine depth.... Meister Eckhart, a Dominican monk, in speaking of this innermost element says, in one of his sermons, among other things, the following: 'The eye with which God sees me is the eye with which I see Him; my eye and His eye are one....' If God were not, I would not be; if I were not, then He were not. It is, however, not needful to know this, for there are things that are easily misunderstood and that can only be thoroughly understood in thought."[19] We should realize that these words of Eckhart that "Hegel liked to quote,"

---

17 This is a quote drawn from Hegel's *The Positivity of the Christian Religion* (Spring 1796), provided by Bloch in his book *Athéisme dans le christianisme*, French trans. É. Kaufholz and G. Roulet (Paris: Gallimard, 1978), 84–85. Cf. Hegel, *On Christianity, Early Theological Writings*, trans. T. M. Knox (Chicago: University of Chicago, 1948), 159. Bloch sets forth his quite peculiar views on Eckhart as a precursor of Feuerbach and Marx (op. cit., 83–86). These theories are of interest only in that they show how a gnosticizing Marxist "misunderstands" Eckhart, despite the accuracy of some of his analyses.

18 This remark, made by Baader a short time before his death, was reported by his disciple-editor Hoffmann, *Sämmtliche Werke*, vol. 15, 159, which we cite from Ernst Benz, *The Mystical Sources of German Romantic Philosophy*, trans. B. R. Reynolds & E. M. Paul (Allison Park, PA: Pickwick, 1983), 6.

19 Vol. 1, trans. Rev. E. B. Speirs & J. B. Sanderson (London: Kegan Paul, Trench, Trübner, 1895), 217–18. The *Lectures on the Philosophy of Religion* were given from 1821 to 1831. The text from the Meister is borrowed in part from the German sermon number 12 in the Quint edition: cf. the English translation of M. O'C. Walshe, *The Complete Mystical Works of Meister Eckhart* (New York: Herder & Herder, 2009), 298.

as J. Hyppolite tells us,[20] may exhibit a certain consonance with the German philosopher's deepest intention: "God is God only so far as he knows himself; his self-knowledge is, further, his self-consciousness in man, and man's knowledge *of* God, which proceeds to man's self-knowledge *in* God."[21] We will go even further. For, as deviated as Hegelian gnosis may be, it nonetheless includes some authentically gnostic aspects. Having done this, Hegel realizes, or rather tries to realize, philosophy's deepest desire: access to supreme knowledge, a desire that religion seems to satisfy only indirectly here below. Any true philosophy, in its primary aim, is therefore gnostic in essence, pursues an intention which seems devoid of religion, and the realization of this intention constitutes its rightful task.

But this should obviously not mean that Western philosophies have actually managed to attain the goal inherent to their essence. Far from it. To the contrary, many of them only based themselves on this aim to resist it and completely expel it from philosophy, as does Kantianism. Other philosophies are obedient to it only by carrying out a total subversion of this aim, and this is eminently the case with Hegelian philosophy. However, as total as the subversion might be, it does not go as far as a complete disfiguring: the caricature is recognizable. This is what makes the true thinking of the philosopher so difficult to grasp and even confers on it an ambiguous character, as is evidenced by the diverging interpretations. This ambiguity is summed up in the question so often asked by commentators: is Hegel's God "the creator of men or their ultimate creature?"[22] Ultimately, nothing can be said about Hegel's philosophy other than what he himself says about it. Only the question arises: is this because he has said everything that could be said about it (a philosophy that has reached a perfect awareness of its own saying), or else because, wanting to say everything, it actually *says nothing*? For speaking is choosing, and this always runs the

---

20 *Genèse et structure*, 523.
21 *Hegel's Philosophy of Mind*, § 564, trans. W. Wallace (Oxford: Clarendon Press, 1894), 176.
22 Jacques D'Hondt, *Hegel* (Paris: P. U. F., 1975), 54; likewise J. Hyppolite, *Genèse et structure*, 525.

risk of unilateralness. Only at this price does speech not entirely collapse into *uselessness* and avoid that dialectical sophistry that thinks itself able to forestall any contradiction by integrating the contradiction as such into its own discourse.

In what then does Hegel's misunderstanding lie, a misunderstanding from which proceeds the radical deviation he caused gnosis to undergo, a deviation such that it has somehow "poisoned" and warped the European mode of philosophizing? We can characterize it in many ways. It has been said, in particular, that Hegel's philosophy is a vast attempt to reconcile everything: the finite and the infinite, time and eternity, spirit and nature, philosophy and religion, the individual and the state, &c. Now, if it is certain that this desire for universal reconciliation corresponds to the intellectual temperament of the philosopher, if the occasional cause is provided by the spectacle of antinomies and separations that Kantianism has everywhere consolidated, one can admit, according to all likelihood, that the model was "proposed" to him by Jacob Boehme's mystical theosophy and, secondarily, by Meister Eckhart. What did he see in this gnosis? A fundamentally more "intelligent" way for considering the grand questions that define the problematic field of the loftiest human speculation, an unnoticed vantage point of Kantian criticism, a vantage point which thereby seemed to him to elude this criticism's jurisdiction.

But the very ones who had exemplified this "more intelligent" point of view seemed, to him, to have adopted and implemented it without any exact awareness of what they were doing, and without scientific rigor, in disorder and confusion.[23] To annex this gnostic light for the benefit of a conscious and organized knowledge, to *mimic* an understanding of gnosis, but

---

23 "Gnosis," Hegel forthrightly states, "has more than one awkward side to it: its metaphysics does not push itself to consider the categories themselves or to develop the content methodically; it suffers from the concept's inadequacy for such wild or ingenious forms and formations...." This has to do with the gnosis of Jacob Boehme, that "powerful spirit," praised by Hegel, at the end of the 1827 Preface to the second edition of the *Encyclopedia*, for having "expanded the content of religion for itself to the universal idea," but Plato, *and even more* Aristotle, must be preferred to these "gnostic and cabbalistic phantasmagorias" (*Encyclopedia of the Philosophical Sciences in Basic Outline*, trans. K. Brinkmann & D. O. Dahlstrom [Cambridge: Cambridge University Press, 2010], 19–21).

on the terrain of eighteenth-century rationalist philosophy, without achieving the initial steps that it presupposes—the uprooting of ordinary knowledge and the existential commitment of one's whole being to the uncreated Light of the Logos[24]—and, by the same stroke, do better than Boehme and Meister Eckhart—that is what Hegel was implicitly proposing. His situation is entirely comparable to the one described by E. Herrigel, in his short book *Zen in the Art of Archery*,[25] when he wants to imitate his master and shoot, like him, "spiritually": he has not yet understood that this is not about carrying out a performance, "from the outside," copying the movement of the hand of the master whose bowstring seems to release of itself without any effort of will, but this is really about entering into non-willing; any cheating disqualifies; God is not mocked. The difference between these two situations is that Herrigel had a master to correct him in this most subtle error, while the young Hegel had nobody to tell him he was amiss: besides, he would not have understood.

ALIENATION OF RELIGIOUS CONSCIOUSNESS AND CULTURAL HISTORY

Hegelianism is therefore a pseudo-gnosis, a gnosis it imitates in its external form and approach, for want of grasping its most profound nature. It is the presence in Hegelian philosophy of this gnostic intention incapable of attaining its object that in our opinion accounts for the way Hegel effects the reconciliation of nature and cognitive subject through culture, and its failure both culturally and philosophically. This is what compels Hegel to consider culture—and essentially

---

24 Here is, for example, how Boehme responds to the question: "How may I come to the suprasensual (*übersinnlich*) life, so that I can see God and hear Him speak?...If you could be silent from all willing and thinking for one hour, you would hear God's inexpressible words.... When you remain silent from the thinking and willing of self (*Selbstheit*)...the eternal hearing, seeing, and speaking will be revealed in you, and God will see and hear through you... Your own hearing, willing, and seeing hinders you so that you do not see and hear God" (*The Suprasensual Life*, in *The Way to Christ*, trans. P. Erb [New York / Mahwah: Paulist Press, 1978], 171). One would search in vain for a similar text in Hegel's works.

25 Trans. R. F. C. Hull (New York: Random House, 1953), 43–48.

Hegel, or the Transformation of Gnosis into Logic

religious culture and therefore symbolism—as an alienation of the spirit's self-awareness, and (his own) philosophy as that which puts an end to this alienation, precisely because it is a phenomenology of the spirit, that is, "picture-thought" assumed by the mind during its historical development. In other words, religious consciousness is still a consciousness unaware of its own truth, and that only the absolute self-knowledge achieved by Hegelianism can save by reappropriating all the pictures (and therefore disguises) of itself that unhappy consciousness has set against itself during its actual history. This is how the theme of religious alienation makes its appearance, to which Feuerbach will give its full scope, and which dominates the host of strategies for neutralizing awareness of the sacred.[26] It consists in subverting the meaning of symbols, which, being signs of the transcendent, are transformed by it into figures immanent to consciousness. This is true for the religious criticism developed by post-Galilean scientific rationalism: "It is just this," writes Hegel, "that Enlightenment [*Aufklärung*] rightly declares faith to be, when it says that what is for faith the absolute Being, is a Being of its own consciousness, is its own thought, something that is a creation of consciousness itself. Thus what Enlightenment declares to be an error and a fiction is the very same thing as Enlightenment itself is."[27] However, Hegel remarks, the human origin of religious representations and ideas, ideas that the *Aufklärung* denounces as erroneous, reveals in fact, in the light of (his own) philosophy, this origin's true meaning; God is indeed the essence of consciousness: faith's "object is also for [Enlightenment] just this, viz. a pure essence of its own consciousness, so that this consciousness does not take itself to be lost and negated in that object, but rather puts its trust in it, i.e., it finds itself as this *particular* consciousness or as *self*-consciousness, precisely *in the object*. Whomsoever I trust, his *certainty of himself* is for

---

[26] On this subject, one can refer to my work: *The Crisis of Religious Symbolism*, trans. G. J. Champoux (Kettering OH: Angelico Press, 2016), 145–247.
[27] *Phenomenology of Spirit*, trans. A. V. Miller (Oxford: Oxford University Press, 1977), 334; *Aufklärung* roughly corresponds to what is called in English "Enlightenment philosophy."

me the *certainty of myself*; I recognize in him my own being-for-self."[28] The *Aufklärung*, denying that religious symbolism relates to a real (invisible) reality, reduces the symbol to being only a product of human consciousness. But this irrational and therefore "monstrous" product will remain inexplicable, ultimately posing a threat to the fine assurance of scientific reason, if one did not succeed in taming it by transforming this foreign presence inside consciousness into a presence connatural to consciousness (although not perceived as such). Such is the general approach for the neutralizing of religious consciousness. This is because scientific rationalism is, in fact, incapable of really neutralizing the consciousness of the sacred. Its proper work is to reduce the sacred to the awareness that we have of it. But even then the sacred somehow remains what it is. Seeing it as a monstrosity of the imagination born of superstitious fear (Spinoza) is still a way of recognizing it for what it gives itself out to be. The reduction with which "phenomenology of spirit" proceeds is much more radical.

But, notes Hegel,[29] the phenomenology of spirit, that is, the knowledge of the pictures under which the mind appears to itself, has not only taught us that religious creations were only a way for consciousness to articulate, without knowing it, its own truth; it also teaches us that this truth is discovered through the forms presented to us by culture. Culture mediates between the cognitive subject and nature. It certainly constitutes an alienation, but a secondary alienation in response to a primary alienation, that of nature, and which amends it. Insofar as cultural forms are posed as objective and autonomous realities, and therefore insofar as they stand on the side of nature, they alienate the mind that does not recognize them as forms of itself. But on the other hand, culture, insofar as it is formation, process, becoming, is torn away from the natural order and necessarily opposes it. Culture teaches the mind, then, that there is something other than material nature, and ultimately allows it to become self-aware; culture is therefore a process, a history. In other words, history is

---

28 Ibid.
29 Ibid.

the spirit's destiny. "The actuality of historical reality" must be taken seriously. The mind is itself only insofar as it is the movement of its own temporal development through the reflecting mirror of culture: "this substance which is Spirit, is the process in which Spirit *becomes* what it is *in itself*; and it is only as this process of reflecting itself into itself that it is in itself truly *Spirit*.... The movement of carrying forward the form of its self-knowledge is the labor which it accomplishes as actual History."[30] History is culture (*Bildung*), education, the training of the spirit by itself, of the spirit in search of its truth, which comes to prevail against the objectivity of nature, that first "other" of the spirit. Nature first appears to us as reality in itself, but, through the mediation of culture, reason discovers that everything is spirit: "Reason is consciousness's certainty of being all reality: this is the essential notion of idealism."[31] Still, this idealism, in order to access its truth, must be discovered as the result of a "long cultural path," that is, as the "coming-to-be of Spirit."[32] Culture, in the sense of a historical development, is therefore indeed the mediation by which the reconciliation of subjective spirit and objective nature is achieved, but on the express condition of being considered as a pure history of the spirit reappropriating all otherness.[33]

These are the two features of the Hegelian solution to the question posed to the philosopher by the existence of religious forms: they constitute an alienation of consciousness, but this consciousness achieves, precisely through them, the coming-to-be of its own truth. How then is this a failure?

THE SOPHISTRY OF BECOMING

If Hegelian gnosis was a true gnosis, that is, one that does not confuse the essence of knowledge with the mental operations by which it manifests itself in the human mind, it would teach that there is not, *basically*, any reconciliation to carry out,

---

30 Ibid., 487–88.
31 Ibid., 527.
32 Ibid., 263.
33 Ibid., 492.

because, in reality, it is achieved from all eternity. This eternal achievement does not, however, as we too often believe, lead to the uselessness of its temporal and human achievement, nor does it constitute a kind of "vain repetition." On the contrary, it makes possible its temporal realization and gives it its whole meaning, "because no one has ascended to Heaven except the One who descended from Heaven."[34] Eternal fulfillment does not precede or follow human achievement. Being timeless, it constitutes its *permanent meaning*; it is its true salvation and its glory, failing which the unfolding of the entire becoming founders in the dust heap of successiveness. But Hegel has nothing but contempt for such a way of seeing things, he who laughs at himself from beyond,[35] and seems to ignore that the whole value of time is that of a saving "now." If there is reconciliation, it can only be immediate and timeless. Immediate, because all mediation—unless it is itself the saving descent of eternal reconciliation—contravenes the terms it wants to unite, and therefore divides them; timeless, because only that which has never been separated is truly reconciled. But Hegel, as we have seen, intends to take the effectiveness of historical development seriously,[36] he wants to think close to becoming. For him, in fact, "the result [is not] the *actual whole*, but rather the result together with the process through which it came about.... the bare result is the corpse which has left the guiding tendency behind it,"[37] a doctrine which is the exact opposite of this saying: "when the sun rises, the night has never been."[38] For, in truth, as René Guénon has shown by relying on the symbolic meaning of integral calculus,

---

34 John 3:13.
35 "Philosophy is... an inquisition into the rational, and therefore the apprehension of the real and present. Hence it cannot be the exposition of a world beyond, which is merely a castle in the air, having no existence except in the terror of a one-sided and empty formalism of thought." *Philosophy of Right*, trans. S. W. Dyde (London: George Bell & Sons, 1896), xxvi.
36 All atheisms fond of the concrete derive strong satisfaction from this concern, as do, today, all Christians who clearly do not intend to lag behind on the topic.
37 *Phenomenology of Spirit*, 2–3.
38 Frithjof Schuon, *Spiritual Perspectives and Human Facts* (Bloomington, IN: World Wisdom, 2007), 174.

Hegel, or the Transformation of Gnosis into Logic

there is discontinuity, from the point of view of the process, between the process and its term. It is only from the point of view of the term or the result that there is continuity and that we can eventually find the process (but transformed, such as it is in itself), just as it is only from the integral that we can determine the particular values of the variable that leads to it.[39] In other words, no process can, by itself, achieve its result. This preexists and "occurs" in it as a vertical descent perpendicular to the line of temporal development, when the conditions are met.[40] Otherwise, this never occurs. Hegel having forbidden himself any recourse to such a solution, he is condemned either to renounce all reconciliation, or else *to pose becoming itself as reconciliation*: "The equilibrium in which coming-to-be and ceasing-to-be are poised is in the first place becoming itself."[41] Becoming is synthesis, the "unity of being and nothingness,"[42] a famous thesis that Hegel even presents as something unnoticed and yet so plainly obvious.[43] A thesis, yes, but a perfectly fallacious one.[44] Becoming is not the synthesis of being and nothingness, it is the very impossibility of

---

39 *The Principles of Infinitesimal Calculus,* trans. M. Allen & H. D. Fohr (Hillsdale, NY: Sophia Perennis, 2001), passim.
40 This general law applies to all physical, biological, or spiritual processes. Thus the *spiritual* soul, even as the life-principle, is not the result of a physico-chemical process, it occurs when the conditions are met. In reality, however, the opposite is true: the maturation of the physico-chemical conditions is already the work of the vegetative and animal soul that is physically and temporally realized in them. Likewise for holiness. Unknown to himself, every man is a saint. It is the invisible presence of this principial holiness that effects the "work of grace" in man and leads him to his end.
41 *The Science of Logic,* 81.
42 Ibid., 76.
43 Ibid., 77–78.
44 Hegelianism is a (visibly unconscious) sophistry in the exact sense that Plato gives to this term in the *Sophist,* where he shows that, given the possibility of speaking about everything, with a semblance of relevance, it can only be a false knowledge, an imitation, a mimetic. *Encyclopedism* is therefore the hallmark of all sophistry. Too often we see today, in the Platonic definition, a distortion and a bias. But the real question—of the greatest difficulty (236e)—is to ask oneself how it is possible that there really exists a false speech, and indeed one which actually gives the possibility of speaking about everything. A careful examination of Hegelianism, this philosophical encyclopedism, would, we believe, partially answer this question. On sophistry, see my book *Penser l'analogie,* 146–61.

their unity, without which, rightly, it would not become. Quite true, here below being cannot be separated from nothingness; but it is no less true that it cannot be united with it either. It is this perpetually defective unity that precisely constitutes becoming, which is thus only the symbol or the image, by its very changeability, of the unchanging and eternal unity of the Absolute. Time passes, or becomes, because (and to the very extent that) it affirms Eternity. There is no other reality than unchanging Reality; but, any affirmation or any manifestation being necessarily distinct from what it affirms, this implies in itself its limitation or negation (as image), which is another way, for Absolute Reality, to affirm that there is no other Reality than Itself. Thus time only exists as long as it affirms Being, but hardly is it manifested when this existence is denied by Being itself. Each affirmative pulsation at the heart of time instantly returns, by vanishing, into sheer Eternity. Time is perpetually consumed from within by the Lord, and that is why *it passes*. And if it did not pass, it would be immutability and Eternity itself.

Basically Hegel mingles time and eternity, and by the same stroke assigns to becoming a task it cannot assume. On the one hand, culture must mediate every reconciliation, but, on the other, being made up of an indefinite number of distinct cultural moments, such that the truth of the preceding moment is solely in the following moment, it follows that this task will never be completed, and therefore, in reality, neither could anyone offer to do this. If the spirit, whose history is "culture" (*Bildung*, education), harbored some transcendence, cultural forms could be at any time a place for reconciliation, for a vertical return to the *Logos*, but also just as well, eventually, a place for a possible fall into "outer darkness." But this is not the case. The only transcendence is a horizontal transcendence, the only surpassing is one effected by the next moment compared to the previous moment; in culture, becoming is thus to itself its own mediation,[45] and alienation is therefore, in reality, final. One could hardly imagine a more hellish and desperate

---

45 *Phenomenology of the Spirit*, 492: "Becoming is ... self-mediating." Sartre says, with nearly the same meaning, that history is totalization.

Hegel, or the Transformation of Gnosis into Logic

enclosure of history within itself. No doubt Hegelian sophistry would retort that, dialectically conceived, the enclosing of time is also its liberation, and indeed time is thus delivered from everything that could limit its power (namely, its status as a moving and defective image of eternity) and is able to reduce everything to its own limits. History becomes the substance of things,[46] history, that is to say, the reified abstraction of temporal fragmentation. While the gnostic perspective, far from denying the future and history, confers a *permanent* value and actuality on the various cultural contents and theses deployed there, Hegelian philosophy reduces them to being only the succession of figures of a consciousness in pursuit of itself and always falling short. This philosophy should have understood, however, that in a purely temporal history nothing happens, nothing truly *happens*. For something really does happen, an *event* really occurs, only if something radically "new" transpires in time. Strictly speaking, there is nothing radically new in time except that which is extra-temporal, that is, that which manifests an irruption of the Eternal. Only sacred events are true events. But Hegel accomplishes for time, everything else being equal, what Aristotle had done for space: intelligible forms are for him purely immanent in becoming and in history, as they were so in bodies and in space for Aristotle. The consequences will be the same: Marx will succeed Hegel as Galileo "succeeded" Aristotle.

Therefore, the reduction of culture to its temporal dimension alone makes the Hegelian solution, in the end, impossible and forces us to speak of failure. But, it will be said, culture as a development of the mind is only one part of this solution; the other, which gives it its meaning, is philosophy itself, which elevates this development to a conceptual self-awareness: Hegelianism is indeed a gnosis, it is a saving knowledge. This is true, and we have already said it. Hegel has repeatedly affirmed this. Cultural alienation is only possibly alienating on condition that it is thought philosophically, that it is known in its truth: as the becoming of Spirit,

---

46 An error parallel to that of Descartes for whom extension is the substance of things.

"history['s] ... fulfilment consists in perfectly *knowing* what *it is*."[47] Besides, if it were not so, one could not even speak of alienation. Philosophy is therefore the science of the spirit in its truth. All the forms assumed by the mind in its development, whether forms of art or religion, limit and alienate the mind in some way. But philosophy "is determined as an understanding of the necessity of the *content* of absolute representation, as well as that of the two forms" of art and religion. In other words, it is "a liberation from the one-sidedness of the forms, elevation of them into the absolute form."[48] So it should be clear that, for the human spirit, the only salvation is the one obtained by philosophical thinking, which is none other, in reality, than precisely the one Hegel unrolls before our eyes; not the one for which Hegelian discourse would be only an image, a reflection, an approximation, but the very one possessed by anyone who thinks, for there is no other thought than that. This consequence, the direct result of his initial misinterpretation of gnosis, Hegel affirms most explicitly: "Philosophy," he says, "is identical to the time in which it makes its appearance. Philosophy does not stand above its time: it is only the awareness of the substantial spirit of its time or, again, the thought about knowledge of what there is in that time."[49] There is no transcendence, therefore, of philosophy in relation to its object. It follows that: "The latest philosophy, chronologically speaking, is the result of all those that precede it and must therefore contain the principles of all of them. This is why, if it is philosophy at all, it is the most developed, the richest and the most concrete philosophy."[50] At the moment when Hegel wrote this text, this was obviously the case with his own philosophy. But, if it is so, such a philosophy can in no way constitute a salvation for the human spirit. And that is why we are forced to speak again about a failure.

---

47 *Phenomenology of the Spirit*, 492.
48 *Hegel's Philosophy of Mind*, § 573.
49 *Leçons sur l'histoire de la philosophie*, trans. J. Gibelin (Paris: Gallimard, 1970), tome I, 173–74.
50 *Encyclopedia of the Philosophical Sciences in Basic Outline*, 42.

Hegel, or the Transformation of Gnosis into Logic

Indeed, it is not in the power of a speculative discourse, *as such*, to deliver the mind from its limits and to wrest man from unhappiness and this anxiety of being in which Koyré saw "Hegel's deepest metaphysical intuition."[51] As an intellective key to transcendent enlightenment, it can only do this by dissolving or breaking down mental barriers and thereby making possible a true spiritual ascent. But that implies that it is referring—and refers us—to its Object, to the permanent actuality of the *Logos*, which cannot be at the end-point of any history of philosophy whatsoever. Surely, the light of the intellect (and therefore possibly the philosophical thought that prolongs it in the dialectical order of discourse) participates in the unsetting light of the *Logos*, but this light is within it only as a reflection requiring the openness and inward orientation of our understanding. And this is even more true for the conceptual prolongations of our spirit. Hegel, dazzled by the discovery of this vestigial light that shines in particular in the purity of the concept, took image for model and effect for Cause. He turned away from the one Sun of spirits to see only the innumerable multiplicity of its reflections on the surface of the mind. It was then that, wanting to save everything by speculative thought alone, he assigned to philosophy the indefinite task of embracing the mobility of relative being in the smallest phases of its perpetual transformations. Now this is a Zenonian task, that is to say, impossible: the indefinite is inexhaustible analytically. In reality the whole Hegelian endeavor, an endeavor of a singular magnitude, amounts to *subjecting* the highest knowledge to the order of the indefinitely relative—to condemn it to follow the smallest twists and turns of the dialectic of becoming, to want to "think everything" explicitly, when there is no limit to conceptual analysis—and such an intention inevitably leads to an arbitrary multiplication of rational links, and therefore to a sclerosing proliferation of fibrous mental tissue. Hence this is, at once, an extreme fragmentation of philosophical discourse and, to curb its dispersing effect, a strengthening of the system that

---

51 *Études d'histoire de la pensée philosophique*, 162, fn 3.

goes as far as caricature. Basically, there is no Hegelian philosophy in the sense that all philosophy aims at the normative intelligibility of the real, that is to say, aims at accounting for what is, by what can legitimately be, which necessarily entails distinguishing the truly real from the apparent real. Hegelian philosophy renounces this primary task to transform itself into a *speculative recording chamber*; it confines itself to noting what becomes, in order to save it conceptually; it represents one of the greatest degradations of thought that one can imagine; it makes the philosopher the servant and even the slave of the "spirit of the times": "This is the present time's point of view, and the series of spiritual figures has thus ceased for the moment.... This series is the true realm of spirits, the only realm of spirits there is... I hope that this history of philosophy might contain an invitation for you to grasp the spirit of the time, which is within us in a natural way, and bring it to light by drawing it out of its natural condition, that is, from its hidden and lifeless existence, and—each in one's own place—consciously shed light on it."[52]

Thus the ultimate confinement of human culture takes place inside the mental and rational cavern. For Kant, "simple reason" still had "borders" that excluded from itself "religious folly." For Hegel, it apparently no longer has any, since he extends reason to the totality of reality and of becoming and appropriates for it even what seems the most anti-rational. But in reality, faced with the scandal of religious consciousness and its representations, Hegel reduced everything to the limits of reason, integrating sacred symbols into its substance as a temporary alienation in the course of its historical realization. We have therefore gone from cultural reduction to a "consciousness-related" reduction, and from a consciousness-related reduction to rational reduction: we must find a reason for what seems devoid of it. Henceforth the general blueprint is ready. Modern and contemporary thought will not change, even if led to give various interpretations. It will always be a question, after the mental (or psychic) confinement of the sacred—because

---

52 *Leçons sur l'histoire de la philosophie*, quoted and translated by D'Hondt, Hegel, 77.

Hegel, or the Transformation of Gnosis into Logic

it cannot be reasonably left at the door of the human spirit as naively believed by triumphant scientism — of finding why such a spirit, oblivious of its true nature, has been able to produce such monsters, through which, however, it can gain access to self-recognition.

THE FAILURE OF THE SYMBOL ACCORDING TO HEGEL

Thus far we have considered Hegelian doctrine as a whole. To conclude, we will briefly examine what it specifically says about the symbol in the literal sense of the term, and we will see the results of our analysis verified.

In his *Lectures on Fine Art*, delivered from 1820 to 1829, Hegel deals specifically with the question of the symbol.[53] This already means that the symbol interests him only from the vantage point of art and not from that of religion, although symbolism concerns the religious as much as the artistic.[54] To our knowledge, his *Lectures on the Philosophy of Religion* does not contain any comprehensive discussion of the symbol.[55] We must therefore delineate first Hegel's concept of art and the place he assigns to it. This concept is also found in the *Lectures on Aesthetics*, in the first volume, devoted to the Idea and the Ideal[56] (and repeated in other works, from the *Encyclopedia* to the *Lectures on the Philosophy of Religion*). Art, religion, and philosophy belong to the "sphere of the absolute spirit." Their content is identical: it is "truth as the absolute object of consciousness." But these three "realms of the spirit" differ in the *forms* "in which they bring home to consciousness their object, the Absolute." These forms are not equivalent. Incapable of working out distinctions, not only without classifying

---

53   *Aesthetics, Lectures on Fine Art*, trans. T. M. Knox (Oxford: Clarendon Press, 1975), vol. 1, Part II, 299–426. This first section of Part II includes an introduction which deals with "the symbol in general," and three chapters which develop the themes announced in the introduction. We will rely mainly on the introduction (299–322).

54   Ibid., 314: "However close the connection between religion and art may be, [here we will] not go over the symbols themselves or religion."

55   Trans. R. F. Brown, P. C. Hodgson & J. M. Stewart (Berkeley, Los Angeles, London: University of California Press, 1988).

56   *Aesthetics*, Part I, 101–4. Unless otherwise indicated, the following quotes are taken from these pages.

them hierarchically, but also without ordering them as so many phases in a progressive development, Hegel sees, in the passage from the form "art" to the form "religion," then from that to the form "philosophy," a continuous and necessary progress in awareness of the absolute. In art, the absolute is captured by feeling, therefore in a direct and immediate way, but as something external. This is why art pertains to the realm of sensory intuition. It "sets truth before our minds in the mode of sensuous configuration," and therefore with individual and particular forms (a particular statue, a particular painted landscape, &c.) which cannot, because of their particularity, "provide a vision of the spiritual." Clearly, art is often religious, and religion often uses works of art. However, it is as pure art that religious truth is attained, as Greek statuary proves: "the poets and artists became for the Greeks the creators of their gods." And, on the other hand, the more religion becomes religious, the more it frees itself from artistic expression.

Religion in fact constitutes a less limited mode of apprehending the absolute: "the '*after*' of art consists in the fact that there dwells in the spirit the need to satisfy itself solely in its own inner self as the true form for truth to take." Art then ceases to be the highest form of the true and the absolute, which a civilization and a community put above everything else: "No matter how excellent we find the statues of the Greek gods, no matter how we see God the Father, Christ, and Mary so estimably and perfectly portrayed: it is no help; we no longer bow the knee."[57] Therefore religion grasps the absolute as a

---

57 Needless to say, each of these statements raises the most considerable difficulties. Two things impress the reader about Hegel: the extent of his cultural information, fruit of an insatiable curiosity, on the one hand; the power of a seemingly indefatigable and never-exhausted dialectic, on the other. But, inevitably, this vast amount of information turns out to be quite fragile and shallow; and above all—because all information depends on its time—the artificial nature of the dialectical construction becomes, in the long run, difficult to bear, and its gratuitousness even ends up discouraging refutation. If the theses that Hegel maintains were true, they would lead purely and simply to the negation of sacred art, that is, of the totality of human art over the entire surface of the earth, with a few historical and geographical exceptions. It is an understatement to say that he did not understand anything about Hindu art or the art of icons ("mummified art devoid of spirituality," *Aesthetics*, vol. 2

Hegel, or the Transformation of Gnosis into Logic

subject which, through *piety*, which is foreign to art, enables religion to become imbued with "what art makes objective as externally perceptible, and the subject so identifies himself with this content that it is its inner presence in ideas and depth of feeling that becomes the essential element for the existence of the Absolute."

However, this interiority is still presented to consciousness as revealing itself externally. All religion moves in the "element of representation." This is why it is surpassed by philosophy, which "does nothing but transform our representation into concepts."[58] Thanks to this, the absolute is grasped by thought. It is therefore thought that unites art and religion, since thought is objective like art and subjective like religion.

Such is the general framework of the philosophy of mind, the first moment of which is represented by art—which does not mean that it disappears completely when the second moment reaches full self-awareness, but that, while not ceasing to "always rise higher and come to perfection," art's "form has ceased to be the supreme need of the spirit."[59] Now,[60] if we consider this first moment in itself, we will be led to distinguish three successive phases that constitute "three chief art-forms": *symbolical* art, *classical* art, and *romantic* art. In general, art is the realization of the idea of the beautiful through a form. Each formal realization only expresses the awareness that the idea of the beautiful has of itself, of its own riches and determinations. In short, the becoming of art is the becoming of the intrinsic content of the idea of the beautiful. The perfecting of the art form is a function of progress in the truth of the idea, and therefore necessarily follows from it. The evolution of art reflects the dialectic of the idea and its expression, depending on whether the idea is inferior (symbolical art), adequate (classical), or superior (romantic) to the form that expresses it. Note that symbolical

---

[published in tandem with vol. 1], Part III, 872), but he still presents a barely recognizable caricature of them: surely it would have been better to say nothing.
58 *Lectures on the Philosophy of Religion*, 145.
59 *Aesthetics*, vol. 1, Part I, 103.
60 Unless otherwise indicated, the following quotes are taken from *Aesthetics*, Part II, 299–322.

art designates the art of the East (Persia, India, Egypt, &c.), classical art is that of Greco-Roman antiquity, and romantic art is roughly identified with Christian art, that is, with medieval or Gothic art (the distinction between Romanesque and Gothic was as yet unknown in Hegel's time),[61] and modern art. This romantic art, by virtue of the infinite richness of its interior content, of its free and purely spiritual subjectivity, proves to be completely indifferent to form![62] The pertinence of such a theory will be appreciated.

What about symbolic art itself now? Symbolic art is that in which the content of the idea[63] is so meager, so indeterminate, so abstract, that it does not find in itself the elements for its outward "adequate manifestation." In other respects, symbolic art "finds itself confronted by what is external to itself, external things in nature and human affairs." It then *seeks* (symbolic art is essentially an *unsuccessful attempt*) to associate, from the outside, abstractions and "undetermined universals," in other words "vague generalities," with the real forms of nature which it alters and distorts "arbitrarily." Thus, "instead of coming to a complete identification, it comes only to an accord, and even to a still abstract harmony between meaning and shape, ... [exhibiting equally] their affinity, their mutual externality, foreignness, and incompatibility." As B. Teyssèdre says summarizing Hegel's thought, "the mind expresses itself so poorly that it seems arbitrary, nature is so distorted that it seems artificial. As somewhat of a relationship must subsist, this comes down to the vague assertion that there is a relationship.... Far from the inside being *embodied* on the outside, like Apollo in the Sauroctonos (Python-slayer) statue, the *emphasis is on the distinction* between unpleasant, or grotesque, or monstrous appearances, and a Spirit about which we know and feel nothing, other than that it is."[64]

---

61 The distinction between Romanesque and Gothic, of Norman origin, would not be prior to 1818.
62 *Aesthetics*, vol. 1, Part. II, 302.
63 For Hegel the content of the idea simply signifies the conscious knowledge that the human mind has of the beautiful.
64 *L'esthétique de Hegel* (Paris: P. U. F., 1958), 58.

Hegel, or the Transformation of Gnosis into Logic

However, this symbolic art develops in three phases: that of unconscious symbolism, which constitutes a pre-aesthetic or "pre-artistic" stage of nature worship and fetishism; that of *symbolism of the sublime* in which the mind, assuming a keener awareness of the absolute, notices above all its inexpressible sublimity, which must nevertheless be expressed with the help of an unworthy material; and lastly, that of *conscious symbolism*, which is also the end of symbolic art, and in which the (implicit) symbol becomes explicit comparison, so that the expressive form is no more than a simple image whose inadequacy to its content is perfectly understood.

Finally, each of these three phases of symbolic art is in turn subdivided into intermediate stages. *Unconscious symbolism* starts from ground zero of art and symbol, where the absolute is not distinguished from the sensible (Persia), passes to quantitative sublimity (India), and ends in symbolism properly so-called (Egypt). The *symbolism of the sublime* perceives the one and the All as omnipresent: it is the affirmative stage of the sublime art of pantheism that was "developed in the most brilliant way in Mohammedanism and its mystical art" and sometimes in "Christian mysticism."[65] In the negative stage, to the contrary, one sings of the Lord's inaccessibility to any concrete representation: this is especially the case with Hebrew poetry. Finally, *conscious symbolism*, through the stages of "fables, parables, and apologues" first, then "allegory, metaphor," ultimately leads to the total and final sundering of meaning and form.

By briefly recalling the Hegelian doctrine, we wanted above all to emphasize the true nature of his concept of the symbol, which seems better in its practice than in its general definitions. Basically, Hegel is an enemy of symbolism. The symbol, he says in a very typical way, is both adequate and inadequate. Adequate, in the sense that what "it is externally already includes the content of the representation it wants to evoke." But also and necessarily inadequate, otherwise it would cease to be a symbol, since, insofar as a symbol, it represents not a concrete object, but a general quality. And so it is, says Hegel, for the

---

65 *Aesthetics*, vol. 1, Part II, 321.

equilateral triangle which has properties adequate to the Trinity, but which has others unrelated to it. Now, these considerations seem to be self-evident until we ask ourselves: what expressive form would be perfectly adequate for its meaning? Necessarily a work in which form and meaning are indistinguishable. And this is exactly what Hegel has in mind when he characterizes *classical art* as having such an adequacy. In other words, in this art (Greek sculpture) the represented god and his statue *are literally only one*: here we have "the identity of meaning and of its concrete expression."[66] With such art "nothing symbolical remains,"[67] and therefore the sensible form must be seen in it entirety for itself, because it is entirely what it is. Whereas symbolic art "cannot find in concrete appearance any specific form corresponding completely with [the idea's] abstraction and universality"; symbolism is therefore based on a "non-correspondence."[68] Basically, Hegel reproaches the symbol for being a symbol. "When this true content and therefore the true [adequate] form is found for art, then the seeking and striving after both of these, wherein the *deficiency* of symbolic art precisely consists, ceases immediately."[69]

Thus is revealed the true meaning of the symbol's dual nature: its adequacy is apparent, its inadequacy real. "In this respect the whole of symbolic art may be understood as a continuing struggle for compatibility of meaning and shape, and the different levels of this struggle are not so much different kinds of symbolic art as stages and modes of one and the same contradiction [of incompatibility between meaning and shape]."[70] Rejection therefore of symbolism goes hand in hand with the rejection of mystery and esotericism, which constitute what remains of symbolism in the perfection of

---

66 Ibid., 433. Gods are strictly nothing but their statues. This conception of the unity of form and content is obviously unsustainable and curiously "unintelligent": it is the physical and numerical unity, which is, moreover, only a pseudo-unity, because there is unity only according to a principle of unification necessarily transcendent to what it unites.
67 Ibid., 434.
68 Ibid., 303.
69 Ibid., 317.
70 Ibid., 317–18.

Hegel, or the Transformation of Gnosis into Logic

Greek art. "The character of the undisclosed [the esoteric, the occult] and the unspoken" are contrasted to the spirit that "is the revealed and the self-revealing. In this respect, the symbolic mode of expression constitutes the other side [the hidden side] of the secrecy [esotericism] of the mysteries, because in the symbolical the meaning remains dark...."[71]

Hegel surely does not envisage any other adequacy of form and content than the one exhibited by Greco-Roman statuary in which the idea "transcends its external existence instead of having blossomed or been perfectly enclosed by it."[72] And, since, on the other hand, romantic art *goes beyond* form and vanishes at the limit as an aesthetic manifestation, it must be concluded that, in Hegel's eyes and whatever he says elsewhere, art as a whole, relative to the becoming of the absolute spirit, is a failure. This cannot have any other meaning than that of a failure of the sensual and bodily as such. In this way Hegelian pseudo-gnosis finally surrenders its secret: it is basically an *angelism* and a *docetism*, like all other caricatures of true gnosis.[73] It is underpinned by a fundamental hostility towards the carnal. With Hegel, the body is not resurrected,[74] the body does not experience transfiguration, while, as a matter of fact, Byzantine iconography is derived on the whole from the Transfiguration of Christ on Mount Tabor, from the glory which the body knows in its essential reality. Far from being a philosophy of reconciliation, Hegelianism is an idealistic monism that endlessly and universally struggles against the impurity of the sensible and the weight of earthly realities. He acknowledges them only under surety of their historicizing reduction. He is esteemed for his concern for concrete and historical efficacy without anyone realizing that this is only a decoy. To perceive in Hegelian efficacy anything

---

71 Ibid., vol. 1, Part II, 469. "Esoteric" and "esotericism" occur in the French translation, not in the German text: *Æsthetik* (Berlin: Aufbau-Verlag, 1955), 454.
72 Ibid., 303.
73 Cf. supra, chap. I.
74 The *Life of Jesus* that Hegel wrote ends with the burial. Christ's resurrection is only the faith that the disciples kept in him after his death. In other words, his (physical) death *is* his (spiritual) resurrection as an ecclesial community (*Hegel's Phenomenology of Spirit*, vol. II, § 784, 588).

other than the deadly intoxication of a reified abstraction, one must already have succumbed to the magic of his conceptual passion. The two thousand pages of *Aesthetics* bear clear witness to this. What are we to think of an art philosopher who coldly asks if the "incongruity between meaning and the immediate artistic expression" in Hindu art should not be attributed "to the deficiency of art, the turbidity of imagination and its lack of ideas"?[75] Not only is it difficult to amass more nonsense and self-importance in so few words, but again such a judgment betrays the underlying sensibility of its author and his rational angelism. It is said that Hegel once wished that trees bordering a road be felled so that the geometry of the straight line could more visibly manifest the purity of the spirit. What displeases him in religious painting is Byzantine art in which he sees, with contempt, only craftsmanship and a traditional and standardized rigidity. What delights him is the ethereal spiritualism of Raphaelite virgins combined with the very human, very individual naturalism of their bodily forms: such is for him the peak of pictorial art, which "can be ascended only once by one people in the course of history's development."[76] That we like Raphael or Correggio is understandable. What is less so is that their works are perceived as the religious and spiritual art par excellence, while what we have here is an objectively secular art that might or might not deal with religious subjects. Yet it happens that the spiritual or sacred meaning is purely nominal and that nothing, or almost nothing, evokes it in the painting itself. What is there that is religious in the "Madonna of the Chair" apart from its title? And we could cite dozens of works from the same period and by the same artists that we are entitled to consider perhaps as exemplary successes in secular art, but that we cannot see ranked as sacred art without a certain bewilderment.[77] True, Hegel

---

75 *Aesthetics*, vol. 1, Part II, 309.
76 Ibid., vol. 2, Part III, 882.
77 There is sacred art, in the true sense of the word, only if the means of expression (materials and the production techniques of these materials, on the one hand, stylistic elements and traditional canons, on the other) are

is not alone in making this mistake and, to the contrary, it is the whole of Western civilization that, at least until the contemporary crisis, shared his opinion. But this phenomenon only testifies to the prodigious weakening of the spiritual sense that post-Galilean Europe experienced, at least as regards the plastic arts (painting, architecture, sculpture).[78] The Raphaelite Madonnas are *only* young Italians (aristocrats, bourgeois, or peasant women); the Christ-child is a chubby baby, athletic if not fat, with a blank stare. As one enthusiastic critic ingenuously puts it: "Raphael's Virgin has lost all the attributes of heavenly nature. The halo that distinguishes her is reduced from a disc to a thread, a thin floating ring... and often this vestige itself vanishes." But—and this betrays the fundamental angelism of this art and of Hegelian aesthetics in particular—Raphael spiritualizes the forms by removing from them any overly natural detail. "Nothing is more delicate than the art by which Raphael avoids, in this tender subject, any allusion to physical things," for example: breastfeeding. "This theme... is overly *natural*, it mixes a too crude idea of function with august ideas.... It is through these exquisite reticences, by dint of tact and modesty, that he was able to put in these Madonnas everything that a human figure can express of the ideal."[79] To which one should respond along with Lanza del Vasto: "Thank God Christians have no ideal. We say: '*Corpus Domini nostri Jesu Christi custodiat animam meam.*'"[80] Nothing

---

themselves sacred, that is, they maintain an ontological and semantic relationship with the reality they are expressing. They are then the object of a ritual consecration that makes their intrinsic correspondence with their model spiritually effective. Since the Renaissance, art may be religious only by its subject or the artist's intention; but art is hardly the objective mediator of a spiritual or divine presence.

78 On this subject, read the reflections of F. Schuon in "Principles and Criteria of Art" in *Language of the Self*, trans. M. Pallis & M. Matheson (Madras: Ganesh, 1959), 102–35.

79 Louis Gillet, *Raphaël*, Librairie de l'art ancien et moderne, 1906, cited by Elie-Charles Flamand, La Renaissance II, in *Histoire générale de la peinture* (Lausanne: éditions Rencontre, tome X, 1965), 109.

80 *Dialogue de l'amitié* (with Luc Dietrich) (Paris: R. Laffont, 1946), 72. In the same book (53), Lanza del Vasto writes that from the beginning of the sixteenth century "the crew of unfortunates who believe they have found [perfection] multiplies, the most illustrious example of which is provided

is more telling, in this respect, than the remark of an art historian comparing these two works of Raphael: the *School of Athens* and the *Dispute of the Blessed Sacrament*, in which "the golden age as a whole is contained": "it is here [in the *Dispute of the Blessed Sacrament*], in the clouds, that Raphael builds the foundations of Religion."[81]

CONCLUSION: THE CONFINEMENT OF THE SACRED

Hegelianism's general meaning is seen now more clearly, to the very extent that the concrete examples of artistic works and the judgments that he brings to them oblige its author to leave his own system, and therefore enable us to do the same and see it as if from the outside. This is not easy, since this system is in itself its own reference, as we have already said and as we will recall in a moment, so that the simple understanding of this philosophy would necessarily be equivalent to recognizing it as total and all-encompassing truth. But this is no longer the case when the system itself refers to realities about which we are well informed, and in relation to which no doctrine, however prestigious, could overawe us. How can we admit that in romantic art, that is, in medieval Christian art "on account of its free spirituality... *the shape is externally more or less indifferent*,"[82] when one also knows the formal rules with which Chartres Cathedral, Notre Dame of Paris, or any other Romanesque or Gothic building are in compliance?[83] Hegelian philosophy is therefore fundamentally anti-symbolist

---

by Raphael, who, gifted with exceptional grace and talent, practices the lie to perfection. The lack of metaphysical anxieties and spiritual certainties bursts forth nowhere as much as in the flowing curves of his broad religious compositions which are as profane as those of the lavish Venetians, but without their carnal innocence and succulent fruits.'

81 Jean Babelon, *L'art au siècle de Léon X* (Paris: Éditions de Clairefontaine, 2000), 81.

82 Hegel, *Aesthetics*, vol. 1, Part II, 302. Our emphasis.

83 This science of architectural symbolism is explained, in particular, in Jean Hani's book, *The Symbolism of the Christian Temple*, trans. R. Proctor (Kettering, OH: Angelico, 2017), the clearest synthesis we have read on this subject. *Initiation à la symbolique romane*, by M. M. Davy (Paris: Flammarion, 1964) as well as her *Sources et clefs de l'art roman* (in collaboration with R. and M. Pernoud [Paris: Berg International, 1973]) are in some respects more complete works, but also more labored, less didactic, and less decisive.

and, by that very fact, destructive of all religion. For there is no religion that does not imply an immanence of the divine in sensual, spatio-temporal forms, and therefore the capacity for these forms to be receptors of the divine.

This does not mean, however, that we can rule decisively between the divergent interpretations of "right-wing Hegelianism" or "left-wing Hegelianism"; one sees Hegel as the great theologian of modern times, the other detects there only an at least speculatively possible, radical atheism. The doctrine of symbolism would objectively side rather with Kojève, who moreover agrees in this with the judgment of Maritain.[84] But, more profoundly, this problem is irrelevant. To ask oneself whether the history of the spirit recounted by phenomenology is that of God or man, is to refer to extra-philosophical realities that are supposed to hold, in the last analysis, the ultimate key to this discourse, its definitive truth. On the contrary, it seems that Hegel's entire effort aims at rejecting this ontological reference, claiming it dispensable. Not by denying these realities, which would be another way of affirming them; but by placing the philosophical discourse in such a place that the question of the concept's ontological reference *loses all meaning*. This place is that of absolute spirit, which, in a certain way, overflows the divine spirit and the human spirit: "The divine spirit and the human spirit have in common what is, in itself and for itself, the universal, absolute Spirit; it is spirit, but also encompasses nature in itself.... The universality of Spirit, to which philosophy and religion relate, is an absolute, non-exterior universality, all pervasive, omnipresent in everything."[85] What Hegel saw in gnosis is precisely a means of escaping the state of radical separation of phenomenon and noumenon in which Kant left philosophy, the

---

84 Maritain has devoted an important study to Hegel in *Moral Philosophy* (New York: Scribner's, 1964), 119–208.

85 Introduction to *Leçons sur l'histoire de la philosophie*, tome I, 202; also, ibid., 146: "There is only one reason, no second, superhuman reason; it is the divine in man." This is true, in a way, just as there is only one light. But it should be added that human reason is not *the* Reason; it is only a reflection or an obscuring of it, and can realize its true essence only by effacing itself in its particular mode so to become identified with its own transcendent substance.

GNOSTICS OF THE 19TH AND 20TH CENTURIES

possibility of accessing a point from which, as André Breton will say more or less, "the subject and the object cease to be perceived contradictorily."[86] Gnosis, however, is nothing more here than the knowledge that philosophy has of itself. This translation of metaphysics into *Logic* "signifies the negation of a transcendent being that reason could know, but which would be an intelligible world opposite reason. *The absolute is subject, not substance; the Absolute is the speculative knowledge of Logic. God is only accessible in pure speculative knowledge, and is only in this very knowledge, and is only this very knowledge.* Theology realized the intelligible beyond intelligence. Hegelian logic knows neither thing in itself, nor intelligible world. The Absolute is deemed to be nowhere else than in this phenomenal world, it is in our own thought that absolute thinking is thought...."[87] The emergence of Galilean science deprived religious symbolism of its ontological referents by destroying any possibility of a sacred cosmology.[88] The proper work of Hegelianism is to deduce all the philosophical consequences brought about by this revolution, and to transform the ontological referent of religious discourse, that is, the thing in itself that Kantianism had maintained—but without being able to *reference it*—into

---

86 Let us recall this declaration, made in the solemn tone affected by the "pope" of surrealism: "Everything tends to make us believe that there exists a certain point of the mind at which life and death, the real and the imagined, past and future, the communicable and the incommunicable, high and low, cease to be perceived as contradictions" (Second Manifesto of Surrealism, in *Manifestoes of Surrealism*, trans. R. Seaver & H. R. Lane [Ann Arbor: University of Michigan, 1972], 123). With Breton, the assertion of this supreme point is combined with a strict materialism "show[ing] no propensity to lapse into the supernatural" ("Ascendant Sign," in *Free Rein*, trans. M. Parmentier & J. d'Amboise [Lincoln & London: University of Nebraska Press, 1995], 105). Breton, moreover, has always evinced the most violent hatred towards religion (Christian in particular). In his *Philosophie du surréalisme* (Paris: Flammarion, 1955), 56, F. Alquié has shown that Breton's constant approval of Hegel, alongside certain errors of interpretation, draws its explicit motive from the Hegelian negation of transcendence. For Alquié, moreover, this was not about a misunderstanding of Hegel on Breton's part, but about the truth of surrealism, which would proceed in the direction of a transcendence of the individual and lived experience.
87 J. Hyppolite, *Logique et existence* (Paris: P. U. F., 1953), 70-71 (the italicized passages are from Hegel); also read § 213 of the *Encyclopedia...*, 282-84.
88 Cf. *The Crisis of Religious Symbolism*, 13-142.

Hegel, or the Transformation of Gnosis into Logic

an interior moment for the becoming of the mind. In such a philosophy, everything is enclosed, nothing is left outside, there is no longer any beyond to the mind, just as with mechanism there is no longer any beyond to the world. The beyond of mind and reason is lodged in reason itself. To the alienation of consciousness from the divine and the religious spheres corresponds the alienation of God from human consciousness: "It is the eternal life of God to find himself, to become for himself, to unite with himself. In this preferment there is an alienation, a decision; but it is the nature of the Idea to alienate itself in order to find itself."[89] However, in the end, all this, in its truth, takes place only in thought: "Thought is the unique sphere where, everything foreign having disappeared from view, the spirit is absolutely free."[90]

This is why, in the final analysis, the process by which "mythological representations" arise in human culture and the process by which God becomes a mythological representation are one and the same. The Spirit is first of all sheer intimacy with itself, an impenetrable interiority. "Then it happens that this Spirit, gathered in upon itself, becomes resolved, differentiates itself from itself, becomes object, becomes objective; in terms of representation: God is Spirit or love (which is identical), that is, God exteriorizes himself, communicates himself, passes into otherness. Then all the appearances of the given, the received, &c., are presented, which is also to be met with in mythology. This is where everything that is historical and everything that is called positive in religion is situated."[91] How could it be otherwise? Since mythologies have no objective referents, they can only be productions of fantasy and imagination. But as soon as they are understood as products of the human *psyche*, it is necessary, in order to ward off the danger represented by the introduction of the irrational within rationality, to explain it as a necessity in universal reason's becoming. "What we first encounter in religion is myth, figurative representations. It contains the true as the

---

89 *Leçons sur l'histoire de la philosophie*, tome I, 131–32.
90 Ibid., 132.
91 Ibid., 206.

spirit *represents* it to itself. Its content is shown to have a sensuous representation, but it is produced by the mind. Myths are therefore not arbitrary inventions of priests for deceiving people, but productions of thought, having the imagination as an organ..., myths are actually the play of fantasy; it is, however, necessary to harmonize in and for itself what they contain of general truths...the spiritual is revealed through the imagination."[92] In fact, these truths cannot be revealed otherwise. The mind needs mythical fictions in order to become aware of its truly divine nature: "for religions and what they contain of mythology are *products of man wherein he has deposited what is most sublime and most profound in him*, the consciousness of what is the truth.... Religions and mythologies are products of reason in the process of becoming conscious; however poor, however childish as they seem, they nevertheless contain reason; they are based on rational instinct."[93] This is certainly true of Greek mythology. In this mythology, a work of the imagination and therefore "seated firmly in the arbitrary," it is "reason that imagines." By such an operation, "the spirit thus represents itself, enlightens itself in accounting for a sensuous existence; this is even more the case with Christian mythology; anthropomorphism plays there a still greater role."[94] Mythology, then, is not only the account of Genesis, but in a general way, all that is marvelous or miraculous, for example the divine manifestation in the Burning Bush: "Thus Moses saw God in the burning bush and the Greeks represented their gods by marble statues or other images." From this standpoint—that of representation—the historicity of Christ is as external as biblical mythology. However, "these images of fantasy or this historical material must not remain in this exteriority, but become for the spirit something of the spiritual order, they must relinquish this exterior existence, which has precisely nothing spiritual about it."[95] Moreover, this is what the death

---

92 Ibid., 196–97. Hegel has always upheld Creuzer's opinion (cf. *Histoire et théorie du symbole*, 21–22), but interprets it within the framework of his own dialectic. This is what he also does in the lectures from which we quote fragments.
93 *Leçons sur l'histoire de la philosophie*, tome I, 231–32. Our emphasis.
94 Ibid., 233.
95 Ibid., 201.

of Christ achieves, in a somewhat unconscious way, at least insofar as (Hegelian) philosophy had not come along to give us its meaning: "Now, however, a further determination comes into play—God has died, God is dead—this is the most frightful of all thoughts, that all that is eternal, all that is true is not, that negation itself is found in God."[96]

We have said enough, we think, to uncover the basis of Hegelian thought. Should we see Hegel as the last of the great theologians?[97] This is what many European thinkers, both Protestants and Catholics, assert, and one can speak, beyond Kierkegaard, of a real "return to Hegel." Or should we see here an integral atheism, in the manner of Kojève? Both are right, but perhaps neither takes seriously enough the radical change with which Hegelian "logic" intends to proceed. Those who theologize are not wrong to point out the difficulties raised by a naively "reified" ontology: to posit God as a being (even the first) among other beings, is equivalent to his rejection and negation. This is why the Hegelian attempt to overcome the dualism of human subject and divine Object seems legitimate to them: it responds to a real need of metaphysical intelligence. From this point of view, it is clear that the Kojevians too easily interpret in the sense of pure atheism all of Hegel's statements concerning the immanence of the divine to human reason, no doubt because they underestimate the importance of an integral theology's demands. Conversely, those who theologize are perhaps too easily convinced about the "Eckhartian" or "Boehmian" content of Hegel's most daring theses. Is this

---

96 *Lectures on the Philosophy of Religion*, Part III, 1. "The Absolute religion," vol. 3, trans. E. B. Speirs & J. B. Sanderson (London: Routledge & Kegan Paul, 1895), 91.

97 "Hegel remains the last great thinker who took Christian Revelation seriously and believed that it should remain for all thinking minds the major site for human reflection." B. M. Lemaigre, *L'objectivité de Dieu dans la pensée hégélienne*, in *Procès de l'objectivité de Dieu* (Paris: Cerf, 1969), 53. The author is of course aware that the Hegelian God seems to "dissolve into the Idea." But he sees this as a misinterpretation: "Hegel in our view in no way denies the existence of God, the fact that he reveals himself to man in order to be known to him" (ibid., 51). We do not think that this thesis can be upheld when taking into account the texts of the lectures on *Aesthetics*, on the *Philosophy of Religion* and on the *History of Philosophy*.

really what the philosopher meant? Is not Kojevian radicalism more clear-eyed? Surely Kojève goes further than the letter of the Hegelian text; or at least he leads the letter of the text to its explicitly atheistic end—which Hegel never does. But is not this the only means of bestowing on it its true and actual meaning? The following question then remains: are those who theologize, in reality, unwitting atheists? And the Kojevians, hyper-theologians without knowing it? Who then is unaware of what? And how, deciding with what criteria, since there is no *outside* to the System?

Confining oneself to the System itself, to its own "Logic," there is no way to answer these questions, since the System's function is to form the locus of absolute knowledge from which *it is precisely no longer possible to pose them*. To continue to pose them is therefore, in a certain way, not to take the System seriously, not to enter into absolute knowledge and to stay with the "element of representation," is to seek in objects external to the System (God, man) for referents that give philosophical discourse its "true" meaning, while, from the vantage point of absolute knowledge, there is no longer any exteriority. This discourse, therefore, has no other referent than itself, it is to itself its own interpreter and its own truth. This is, in our opinion, the essential *thesis* of all Hegelian philosophy.[98] However, there is at least one thing that is external to the System, and that is the System itself as a determinate cultural production. There is at least something that *exists* and becomes the object of knowledge, and that is the Hegelian system, which is precisely what we are seeking to understand and to penetrate, because it is a problem. Insofar as Hegel ex-*poses* his philosophy *before* men, he makes it, in its very historical appearance, as if external to all

---

98 One could say, to use an expression of Hegel himself in the *Encyclopedia*: such is the esoteric meaning of this philosophy (cf. the "remark" in *Philosophy of Mind*, § 573, 183–84). This "remark" is important because Hegel comes to the defense, not only of Spinoza, but also of mystical texts, like the *Bhagavad Gita* or the poems of Rumi, against the reproach of pantheism. At the same time, it is his own system that he exonerates, to the very extent that he perceives his thought's kinship with these expressions of "Eastern mysticism," all the while affirming the superiority of the philosophical (Hegelian) point of view. The charge of pantheism basically corresponds to a mere exoteric understanding.

intelligences that will have become cognizant of it.[99] In other words, Hegelianism would be right only if it did not exist as Hegelianism, if it stood aside before its own self-evidentness. Such is the case with true gnosis, which is, as we have recalled, rightly ineffable. There is no vantage point on reality. Reality is itself its own vantage point. Just as it is for light, the most adequate symbol of true gnosis. Who sees the light? It is in itself pure transparency, elusive; invisibly present, however, since it exerts an action, and if it were not "there," there would no longer be any vision. And yet it is no less true to say that everywhere it is the light that we perceive of the light, since we only see what each thing reflects. Thus the light precedes us, "behind" and "ahead." Our eye perceives only by directing its gaze in a direction that follows the luminous rays, but, at the same time, what comes to the fore are these same rays sent back by the object. But, as we well know, neither the source of light—for us the Sun—or the illuminated object radiating its colors, are *the* light. However, without a light source, no light, and without an illuminated object, no evidence of its existence. If we apply this symbolism to gnosis, it means that true Gnosis precedes all its expressions, which are only particular mirrors of it. We are ever speaking as sons who have received knowledge from the "Father of Lights." The Word is sonship, as the trinitarian mystery teaches. As a result, every truly gnostic (or metaphysical) doctrine is only a temporary place of manifestation for informal Gnosis, pure Knowledge. Similar to a prism immersed in an ocean of infinite light, it focuses and refracts this light, it makes it manifest, reflects its rays for a determined group of men, but also and necessarily splits up what is one and deflects what is straight. On the other hand, this symbolism also means that true Knowledge, absolute Knowledge, far from reducing transcendent and objective

---

99 This is also the strategy that Kierkegaard seems to adopt against Hegel: "...the best way to proceed is...never to take Hegel's logic at the level of its (rational) rightness, but in the fact of its existence" (Pascal Marignac, La figure de Hegel dans le *"Post-Scriptum"* de Kierkegaard, in Revue de l'Enseignement Philosophique, year 31, num. 4 [April–May 1981]: 9). To which we will add that it is precisely the radical "logic" of Hegelianism that accentuates its own "existentiality" and makes it problematic.

referents, enlightens them, causes them to emerge out of night and indistinction, in short gives them existence *without contradiction*. Just as by light and in light objects are *posited in themselves* in their mutual exteriority, so by and in superessential Gnosis, these objective realities which are "God," man and the world, are posited in themselves in their irreducible otherness, without this otherness causing a problem. It is only for want of ascending to the intuition of pure Knowledge that is super-ontological, that which Plato calls the "Idea of the Good which is beyond being and essence," that theology and philosophy come up against the contradiction of subject and object. But when one has ascended to this "Knowledge" that surpasses any affirmation as well as any negation, any position as well as any reduction, one understands that the field of the Real is truly beyond all limitation and therefore that all limitations find within its bosom the *possibility* of existing, and particularly the first of all, the ontological determination. It must also be emphasized that without this ontological self-determination, we humans would have no notion, no intellective perception, of the superessential Gnosis that exceeds all knowledge, just as without the Sun, we humans would be unaware of light's existence. In other words, it is the God of ontotheology who reveals to us (and thereby veils) the more than luminous darkness of the superessential Thearchy. As we learn from the word that resounds in the pyre of the Burning Bush: "I am He-who-is," which implies both identity and difference between "I" and "He-who-is"; Being is the first "attribute" of God and the last, the one that makes him known. This means: when the intelligence attains Pure Being, *know* that it is I-Myself that it attains, because this Pure Being is I-Myself who "am" this very being, that is, who "causes" It "to be." God is the One who gives "existence" to Pure Being.[100] However, He cannot

---

[100] We obviously do not exclude any other interpretation of the biblical saying: "*Eheyeh asher eheyeh.*" Without wishing to enter into a debate that fills, by itself, libraries, we will point out that it is not impossible, according to grammarians, to understand the Name YHWH (which derives from the "definition" given to Moses) in the sense of a causative: "He who causes to be, He who calls into existence," an interpretation they reject however because the object of divine action is not indicated, and also because "no causative form of this verb is

Hegel, or the Transformation of Gnosis into Logic

be "reduced" to this ontological hypostasis.[101] God is "more than It" since He can give It as his Name. But it is not other than Him. However, for Him, for the superessential Thearchy, there is no Name. And this is why Gnosis can declare:

> The Way that that can be told
> Is not the Way
> The Name that can be pronounced
> Is not the Name
>
> The Nameless
> Made Heaven and Earth appear
> The Named
> Is Mother of the Ten Thousand Beings.[102]

For, as Eckhart says "God (the Named, the Being) *becomes* when all creatures say 'God.'"[103]

We will conclude by quoting this beautiful text from the *The Recorded Sayings of Ch'an Master Lin-chi*, which clearly shows that, in the light of the doctrine of pure Knowledge, everything

---

known elsewhere in Hebrew" (A. Clamer, *La sainte Bible*, tome I, part 2 [Paris: Letouzey and Ané, 1956], 83). Moreover, it is generally considered that the "I am Being" translation of the Septuagint is too philosophical, a nuance foreign to the Hebrew mentality. This last so often repeated argument seems, in itself, highly questionable. On the other hand, it does not match the facts. Qumram texts actually bear witness against this. On several occasions God is called Being: "The Eternal Being [is] the support of my right hand" (*The Community Rule* XI, 4); "The Eternal Being, my eyes have beheld" (ibid., XI, 5); "The oracle of Being" (*Hymns*, XII, 9; *Les textes de Qumrâm*, trans. and annotated by J. Carmignac & P. Guilbert [Paris: Letouzey and Ané, 1961], vol. 1, 76 and 264). We can therefore accept the meaning of being, which we will understand in the active sense: an act of being or ontological self-affirmation. This act of being (*actus essendi*) is the primordial act of God, so that there is no need to ask oneself what is the object of divine action, since this object is being itself. And it is thanks to this principial *Esse* that we can "know" God, and therefore also recognize him. It is the *sign* that gives us access to this knowledge, the *Name* within Which is hidden the mystery of the super-essence, this Name that Moses asks God to give him so that the Jews might know Who it is and recognize the One who sends him—which would not make sense if they did not already know that Name and its meaning. These themes are clarified and developed in *Penser l'analogie*, chap. X.
101 "Hypostasis" is taken here in the Plotinian sense (degree of reality) and not in the theological sense of "person."
102 *Tao Te King*, trans. Claude Larre (Paris: Desclée de Brouwer, 1977), 17.
103 *The Complete Mystical Works of Meister Eckhart*, trans. M. O'C. Walshe (New York: Crossroad, 2009), Sermon 56, 293.

changes and nothing changes, and that, in its deepest reality, this Knowledge does not change, involves no reduction, no suppression, but on the contrary, allows It alone to allow all otherness to subsist by opening up the "infinite space" of supreme Reality: "The master gave an evening lecture, instructing the group as follows:

a. At times one takes away the person but does not take away the environment.

b. At times one takes away the environment but does not take away the person.

c. At times one takes away both the person and the environment.

d. At times one takes away neither the person nor the environment."[104]

And so our reflections on Hegel bring us back to our starting point, that is, to gnosis. It is both the honor of Hegelian philosophy and its pitfall to have forced us to do so: honor, because there is surely no other European philosophy which has *tried* to approach pure Knowledge so tenaciously, and this is why it can induce a feeling of having "exhausted" philosophy; but also pitfall, to the very extent that Hegel ultimately understood this supreme Knowledge only in the form of a "logic."

---

104 *The Zen Teachings of Master Lin-chi*, trans. B. Watson (Boston & London: Shambhala, 1993), 21.

CHAPTER 5

Ruyerian Gnosis, A Religion of the Scientific Age

DOES RAYMOND RUYER DESERVE TO APPEAR in a book devoted to gnosis? We think so. True, the general tone of his discourse is foreign to what we most often identify as pertaining to gnosis. Historians of gnosticism, such as Simone Pétrement, Michel Tardieu, Jean-Daniel Dubois, and a few others, have not failed to point out and even denounce Ruyer's usurpation of the term. And there is surely nothing in his work that expressly bears any resemblance to the religious currents thus designated. Two points should be noted however: on the one hand, as we will show in the third part of this book, we do not think one can rest content with a "nominal" definition of gnosis: it is not just a label, and the philosopher should not relinquish the search for its essence; that is why it is legitimate to want to identify its presence elsewhere than in duly validated domains. On the other hand, we are almost certain that the historians we have mentioned (with the exception of Simone Pétrement) have only a very superficial knowledge of Ruyer's philosophy, which is one of the twentieth century's most powerful intellectual endeavors. What we have here is arduous thinking in the guise of easy, not very technical, language tinged with humor, but which requires a protracted effort to understand.

So it is not just on the strength of the title of his most famous work that we are inviting Ruyer to be among the great gnostics of modern thought; it is first of all on the basis of his doctrine's content. Besides, as previously noted, and to be repeated later, there is something gnostic in every philosophical approach when it wants to go right to the very end of its intention, to the extent that gnosis, in its essence—not in all its stages—is the truth of knowledge [*connaissance*] (of "co-birth" [co-naissance]). And this obviously applies to scientific knowledge, and in the highest degree to the modern science of quantum physics, to the very extent that it seeks to think about reality as it is revealed and such that it forces the physicist to recognize the inseparability of the observing subject and the observed phenomenon. He has to then surrender any claim to the materialist postulate of a reality merely spread out in space and completely foreign to the knowledge of it acquired by human intelligence. This is indeed the epistemic situation imposed by contemporary science and that no longer has anything to do with nineteenth century scientistic mechanicism (which went wholly unperceived by Guénon). Of this epistemic situation, the greatest physicists of the twentieth century were clearly aware. Niels Bohr, Heisenberg, Schrödinger, Bernard d'Espagnat, Fritjof Capra, Costa de Beauregard, &c., have striven to take this situation into account while rebuilding, with more or less success, and sometimes inspired by more or less well understood oriental doctrines, a new vision of reality that breaks with the objectivist materialism of prior physics. A fairly exact idea of this vision of reality was advanced by the famous Cordoba Conference (1979).[1] However, in our opinion, none of these reconstructions has provided such a conception of cosmic reality as well-wrought, as ample, and as rigorous as the one worked out by Ruyer from 1937 (*La Conscience et le Corps*) until his death in 1987. He was, it is said, "the Leibniz of our time."

But this cosmological gnosis is not only endorsed by its intrinsic importance and by its truth (at least where cosmology is concerned), it also concerns very directly our search for true gnosis, to the extent that cosmology and theology, according to Ruyer, are really only one, and where this philosopher had the somewhat unusual ambition to lay the foundations of a scientifically acceptable religion: not a religion of science, but the updating of the religious or, if one prefers, theological implications actually contained in the ideas of contemporary science. In this regard, and in its general aim — not in its

---

[1] The proceedings of this conference were published under the title *Science et Conscience: Les deux Lectures de l'univers* (Paris: Éditions Stock, 1980).

content—Ruyer's approach is similar to that of Teilhard de Chardin, another gnostic cosmologist to whom we will return in our third part. It is therefore necessary to take quite seriously *The Gnosis of Princeton*'s subtitle: "Scholars in Search of a Religion," and absorb its full impact. This is what we will try to show, before presenting a critical assessment of this gnosis.

THE HISTORY OF A TITLE

Everyone knows today that the title, *The Gnosis of Princeton*, is misleading. Those who knew Ruyer, whether they were his students, colleagues, or friends, or all three, were informed from the start. Ruyer made no secret that he was looking for a fable likely to strike the public, and draw its attention to the theses he had been expounding for such a long time, since *La Conscience et le Corps* and *Éléments de psychobiologie*, and which gained, in our opinion, their most accomplished expression in *Neo-finalism*, without obtaining from scientists, and even philosophers, a critical success. The idea occurred to him to attribute his own ideas to a mysterious group of American scholars, for whom he would somehow only be the scribe, convinced that thus his own theses would appear much more remarkable and would in fact be much more noticed. On the choice of the word *gnosis* he hardly wavered. His knowledge in the matter was not very extensive, and besides, Ruyer, whose knowledge in scientific matters was considerable, was hardly interested in historical scholarship. He obviously knew the classic work of Leisegang; he also relied on information that his truly global curiosity brought through chance readings. Moreover, the term gnosis is not taken by him in a very precise historical sense—insofar as such a sense exists. He uses it in the broad sense of a relatively reserved or secret knowledge whose possession transforms those who hold it and brings them true intellectual salvation by giving them access, as much as possible, to a supersensible order of reality. Ruyer is not primarily concerned with this word and takes little care to justify it: a few lines only at the beginning of the book,[2] where he points out that the gnostic label is provisional, and may be

---

2 *La Gnose de Princeton*, 10. Our references are to the original edition (Paris: Fayard, 1974). The work was reprinted by Hachette in 1977.

altered. The appeal of the concept is both in its vague, mysterious character and in the fashionable resurgence it enjoys today, even though Ruyer very much wished to stand apart from all currents now grouped under the term *New Age*.

Indeed, a more in-depth historical study would have shown that the use of such a controversial word had many drawbacks as well, not the least of which is, exactly, the underlying misocosmism, or at least what might be characterized as such, of many gnosticist doctrines; whereas Ruyerian religion is defined as a "cosmolatry,"[3] and can be considered, according to an expression we have recorded from the very mouth of the philosopher, as a "semi-pantheism." The Ruyerian world is divine, or even: the Ruyerian divine is cosmic; it is, in any case, inseparable from the cosmos, without however being fully identical to it. So there is some paradox in calling by the same name a doctrine of the twentieth century and that of Marcion or Basilides who saw in the world created by the demiurge the preeminent work of evil (hence their condemnation of the biblical God, the Jewish God) and who considered the soul's sojourn in this corporeal world as a punishment and a forfeiture. Ruyer is not unaware of this very basic data. He has even treated it rather extensively, however historically allusive, in a chapter of *Dieu des Religions. Dieu de la science*, entitled: "Naturalism and Gnostic Dualism," the conclusion of which is that the "creative descent, if it is one, is devoid of all the pessimistic harmonics of the gnostic fall."[4]

However, in *The Gnosis of Princeton*, it seems the opposition between the cosmolatry of the neo-gnostics and the misocosmism of ancient gnosticism is nowhere indicated, which, in the end, is somewhat surprising. Scholar-historian of gnosticism, Simone Pétrement has clearly underscored this: "The 'new gnosis' which, according to Ruyer, was being developed among some Princeton scholars, clearly seems... the very opposite of gnosticism. The religion of these scholars seems to be a cosmic religion, faith in a spirit immanent to the world, nearly what the Stoic religion was in Antiquity. This is why they make no room

---

3 Ibid., 7.
4 Paris: Flammarion, 1970, 106.

for Christ in their belief. The god whose existence they admit is a god known directly, manifesting itself directly in the facts of the world. Gnosticism, to the contrary, far from not being Christian, could be regarded as a doctrine absolutely centered on Christ, in the sense that it is the doctrine that God can be known only through a Savior or Mediator having human form."[5] Simone Pétrement is surely misinterpreting in part Ruyèr's thinking by reducing it to a cosmic religion: Ruyer always affirmed the existence of a God purely invisible and devoid of "nature." But her reaction betrays the embarrassment of the specialist when faced with a certain use of the word gnosis.

However, Ruyer's usage is devoid of neither reason nor historical basis. As for reason, what impels Ruyer to use this term to designate the doctrine he attributes to American scholars is, we think, because gnosis is situated at the interface between philosophy and religion. And in doing so, Ruyer is indeed referring to a historical tradition, although relatively recent, which consists in using the term gnosis to designate more or less esoteric currents that claim to be custodians of a true and universal knowledge, bearing on the ultimate principles of reality, like metaphysics, but providing those who have it, unlike merely secular or positivist science, with a kind of salvation, just like religion.[6]

This is a meaning found in the German philosophical tradition, in particular with Hegel, to characterize the work of Boehme,[7] or with Franz von Baader, who, moreover, considered himself a Christian gnostic.[8] That said, one should obviously not forget the more immediate reasons why Ruyer had to use a somewhat mysterious term, in the vague sense, yet with a whiff of sulphur, all characteristics likely to pique the curiosity of the public, to render uncertain, or even impossible, attempts at identification or verification, and at the same

---

5 Le Dieu séparé – Les origines du gnosticisme, 106.
6 This is also the thesis of M. Gex, "La Gnose de Princeton. Une synthèse de la philosophie et de la religion," in Revue de theologie et de philosophie, Lausanne, no. 114 (1982): 415–26.
7 Hegel, Encyclopedia of the Philosophical Sciences in Basic Outline, Preface to the second edition, 16-19.
8 Cf. infra, 139–140.

time to clearly differentiate this religion from a Christianity that Ruyer rejected.⁹

As for the geographical location of this Princeton gnosis, it must be admitted that this time it was only for publicity purposes: then again, Ruyer had wavered between Pasadena and Princeton, having no more of a connection with the scholars of the first university than with those of the second. But the thought that Einstein had taught at Princeton ultimately won out over everything else.

THE NATURE OF THE RUYERIAN PROJECT

Such are the facts. It would be wrong, however, to see here only an ingenious scheme intended simply to ensure the success of a work. On the contrary, we believe that it is necessary to take this "literary prank" very seriously and to delve further into its significance. Raymond Ruyer was surely not devoid of a sense of humor and had certainly not forgotten the tradition of the "prank," a tradition into which he was initiated with his stay at the École Normale Supérieure. And the idea of mystifying the Western intelligentsia, so conceited and ultimately so credulous before the idols of the moment, could only appeal to him. But Ruyer was also decidedly serious minded, and this "mystification" does not seem gratuitous. It even corresponds, we think, to a real necessity, if one at least takes into account the philosopher's real intentions.

And first of all, one point is beyond dispute: Ruyer attached the greatest importance to the theses set out in this book. They are for him the expression of pure and simple truth, and a truth that he believed to be based on the most certain of rational demands. This point is fundamental. However astonishing, the views expressed by the philosopher do not derive from any mystical illumination or transcendent revelation, the possibility of which Ruyer completely rejects: for him, they logically follow from the most recent science and

---

9 Michel Tardieu, Jean-Daniel Dubois: *Introduction à la littérature gnostique*, tome I, 33–34. The learned authors of this essential work do not see anything else in Ruyerian "gnosis" than the usurpation of a term for advertising purposes, which to us seems quite inaccurate.

impose themselves with the obviousness of what he himself has called an anti-paradox.[10]

If it is in fact permissible to speak of a Ruyerian methodology, we would make it consist almost entirely in bringing to light the hidden anti-paradoxes of our cognitive operations and in our submission to their irrefutable truth. During one of the last conversations I had with him in November 1983, he had spoken of a new book he had just written, entitled *L'embryogenèse du monde et le Dieu invisible*, with which, he said, "I have gone one step further." "But," he added, "I despair of having my point of view accepted by current science. I would have liked to have one thing understood: what a domain of survey, a field of consciousness is; I have not succeeded, I have come to terms with this state of affairs. Positivist scientists are fools, genetic materialism is inept. But I am resigned, they cannot understand."

The necessity about which we speak could be characterized not as a mystification, but as a *mythification* required by every founding of any religion whatsoever, or, if not of a religion, at least of a religious current. And so we come to the heart of our subject.

Surely our thesis will seem extravagant, exorbitant, disproportionate, and incongruous. It is hard to imagine that a university professor, a philosopher, an opponent of any idea of transcendent revelation, refractory to all religious pathos ("I am," he told me one day, "a theoretical animal"), a resolute skeptic, a culture-loving scientist, someone passionate about technology (he attached much importance to the history of technical development), can be seriously considered as desirous of founding a new religion. And, of course, nothing is further from the Ruyerian approach than that of a Jewish prophet or a mystic, all attitudes for which he had as much abhorrence as for Sartrean existentialism. And if the founding of a Church is involved, with a cult and rites apt for evoking a more or less sacred atmosphere, with a hierarchy, dogmas, a calendar, and even excommunications, we cannot actually speak of Ruyer

---

10 Cf. *La Gnose de Princeton*, 21–22; also *Neo-finalism*, 1–7; *Les Cent prochains siècles* (Paris: Fayard, 1974), 39–142; *Les paradoxes de la conscience et l'information* (Paris: Albin Michel, 1966).

as the founder of a new religion. That would be ridiculous.

But it must be understood: even though Ruyer has, in fact, no intention of founding a new religion, he does have the firm purpose of leading his readers to an awareness of the religious or quasi-religious dimension inherent to scientific knowledge whenever this knowledge, identified with philosophy, finally discovers the place of reality that it had only seen upside-down until then. And that is why this sought-for "religion" of scholars is quite truly a gnosis in one of the recognized senses of the term.

COMTIAN SYNTHESIS AND RUYERIAN SYNTHESIS

Ruyer's endeavor, as we can see, is very different from that of Auguste Comte founding the religion of humanity, although both endeavors admit of an identical starting point, which is the taking into account of science. But, that said, everything else sets them in opposition, and one would even be justified in asking if in some respects Ruyer did not see himself as the anti-Comte par excellence.[11] Auguste Comte retains everything of religion, except the properly theological core. On the contrary, Ruyer retains almost nothing of religion, except that theological core, which it would be perhaps even more appropriate to call theosophical. Certainly, Auguste Comte rejects the term atheism: "The appellation atheist," he wrote to John Stuart Mill, "fits us only if one restricts the term to the narrow etymological meaning... for truly the only thing we have in common with those so designated is that we do not believe in God. In no way do we share their vain metaphysical dreams concerning the origins of the world or of man."[12] Ultimately, for him, this involves effecting, through the study of a suitably systematized history of science, a "reform of the understanding," the birth of a truly positive spirit in which the question of God will no longer have any meaning and will no

---

11 Ruyer presented his point of view on Comte in chapter III of *Dieu des religions, Dieu de la science*: "The vital realm of animals and the religious world of man," 45–54.

12 *The Correspondence of John Stuart Mill and Auguste Comte*, ed. and trans. O. A. Haac (New Brunswick, NJ: Transaction Publishers, 1995), letter of July 14, 1845, 320.

longer have to be discussed.[13] In other words, what Auguste Comte retains of science is essentially the methodological form of its historical approach and its educational efficacy for the human mind.

On the contrary, what Raymond Ruyer retains of science is its content, and, particularly in *The Gnosis of Princeton*, the content of physical science, which is rather new. Until then Ruyer had been concerned mainly with biology, his knowledge of which, it should be emphasized, was quite extensive, more extensive than his knowledge of physics, as he himself readily admitted. Paradoxically, however, it is precisely physical science that Auguste Comte regarded as the most contrary to theology,[14] which, according to Ruyer, should lead to a theologization of scientific knowledge and which provides him with the opportunity to set forth "his" religion. Basically, what Ruyer proposes, in a certain manner, is to "reverse" the law of the three states. Whereas for Comte, the consideration of the progress of science educates the human mind and necessarily leads it from the theological to the positive, passing through the metaphysical, for Ruyer the consideration of Einsteinian cosmology, just like quantum physics, necessarily leads the human mind from the positive state, where the punctuality of phenomena is recorded in the here-and-now and according to a "step by step," to the theological state where the world as a whole, viewed in the thematic unity of the space-time continuum, is *in reality*—that is, if we would view it as truly real—the visible dimension of God, the cosmic brain of which God is the thought: "God is the Spirit restored to its fundamental and primary place, despite the 'emergentist' appearances that mislead superficial cosmogonies. The Spirit becomes a material keyboard, before playing its melodies on itself become a keyboard. God is Thought for which the constituted world is the brain."[15] Here, as with Auguste Comte, science plays the

---

13 *Philosophie première. Cours de philosophie positive* (Lectures 1 to 45), presentation and notes by Michel Serres, François Dagognet, Allai Sinaceur (Paris: Hermann, 1975), 26.
14 Ibid., 24: "Theology and physics are so profoundly incompatible, their conceptions possess a character so radically opposed..."
15 *The Gnosis of Princeton*, 173. And let us not forget that what is ontologically

role of a decisive conversion factor, but in the opposite direction. To the three successive states of Comtism correspond the three chief instances of Ruyerian thought: science, philosophy, religion, three instances which basically cover the same reality. Frankly, this identity appears in its fully practical efficacy only with *The Gnosis of Princeton*. Before the publication of this book, Ruyer above all affirmed, and in the strongest way, the non-separation of science and philosophy: "This involves," he states in the only important text where he formally presents his own thought, "a collaboration with the progress of knowledge by working towards an undivided Philosophy-Science, capable of criticizing itself and generalizing itself—with or without a 'specialist in generalities'—to the extent that reality is disclosed in its inexhaustible subtlety."[16] Surely, in works prior to *The Gnosis of Princeton*, the theologian is often brought in. And God is present in all his books since at least *La Conscience et le Corps* and the *Eléments of psychobiologie*. Several of the later books (*Genèse des formes vivantes*; *Néo-finalisme*; *Dieu des religions, Dieu de la Science*) actually represent various excerpts from a huge work on God the very size of which made it difficult to publish and of which Ruyer has published only the more important parts; the last one published in 1970, *God of Religions, God of Science*, had even remained for nearly twenty years in manuscript state.

Now, it is interesting to make a comparison, as brief as it may be, between this last work and *The Gnosis of Princeton*, which appeared four years later. The very title *God of Religions, God of Science* heralds, if not an opposition, at least a distinction between the two realms. The book's viewpoint is that of a *speculative* approach. Ruyer describes what for him constitutes the true theology of the various religions, which are basically the mythical modes of expression for an awareness of *Natura naturans*, and hence of the encompassing supernatural totality, the ultimate meaning of all the thematic activities that inform and constitute the *Natura naturata*. He thus shows how religion and science come together, but provided both are reinterpreted

---

primary is Thought and not the brain: "the Spirit becomes a material keyboard."
16 "Ruyer" in *Les philosophes français d'aujourd'hui*, ed. D. Huisman & G. Deledalle (Paris: SEDES, 1959), 275.

in the perspective of Ruyerian philosophy, that is to say, that religion be rid of its dogmatisms, its superstitions, like belief in a Savior (whether Buddha or Jesus), and that the science be rid of the philosophical absurdities of mechanistic materialism and its dogmatic atheism.

We find thus stated in this work the — necessary — overturning of Comte's principle of the three-states law, states that moreover, with Ruyer, are posited as three permanent instances that he names: science, philosophy, and religion. Religion is in fact, Ruyer asserts, "at all levels philosophical in essence, in the sense that this involves the relationship of man with the total universe." Once this philosophical essence is clearly identified, the truth of its relationship with the scientific vision becomes apparent: "However it may differ from the scientific vision, the religious vision of the world remains deeply akin to it in that it is 'theoretical' in intention. In a certain sense one can say of religion what used to be said about philosophy: it is a totally unified knowledge."[17] True, in some respects Ruyer's approach does not aim to restore such a conception of philosophy. It does not, however, claim to confuse the instances, but to clarify how it is possible to cross from one to the other, because all three overlap one same and unique reality. Recalling the convergence of Jung and Mircea Eliade in the shared use of the word "archetype," Ruyer concludes: "Here again we are moving from the natural — spatial and transpatial — to the religious world through totalization. The world of religion is total in all dimensions, both physical and metaphysical. It is enough that the archetypes of human behavior are themselves grasped against the backdrop of a total Archetype, for one to be in the religious sphere and for metaphysics to become theology."[18]

What more or what else is there then in *The Gnosis of Princeton*? As for the content of Ruyer's theses, there is little. The substance of the doctrine is identical, and many analyses are similar. However, two points can be underscored. On the one hand, more than in any of his books, Ruyer deals with the

---

17 *Dieu des religions*..., 61 and 63.
18 Ibid., 67.

problems of contemporary physics, and so directly addresses questions he had only occasionally treated previously. On the other, he proposes, in *The Gnosis of Princeton*, no longer to describe religion, in general, from data provided by the history of religions, the study of comparative religions, the psychology and psychoanalysis of the *homo religiosus*, were it just to develop his own idea of religion's essence, but clearly to propose a kind of new religion, actually practiced, whose dogmas, or rather basic articles of faith, will be provided by data from contemporary physics. Ruyer has crossed over here from the stage of spectator, or philosophical observer, to that of actor. The difference, in some ways, is considerable.

FROM THE GOD OF LIFE TO THE GOD OF THE COSMOS

Why did he have to tackle the study of physics to somehow dare to "take the plunge"? There is no doubt about the answer, and it is twofold.

First, physical science deals with a deeper, more cosmologically decisive layer of natural reality: of course, biological and especially embryological phenomena thrust upon us the idea of an informative and finalized activity according to specific and quasi-archetypal themes. However, these themes themselves seem to work on and organize an inert matter more primitive and more determining than the biological, which matter besides, in its atomic constituents and subatomic components, necessarily refers to a general cosmology, to a totalizing conception of space-time. Biology, and still more psychology, which is inseparable from it, provide explanatory models for thinking about reality in the act of becoming real, the most enlightening model of which remains that of consciousness, or of the field of consciousness. But it is physics that poses the most radical questions regarding the world envisioned in its own subsistence and its nature as universe, that is, in its reality as an all-encompassing totalization. Jacques Merleau-Ponty—much read by Ruyer—and a few others have shown not only the emergence, along with Einstein and contemporary physics, of a new cosmology, but above all the rebirth of cosmology as such, which had disappeared with the establishment of

Galilean physics: for a mechanistic physics, in fact, the world is merely an indefinite spatio-temporal container, without form, without property, and without physical relationship with any of the phenomena that occur there.

Second, the physicists themselves, much more than biologists, behave like metaphysicians and do not hesitate, whenever basic physics is involved, to engage in vigorous philosophical assertions. How many times have we not heard Ruyer protest against the strict mechanicism of a Monod claiming to reduce all living phenomena to the functioning of molecular structures, and to lament that he did not transform himself into a physicist: "why does he remain at the molecular level," he wondered, "and why does he not go down to the atomic and subatomic level? He would then see that these molecular structures by no means constitute stable material systems, like the parts of a clockwork mechanism, but that the unity of their specific subsistence is energetic and ultimately semantic in nature."[19] Thus many American, English, German, or even French physicists were trying to develop a vision of the cosmos that was not materialist, who deliberately broke with local ("inch by inch") mechanistic determinism, and who, with Heisenberg or Schrödinger for example, could even go as far as a certain subjectivist idealism. Their approaches somehow empowered Ruyer to lead his own theses to their conclusions, at the same time that they gave him an opportunity to rectify the physicists' philosophical "naiveties" that still kept them prisoners of their anti-materialism.

Finally, in third place, even though Ruyer rejected the subjectivist idealism of a Schrödinger, in the name of what he himself one day in our presence called "an objective idealism,"[20] he did

---

19 "The atom needs neither material nor subordinate technics. It has no organic needs. Its 'soul'—its undulatory laws—has not fallen into a body, for the reason that its 'body' is in ceaseless formation by its 'soul.' The atom has no concern for nutrition or reproduction. It does not die, and it does not kill. It leaves no corpse. Atoms of mud are neither muddy nor dirty. Rather, they are a kind of pure music" (*Dieu des religions, Dieu de la science*, 104).

20 The expression was claimed by Schelling to define his own position relative to Fichte's subjective idealism and Hegel's absolute idealism (*Darstellung meines Systems der Philosophie* [Jena & Leipzig: Gabler, 1801], Werke, IV, 109).

retain from this interpretation the scientific fact that had given birth to it and that was the basis of the new cosmology: the impossibility of separating the spectator from the spectacle, the subject from the object, the observation of the physically real from the reality observed. The observation itself must be regarded as a possibility actually included in the cosmos, it is an event *of* the cosmos itself included in its overall possibility, not the effect of an observer from an extracosmic position. In short, *observation* is actually *participation*.

Here we touch on a basic point. It is through the conversion of observation (illusory reverse side) into participation (real right side) that scientific knowledge begins to be transformed into gnosis and reveal its fundamentally religious nature.

Explaining the expression "basic cosmology" by which Ruyer's gnosis defines his endeavor, Ruyer states: "It is not about establishing a kind of minimal cosmology (or religious philosophy). This is even less a 'religious science' or a 'scientific religion.' What the gnostics mean is this: a cosmology, being totalizing for space and time, should totalize the observers as well as the observed, the points of view as well as the points viewed, the 'Ego' as well as the 'here-and-now.'"[21]

Cosmic participation, or the cosmos as participable by and for human consciousness, leads then to gnostic wisdom, hence to the definitive fulfillment of gnosis, under the form of what Ruyer calls "psychosynthesis" as opposed to psychoanalysis.

SEMANTIC PARTICIPATION, THE KEY TO RUYERIAN GNOSIS

Ruyer, who had already developed the notion of knowledge and information by participating in an important article entitled "Les observables et les participables," returned to this doctrine in *The Gnosis of Princeton*.[22] It seems the key to this cosmologist's gnosis that forms the basis of his thought. To know is not just to posit an object in front of oneself, even though this is the only mode of knowledge recognized by

---

21 *La Gnose de Princeton*, 24.
22 *Revue philosophique*, tome CLVI, 1966, 419–50. The comparison of this article with pages 127 to 130 of *La Gnose de Princeton* shows that Ruyer has reused important passages from this article (with minor changes).

science. More really, more fundamentally, it is to be informed, that is, to receive within oneself a form, a meaning, that creates meaning within us and therefore a meaning in which we participate. If knowledge were merely external observation, it would be aware of nothing, of a sheer succession of incoherent, event-based punctualities. To grasp a meaning, a form, is necessarily to *be* grasped, to be mentally and semantically adapted and informed by what is grasped. In this way we can move from cognitive participation to psychobiological participation and even to cosmological participation, since there is no essential difference among them. To participate is, then, not only to know through information, it is also to exist. Every real individual being, that is, one that self-surveys and is self-possessed (an atom, a molecule, a bacterium, a tree, &c.), and which is not a cluster, without state unity (a mound of earth, a cloud) — every real being only exists by participating in the specific themes that define its temporal identity, the norms of its activity, the nature of its formative instincts, just as the speaking subject only discovers a word on condition of participating in the language that speaks within him. On the basis of this participation and its various modes, a being somehow explores and discovers the demands of its own nature, experiences culture, the world, and even the world beyond, and the Will of the supreme Norm, of universal Consciousness. Here gnostic participation truly gains access to its religious dimension. "In all religions," writes Ruyer, "God is a Participable rather than an Observable. This is therefore an Unknowable in the ordinary sense; all traditional religious experiences are, in a sense, psychological experiences, transposed mythically.... But one can also — *this is the entirety of the New Gnosis* — deem that the psychological, biological, and linguistic experience of participation is a kind of natural *revelation* with religious value."[23] And Ruyer concludes with this quite significant statement: "Gnosis consists in wanting to have both participables and participation enter into science, just as into religious philosophy, through the front door, not by the back door of a suspect, barely scientific, and vaguely

---

23 *La Gnose de Princeton*, 129.

occultist psychology, but through the front door of microphysics, developmental biology, comprehensive psychology, and non-Pavlovian linguistics, that of B. L. Whorf or N. Chomsky. It consists in showing that science reveals participation, but only by seeing it through its reverse side."[24]

We now have a better glimpse into the breadth of Ruyer's endeavor: it is extremely ambitious, and, in a certain way, one can even judge it exorbitant. Ruyer not only intends to embrace in a single unitary vision all areas of human thought: physics, biology, psychology, philosophy, religion, wisdom — and one might well think that he has actually succeeded — but he is also proposing neither more nor less than the opening up of a new religious perspective, a new path to the divine, a new gnosis, which is scientifically "credible," and therefore philosophically possible. This quite extraordinary dimension of Ruyer's endeavor has often been misunderstood for several reasons: those who believed in the existence of the Princetonian gnostics attributed the establishment of this "new religion" to American scholars (for whom Ruyer was only the secretary); those aware of the fable saw in it an amusing subterfuge to gain the reader's attention on themes repeatedly set forth by him. All this is, moreover, incontestable in some respects. The fable relies on a background of truth to which, by an inducing effect, it has precisely ended up giving shape: great physicists subscribe to many of Ruyer's theses and are clearly recognized therein. On the other hand, this fable stirred a world-wide interest in the thought of the philosopher: the intended goal was achieved. But, if we take this thought truly seriously, we have to go further. This fable was not only possible and desirable, it was also necessary, and necessary both negatively and positively.

Negatively, in order to forestall and rectify the very temptation frequent among many scholars to refer to Eastern religions and mystical currents more or less well understood or overestimated, by offering them a much more rational and scientifically plausible religion. Ruyer is basically saying to scholars: no need to go looking for a religion in the East, you

---

24 Ibid., 130.

just have to look at the science right under your nose. So there is now a positive need to awaken the reader to an awareness of the true nature of participation. What is gnosis, in fact, if not an awareness of participation? And what is participation, in the final analysis, if not a participation in God? Such are the points that we would like to recall in concluding.

ELEUSINIAN INITIATION

As for Ruyer's intention to develop a "basic religion," that is, to make the reader aware of the intrinsically religious nature of our basic vision of reality when restored to its proper place, he himself explains it quite clearly: this does not involve fabricating from whole cloth a new religion, but creating the conditions for the emergence, among our contemporaries, of a gnostic consciousness.[25]

That the new religion is based on a "credible," rationally "acceptable" theology, he expressly asserts on several occasions.[26] At any rate, participation or, basically, participation in the divine, is the major principle with all his metaphysics. Just as the universe—insofar as it is perpetually being made and realizing the transpatial and transtemporal themes that particularize its nature—is God visible, what we can see of God, so intelligence—insofar as it seeks to grasp a meaning, that is, participate semantically in divine information—ultimately thinks "from God," as Ruyer himself said to me one day, that is to say, is thought by God, the Sense of the senses[27] in its very act. So what should the Ruyerian gnostic do? Or rather, what can he not do? Here we touch on the most fundamental point of the need for Ruyer's mythification, because it is out of this need that the contents of Ruyerian gnosis intends to justify, by founding it, the mythic form with which it has been expressed. And indeed, since the Ruyerian gnostic is not an observing theoretician, but a participating theoretician, the intellectual task incumbent upon him cannot be to propose dogmatic theorems to be believed, but rather semantic themes

---

25 Ibid., 19.
26 Ibid., 70, 73, 130, &c.
27 Cf. *Neofinalism*, 135 and 240.

to research and fathom. Since God is, in some respects, the universal "mother tongue," composing the nature and the order of things, all the gnostic can do is try to learn how to speak this language. God does not say anything, but He speaks in every intelligence that tries to spell out the universe. "God," Ruyer declares, "is not a Boss, or a suspect Speaker, but a mother tongue or primordial language behind all languages, and... he is not a mythical being, precisely because he *founds all the mythoi*. God is the Universal participant... a Tongue that is spoken, not by imitation, but by participatory invention."[28]

Since God founds all the *mythoi*, he also founds Ruyer's *mythos* of Princetonian gnosis. What is in fact the mythical Princeton gnosis if not an attempt at exploration with a view to semantic participation? The question of the truth or falsity of the fable imagined by Ruyer no longer has to be posed as that of the truth of a specific predatory or sensory organ invented by nature, or a specific religious myth invented by culture. The Princeton gnosis is not a biological but a philosophical agent intended to enable an exploration and capture of the universal divine semantics, which is, in a certain way, true of all metaphysical works, but which is explicitly asserted here. For the gnosis of participation cannot be taught in the anti-gnostic manner of an objective description and according to the logic of what is observable. The teaching of gnosis can only be taught in a gnostic way, that is, by participation, and by participation in the very game of gnosis; which means that this is basically an initiation. And not only is *The Gnosis of Princeton* as a whole a game, a game of a mythical scientific gnosis, a game that Ruyer suggests his reader play by having the reader think and muse about the existence of this mysterious group, but the book is itself also a game by which Ruyer attempts to initiate himself into gnosis, the mythological device that enables him to usher his metaphysics and his theology to their conclusion, which in fact implies that he goes as far as established religions, but according to a philosophically acceptable mode.

The gnostic Church is therefore as real as it is invisible. In this Church, Ruyer tells us, "each one initiates himself, at his

---

28 *La Gnose de Princeton*, 139. Our emphasis.

own moment, reinvents the Rule, as in the card game invented by one of them (the game 'Eleusis'), where you have to guess the rule, not apply it shrewdly."[29] And he concludes: "The New Gnosis is like Eleusis: each one initiates himself. Each is in turn, or at the same time, player and master of the game, a kind of free and mutual co-optation — and yet strict because the rule is subtle. These gnostics further believe that their initiation system represents the very system of real existence, where each being must discover by himself, taking the initiative, what is expected of him by the unknown Gamemaster."[30]

One could not be clearer. And that is why the subtitle does not only include the terms "scholars" and "religion," which we have attempted to comment on; it also includes the term "search," whose meaning is discovered now more clearly: the gnostic religion is, in fact, neither foundable, nor institutable. It can only be sought.

The myth of this Princeton gnosis, at the end of our reflection, therefore appears for what it is, that is to say as one of those "montages" thanks to which the wisdom of the neo-gnostics seeks to understand what it can of the divine *Sophia*. At least one will be convinced if one strives to interpret this myth in its own light, to read Ruyer as ruyerily as possible. This is what we have tried to do. Just one question is to be posed then: since the function of a myth does not lie in its truth but in its efficacy and semantic fruitfulness, we are entitled to wonder if the gnosis of Princeton is an efficacious montage?

RUYERIAN GNOSIS: A "COSMOLOGISM"?

The Ruyerian or, if you will, 'Princetonian' gnosis constitutes, in the eyes of its author, the only remedy for "the religious crisis of our time," which "is first and foremost a crisis of all the myths that contradict scientific knowledge." The existing religions are in fact only "disqualified and unbelievable myths." Scientific Gnosis alone has any future for itself, because it is the only "accommodating" myth.[31] That the God of science

---

29 Ibid., 12.
30 Ibid., 13.
31 Preface to the new 1977 edition of *La Gnose de Princeton*, 15.

is such as Ruyer "tells" it, can be admitted in many respects: this God is cosmologically plausible and consistent. But is it also so with respect to theology and metaphysics? There are two points to be taken into account here.

First of all, one cannot help but stress the extremely casual way in which Ruyer rids himself of the old religious doctrines by viewing them as "disqualified and unbelievable myths." That there are religions of mythological nature is obvious for Greek religion, Hinduism, and some aspects of Buddhism or Shintoism. But others present themselves expressly as historical revelations. This is the case, in particular, with Judaism and Christianity. The most indisputable positive data prohibit us from seeing only myths there, even if every mythical element, that is to say involving the symbolism of the cosmos, is not absent from it—which is, moreover, perfectly legitimate. What should we make of this data? What, in fact, does the ruyerian gnostic make of it? The truth is he makes nothing of it, he ignores it. To our knowledge, and even where he could have spoken about it in *God of Religions, God of Science*, Ruyer never deals with a historical (or non-historical) religion in itself. He may go on at length about the Tao or the Logos, but about Moses or Buddha, never. He does not say anything about Jesus Christ, what he did and taught, about the apostles or the preaching of the kerygma, about Christian Tradition and the Church, nothing of this immense story that nevertheless poses a certain number of questions to the philosopher: from where does it come? how was this possible? is this madness? superstition? a lie? and how could Christ utter words that no one had said before him, and which, two thousand years later, still have a ring of eternal novelty?—to all this factual data Ruyer pays no heed. To put it bluntly, his "God of science" seems as convincing as his "God of religions" seems approximate, in particular for want of having devoted to the study of religions and their history the scrupulous attention he has devoted to the study of physical and biological facts. One day he himself told me that, of the entire Bible, he did not believe one word (but he admired the literary work): this is easier to say than to uphold rationally.

As for seeing in Jesus Christ, according to his own admission, only a kind of "hippie," beyond any provocation, this betokens, for a philosopher, a curious lack of spiritual insight. For all these reasons, the future of scientific gnosis as replacement myth seems, in reality, much more uncertain than that of the established religions.

But we must now come to the second point, to the (necessarily succinct) examination of this gnosis in relation to its theological and metaphysical validity, in other words to its ability to assume speculative responsibility for the most fundamental aspects of human experience and give them meaning. It seems that, in some respects, we are rather off the mark. Ruyer certainly has a sense of cosmic religion, but he rejects the sacred insofar as it would be the fruit of the initiative of a personal God communicating with a human person: he neither believes in a God supernaturally revealing himself, nor in the reality of personal beings. His God is transcendent to the world only insofar as he remains unknown to us, that is, insofar as his immanence to the universe exceeds this universe. Can anyone even still speak of immanence? Does not this imply that someone may distinguish between the reality of the world and that of God? Now, for Ruyer, the world is God; this involves, however, a semi-pantheism, to the extent that the world is only "God visible,"[32] the only one we will ever know, since there is no immortality of the soul.

In order to highlight the limits of this gnosis and the one-sidedness of his reading of reality, we cannot avoid asking ourselves about what constitutes the basis of his doctrine, about his central intuition. We mentioned it in passing; it must now be considered for itself. This intuition is the following: the fabric of reality is in the nature of a field of consciousness; from this view, which we believe to be correct (as for psycho-corporeal reality), everything else follows.

---

32 On this point, and a few others, Ruyer was inspired by the concept of the "Primordial God" and "consequent God" of the mathematician and philosopher A. N. Whitehead, as well as the writer Samuel Butler, for whom he professed great admiration: cf. *God the Known and God the Unknown* (London: A. C. Fifield, 1909).

The field of consciousness thesis answers an objective problem: it is impossible to account for the real unity of a physical (a molecule, for example) or biological being (a protozoan, a cat) in a purely mechanistic way; the only solution is to represent this state of unity as being in the nature of a field of consciousness, such as the experience provided by visual perception (or any other perception). This solution, however, runs up against the deeply rooted conviction that any field of consciousness requires a conscious subject who "gazes" at this field, and the presence of which in things is quite hard to admit. However, according to Ruyer, this is a tenacious prejudice without any real foundation: it simply comes from erroneously imagining that the "gaze" of consciousness is similar to the way in which our bodily eye sees things. Take as an example of a field of consciousness the vision I have of my desk: in order to be "seen" (known) this vision has no need as yet of an intellectual gaze that would traverse its "vision-expanse," it *knows* itself immediately. It constitutes what Ruyer calls a "domain of absolute survey," that is, one that is not relative to what it "surveys," which is not transcendent to it like the bodily eye is vertically above what it regards: there is no eye of consciousness. Thus, rid of its illusory subject-observer, the field of consciousness can serve as model for conceptualizing the real unities of the universe as actual "subjectivities," but without a subject.

Does this reading vigorously touch reality in one of its fundamental aspects? We think so. Does it follow that it is applicable as such to the case of human beings and their acts of consciousness, and that we can consider any field of consciousness, in man, as a subjectivity without a subject?[33] Is the subject, the person, only the image, transposed into consciousness, of "our body reduced to the state of a metaphysical point"?[34] Does Ruyer, who rejects the immortality of the soul, also reject the reality of the "I" of the being-person? This question is not easy to answer. His work includes texts that go in the direction of a certain transcendence of the "I," and even of consciousness. "We

---

33 This is Michel Piclin's expression in his article "Conscience et Corps," in *Raymond Ruyer. De la science à la théologie* (Paris: Kimé, 1985), 162.
34 *La Conscience et le Corps* (1937) (Paris: P. U. F., 1950), 6.

should vehemently deny... a point of observation external to the sensory field. But we should affirm no less vehemently the existence of a sort of a 'metaphysical' transversal to the entire field, and whose two extremities are the 'I'... on the one hand, and the guiding Idea of organization, on the other."[35] As for consciousness, he seems to admit that it is not absolutely identical to the field of consciousness (this much is certain, as we will see): "Consciousness is truly consciousness only insofar as it contains more than its instantaneous perceptible content."[36] Likewise, in *Animal, Man and the Symbolic Function*, he defines consciousness as a "psychic distance": "Man begins with the fact of consciousness, that is, with the fact 'that man is capable of standing at a distance from himself; that he knows himself and grasps his own point of selfhood from outside himself, moves away from himself, that he knows himself from a point external to himself.'"[37] Our purpose is not to seek to reconcile these three texts with those cited previously. There may be a hesitation in the thought of Ruyer. We believe, however, that his doctrine inclines rather in the direction of the field of consciousness without looking back, as it goes more in the direction of a God-Order than in that of a God-Person (which he admits, all the while rejecting the "personified God" of the "Yaweh or Jupiter" type).[38] It is moreover uncertain whether we should see in the mention of the "transversal metaphysics" anything other than the intelligence culminating in "Platonic" realities, and not a designation of the "I" as person-being.

This is why, at the risk of misinterpretation, our critical examination will keep to the often repeated descriptions of the field of consciousness as a domain of absolute survey, and therefore to the subject considered as a perceptual illusion.

According to Ruyer, therefore, we imagine the gaze of consciousness as modeled on the gaze of our bodily eye (unduly transposed into the psychic realm) which is always at a distance

---

35 *Neo-finalism*, 99.
36 Ibid., 138.
37 Paris: Gallimard, 1964, 122–23; the quote, in Ruyer's text, is from Van der Leeuw, *Religion in Essence and Manifestation*, vol. 1, trans. J. E. Turner (New York & Evanston: Harper & Row, 1963), 346.
38 *Dieu des religions, Dieu de la science*, 149.

from what it sees; this is a faulty image to the extent that the field of consciousness is in reality and by definition immediate knowledge of itself and therefore does not need to be viewed "from a distance" in order to be known—that much is indisputable. But that the idea of a conscious subject, that is, of a being-person, is also only the imaginary product of an undue transposition seems altogether impossible. Consciousness, in fact, is not only a "field of consciousness," an "absolute surface" without depth, it is also indisputably a self-awareness as consciousness, and not exclusively consciousness "of a field." Being self-aware as a purely consciousness-related capacity, which is called reflective (or reflexive) consciousness—and this is a mark of the mind being self-knowing—self-awareness is, thereby, consciousness of non-self, object consciousness, awareness of something that is "in front of *me*," and not only in front of (my) body. Certainly, the self-of-consciousness is not known by the mind with the same knowledge by which it knows the "vision-expanse." This self is rather "pre-known" by intuitive and spontaneous induction, and this is precisely because we cannot grasp it (that which grasps everything) as a piece of information (since it is uniquely through it and for it that there is rightly any information), and this is precisely why we are aware of it as a kind of "behind me" transcendence. One might say that Ruyer seems to somehow conceive of the subject only as an object: object-consciousness before an object-thing, which logically leads him to reject its existence and to underscore its contradictory nature. However, this is not how the self, the person-being, is inferred, but as something without which there would be no object, and therefore as something thanks to which there is objectivity and distance.

We have come to the crux of the matter. Ruyer's hypothesis of an undue transposition, at the psychic level, of the perceptual situation of the bodily eye relative to the object seen, in reality presupposes what it claims to account for. Because, in truth, by no means do we have the primary experience of a thing before an eye, *since the eye cannot see itself.*[39] A thing is

---

[39] Ruyer is obviously affirming that "in seeing objects we (almost) see our eyes" (*Paradoxes de la conscience et limites de l'automatisme*, 67–68). This is to overstate

not before (my) eye, it is before me, otherwise there would be neither the thing (or *my* eye) any longer, but only states of sensation. The eye does not know itself seeing, that is, in the very act of its seeing, while consciousness knows itself as consciousness in the very act of its knowledge of something, and therefore cannot but be distinguished from it. Not that it would then posit itself as a knowing object facing a known object, but as that by which there is a known object. Ruyer's explanation must therefore be reversed: it is the relative transcendence of consciousness with respect to fields of consciousness that accounts for the perceptual situation of visual experience, and such is its essence. Consciousness is structurally objectifying, and this means, under another form, that all distance is primarily spiritual—even more, that true distance, real distance, is only spiritual in nature.

It seems that here certain discoveries of recent physics could, on the contrary, support the thesis that we support. We would like to speak about what has been called the *inseparability principle*, highlighted, in particular, by the physicists Bell (C. E. R. N.) and Shimony (Boston University), and demonstrated experimentally by Alain Aspect in 1983. This principle states that if "we want to conceive of reality as having spatially localizable parts, then, if some of these parts have interacted in some specified ways in the past, they will somehow continue to 'interact,' regardless of how far apart they may be [and this by means of an instantaneous influence]."[40] This principle is entirely in line with the Ruyerian cosmology. But, insofar as it shows that the notion of distance is not able to

---

the argument: to see the edge of your eyelashes is not to see your eye (and besides there are eyes without eyelashes).

40 Bernard d'Espagnat, *In Search of Reality*, trans. A. Ehlers (New York: Springer-Verlag, 1983), 25. [Bracketed segment of quote absent from the English translation—trans.] According to an image taken from Olivier Costa de Beauregard, "two dice roll out of the same cup (two photons are emitted by the same source), and if one stops with the six showing (if one of the photons turns at a certain angle), *the other one also stops with the six showing* (the other photon simultaneously rotates at the same angle)." How can the second photon simultaneously "know" what the first one is doing and do it at the same time? (Charles Hirsch, "Des jumeaux très particuliers," *La science et ses doubles*, Joël André, ed. [Paris: Autrement, 1986], 130).

be established physically, since we cannot physically separate two "points" from each other, everything is occurring as if they were always united spatially and temporally. In such a case only the distinction between spiritual entities remains to account for the indisputable notion of distance: "a distance," writes Bernard d'Espagnat, "does not intrinsically *exist* between certain elements of independent reality. We ourselves situate it, so to speak, between the elements of *empirical reality*, or, otherwise stated, in the *picture* of reality that we devise for communication and other uses."[41] But, if it is we ourselves who situate it, then this "distance" is in us first, not spatially of course, but spiritually. The only punctualities truly distinct and separate from each other are spiritual punctualities, those actualized by human beings, separable and separate because each one is defined by its incommunicable interiority, but also, for that very reason, each can be united with others.

There is therefore no undue transposition, there is, on the contrary, the legitimate translation of conscious distancing into spatial distance, inasmuch as our senses are essentially bodily modes of consciousness and structured by it. It is the bodily world that is an image, a translation, of the psychic and spiritual worlds, not the reverse. According to the most rigorous laws of symbolic realism, it is conscious distancing that becomes physical distance, it is spiritual transcendence that becomes geometric verticality, just as, conversely, Christ can achieve his actual exit from the visible world only by ascending along the vertical "until a cloud hides him from view" (Acts 1:9).

Consideration of vertical symbolism is here of great interest. We could sum up our whole meditation in the following way: geometrically speaking, in order for there to be distance, at least two points are needed: if there are in fact two, this is because they are distinct, and, between two purely spatial entities, there is no other distinction than that of their distance. But, to determine two points on a straight line, we must lower the perpendicular at each of these points, otherwise no point is determinable. It is not by remaining on the straight line or

---

41 Ibid., 49–50. Author's emphasis.

plane that contains it that we can find the end-point we are seeking, for this line, being indefinitely divisible, its course will never meet the punctual term. A point is only the meeting of the vertical with the horizontal line. This point, the foot of the perpendicular, this is the image of the vertical view from the horizontal: what the horizontal "sees" of the vertical. And so it is with the unicity of the person-being. Consciousness is not the person-being, it is only its illumination. What it illuminates, what it knows on the plane of its mental life, is the trace of a transcendence, the foot of the vertical that establishes it and links it to the Unique. The spiritual punctuality of the person is determined by the creative gaze that the Unique lowers down upon it and of which ordinary consciousness knows only the ontological trace, but which it intuitively infers to be extended up to the One. And this is — our person — that relationship of love and adoration that ascends along the creative ray: the creative ray, which is God's gaze of love on his creature, is converted into a person-being and the person-being, through its spiritual ascent, with each stage of its ascent, actualizes this person-being by converting it into love.

Strictly speaking, we must therefore restore to consciousness the inalienable transcendence of God's gaze, that is, once one agrees to view the person in his or her truly metaphysical nature. Surely we can never comprehend it as such, since it is that which comprehends everything; we can only actualize it, with the grace of God. And this is "becoming yourself": insofar as "substance," the person is "act." This person-being clearly must be presupposed, however, by intuitive inference and according to the very nature of the intelligence that is the innate sense of being, for our eyes do not see being and no data imparts it to us: we discover that we know it on the occasion of every encounter with an object and every taking of self-consciousness. It is basically transcendent to all knowledge: a deep below of things from which they come towards us, a deep in back of our consciousness out of which we go towards things.

Only thus can we accede to the other reading of reality we indicated at the outset of our meditation; this reality which is not only composed, as it seems in the Ruyerian universe, of "fields of consciousness," or "natures," or "domain regions," or "self-creating forms," but which is also made of absences, voids, otherness, and therefore of falls, abandonments, derelictions, of tensions and dramas, to the very extent that being, the touchstone of our desire, of our will, of our intelligence, is everywhere immanent and everywhere transcendent, everywhere present and everywhere absent, always in the depths. So it is ultimately the taking into account of the mystery of being that alone can explain this other and undeniable aspect of reality, because, under the effect of its weight, reality widens at the same time as it rises under the effect of its attraction, bringing man and things into a true metaphysical gravitation. This mystery of being is not the product of a speculative construction, although it requires a difficult philosophical effort to be, as much as possible, discerned and formulated with some rigor: it is indeed everywhere, at the end of all our thoughts just as at their origin. One can neither invent or be rid of it.

Now Ruyer's gnosis[42] seems blind to the feeling of reality's "ontological depths," in which it sees only an "effect of axiological relief," that is, the effect produced in us by the vision of opposing values. This is a strange insensitivity to the play of being, to the yonder side of everything that is given and slips away, and by which all reality comes to us at the same time that it both lingers and flees towards its source. We are speaking here not only of a particular being, but of being as such, of the being of each being, which, as the principle of each individual reality, is necessarily supra-organic, that is to say truly metaphysical. It indeed seems that Ruyer never took into consideration this being, and that he ever conceived of beings only as natures. Even less was he inclined to consider First Being as a "pure act of being," according to the formula of St. Thomas Aquinas (*actus purus essendi*). He had, moreover, only mockery and disdain for what Gilson has called the "metaphysics of the Exodus," and saw in the revelation of the Burning

---

42 After *La Gnose de Princeton* (1974), Ruyer explicitly mentions the group of "Princetonian gnostics" in two other works: *Les cent prochains siècle—Le destin historique de l'homme selon la Nouvelle Gnose américaine* (1977), and *L'Art d'être toujours content—Introduction à la vie gnostique* (1978). These two books were published by Arthème Fayard.

Bush, "I am He who is" (*Sum qui sum*), only a language game and the mental intoxication of a somewhat overly enthusiastic scribe. However, and just as previously for the vertical, it is not through the sublimism of transcendence that we "posit" Being outside of all nature, but it is Being itself, inferred in the radicality of its infinite Act (because not limited by any nature) that necessarily founds all transcendence relative to all nature, founds already the participatory transcendence of the person in relation to his individual form of natural existence in the world. Otherwise, the very idea of transcendence would be only a forever inexplicable illusion.

Finally, we should be mindful that what we have called "the other side of reality" is not just composed of absence, remoteness, distancing, contingency, otherness (which existentialism—Ruyer loathed it—emphasized excessively), it is also composed, *and by that very fact*, of presence, of bringing together, hope, "coming towards," and love. Now, there is no possibility of presence except through the person, there is no "here" and no "now," no "present," except through the occurrence of a person's transcendent act. Ruyer speaks of the world of the "here and now" as that of a purely physical reality. But if the here and now had only a physical or spatio-temporal determination, there would be no basis for their unicity; as we have seen, they would be indeterminable and therefore could not exist. Just as there is no means to determine a point on a line except by the vertical that crosses at this point, likewise every local presence and every temporal present exist only through the supervening act, in space and time, from the transcendent person in space and time. It is not the world that situates us first, it is we who situate the world.

Ruyer's gnosis is basically cosmological. Granted, his vision of the world is one of remarkable breadth and astonishing precision. However, in view of some of its aspects, of some of its denials, we might wonder if we are dealing with a "cosmologism." In any case, it seems that by rejecting the immortality of the personal soul and foreswearing any possibility of a sacred revelation, Ruyer offers us a gnosis without hope and a God without love.

CHAPTER 6

Gnosis and Gnosticism in René Guénon

ONE MIGHT SURMISE THAT THE QUESTION of gnosis *and* gnosticism occupies, in René Guénon, only a very secondary place. And, if we keep to the texts, this is altogether accurate, since he has devoted only a few articles to this question.[1] However, once it is noticed that gnosis designates nothing but metaphysical knowledge or sacred science, we have to admit that Guénon deals, so to say, only with this, and that it represents the essential axis of all his work. This is why one could say that Guénon's main effort is to strive to restore the term gnosis to its authentic meaning of sacred knowledge, and that, in this sense, despite sometimes questionable formulations, he was able to communicate the idea. For want of the "ideal type" of orthodox gnosis procured by his work (with a

---

1 The essential references for these two terms are the following (we give the titles in alphabetical order, chronological order having no significance for posthumous collections, and according to the pagination of the edition indicated): *Insights into Christian Esotericism*, trans. H. D. Fohr (Hillsdale, NY: Sophia Perennis, 2001), 35, 41, 43; *Comptes Rendus* (Paris: Ed. Traditionnelle, 1973), 119–21; *The Multiples States of the Being*, trans. H. D. Fohr (Ghent, NY: Sophia Perennis, 2001), 25, fn 10; *Studies in Freemasonry and the Compagnonnage*, trans. H. D. Fohr, C. Bethell, & M. Allen (Hillsdale, NY: Sophia Perennis, 2004), 47–50, 192, 198 [Trans.—Some of the book reviews were not translated for the single volume English edition]; *Études sur la Franc-Maçonnerie et le Compagnonnage* (Paris: Ed. Traditionnelles, 1964) tome I, 181, 243, 249; tome II, 170; *Traditional Forms and Cosmic Cycles*, trans. H. D. Fohr (Hillsdale, NY: Sophia Perennis, 2001), 44, fn 9, 55; *Man and His Becoming according to the Vedanta*, trans. R. C. Nicholson (Ghent, NY: Sophia Perennis, 2001), 142, fn 8; *Miscellanea* (Hillsdale, NY: Sophia Perennis, 2003), 12, 146–48; *Symbols of Sacred Science*, trans. H. D. Fohr (Hillsdale, NY: Sophia Perennis, 2001), 106, fn 7. These indications are not exhaustive, but somewhat more complete than those given by André Désilets, *René Guénon: Index, bibliographie* (Quebec: Les Presses de l'Université Laval, 1977). As such, this work will be of great service to any reader of the Guénonian corpus. [Trans.—The entire corpus may be searched online: http://www.index-rene-guenon.org/]

few corrections), it is doubtful we could truly have gotten our bearings in the welter of gnostic currents.

As already pointed out,[2] the term gnosis was discredited from the outset by the deviant use made of it by certain philosophical-religious schools of the second century AD which, for this reason, have been classified under the general designation of gnosticism. With regard to Christian faith, the two things seem to be so linked that one cannot conceive of one without the other, and it will be said that there is in reality no other gnosis than the one exemplified by the gnosticism of a hundred faces. But, as a basically not at all surprising consequence, opponents of Christianity will adopt the same attitude, and will claim to recognize in gnosticism, which they identify with true gnosis, a tradition prior and superior to any revealed religion.

But Christianity and anticlericalism are not alone in professing this confusion between gnosis and gnosticism. Did not Guénon himself, in the first part of his adult life, strive to resuscitate gnosticism, at least under its Cathar form, by participating in the forming of a Gnostic "Church," of which he was (validly or not) one of the bishops? He who always seems to want to distinguish the purity of gnosis from the impurities of gnosticism, had he not been a member of a neo-gnostic organization, the alleged heir to an ancient tradition, an organization animated moreover by an unequivocal anti-Catholicism?

Was there a change in Guénon's attitude? Or must we indeed allow that, as he himself wrote to Noële Maurice-Denis Boulet, he "had entered this milieu of *Gnose* only to destroy it"?[3] We will

---

2 *Love and Truth*, 401.
3 *L'ésotériste René Guénon. Souvenirs et jugements*, published in *La Pensée Catholique*, no. 77 (1962): 23. This study, published in nos. 77–80, is not only a source of valuable information on Guénon's life, but also represents the most attentive effort at understanding that any Thomist philosopher has given to his doctrine. It is regrettable in this regard that the book by Marie-France James (*Ésotérisme et christianisme autour de René Guénon* [Paris: Nouvelles Editions Latines, 1981]), who wants to be so rigorous on the plane of historical science, and which certainly represents a considerable sum of research, otherwise evinces an almost total misunderstanding of metaphysical doctrines, in particular that of the multiple states of being, a misunderstanding such that it makes many pages of this book altogether unintelligible. For example (158), recalling that

see that in keeping to the texts, there was a change, in certain respects, that should not rule out all continuity, far from it. We think in fact that, as regards the pure idea of metaphysics, Guénon has hardly changed and that he was rather soon in possession of the major concepts that were to dominate his work. However, the forms in which he expressed these concepts may have varied considerably because all language is dependent on a culture, and therefore on an intellectual history.

Choice of expression derives then from calculations about opportuneness of which it is nearly impossible to gain any idea, and which itself depends on the knowledge we have of this culture and this history. Such knowledge, bearing on facts, can only be progressive and empirical; it depends also, and necessarily, on a certain affinity of the knowing subject with the known object. So much so that apart from religious orthodoxy guaranteed by the authority of the magisterial tradition, the meaning of any cultural form cannot be immutably defined; it changes with the accuracy of our information and our individual predispositions, or can even be permanently deferred when the question is decidedly too muddled. And, as is known moreover, Guénon never lingered where it did not seem possible to obtain sufficient clarity.[4]

---

for Guénon, what is said theologically about angels and demons can be said metaphysically about superior and inferior states of being, she concludes from this that he is thus likening "man to what is said of 'heavenly hierarchies' in an Origen, a Clement of Alexandria or a Dionysius the Areopagite." For M. F. James, "these two approaches are meant to be the confirmation of a preternatural (parapsychology, magic) and even rightly spiritual (theurgy) terrain." But she does not see, on the one hand, that the superior states of being concern something quite different than parapsychology—which, as far as it has meaning, in no way surpasses the human degree of existence—since they denote essentially the spiritual worlds and even the "divine world," and on the other hand, that the aforesaid doctrine has precisely for its purpose to explain why, all while realizing the totality of being, man does not have to become an angel in the proper sense of the term (*The Multiple States of the Being*, 70). To which should be added the discomfort occasioned by a book that claims to denounce Guénon as a satanic agent (332-33, and mostly 361), but in which, for 479 pages, he is only called "our friend." Not to mention other oddities.

4 This is the case, for example, with the enigma of Louis XVII, the message of Our Lady of La Salette, the origins of Christianity, &c. Obviously these are issues of quite unequal importance. Concerning Christianity, we do not see how, more than for any other religion, someone would have good reason

ENCOUNTER WITH THE NEO-GNOSTICS

Guénon's own interest in gnosticism and gnosis, it must be said, seems to begin by being rather exactly in harmony with that of his time, that is, with the idea formed of the two terms by a certain cultural fashion between 1880 and 1914. Note well, it was also during this time that the scientific historiography of gnosticism was worked out, with its two major trends, that of Harnack on the one hand, who sees in gnosticism "a radical and premature hellenization of Christianity,"[5] a hellenization the Great Church will achieve with more wisdom and slowness; that of Bousset and Reitzenstein on the other, who, struck by the resemblance of Christian gnosticism to Egyptian, Babylonian, Iranian, and Hermetic religious manifestations, speak of a pre-Christian gnosis and see in the gnosticism of Valentinus, Basilides, or Marcion a kind of "regression of a hellenized Christianity towards its Eastern origins,"[6] in short, an "orientalization"[7] no less radical than the hellenization of Harnack. However, this boom in gnostic historiography goes hand in hand with a certain style of gnosis, which specified its essential features especially in the first part of the nineteenth century—at that time the more or less "occultist" meaning of this term, a meaning retained henceforth in the use made of it by most pseudo-esoteric circles. This is not the case in the seventeenth century. At that time, Fénelon could still try to take up Clement of Alexandria's perfectly orthodox vocabulary and identify the mysticism of pure love with the gnosis of the Church Fathers. True, his short work, *Le gnostique de saint Clément d'Alexandrie*, in which he provides a masterful exposition of the doctrine of the great Alexandrian, remained

---

to speak about "the almost impenetrable obscurity that surrounds everything relating to the origins and early stages of Christianity, an obscurity so profound that, upon reflection, it seems impossible that it should simply have been accidental, but more likely was expressly intended" (*Insights into Christian Esoterism*, 5). Reading the *Acts of the Apostles* in no way gives such an impression. See *Christ the Original Mystery*, 102–6.

5 *Lehrbuch der Dogmengeschichte*, Tübingen, 1886, pt. I, 162; H. C. Puech, ibid., 143.
6 H. Lietzmann, *Geschichte der alten Kirche*, I, *Die Anfänge*, 1932,317; H. C. Puech, ibid., 144.
7 Reitzenstein-Schaeder, *Studien zum antiken Synkretismus aus Iran und Griechenland*, 1926, 141; H. C. Puech, ibid., 144.

unpublished for a very long time, Bossuet having opposed its dissemination.[8] Nevertheless Bossuet himself is not offended by the use of the term and strives only to bring its meaning back to the plane of common theology: "I do not see," he says, "why some other subtlety must be intended, under the name of gnosis, nor any other mystery than the great mystery of Christianity, well known by faith, well understood by the perfect, on account of the gift of intelligence, sincerely practiced and shaped by habit."[9] Apparently, as Saint-Simon attests, at the court of Louis XIV the term gnosis meant the doctrine of Fénelon;[10] however, the "compromising" nature of the term seems accentuated over time. The reasons are not hard to guess.

Fénelon's failure in his effort to restore life to the gnosis of St. Clement of Alexandria, by relating it to the mysticism St. Teresa of Avila and St. John of the Cross, as well as to the doctrine of pure love, will end up, in the nineteenth century, enabling only one meaning of this term to survive, the condemned meaning. Thus, on the Christian side, at least in general opinion, 'gnosis' is gradually assimilated to 'gnosticism,' and hardly designates anything but a heresy,[11] at the same time as, on the side of the free-thinkers, the term gnosis, which has lost its orthodox meaning, will be recovered by opponents of Christianity. Already, in the eighteenth century century, heresiarchs take the form of heroes for free thought. They are deemed either Christian philosophers who seek to shake off

---

8 Published with an introduction by Fr. Paul Dudon, S. J., *Études de Théologie historique* (Paris: Beauchesne, 1930). Fénelon's text occupies pages 163–256. This is a manuscript notebook that remained unknown until its discovery by Fr. Dudon in the Saint Sulpice library. Neither Fénelon, nor Bossuet, in their public quarrel, ever made the slightest allusion to it. Bossuet, however, quoted and refuted it in his *Tradition des nouveaux mystiques*, but without naming the author. Fénelon having yielded, Bossuet refrained from publishing his own work, which only saw the light of day in 1753. This question will be taken up again in chap. 8, 268–69; see supra, chap. 3, 39–40.

9 *Tradition des nouveaux mystiques*, chap. III, sect. 1, Dudon, ibid., 25.

10 Quotation in É. Littré, *Dictionnaire de la langue française*, under the word "Gnosis." Does not this text of Saint-Simon prove that the use of gnosis as another term for quietism was more common than ordinarily thought?

11 Perhaps it is no coincidence that, let us recall, the term gnosticism appears only in 1828 (in the Protestant university scholar Jacques Matter's work, *Critical History of Gnosticism*, Levrault, Paris).

the yoke of dogmatic discipline and would not appease the credulity of the vulgar, or else pagan philosophers thoughtfully applying the needs of reason to the obscure images of faith. Besides, the esoteric elitism of gnosis flatters the vanity of the libertine. The more the society of the *Ancien Régime* was dechristianized, the more religion was reduced to a simple, still ubiquitous façade, the "gross dupery" of which was upheld less and less. Good for the simple, as Voltaire asserts—he who amused himself on Sunday playing the country priest in front of his peasants, religion's power being without effect on a superior mind that turns, with a sense of complicity, towards the ancient heretics, and even, beyond Christianity, towards ancient paganism. From this point of view, every esotericism can only be heterodox and the bearer of mankind's hopes in its long struggle for "light." Then came the French Revolution, the anti-religious hatred of which inflicted on the Catholic Church, the oldest institution in the West, the most terrible blows in its history. In one year, between 1793 and 1794, this institution completely disappeared from French soil,[12] and will *never* regain its former splendor. With the façade cast down, in the spiritual wilderness of a most sinister age, a certain mystical neo-paganism had a stroke of luck, but only succeeded in filling the scattered pieces with a pompously insane rhetoric.

A while later, a current developed in Germany, romanticism, which in some ways is the antipodes of revolutionary atheism, but which will eventually combine with it to form now and then a kind of anti-Christian esotericism. This romanticism, in rediscovering Meister Eckhart and Jacob Boehme, revived the idea of a purely spiritual inner knowledge, to which it will intentionally give the name of gnosis. The best example, in this respect, is surely that of Franz von Baader, who moreover distinguishes clearly between a pseudo-gnosis of diabolical origin and true Christian gnosis: "It is true that there is a pseudo-gnosis," he says, "and a book [of Louis-Claude de Saint Martin] ... speaks to us clearly enough about one such school of Satan spreading out dreadfully among us, but that is exactly why there is and

---

12 R. Taveneaux, *Le catholicisme post-tridentin*, in *Histoire des religions*, tome II (Paris: Gallimard, 1972), 1108–12.

there was always a true gnosis."[13] Also, in Hegel, Boehme's work is defined as a gnosis, but one that, in order to become perfect, be transformed into pure philosophy.[14] We can then imagine that, in the intense circulation of ideas taking place in Europe in this first half of the nineteenth century, gnosis comes to designate an esoteric knowledge, superior to that of Christian dogmatics, and which makes any official religion useless because it dispels its mystery. This gnosis, the mystical foundation of anticlerical ideology, is convinced of reconnecting with a secret tradition, an exemplary victim of ecclesiastical hatred, and rediscovering the life-giving soil of our most authentic cultural roots, those not poisoned by Judeo-Christianity, or that Roman centralism had failed to root out. An unmistakable witness to this idea is the article that Pierre Larousse's *Grand Dictionnaire universel* devotes to *gnosticism* (already an accepted term): "We would be wrong... in believing that gnosis is essentially a Christian fact. By its origin, purpose, and efforts, it is much broader that any one religion could be; it is free thought seeking to explain at the same time the world, society, beliefs, customs, all with the help of tradition; which shows that free thought must not be confused here with rationalism." Then, after having asserted that its similarity to Buddhism proves its Indian origins,[15] he declares: "Gnosis was not a Christian heresy, but indeed the philosophy of Christianity itself:... to Christians gnosis said: 'your leader is an intelligence of the highest order, but his apostles did not understood their master, and, in their, turn, their disciples altered the texts left to them.'"[16]

---

13 *Tagebuch*, Weiern, January 31, 1787; *Sämmtl. Werke*, Bd. 11, 126 sq; cf. E. Benz, op. cit., 104.

14 *Encyclopedia of the Philosophical Sciences in Basic Outline*, 19. In the same way it has been shown that everything *Second Faust* owed to gnosis Goethe had learned about in the *History of the Church* by Gottfried Arnold.

15 Moreover, this is a theme to be met with since the eighteenth century, particularly in regard to possible connections of Buddhism and Brahmanism with the Fénelonian and Guyonian love mysticism, which in no way seems to deserve the reproaches that Guénon directs at it. Recall that the first mention in the West of the Buddha is found in St. Clement of Alexandria, *Stromata* I, chap. XV.

16 Obviously we must not ask how it is possible that an "intelligence of the highest order" was so greatly mistaken in his choice of witnesses.

Gnosis and Gnosticism in René Guénon

Such is, roughly, the idea that those we have called the "anticlerical mystics" had of "gnosis," and with whom the young Guénon entered into contact. The more they disdain to be informed about it historically, all the more confidently they speak about it, so convinced are they of being the only ones who really know how matters stand. For as universal as their idea of gnosis might be, they clearly intend however to place themselves in doctrinal continuity with what begins to be called gnosticism, that is, the heretical Christian schools. They generally present this doctrine as an emotional reaction to the scandal that is the existence of evil. This is undeniable, but insufficient. Objective evil, present in creation, a creation that seems to them irremediably defiled, is so keenly felt to be unjustifiable only in correlation with a dramatic overemphasis on saving interiorization: these two excesses, one objective, the other subjective, mutually condition each other. This interiority feels obliged to deem all material creation evil, and the disqualification of creation leaves an inward flight as our only salvation. The result of this is, as we have shown above,[17] an anti-creationist angelism necessarily accompanied by a Christological docetism: how could God have made himself truly flesh if the flesh is entirely evil? Accordingly, the biblical creator is just a demiurge, an evil god, that it behooves us to reject along with the entirety of the Old Testament and St. Paul's theological rabbinism. These themes are well known. They reveal, with regard to metaphysical doctrine, a complete misunderstanding of the mystery of divine immanence in cosmic exteriority, because, as the Koran teaches: "He is the First and the Last, and the Outward and the Inward, and He knows infinitely all things" (57:3).[18] As we see, according to the Koran, God's "infinite gnosis" consists precisely in radical unity and the strict implications of immanence and transcendence, the without and the within. And yet, some of these ideas are found in the very first texts of Guénon-Palingenius,

---

17 See chap. 1: "Christian Gnosis and Anti-Christian Gnosis."
18 See, on this subject, F. Schuon: "The Cross of Space and Time in Koranic Onomatology," in *Form and Substance in the Religions* (Bloomington, IN: World Wisdom, 2002), 69–84.

and one can understand why he could have implied one day that he no longer had anything in common with the one who had voiced them.[19]

We will give no detailed account of the history of the gnosticism revival as seen in France at the end of the nineteenth century. This history is yet to be written. However, we find the main elements in the various works devoted to Guénon, works that explain how Guénon became acquainted with this gnosticism.[20]

Around 1880, Lady Caithness, Duchess of Pomar, a member of the Christian Theosophical and Esoteric Society,[21] organized spiritualist seances in her mansion on the Rue Brémontier, in Paris, during which they were fond of summoning the shades of the great departed: Simon Magus, the father of gnosticism according to St. Irenaeus, Valentinus, Apollonius of Tyana, &c. Occasionally in attendance at these seances was an archivist and man of letters with an impressionable and somewhat unstable temperament named Jules Doinel. "One evening in the autumn of 1888,"[22] the spirit of Guilhabert de Castres, Cathar bishop of Toulouse,[23] appeared, who conferred

---

19 Voile d'Isis, February 1933, included in Études sur la Franc-maçonnerie et le Compagnonnage (Paris: Ed. Traditionnelles, 1964, tome I, 215.
20 We will cite in particular: P. Chacornac, The Simple Life of René Guénon, trans. C. Bethell (Hillsdale, NY: Sophia Perennis, 2001); J. P. Laurant, Le sens caché dans l'oeuvre de René Guénon (Lausanne: l'Âge d'Homme, 1975); J. Robin, René Guénon. Témoin de la Tradition (Paris: Guy Trédaniel, 1978); Marie-France James, Ésotérisme et christianisme autour de René Guénon (Paris: Nouvelles Éditions Latines, 1981); same author, same publisher, Ésotérisme, occultisme, franc-maçonnerie au XIXème et XXème siècle, 1981 (a prosopographic mine). Works devoted to Guénon have now increased considerably, both in France and abroad. The last in date, by the scope and accuracy of its information, will surely long remain the best: Jean-Pierre Laurant, René Guénon—Les enjeux d'une lecture (Paris: Dervy, 2006).
21 Guénon devoted a chapter of his Theosophy: History of a Pseudo-Religion (Hillsdale, NY: Sophia Perennis, 2003) to this curious person (164–91).
22 According to M. F. James, Ésotérisme, occultisme..., 102, J. Robin gives 1889 (op. cit., 65) and J. P. Laurant, 1890 (Sens caché..., 46).
23 Guilhabert de Castres, whose existence is attested as early as 1193, is one of the most eminent figures of Catharism, "Fils majeur"—that is, first coadjutor—of Gaucelin, bishop of Toulouse, whom he succeeded about 1220, leaving Fanjeaux at that time, where he resided, for the episcopal city. He died at Montségur about 1241; cf. Michel Roquebert, L'Épopée cathare, tome I. 1198–1220: L'invasion (Toulouse: Privat, 1970).

on Doinel the mission of restoring the Gnostic Church and, to do this, invested him with the office of patriarch.[24] Other revelations and some verifications convinced Doinel of the authenticity of his initiation. At the instigation of a friend, Fabre des Essarts, a gnostic assembly was held at Paris that recognized Doinel as patriarch under the name of Valentinus II. Later he himself conferred the episcopal dignity on Fabre des Essarts (Synesius),[25] on Gérard Encausse, founder of Martinism, and a few others. Doinel, however, seems to have always been eager to bring the Gnostic Church closer to the Catholic Church. In 1894, he even went so far as to recant, and handed his episcopal pallium over to the bishop of Orléans.[26] That is why, in 1895, Synesius succeeded him as Patriarch of the Gnostic Church, and who, in turn, conferred the episcopal consecration on Leon Champrenaud, Albert de Pouvourville,[27] Patrice Genty, &c. It was during the Spiritualist and Masonic Congress of 1908 that Guénon met Fabre des Essarts. He asked to enter this Gnostic Church, and in 1909 was consecrated bishop of Alexandria under the name of Palingenius.[28] Synesius then founded a review, *La Gnose*,

---

24 Such a mode of communication of initiation is, according to Guénon, not impossible; cf. *Perspectives on Initiation*, trans. H. D. Fohr (Hillsdale, NY: Sophia Perennis, 2001), 64–65. It is not unlike the mode presiding over the renewal of the Order of the Temple in 1908, the head of which would be Guénon.
25 M. F. James, in *Ésotérisme, occultisme...*, indicates two different dates for this consecration: 1892, 103, and 1889, 114.
26 This conversion will be followed by a return to gnosticism, and perhaps a new abjuration. He died in 1902.
27 On Pouvourville, read J. P. Laurant, *Matgioï. Un aventurier taoïste* (Paris: Dervy, 1982). According to information provided by Robert Amadou (M. F. James, *Ésotérisme et christianisme...*, 81), J. Doinel, in addition to a consecration in subtle mode, would have received, quite regularly, the episcopal seal from a bishop of the Church of Utrecht. According to J. P. Laurant, op. cit., 91, he would have been the bishop of Antioch. See, however in Appendix I, 205, a denial by Robert Amadou.
28 At the same time, Guénon, already a Mason and affiliated with the Martinism of Papus, received from the "beyond," from Jacques de Molay, the mission to revive the Order of the Temple and be its head (Laurant, *Le sens caché...*, 46). This Renovated Order of the Temple (O.T.R.) makes extensive use of the means of mediumistic communication. He continued his work in the midst of many quarrels and excommunications (especially with the followers of Papus, who accused Guénon of dark maneuverings). At the end of 1911, "on the order of his masters," Guénon announced the dissolution of

the management of which he entrusted to Guénon, and the publication of which ceased in February 1912. These are the facts, as much as we were able to reconstruct them.

As for the doctrine of the Gnostic Church, it is in all points in conformity with the theses of the gnosticism of the first centuries: anti-Judaism and anti-Jehovism, renewed accusations against the Church Fathers, who have "twisted in a thousand ways the teachings they have received," anticlericalism, etc.[29] Incontestably these theses are in contradiction with Guénon's later teaching. How could he make them his own? Guénon's successive or simultaneous affiliations with various pseudo-esoteric organizations are usually explained as an inquiry intended to verify their initiatory claims.[30] Besides, Guénon himself presented things in this way and speaks of "investigations we were obliged to undertake...," that is, about initiatory regularity.[31] It is true that in another text he states: "If, at a certain time, we had to penetrate into such or such a circle, it was for reasons that concern us alone,"[32] which does not contradict the previous assertion, but is certainly less explicit. We recalled, on the other hand, the statement he made to Noële Maurice-Denis Boulet, according to which he had entered into the Gnostic Church to destroy it.[33] It might seem impossible to dispute the convergent meaning of these assertions; let us therefore admit that Guénon, with serious intent, investigated the esoteric claims of the organizations in question, and endeavored each time to make public their illusory character.

---

the O. T. R. (M. F. James, *Ésotérisme et christianisme*, 99). J. Robin sees in this O. T. R. a possible solution to the problem of the "sources" of the Guénonian work (op. cit., 50 ff). We are however justified in thinking that all this looks quite annoyingly close to spiritualism.

29 M. F. James, op. cit., 82; J. P. Laurant, op. cit., 52–53. Cf. Appendix II, 207.
30 P. Chacornac, op. cit., 33; Robin, op. cit., 45, 135, &c.
31 *Perspectives on Initiation*, 34.
32 *Études sur Franc-Maçonnerie...*, Tome I, 197.
33 Cf. supra, 144, fn. 1. For J. Robin, this statement does not mean a disavowal by Guénon with regard to the initiatory regularity of the Gnostic Church, but only the concern to prevent this organization, authentic but dying, from falling into the state of a psychic corpse at the hands of the satanist Bricaud, a defector from the Gnostic Church and founder of a schismatic church under the name of John II, op. cit., 196–98.

Was it necessary, for this, to penetrate inside each of their associations? Was not a critical review of their declared, clearly anti-traditional doctrines enough? No doubt we must assume that some appearances can be deceiving or confusing.[34]

We must therefore conclude that Guénon never did make his own the doctrines in question, unlike our previous assumption, and he only seemed to put up with them for the time necessary for his investigations—a conclusion that seems to be confirmed by certain texts of Palingenius who, for example, declares in 1911: "we are not neo-gnostics... and, as for those (if any) who claim to adhere solely to Greco-Alexandrian gnosticism, they do not interest us in the least."[35] Likewise, it is certain that in many articles from this period—everyone has underscored this—we find doctrinal elements identical to those formulated by the mature Guénon. Moreover, Guénon himself declared, in 1932, in the continuation of the text cited above about the personal reasons he had to "penetrate into such or such circles": "whatever are the publications where our articles have appeared, whether this is 'at the same time' or not, we have always set forth exactly the same ideas upon which we never have varied."[36]

And yet, it is quite difficult to reconcile certain statements from the 1909–1913 period with those of his later work. If we believe, as we said at the beginning, that on the essential, that is, on pure metaphysics (or gnosis), Guénon hardly ever varied, we are obliged to say that his judgment on what we broadly call traditional forms changed.

---

34 Is not this the case with Masonry, or at least some of its obediences whose atheistic and progressive ideology, with regard to Guénonian criteria, should be immediately condemned? As a matter of fact, Guénon's own initiatory "errors" should not surprise us beyond measure once we admit that a human destiny can know contradictions and reversals: a life does not unfold like a mathematical theorem. But we must admit that a certain Guénonism would confer on some discordances, inevitable in anyone's existence, the value of an infallible teaching, at the cost of really excessive hermeneutical ingenuity (e.g., Robin, op. cit., 193), which strives to attenuate the yet very clear meaning of Guénon's statements in *Insights into Christian Esotericism*, 41, fn 14: "These neo-gnostics have never received anything through any transmission whatsoever..."

35 *La France anti-maçonnique* of August 26, 1911, quoted by J. Robin, op. cit., 19.

36 *Études sur Franc-Maçonnerie...*, tome I, 197.

A few years ago, in an article judicious in every way, Jean Reyor stressed how much the publication of some texts prior to 1914 might baffle readers of Guénon, who, "in his ripe age, no longer meant to show solidarity with all the positions taken in his youthful writings."[37] When he affirms, for example, in the review *La Gnose*, that "by no means does Tradition exclude evolution and progress," that the goal of the Great Work is "the integral accomplishment of progress in every domain of human activity," that Masons do not have to recognize "the existence of any God," [38] that moreover "the God of anthropomorphic religions... is not only irrational but is even anti-rational," and that "it is incorrect to identify... the anthropomorphic God of Christians with *Jehovah*..., the Hierogram of the Great Architect of the Universe himself," whose name can be replaced by that of Humanity,[39] and other oddities, one is entitled to wonder, without ill-will, whether these words are reconcilable with those found in *The Crisis of the Modern World* or in *The Reign of Quantity and Signs of the Times*. It is impossible to answer yes, even if Guénon specifies that, by humanity, we must understand the "Universal Man," and even if reason can be deemed "higher reason," to use an Augustinian expression, which is also the case with the word *manas* in Shankara or in the *Samkhya*.[40]

Also, as a matter of fact, these differences lie more with a general tone, revealing an attitude, than with particular doctrinal points. The use of the vocabulary of anticlerical rationalism proves above all that Guénon had still not broken away from certain influences and environments whose language he adopted in some respects. This he will no longer do after 1911–1912, when he definitely broke with the Western organizations to which he belonged, or took steps to dissolve them. This change in attitude is not just about notions of progress, evolution, and rationalism, which one could characterize well enough as free-thought ideology. It also concerns something much more important,

---

37 "René Guénon et la Franc-Maçonnerie. À propos d'un livre recent," published in the review *Le Symbolisme*, num. 368 (Jan.–Feb. 1965): 117.
38 *Studies in Freemasonry...*, 43–46.
39 *Ibid.*, 15–17; this thesis, which can be read for example in George Sand (*Consuelo*), comes mainly from Pierre Leroux: *De l'humanité*, 1840.
40 Cf. Guénon, *Man and His Becoming according to the Vedanta*, 64 and 66.

namely the attitude of Guénon with regard to religion in general and Christianity in particular. Assuredly, this attitude will remain quite critical. But one perceives, in the young Guénon, an indifference — not to say scorn — towards religions and their God, which appears absent from the major works of his maturity. What is missing from Palingenius is not the notion, but perhaps the living and concrete sense, of Tradition, and therefore respect for the sacred forms in which this is expressed. Certainly, the doctrinal content of his major works is already more than sketched out in the articles of *La Gnose*, and one is right to point this out. But the atmosphere of thought is somewhat changed. In 1911, Palingenius affirms: "We cannot consider metaphysical truth to be anything other than axiomatic in its principles and theorematic in its deductions, and therefore just as rigorous as mathematical truth, of which it is the unlimited prolongation."[41] In 1921, René Guénon wrote: "logic and mathematics may be said to be the two sciences having the most real affinity with metaphysics; but from the very fact that they come within the general definition of scientific knowledge ... they are still radically separated from pure metaphysics."[42] Meanwhile, the transcendence of metaphysics over everything else is greatly accentuated, because its nature as sacred tradition and its primordial origin, already explicitly affirmed, led Guénon, perhaps following a certain event, to have a more clearly hierarchical awareness of its principial supereminence.[43]

---

41 Article in *La Gnose*, October 1911: "Scientific Ideas and the Masonic Ideal," in *Studies in Freemasonry...*, 2.
42 *Introduction to the Study of Hindu Doctrines*, trans. M. Pallis (Ghent, NY: Sophia Perennis, 2001), 95.
43 In his article "Gnosis and the Spiritist Schools" (1909–1911), Guénon already affirms: "Gnosis must therefore... base itself only on the orthodox Tradition contained in the sacred books of all peoples, a Tradition that in reality is everywhere the same despite the various forms with which it is clothed." But he writes again: "In its widest and highest meaning, gnosis is knowledge; therefore true gnosticism cannot be a particular school or system" (*Miscellanea*, 147 and 146). The first quote is purely Guénonian and breaks, in fact, with gnosticizing occultism; the second employs the term Gnosticism, which Guénon will reject entirely. Similarly, in the same article we find quite mind-boggling, but highly revealing declarations. Responding to one of his detractors (although he had formally forbidden himself "any polemics"!), Guénon notes the essential points of divergence: first the rejection of a "personal," necessarily anthropomorphic

GNOSTICS OF THE 19TH AND 20TH CENTURIES

One last example will completely convince us of this change in tone and of the distancing of his thinking from the gnosticism of his youth. This is provided by the celebrated article *The Demiurge*, considered Guénon's first doctrinal work, proving moreover that in 1909, he was, as they say, in full possession of his doctrine. However, if we read this text attentively, we observe a considerable divergence with later texts, at least on one truly significant point.

We will at once point out that the very title of Demiurge and the mention, at the beginning of the article, of the problem of evil, for which this Demiurge is charged with providing a solution, typically derive from gnosticism: the Demiurge is the creator of an evil world. In truth, when we take cognizance of the presentation's details, we see that the central, basically orthodox, idea could dispense with the language in which it is clothed. This is proven by the complete disappearance of this "personage" in later works.[44] Although, in 1909, he identified "the sphere of this same Demiurge" and "what we call Creation," although "all elements of Creation... are contained within the Demiurge himself" who can therefore be "considered as the Creator,"[45] in 1921 the identification of the Demiurge with God the creator is regarded as a "theological heresy" and a "metaphysical absurdity."[46] This absurdity is moreover peculiar to gnosticism: one should not, says Guénon, "put (the Great Architect of the Universe who is 'only one aspect of divinity') in the same category as the gnostic idea of the 'Demiurge,' which would give him a rather 'malefic' character...."[47] "One must at least choose" between Creator and Demiurge.[48]

God and even the word itself; then he continues: "We will say as much of his idea of Christ, that is to say a unique Messiah who is an 'incarnation' of the Divinity; we on the contrary recognize a plurality (and even an indefinite number) of divine 'manifestations' which are not in any way 'incarnations,' for above all it is important to maintain the purity of monotheism, which cannot agree with such a theory," 166). One sees that on occasion Guénon does not recognize the importance of sacred books which teach that "the Word became flesh."

44 But one still finds the adjective *demiurgic*.
45 *Miscellanea*, 10.
46 *Introduction to the Study of Hindu Doctrines*, 91.
47 *Études sur Franc-Maçonnerie...*, tome II, 142.
48 *Traditional Forms and Cosmic Cycles*, trans. H. D. Fohr (Hillsdale, NY: Sophia Perennis, 2001), 93.

But the point that seems most significant concerns what Guénon calls in *The Demiurge* the "pneumatic world," distinguished from the "hylic" world and the "psychic" world. Relating these gnostic (and Pauline) designations to the doctrine of *Vedanta*, he writes: "The one who has become aware of the two manifested worlds, namely the hylic (the totality of gross or material manifestations) and the psychic (the totality of subtle manifestations), is twice-born, *dvija*. But the one who is aware of the unmanifested universe or the formless world—that is, the pneumatic world—and who has achieved the identification of himself with the universal Spirit, *Atma*, he alone can be called *yogi*, that is to say united with the universal Spirit."[49] And some lines further, he establishes the correspondence of these three worlds with the three states of waking, dreaming, and deep sleep. In such a cosmology, manifestation therefore includes only two worlds, corporeal and psychic, the pneumatic world being unmanifested, and "the Pleroma, neither manifested nor unmanifested." Now, as we know, and according to *Man and His Becoming...*, universal manifestation includes three worlds, the third being formed by intelligible or informal realities. In comparison to the gnosticizing conception of *The Demiurge*, the manifested universe is thus augmented by an additional degree, one that India calls *Mahat* or *Buddhi*. Consequently, the state of sleep deep (*sushuptasthana*), which is the state of Prajna (the "Knower"), no longer corresponds just to the unmanifest degree of pure Being, but also encompasses informal manifestation: "*Buddhi* must be in some manner included in the state of *Prajna*."[50]

However, what should be noted above all is that the addition of a degree of reality to universal manifestation completely changes its meaning: the cosmic pessimism of gnosticism is rejected, for, if creation includes the pneumatic or the intelligible, then there is at least one degree of the universe resplendent with the beauty of its created perfection, and where its fundamental goodness is revealed. The essences, insofar as informal realities, are "ultimately none other than the very

---

49 Miscellanea, 14.
50 Man and His Becoming..., 99.

expression of *Atma* in the manifested order,"⁵¹ and conversely, we will say, the expression of the manifested order in *Atma* of the principial possibilities of creation, directly illuminated by the divine Sun.⁵²

Here we see the full, truly decisive importance of the affirmation of the intelligible world that alone can save the cosmos from an indefinite dispersal into the outer darkness, at the same time that it saves human knowledge from its crumbling into the insignificance of nominalism.

We have said enough now about Guénon's connections with gnosticism. Henceforth his attitude will no longer vary and will even only get stronger. We could summarize this attitude by the following two points: (1) the condemnation and final rejection of the neo-gnostics; (2) a prejudicial and invariable distinction between gnosis and gnosticism. And if gnosis is defined as the pre-eminent metaphysical knowledge, gnosticism, with some differences in various texts, is defined, in a rather pejorative way, like the complex of heretical schools that historians designate by this name. The most explicit text that Guénon devoted to this is in *East and West*. He states, in particular: "It is rather hard to know now the precise nature of the somewhat varied doctrines which are classed together under the term 'gnosticism,' and among which there would no doubt be many distinctions to make; but, on the whole, they seem to have contained more

---

51 "Spirit and intellect," in *Miscellanea*, 27.
52 Attentively reading the Allegory of the Cave in Plato, we see that there are on the one hand the puppets whose shadows are projected on the rear wall's surface, and on the other the men and women, hidden by a wall, who bear these puppets on their shoulders. Although Plato identifies the puppets with the Ideas (or essences), he says nothing about those people who make them move and speak. We must therefore distinguish between manifested Idea-essences (or intelligible forms), and unmanifested Ideas that are to be identified with the divine possibles. The manifested Ideas are still part of the Cosmic Theater (samsaric *Maya*), and must be surpassed to go to the supreme Good, which is, says Plato, "beyond being" (or essence: *ousia*). The puppet-bearers can only be seen starting with the Good, which means it is only from the vantage point of Above-Being that the principial root of the multiple can be grasped in its own ontological Unity. Starting with the created, even the loftiest spiritual manifestation, Being "appears" as the exclusive Unity of created multiplicity. Starting from Above-Being, the "internal face" of Being appears as the determinative synthesis of the innumerable (non-quantitative) multiplicity of archetypal possibilities. See *Penser l'analogie*, 162–92.

or less disfigured Eastern ideas, probably misunderstood by the Greeks, and clothed in imaginative forms which are scarcely compatible with pure intellectuality; it would assuredly cost little effort to find things more worthy of interest, less mixed with heteroclite elements, of a much less dubious value, and much more surely significant."[53]

But what of the event previously alluded to that played the role of catalyst in Guénon's attitude towards pseudo-esotericism and religious forms? Our reply will be that it very likely consists in his connection with Sufism. It was in 1912, according to the indications provided by the dedication to *The Symbolism of the Cross*, with the date confirmed by a letter, that Guénon received initiation.[54] We think this to be the decisive event, not from a doctrinal point of view, but from a spiritual point of view, that is, for that which concerns the commitment of one's being as a whole to the Truth. How, in fact, could we not notice that it is at this date that Guénon definitively breaks with marginal elements of esotericism to join a regular initiatory lineage? It is also this initiation that communicates to him a sharper and more concrete consciousness of requirements from the traditional point of view, since it seems that, according to Jean Robin's title, René Guénon never wanted to be anything else than a "witness to Tradition." Still other no less significant coincidences could be noted (for example, the abandonment of the "Palingenius" pseudonym for that of "Sphinx"). Anyhow, this event seems analogous to the one that will occur in 1930 with his departure for Cairo, and which will bring about his immersion—as much as his nature allowed—in a truly traditional atmosphere. "Blessed are those who have not seen and who have believed!" But there are some things you only understand after seeing them...[55]

---

53 Trans. M. Lings (Hillsdale, NY: Sophia Perennis, 2001), 144. In 1931, he even affirms: "we have ever experienced only a quite mediocre interest in gnosticism, first because it is very difficult to know exactly what it was in reality, and then because in any case *its Greek form is most repulsive to us*" (*Comptes Rendus*, 119; our italics). As observed, the Greek form is repulsive to Guénon, but such a sentiment does not constitute a guarantee of objectivity.

54 J. Robin, op. cit., 69.

55 The Proceedings of the international conference of Cerisy-la-Salle (13–20 July, 1973): *René Guénon et l'actualité de la pensée traditionnelle* (Braine-le-Comte:

GNOSIS: SACRED INTELLECTUALITY

The distinction between gnosis and gnosticism, thereafter advocated by Guénon, has become the rule. In fact, the participants in the *Colloque international de Messine sur les origines du gnosticisme* agreed to define this term as designating "a certain group of systems of the second century AD which everybody concurs in so naming," while gnosis signifies "knowledge of the divine mysteries reserved for an elite."[56] This distinction must suffice for an understanding of what true gnosis is and to disentangle it from its gnosticist corruption.

To truly show the significance of orthodox gnosis, and what its importance and function is, it would be necessary to retrace the entire history of Western philosophy,[57] from its Greek origins down to its most curious contemporary forms. This history alone, we think, which is also in certain respects (at least since the end of the Middle Ages) that of Christian theology, would enable us to see what is at stake in this question. Instead, we will be content with a brief characterization.

The idea of gnosis is that of a supernatural and unifying knowledge of Divine Reality. These three elements are in fact necessary for its definition:

(1) Divine Reality or infinite and perfect Reality, because all knowledge is specified by its object, and because the object of gnosis is none other than the pre-eminent Object, the absolutely real;

(2) unifying and identifying because, differing from every other knowing, there is only gnosis if there is transformation of the knowing subject and union with the known Object: whereas ordinarily knowledge, operating by abstraction, leaves the very being of the knower outside itself, here it specifically takes

---

Éd. du Baucens, 1977), contains in this respect important testimonies, especially that of Nadjmoud-Dine Bammate.
56 *Le Origini dello Gnosticismo*, Colloquio di Messina (Leiden, 1967), xxiii.
57 Obviously we include in this concept of philosophy much that Guénon has set aside from it. The usage of this term, literally signifying "love of *Sophia*" and therefore a sapiential quest and concentration upon its divine mystery, is imposed on us and guaranteed by the Platonic tradition, which represents one of the chief expressions of universal metaphysics. In speaking of philosophy, Plato did nothing but recover a term whose inventor was (in Cicero's words) Pythagoras himself.

place only through a deifying participation in what it knows;

(3) supernatural, metaphysical, super-rational, or sacred knowledge because, while still belonging to knowledge, like any speculative act whatsoever, it is completely distinguished from it by its mode, which is that of the pneumatized (or spiritual) intellect. To tell the truth, it is distinguished from other modes to the extent that, within itself, it realizes the perfection of every cognitive aim.

This conception of a sacred intellectuality is basically the one implemented by Plato and Neo-Platonism: a knowledge that is a conversion and involves the entire being, in such a way that the degrees of knowledge are so many hierarchically ascending states of being. The symbol of the Cave teaches this, as well as the Plotinian doctrine of the hypostases. And such is, quite explicitly, Plato's definition of philosophy, a conception that will collide with two kinds of disputes, one in the name of intellectuality and the other in the name of the sacred.

Objections concerning the speculative order were the work of Aristotle, who inaugurated, in the history of Western thought, what can be called "profane science," that is, an exclusively abstract functioning of knowledge.[58] Surely, science itself is still for him objectively connected to metaphysics, at least in some principles of the ontological order. But the study of logic (the *Analytics*), invented by Aristotle, holds first place. On the other hand, knowledge, whether physical or metaphysical, is one and is differentiated only as a function of the various modalities by which it abstracts known reality.[59] One can see all that separates such a conception from that of Plato. For Plato, to know is to know what is. The truth of knowledge varies as a function of the reality of its object. Essentially there are, then, degrees of knowledge strictly corresponding to the degrees of reality, such that every lower degree is ignorant of the degree

---

58 We have expanded on this question in *The Crisis of Religious Symbolism*, 41–43.
59 Aristotle distinguishes between "first philosophy" (or "theology") and "second philosophy." But, even if the object of the one (being qua being) differs from the object of the other (physical being), their knowledge is one. There is, he says, the same relationship between metaphysics and physics as in mathematics between arithmetic and geometry (*Meta.*, IV, c.2, 1004 a5). The abstraction is either physics, mathematics, or metaphysics.

above: there can be no true knowledge of what truly is not, that is, no knowledge of becoming. Only knowledge of the Absolute (the Unconditioned, *Anhypotheton*) is knowledge absolutely. It is knowledge of the Supreme Good, "beyond being" (*epekeina tes ousias*, *Republic* VI, 509b), but this requires the actualization of the intellect (*nous*) and the abandonment of discursive knowledge (*dianoia*). In other words, because every true knowledge is desire for being, the intellect can know nothing (truly) of what it cannot be identified with. Now, can man become a stone, a tree, or a cat? No. Consequently there is no perfect knowledge of the stone, tree, or cat (qua physical and sensory beings).

To the contrary, it is in the physical realm that Aristotle wants to obtain a scientific certainty. One sees in what sense the formula in *On the Soul* — "the soul is all that it knows,"[60] which Guénon likes to quote — must be understood. It cannot mean an entitative union of the soul with its objects of knowledge; nor could it be considered as an unconscious revelation of Aristotle's, signifying more than he thought he was expressing. Yet the exact formula actually includes the adverb *pos*, "in some manner" (*quodammodo*).[61] And if the soul can be, in the cognitive act, *quodammodo*, all things (stone, tree, cat), this is precisely because the act of knowing extracts the intelligible form from the known being. In other words, it is because it is, *entitatively*, nothing of what it knows, that the soul can be, *intentionally*, identified with everything known. For Aristotle, knowledge is realized by a process of abstraction that "disexistentiates" the intelligible form, tears it out of real and concrete being, and so enables it to exist in the soul to which it is united by "informing" it. The intelligible form is then nothing but what is

---

60 For example, *Introduction to the Study of Hindu Doctrine*, 115. In a general way, Guénon gives preference to Aristotle to the detriment of Plato, who visibly irritates him. In his "Discourse against Discourses" (*Études Traditionnelles*, num. 428, 247), he even asserts that Plato's dialectic is only a "vain amusement" and that "it could lead to no truly profound conclusion," which is, all the same, rather perplexing. It can then be understood why he declares that Western metaphysics is "incomplete in character," "which furthermore is to all intents and purposes limited to the doctrine of Aristotle and the Scholastics" (*Introduction to the Study of Hindu Doctrines*. 93). No comment!

61 For example: *On the Soul* (III, 8, 431b 21) "he psyche ta onta pos esti panta," "the soul is, in a certain manner, all beings."

called a concept.⁶² But if, in what concerns the sensible world, Aristotelian analysis only expresses the pure and simple truth, it no longer does the same for knowledge of the intelligibles (the separate existence of which Aristotle denies) and above all the Supreme Intelligible that is God, recognized by the Philosopher in some manner, without however drawing out all the consequences. This difficulty of Aristotelian thought is clearly manifested in the very classical problem of knowing whether it has two first philosophies—ontology (or general metaphysics), and theology (or special metaphysics): is being, inasmuch as being, being in general or God? However that might be, in the West and from the thirteenth century on it is Aristotle's philosophy that provides the general conception of what a science ought to be at the very time that science is providing the model for all true knowledge. To know is to know an object, that is, something that, in its being, is completely distinct from the knowing subject. Now this scientific model, progressively transformed in the course of the sixteenth and seventeenth centuries, with Galileo and Descartes in particular, despite some resistances, has appeared little by little as a model rather exactly in accord with certain aspects of Christian revelation.

Christianity's irruption into the cultural field of antiquity entailed, as we know, considerable changes. The very idea of the sacred, among others, was profoundly altered. With faith in Christ and his deifying grace, there was manifested in the very bosom of the pagan mentality a type of relationship with the divine never experienced by Greco-Roman humanity. The potent figure of Christ concentrated within itself the totality of the sacred. By the same stroke the other forms of the sacred were, if not divested of, at least demoted from their primacy, whether cosmic or human forms are involved. This is why it could be said that the appearance of Christianity was a major factor in the "disenchantment of the world," even though such views are too general to be altogether exact.⁶³ What remains,

---

62 We are simplifying a complex doctrine according to what appears to be its general meaning, without excluding that this doctrine might conceal some virtualities of gnosis.
63 We acknowledge that this remark might just as well be applied to the current study, which summarizes fifteen hundred years of Christian thought in a few lines.

however, is that a certain desacralization of knowledge likewise forced its way through, to the extent that it was not so much the intelligence as the immortal person that was involved in the grace of salvation. Until the arrival of Aristotle's works in the thirteenth century, the effects of the (relative) "laicization" of knowledge had been as if neutralized by the long ascendancy of a diffuse Platonism carried by the thought of St. Augustine. But with Aristotle a new noetic model asserted itself, a model that seemed to justify as correct the distinction between knowledge and faith and to repudiate any notion of a sacred knowledge; hence the interest it presents for certain tendencies in Christianity.

In many respects, the colossal work of St. Thomas will enable the equilibrium between the mystical intellectualism of Plato and the speculative naturalism of Aristotle to be safeguarded. But this equilibrium, like every equilibrium, is fragile, and this is so from two quasi-antinomic points of view: one denies the real distinction between science and faith, the other accentuates it even to contradiction, with both points of view interfering with each other. Besides, this is not truly a matter of two possibly comparable points of view, but rather of a requirement of the nature of things in the first case and following from their "culture" in the second. Actually, the non-distinctive point of view is not the result of a theoretical decision, but necessarily imposes itself: faith is knowledge in its very essence, and knowledge inevitably includes a dimension of faith, as an adherence of the being to what it does not yet see. Thus is proven, in science as in faith, the *presence* of a common and irreducible *kernel of gnosis*. Nothing could lastingly modify this fundamental datum. As for the second point of view, and according to the very history of Western thought, it only brings about, by radicalizing it, the methodical separation of science and faith, obviously to the extent allowed by the nature of things. This means that science is progressively defined as a non-faith, and faith as a non-science.

Faith proclaimed as a non-science is actually what is realized by the Lutheran protest with its conception of a purely fiduciary faith, faith as pure blind confidence, and the rejection of every *ratio theologica* in the name of the deep-seated wickedness of fallen nature, and of a kind of mystical existentialism.

Science proclaimed as a non-faith is first realized (perhaps involuntarily) in Cartesianism, which, as a philosophy and despite some reservations, definitively marginalizes theology. However, one must await Kant for this exclusion to be philosophically integrated with the conceptual act as such. This means, not only that every religious preoccupation is foreign to the cognitive act—which for a philosopher of the Enlightenment is self-evident—but, more radically, that the ontological quality of knowledge, which would in fact imply a kind of faith, is rejected, since the being of things is not seen and is only apprehended by intuition: this is the ontological neutralization of all knowledge.

The theological repercussions of Kantism, despite or because of the "pseudo-gnostic" reaction of Hegel, leads to the Bultmannian approach and the so-called death of God theologies: every concept is an alienating abstraction, even that of God (or any dogma whatsoever, Trinity or Incarnation); faith is merely lived experience, having no other end than to goad human existence to an awareness of its irremediable contingency.

Surely it is here that the meaning of the Guénonian endeavor is revealed to be more topical, to the extent that it intends to speak about a mode of knowledge, gnosis, wherein knowing subject and known object can be united. Topical, yes, because the intellectual situation of the West is precisely that of a progressive divorce of knowledge and being, a divorce that ends by raising this situation into a principle. To apply a remedy here is not easy. And yet attempts have been made in this direction: that of Hegel, for example, who proposes to reconcile being and knowledge by reducing the former to the latter, or that of Ruyer, who makes science and metaphysics identical; they do not end up with a true gnosis: the first attempt leads to the idealist illusion, the second to a quasi-pantheistic naturalism.[64] Outside of these few attempts, modern philosophy, in its entirety the heir of Kantism, does not conceive of a knowledge [Fr. =

---

64 The case of Teilhard de Chardin, close in certain respects to that of Ruyer, will be brought up briefly in chapter 9, 299–302.

connaissance] that does not posit its object as completely "other" (an observable and not a participable): the idea of "knowledge" [Fr. = *co-naissance*, lit. "born together," "shared birth"] is derived from poetry, not science. Likewise, for the theologians, to speak of a union of human subject with divine Object is derived from mystical language, not a speculative elaboration. Guénon's originality is, to the contrary, to remind us that there can exist another type of knowledge, intellective in nature and not simply poetico-mystical (in the ordinary sense of these terms) that, at least in its essence, is a veritable participation of the knower in the Known, without for all that having to resort to idealist monism or pantheism. Assuredly, the Guénonian presentation of gnosis harbors aspects, whether latent or explicit, of intellectualist, if not idealist reduction. Thus, to declare that metaphysics is not content to affirm the unity of being and knowing, but that it realizes it, is to cross, without saying so, from the speculative to the operative: meanwhile, the term metaphysics has changed in meaning. What remains, however, is that Guénon has known how to open up, within the closed horizon of Western epistemology, the possibility of a "new" mode of knowing. New, yet this mode is traditional, that is, sacred as well. It is in its depths a participation in the uncreated light of the divine Word which enlightens every man in this world.

GNOSIS AND THE POSSIBLES

But the Guénonian doctrine not only characterizes the nature of gnosis as a *sacred* knowledge, it also intends to specify its function as *knowledge*. Knowledge is defined by Guénon as a function of reality. Only what man can actually take cognizance of is actually and fully real to him, everything else cannot be defined as possible. Knowledge is thus "realizing," not in the idealistic sense in which knowledge would create the real, but in the sense that, through it alone, there is something real for human beings. The real is strictly correlative to the act by which one apprehends the real. It is not *posited* contradictorily *in itself* by a theoretical assertion that forgets that the entire autonomy and independence of reality that it posits is nevertheless dependent on the act by which it posits this, which philosophical criticism will be only too happy to point out. In other words, and to express this less abstractly: any assertion about the absolutely and infinitely Real seems to sin both by excess and deficiency: by excess since, being relative, it says more than it has the right to do; by deficiency, since this Absolute is nothing more than an assertion.[65] To the second difficulty we can answer quite classically that it is not the human intellect that asserts the divine Absolute, but the Absolute itself that asserts itself in each intellect: the *Verbum illuminans*. As for the first difficulty, the answer is more "original," or at the very least more explicit than usual. Moreover, it is not easy to explain and will take us rather far afield.

Guénon will formulate this answer in *The Multiple States of the Being*. The book begins with a chapter dedicated to the famous distinction between Infinity and universal Possibility, a distinction which, moreover, is real only from our own viewpoint, since, from the viewpoint of the Supreme Principle, universal Possibility is nothing but Infinity, and yet neither is this an arbitrary distinction, since it corresponds to two "aspects" of the Supreme, an analogically active aspect and an analogically passive one. This is not the place to seek out the origin of this distinction,[66] which is rather Tantric than Shankarian,[67] but we have to ask ourselves why Guénon introduces the concept of universal Possibility. What is its interest? Of what use is it? Is not the concept of Infinity enough? Guénon gives an initial response by declaring that, from the viewpoint of universal

---

65 Only those who have never asked about the meaning of a *koan*, or the meaning of the "oneness of witnessing" (*wahdat al-shuhud*), a oneness that the witness El Hallâj could realize only through his own crucifying extinction, only those will find these remarks pointless or sophistic. The question is clearly: what is Buddhahood? or again: how are we to "say God," or be "theo-logos"?
66 This is nothing but what scholasticism calls a virtual distinction, that is, neither real, nor solely of reason.
67 There is very little mention of the Shakti of Brahma in Shankara's essential work, the *Commentary on the Aphorisms of the Vedanta*: once in II, I, 14, according to G. Thibaut's index (*The Vêdânta Sûtra of Badarayana with the Commentary by Shankara* [New York: Dover Publications, 1962], 2 volumes). It is tantrism, and Abhinavagupta's tantrism in particular, that will fully develop the doctrine of what A. K. Coomaraswamy has called the "Divine Bi-Unity" (*Coomaraswamy 2: Selected Papers, Metaphysics*, ed. R. Lipsey [Princeton: Princeton University Press, 1977], 231–40).

possibility, "there is no determination here either, or at least only the minimum required to render [the Infinite] actually conceivable to us."[68] In short, we cannot actually conceive of the Infinite in itself. When we think about Infinity, we are actually thinking about "universal possibility," in other words about "that which can be absolutely anything," "that which cannot limit reality in absolutely any way" and which is basically another way of speaking about the "absolute non-contradiction" of the idea of Infinity, since what is impossible is what implies contradiction.[69] We learn next that this minimal determination corresponds to an "objective" aspect of Infinity, which Guénon identifies with passive perfection. Whatever it may be, universal possibility necessarily encompasses whatever surpasses Being, since Being or principial determination is logically set in opposition to what is not. Thus, Being is not "beyond" all contradiction, it does not realize absolute non-contradiction, another term for universal Possibility. For the Supreme to be absolutely non-contradictory, such that nothing can contradict it, it is therefore necessary that it exceed the first of all determinations and embrace what is beyond Being, which Guénon designates as Non-Being. Such is the logic of Infinity. And so it appears that the viewpoint of universal Possibility is hardly a determination, which only truly begins with Being, but we must rather consider it as the universal *determinability* of the Principle, in itself absolutely undetermined (or superdetermined), were this even through a principial determination of Being.

Concerning the possible in general.

However, the very expression of possibility conceals an ambiguity. On the one hand, it assumes its meaning only by its distinction from the notion of "reality": whatever can be made real is possible, otherwise one does not see with respect

---

68 *The Multiple States of the Being*, 10–11.
69 In order to comment in detail on these very dense pages, we need to stress their Leibnizian background, pages 11 and 12 in particular, where Guénon, according to the pledge of Leibniz (*New Essays on Human Understanding*, IV, chap. 10, §7) shows that the idea of Infinity is both possible (non-contradictory) and necessary.

to what that which is called "possible" would be so; moreover, Guénon speaks constantly about the possibles, about their "realization." But on the other hand he also speaks of the possibles as such, in themselves, and goes so far as to assert that "the distinction between the possible and the real, upon which many philosophers have placed so much emphasis, thus has no metaphysical validity, for every possible is real in its way, according to the mode befitting its own nature."[70] There is no inconsistency here and, in doing so, Guénon is following the most classical philosophical tradition, especially the one exhibited by scholasticism. The term "possible" undoubtedly implies a rapport with an eventual realization, but we can also consider the entity which, in itself, constitutes the possibility of a thing and to pass, in short, from adjective (something is possible) to noun (something is *a* possible). In other words, it is perfectly legitimate to consider the possible by putting in parentheses its relationship to its realization. It is even essential, if we want to examine in just what precisely does the possibility of what is possible consist. But, of course, even viewed in this way, the possible retains, it is implied, a relationship that unites it with its eventual realization.

Now what about this possibility? Before going further, a distinction must be made. Possibility can be considered in two ways: either it is a relative (or extrinsic) possibility, or a so-called "absolute" (or intrinsic) possibility. The possibility of flying is relative to birds, that of speaking is relative to man; the possibility of a square or a circle, on the contrary, depends only on the definition of the circle or square, on their essence; that is, in short, on the non-contradiction of the elements that compose it. As for non-contradiction, it tells us of the essence insofar as conceivable, since the contradictory is inconceivable: we cannot conceive of a circular square. This obviously has to do with this "absolute" or intrinsic possibility, also called logical or metaphysical possibility: the possible is the non-contradictory and therefore the conceivable. From this point of view, its reality is that of a concept, of the thought that conceives of its essence and formulates its definition.

---

70 *The Multiple States of the Being*, 17.

Is this always the case? It all depends on the viewpoint one adopts on the nature of the real. If you are an atheist and a materialist, you have to answer yes. The possible, in itself, has existence only out of the conceivable. It is different if we admit of a Creator God. Because then the possibilities or essences of things are the Ideas (models or exemplars or archetypes) according to which the Divine Word *thinks* the world and all creatures. The only thing that God cannot think is the contradictory. But this in no way limits the power of God since the contradictory is a noughting of reality. In this sense, theology speaks of the Word as the "place of the possibles." Again, these possibles must not be represented in divine Understanding as a numerable multiplicity of entities, distinct and separate from each other. These possibles are, says St. Thomas Aquinas, all the ways in which the divine essence knows itself and therefore is also known as participable by creatures. "[God] knows His own essence perfectly, He knows it according to every mode in which it can be known. Now, it can be known not only as it is in itself, but as it can be participated in by creatures according to some degree of likeness. But every creature has its own proper species, according to which it participates in some degree in likeness to the divine essence. So far, therefore, as God knows His essence as capable of such imitation by any creature, He knows it as the particular type and idea of that creature."[71] But, in God, everything is God. So the possibles in God, or Ideas of all possible creatures, are God himself: "the creature, as existing in God, is the very essence of God."[72] God is one and infinite. It follows that:

(1) The possibles in God are real from the very reality of God, and therefore Guénon is right to argue that, *metaphysically*, the distinction between the real and the possible is not valid;

(2) The divine possibles are one, and, although perfectly distinct, do not constitute a numerable multiplicity;

(3) These possibles are "infinite," like God himself.

According to an expression borrowed from Father Sertillanges, we must say that, for St. Thomas, God is an *infinity of*

---

71 *Summa Theologiae*, I, Q. 15, a. 2.
72 *De Potentia*, Q. III, a. 16, ad 24; *On the Power of God*, trans. English Dominican Fathers (London: Burns Oates & Washbourne, 1932), 234.

possibility (in the singular). Infinite possibility is, in God, God himself.[73]

As we can see, Thomist theology seems to agree with Guénonian doctrine: to speak of an "infinity of possibility" or of "universal possibility" is quite the same. But this agreement goes a little too far. Of course, there are differences, as we will see in a moment. Yet we would almost be tempted to ask if Guénon has not borrowed from a certain Thomism — of which he only had a very superficial knowledge — some elements relating to the most difficult aspects of his metaphysics: we intend to speak about the notion of "possibilities of non-manifestation," which will be dealt with now. However, before dealing with this, we must address some objections.

Concerning the pure possibles according to St. Thomas Aquinas.

The objections to which we are referring have been formulated, whether publicly or privately, by Frithjof Schuon.[74] While, for Guénon, the possibilities of non-manifestation pertain to the highest order and are situated at the properly metaphysical level, exceeding (infinitely) the level of being,[75] for Schuon they designate — and to the very extent one is intent on giving them a meaning — only "possibilities of absence" at the level of the most empirical manifestation: according to Schuon, what is not manifested is the "possibility

---

73 Jacques Chevalier (*Histoire de la pensée* [Paris: Flammarion, 1956], tome II, 777) specifies, in following Sertillanges and in fidelity to the text of Thomas: "When therefore one says of divine knowledge that it is the cause of things insofar as it unites with the divine will which, among all the possibles, freely decides to realize some of these rather than others, we must be careful not to believe...that there is in God an *infinity of possibles* that God conceives of, then from among which he chooses certain of them to project into being: God is an *infinity of possibilities*, as he is an infinity of being; or, if you will, the possibility that is in God is God himself." This text sounds like a response to the "crude" interpretation given by Fr. Pègues in his commentary of *Summa Theologiae*, I, Q. 14, a. 8 and a. 9, quoted by F. Chenique: *Sagesse chrétienne et mystique orientale* (Paris: Dervy, 1996), 340.

74 For example in his "Critical Remarks" published in *Dossier H: René Guénon* (Lausanne: L'Âge d'Homme, 1984), 63-64, or in *From the Divine to the Human*, trans. G. Polit & D. Lambert (Bloomington: World Wisdom Books, 1982), 43 ff: "The Problem of Possibility."

75 *The Multiple States of the Being*, 31-38.

of non-manifestation." A particular basket can contain apples: it is a possibility of manifestation; but it can also be empty: this is a possibility of non-manifestation, which Schuon calls a privative possibility.[76]

This rejection of a notion that, for a Guénonian, is essential to a resolutely meontological (or superontological) perspective, and which is, in this regard, indicative of the more ontologizing (and cataphatic) tendency in Schuonism—this rejection, we say, actually stems from a divergence on the very notion of possibility. For Schuon "that is possible which can either be or not be"; this is what the word "means in an immediate manner."[77] Now, if this is in fact the current meaning of the term, it is also a vague meaning and therefore difficult to use in philosophy. To be convinced of this, all it takes is a basic consideration: what Schuon defines in this way is not only the *possible*, it is also the *contingent*, and everyone knows that a strict definition must be appropriate to the defined object alone. When we say: what "can be" is possible (and which is therefore considered regardless of its *de facto* existence), it is pointless to add: "or not be," otherwise we are defining something other than possibility. Possibility is not expressed by the *or* (which says eventuality, contingency, non-necessity), it is expressed by the *can*. The Schuonian analyses are not without relevance, for example when he rightly asserts that the *esse* of St. Thomas "does not necessarily have [a] limited meaning since it can embrace both aspects," that is, the aspects of Being and Beyond Being.[78] But these analyses suffer from, not a faulty (in some respects it might harken back to Aristotle) but an insufficiently worked out definition

---

76 *From the Divine to the Human*, 48.
77 Ibid., 44.
78 Ibid., 47, fn 5. Witness this well-known text: "This name, the One *who is*, expresses the absolute Being, undetermined by anything added to it; this is why Damascene says that this does not signify what God is, but that it signifies an infinite ocean of substance, as if indeterminate. This is why, when we approach God by way of negation, we first deny to him any bodily realities; then the intellectual realities themselves, such as are found in creatures, like goodness and wisdom; in our minds there remains then just the assertion that God is, and nothing more; our mind also finds itself somewhat perplexed. Finally, we deny God this existence itself, such as it is in creatures; thus he dwells for us in a darkness of ignorance in the bosom of which we unite ourselves with him in the highest way, as Dionysius says." *In I Sent.*, dist. 8 Q. 1, a. 1, ad 4.

of the possible. On the other hand, the Guénonian discourse, as a whole, conforms roughly to the terminology of scholastic philosophy. With this approach involving *modalities* of judgment, that is, the various *modes* in which a predicate is said to belong to the subject, this philosophy classically distinguishes *two* pairs of opposites: on the one hand the possible and the impossible, on the other the necessary and the contingent—this said without considering the difficult problems posed by this quaternity (Is it reducible?), as well as by modal logic in general.[79] Possibility and impossibility, understood in the logical and metaphysical sense, concern the essence insofar as it is, whether conceivable or inconceivable: a "circular square" *cannot* be, we cannot imagine it, it is impossible. Necessity and contingency concern existence: whatever cannot but be is necessary, whatever may not be is contingent.

That said, we come back to the possibilities of non-manifestation question. Consideration of such possibilities—or, in any case, analogous possibilities—is necessary since we take into account the divine essence as an infinity of possibility, or, in Guénonian language, as universal Possibility. Guénon's argument seems, in this regard, identical to that of Thomas Aquinas: God being an infinity of possibility, it is impossible for this infinity to be exhausted by its created manifestation. "God," says St. Thomas, "knows things other than himself insofar as his essence is the likeness of the things that proceed from him.... But since ... the essence of God is of an infinite perfection, whereas every other thing has a limited being and perfection, it is impossible that the universe of things other than God equal the perfection of the divine essence."[80] So there is necessarily in God a non-quantitative multitude of possibles that will never be created beings and that St. Thomas calls "non-beings." These are pure possibilities that "God has decreed never to make."[81]

---

79 François Chenique, *Éléments de logique classique* (Paris: L'Harmattan, 2006), 150 ff; by the same author: *Sagesse chrétienne et mystique orientale*, 333-44.
80 *Contra Gentiles* (Pegis trans.), I, 66, §4; cf. our book *Penser l'analogie*, 89-117.
81 From *De la Vérité* [*Disputed Questions on Truth*], Question 2: "God's Knowledge," art. 8, answer (Paris: Cerf, 1996). It is in this book, remarkably translated into French and commented on by Father Serge Bonino, that St. Thomas dealt most with this theme.

But in St. Thomas this argument is also based on Scripture. St. Paul says in fact (Rom. 4:17): "[God] calls the non-beings as beings (*ta me onta os onta*)," which will be translated (Osty): "God calls those things that are not as if they were," that is to say: things that are not, God calls them into existence. But the Latin version—read by St. Thomas—*Deus vocat ea quae non sunt, tamquam ea quae sunt*, which is moreover a literal translation, can be read: "God calls the things that are not, as well as those that are." The "things that are," these are the beings that possess, have possessed, or will possess actual existence—that which is, has been, or will be created. Things "that are not" are the non-beings (*non entia*) that "neither are, nor will be, nor were," but "that are nevertheless in the power of God," since He "calls" them. Although devoid of created existence, they are not devoid of being: "Whatever he himself can do, all are known to God, although they are not actual."[82] "Privative possibilities," possibilities of absence are not involved here, as Schuon presupposes, but indeed possibles in a quite real sense, even though never existentiated. We can even say, given divine infinity, that they represent a domain incomparably more immense than that of actual creation. These non-beings God knows from a knowledge that theology calls "of simple intelligence," and not from a "knowledge of vision": God conceives them, but does not "see" them as He sees existing beings, although this distinction between two knowings only makes sense from the viewpoint of known objects: in itself the knowledge of God is one.[83]

One might agree that the doctrine of St. Thomas on the "possibilities of non-creation" (but this designation, as we will see, is a betrayal of Thomistic doctrine) seems oddly in accord with that of Guénon: "If one should ask," declares Guénon, "why all possibilities need not be manifested, that is, why there are at the same time both possibilities of manifestation and the possibilities of non-manifestation, it would suffice to answer that the domain of manifestation, being limited by the very fact that there is a totality of conditioned

---

82 *Summa Theologiae*, I, Q. 14, a. 9.
83 Ibid.

states—an indefinite multitude moreover—could not exhaust universal Possibility in its totality, for it excludes everything unconditioned, that is, precisely what matters most from the metaphysical point of view."[84] We could probably, with regard to universal possibility, have reservations about the relevance of an expression such as "in its totality," to the extent that infinity cannot be totalized, which would imply, it seems, its finitude. St. Thomas was quite aware of this difficulty. He asks the question: does God have a *comprehensive* knowledge of Himself, that is, a knowledge which embraces his essence in its totality? If yes, this essence is finite; if no, God, being infinite, does not have a full comprehension of Himself. He replies that, in God, being and intelligence are only one, and therefore the act of divine understanding does not enclose the infinite being that it "comprehends": it is strictly equal.[85]

Are pure possibles uncreatable?

Let us move on now to those language difficulties that are perhaps not unrelated to the all too facilely mathematical slant of Guénon's discourse, and consider these possibilities of non-manifestation "in themselves." Are these the "pure possibles" (*mere possibilia*) of scholastic tradition, the possibles considered independently of any relation to any existentiation whatsoever? It is clear, as the parallel we have drawn indicates, that there are many analogies between the doctrine of St. Thomas and Guénon's on this subject. We are not the first to point this out. Quite significantly, this connection was pointed out from the start, *even before* Guénon had laid out his thought in *The Multiple States of the Being* in 1932, by a friend, Noële Maurice-Denis, whom he had met in November 1915, at the Sorbonne, in Professor Gaston Milhaud's philosophy of science course, and with whom he maintained a correspondence of great philosophical interest from 1917 to 1924.[86] Noële Maurice-Denis who, in 1923, will add to the name of her father (the

---

84 *The Multiple States of the Being*, 15–16.
85 *Summa Theologiae*, I, Q. 4, a. 3.
86 Gabriel Afsar (*Études Traditionnelles*, n° 427, Sept.–Oct. 1971) announced the upcoming publication of around 40 letters and provided the first one (12-Aug-1917). Nothing has come of this.

painter Maurice Denis) that of her husband Robert Boulet, defended a thesis in scholastic philosophy (the first woman to obtain this doctorate) on *L'Être en puissance d'après Aristote et saint Thomas d'Aquin*, published in 1922.[87] We find in this work an echo of the intellectual exchanges, whether orally or by letter, kept up by the two friends. She writes in particular: "It is, it seems, in a sense very akin to Thomistic thinking on this subject [the notion of the possible] that the Brahmans of India distinguish within 'universal Possibility' both 'possibilities of non-manifestation' and 'possibilities of manifestation,' and this relationship does not seem devoid of interest."[88] In a more precise manner, and supported by more information (Guénon's work being known today in its entirety), François Chenique develops the same thesis in a study titled "The Possibilities of Non-Manifestation and the Pure Possibles."[89] After quoting some texts by Guénon, which, frankly, seem to protest

---

[87] Editions Marcel Rivière, 235 pages. The previous year, the same editor had published Guénon's *General Introduction to the Study of Hindu Doctrines*. Noële M.-D. Boulet also wrote reference works on the history of the liturgy and Christian archeology (Pius XII prefaced one of them). She died in 1969.

[88] Page 186. Noële M.-D. B. was therefore already well informed about the Guénonian vocabulary, since she provides us with the first written attestation of the notion of "possibility of non-manifestation," which Guénon, unless I am mistaken, will explicitly propound only in 1925 in *Man and His Becoming according to the Vedanta* (102, 150). This notion is certainly present in the first article of Guénon ("The Demiurge," *La Gnose*, Nov. 1909), but only implicitly. By attributing this concept, in a quite vague way, to the "Brahmins of India," without further clarification, Noële M.-D. B. is thus referring to Guénon in whom alone she sees an authorized interpreter of *Vedanta*. We can however ask if the *Vedanta* actually employs such a concept. The opposition *vyakta* / *avyakta*, "manifested / unmanifested" is quite classic, but the notion of "possible," in the sense of "principial reality," seems hardly worked out, even if found there (India speaks rather of "germ," *bîja*). It therefore seems obvious that Guénon, to formulate his metaphysics, borrowed the language of St. Thomas, thus conferring, on a supposedly Oriental theory, an allure acceptable to a European mentality. Conversely, Western theologians have been able to find in this exposition, besides great analogies, something to shed a brighter light on certain aspects of the doctrine of St. Thomas. This is probably the case with Fr. Sertillanges' quite important formula relating to God as "infinity of possibility," inasmuch as this illustrious theologian had 'given a 'favorable assessment' on the place of Guénon's metaphysics," according to a letter from Guénon to Noëlle M.-D. B. of January 3, 1918; according to Xavier Accart, *Guénon ou le renversement des clartés* (Paris: Archè Milano, 2005), 62.

[89] *Sagesse chrétienne et mystique orientale* (Paris: Dervy, 1996), chap. XVII.

against this interpretation, he concludes: "These possibilities of non-manifestation seem to be the same thing—if the word 'thing' is fitting—as the pure possibles or *mere possibilia* of the ancient theologians."[90]

We do not think, however, that such a comparison is warranted in all respects. We will, of course, grant that the terminology, on both sides, exhibits a close kinship—and for good reason—especially if we go into a little more detail than we have done so far about what the "pure possibles" are.

Literally, *mere possibilia* means "the purely possible" (*mere* is an adverb), that is, the possibles that are nothing but possibles. The Ideas or divine exemplars of everything that exists, has existed, or will exist in creation are called *possibilia*: these possibles therefore have a reality in God and also a created reality: either present, past, or future. The Ideas or exemplars that have eternally no other reality than that of divine possibles are called *mere possibilia*, "purely (or simply) possibles." This distinction, which is standard in theology, does not exactly correspond to that between beings and non-beings, as we indicated at the outset for the sake of simplicity. It should now be emphasized that, for St. Thomas, the name "non-beings" (*non entia*) happens to be applied to two kinds of objects: on the one hand, to what does not have existence currently, but which has existed or will exist, while on the other, to what never was, is not, and never will be.[91] Obviously, only the second kind of non-beings can be referred to as "purely possible," although, unless I am mistaken, the phrase *mere possibilia* is not found in St. Thomas or St. Bonaventure. The first kind of non-beings, which in God are *possibilia*, does not interest us directly here: it concerns the problem of future contingent beings and the knowledge that God has of them.

As for the second kind of non-beings, that of the *pure* possibles, it is precisely the concept that Christian theology has formed of them which does not allow us to identify them with Guénon's possibilities of non-manifestation. We say "Christian theology" because, in fact, it was a question debated by many

---

90 Op. cit., 343.
91 *De Veritate*, Question 2, art. 8; Bonino, *De la Vérité*, 303.

medieval thinkers. All, and in any case the greatest, envisaged nothing else, under the term "pure possible," than the *possibilities of creation* that will not be created: they are *creatables*, otherwise the very idea of the possible would lose its meaning. Certainly, there is some paradox in asserting the reality of a forever uncreated creatable. But we are forced to because, as we have said—and this is the argument that St. Thomas and St. Bonaventure return to tirelessly—no creation can exhaust the infinite richness of the divine essence: "Of those which neither have been, are, nor will be—which He has decreed never to make—He has a kind of speculative knowledge [knowledge of simple intelligence]. And although one can say that He sees these things as within His power, since there is nothing He cannot do,[92] it is more appropriate to say that He sees them in His goodness, the end of all that is made by Him; for He sees that there are many other ways of communicating His goodness, besides those He has already communicated to existing things, having existence, past, present, or future, because all created things cannot equal His goodness, no matter how much they seem to participate in it."[93]

The pure possibles of St. Thomas are therefore by no means (in Guénonian language) "unrealizables" or "non-manifestables," which would be equivalent to limiting *a priori* the divine omnipotence. It is not by virtue of their nature that they remain in the state of pure possibles, it is by virtue of the decree of the divine will. Thus is safeguarded the transcendent mystery of creation, which no human intellect can fathom, and which only the knowledge of God knows—knowledge that embraces the "things which are not, will not be, have not been, *but which can be (sed esse possunt)*."[94]

It is therefore not the nature of the pure possible that would somehow impose its law on the Creator: "Numerous entities, non-existent in the order of reality, are subject to the divine power. Now, whoever does some of the things that he can

---

[92] And therefore God could have created them.
[93] *De Veritate*, Question 2, art. 8; Bonino, *De la Vérité*, 305.
[94] *Quodlibetal Questions*, III, q. 2, a. 1; Bonino clarifies: "that is to say the pure possibilities that never exist *in sua propria*"; Bonino, *De la Vérité*, 583.

do, leaving others undone, acts by choice of His will, not by necessity of his nature. Therefore, God acts by His will, not by necessity of His nature."[95] Consequently, it cannot be said, according to the conception of St. Thomas, that "the pure possibles somehow 'preexist' in the knowledge that God has of his essence."[96] St. Thomas himself contests this opinion: "Our knowledge is received from things, and, by its nature, comes after them. But the Creator's knowledge of creatures, and the artist's of his products, by its very nature, precedes the things known. Now, when what is antecedent is removed, what is subsequent is likewise removed; but the opposite is not true. Hence, our knowledge of natural things cannot be had unless these things previously exist; but the actual existence or non-existence of a thing is a matter of indifference to the intellect of God or that of an artist."[97] The possibles, whether this involves relative possibles or pure possibles, are all modes according to which God knows that his essence is participable by creatures; they are all forms of the intelligibles existing in God as exemplars of his imitability: they are coeternal with the act by which the divine intellect knows them because they are one with it: "the intelligible species itself [the purely possible] is the divine intellect itself, and thus God understands Himself through Himself."[98]

Is not the possible "prime matter" an uncreatable?

However, Noële Maurice-Denis believed she could maintain that the pure possibles of St. Thomas, at least some of them, are not only eternally unrealized, but, by their very nature, are inherently unrealizable. "And yet, if all the possibles," she writes, "are not realized, neither are all realizable, and this for different reasons. Some possibles correspond to metaphysical principles uncreatable as such and in their pure state, even though necessary for the creation of certain beings (this is the case with prime matter), others, creatable in themselves,

---

95 *Summa contra Gentiles*, II, 23, 3; GF., 122.
96 François Chenique, op. cit., 343.
97 *De Veritate*, Question 2, art. 8; Bonino, *De la Vérité*, 304.
98 *Summa Theologiae*, I, Q. 4, a. 2.

are not so in fact... because they include an indeterminacy that is contrary to the mode by which God wills to create."[99] If this is true, we find ourselves in the presence of real possibilities of non-manifestation in Guénon's sense, and it is surely under his influence that Noële Maurice-Denis sought to draw Thomas to this side—all the while recognizing that "the thought of St. Thomas... little developed on this point, [has] remained mysterious."

But this interpretation seems quite problematic: it devalues a few perfectly explicit texts. St. Thomas even devoted an entire article of the *Summa Theologiae* to demonstrating that first (or "prime") matter is created; it is therefore impossible for him to classify it among the uncreatables. In Article 2 of Question 44 (Prima Pars), he asks: "Is primary matter created by God?" The answer is the following: God is cause not only of a being's form, something lacking in matter by itself, but also of being itself; but matter pertains to being, however negligible it may be; "thus it is necessary to say that also primary matter is created by the universal cause of things." And likewise, in Article 1 of Question 46, to those who maintain that neither matter nor heaven could be generated, he replies that "matter and heaven were produced into being by creation." This is true, and this is because prime matter is not created as an independent and separate reality, since it cannot exist all alone, but only as what is given shape by form, as the form's condition of existence (for all beings composed of form and matter): "if matter is in some manner something of being, it has been caused by God, it has been created, or rather co-created with the form."[100] Being created, or rather co-created, matter therefore has in God a model, an archetype, an Idea, which means that "possible-matter" is, in God, a certain mode of likeness to the divine essence: "matter," writes St. Thomas, "in a sense reflects the divine essence,"[101] because, although pure potentiality, it is not nothing, and, through its participation in being, has a likeness to God. "Although matter as

---

99 *L'Être en puissance selon Aristote et saint Thomas d'Aquin*, 185–86.
100 *De Veritate*, Question 2; Bonino, *De la Vérité*, 234.
101 *Quaestio de Potentia*, q. 3, a. 1, ad 13; *On the Power of God*, 87.

regards its potentiality recedes from likeness to God, yet, even insofar as it has being in this wise, it retains a certain likeness to the divine being."[102] This is why it possesses its Idea in God, inseparable however from the Idea of the hylomorphic compound (that is, the Idea of "matter and form"): we cannot consider matter *in itself*: "Since, however, we hold matter to be created by God, though not apart from form, matter has its Idea in God; but not apart from the Idea of the composite [of matter and form]; for matter in itself can neither exist, nor be known."[103] Thus, matter being created (or rather concreated), its Idea (insofar as a divine possible) would not be that of an uncreatable. We cannot therefore classify this Idea among the number of eternally uncreated "pure possibles." As for these pure possibles, which are not exemplars of any created realities, neither are they, as we have seen, uncreatables: "When it comes to what is not, will not be, and has not been, God has no practical knowledge [relative to their created actualization], except virtually (*nisi virtute tantum*), of things which neither are, nor will be, nor have been."[104]

That only divine freedom draws a line of demarcation between creatables.

True, one might wonder if the notion of a creatable eternally uncreated is indeed understandable. Regarding the beings of nature, it does not seem so: it is impossible that what can be produced is never produced,[105] assuming a long enough time. In the divine order, however, the same is not true. On the one hand, the consideration of divine infinity requires

---

102 *Summa Theologiae*, I, Q. 4, a. 11, ad 3.
103 *Summa Theologiae*, I, Q. 15, a. 3, ad 3. What is the Idea of matter in God? We could view it as the archetype of all likeness, as the possible "likeness," the principle of divine imitability as such, or, at least, as a mode or aspect of this imitability, that is, basically, of "principial otherness": matter, by offering form the possibility of its created actuation, makes it "emerge" from its purely intelligible identity. We are referring here to pages 357–60 of *Love and Truth*.
104 *Summa Theologiae*, I, Q. 15, a. 3, ad 2.
105 *Summa Theologiae*, I, Q. 48, a. 2. The same thesis is found in Aristotle: *On the Heavens*, I, 12, 283a24; trans. W. K. C. Guthrie (Cambridge, MA: Harvard University Press, 1960), 125. In a slightly different sense, cf. Leibniz, *Discours de métaphysique et autres textes* (Paris: Flammarion, 2001), 327–33.

us to admit that no creation can exhaust the possibilities of likeness according to which God is participable; this is the primary and strongest reason invoked by theology in favor of the existence of pure possibles. On the other hand, since pure possibilities are creatables (eternally uncreated) we must appeal to the free decision of God, that is, to his will, for drawing a line of demarcation between uncreated creatables and created creatables, and not to the nature of each possible, since, *a priori* and with regard to creatability, there is nothing to distinguish the one from the other. By positing divine freedom at the root of the created's being, we take into account the contingency of the creature that does not have its raison d'être in itself, that is, in its determinate nature (its essence), in other words in the nature of the possible that it manifests.

We might also wonder if this is not the only coherent solution, contrary to Guénon, who declares: "every possibility that is a possibility of manifestation must necessarily be manifested by that very fact... inversely, any possibility that is not to be manifested is a possibility of non-manifestation."[106]

If this is so, if the possibilities of non-manifestation are *by themselves* (and not by a divine decree) *impossibilities of manifestation*, what is the benefit then, in order to take into account their principial reality, of drawing arguments from the infinity of universal possibility in opposition to the finitude of manifestation? However, as we have seen, this is what Guénon does; but this is unnecessary, since the specific nature of these paradoxical "possibilities" is enough to explain their absence in manifestation. Otherwise, to say that the uncreatables cannot belong to creation is sheer tautology: this does not clarify anything. For the finitude of the created to exclude from itself a set of possibles, these possibles would have to be creatable.

As we have already hinted, this appeal to divine freedom can seem an evasion coupled with anthropomorphism. But is any human discourse capable of saying more about it? Recognizing the limits of our speculations, implicitly acknowledged in the recourse to God's unfathomable decisions, is always preferable to pseudo-solutions of an overly formal metaphysics. This

---

106 *Multiple States of the Being*, 15.

recognition of limits introduces into doctrinal discourse a reserve and reverence that explicitly deals with the inexpressible portion. Of course, Guénon does not forget this portion, he even mentions it on numerous occasions. However, his discourse, which tries to be supreme and unsurpassable, rather gives the impression of leaving nothing unsaid. As for anthropomorphism, it obviously needs to be corrected, as much as possible, by virtue of analogy: insofar as will and freedom are perfections, they necessarily belong to God in a supereminent way that has only an analogical relationship to what we experience by these terms.[107] Moreover, the dependence of the created creature on the divine decree of existentiation—a non-reciprocal relationship, says St. Thomas—conveys the radical contingency of all created existence. Why one particular creatable is created, and not another, amounts to asking: why is this or that being what it is? To this question there is no answer: at the root of creation stands something unintelligible, a secret belonging only to God.[108]

With Guénon, to the contrary, everything is regulated by an iron logic, a kind of necessitarism quite close to that of Spinoza, at least in some respects. On the one hand, all possibles are endowed with a determinate nature that controls the destiny of each of them, radically distinguishing them from each other and thus forming them into a kind of principial (non-quantitative)

---

[107] Christ speaks of the will of the Father: this apodictically founds the attribution of will to God. Guénon also gives a metaphysical meaning to the notion of freedom (in the last chapter of *Multiple States*). But his presentation harbors obscurities, as André Conrad showed in issue num. 49 of the *Cahiers de l'Herne*. The "god-ish" perspective (the exoteric perspective for Guénon) enables us, on the contrary, to consider a kind of transcendence of God in God who frees his absoluteness from any subjection to determinations, even the most essential.

[108] To enter into this secret, one must renounce the *why*. A Christian Platonist, concerned about the raison d'être of a creature, finds it in the Ideas or divine possibles. This ascent is all well and good. But then what about after that? Can we still ask: why the principial rose? This is an unanswerable question, a question that confronts us with an essential contingency. To renounce the why is to renounce thinking, which always says "what?" or "why?" To think something is to think about its possibility. Having attained the essences, thought shuts its eyes and is silent. Stunned by the supreme thusness of everything, thinking finds itself delivered from itself.

multiplicity; on the other hand, here God has, in a way, nothing more to do: the manifestable manifests itself by virtue of its nature, and conversely for the non-manifestable.[109]

The difficulties of a totalizing metaphysics.

Is this logic flawless? We spoke of a formal metaphysics; it seems in any case "totalizing" in nature. Guénon defines wholes, or sets, according to a hierarchy of envelopes whose consistency does not seem easy to grasp. We can also wonder if the wholes thus defined correspond to realities (have an ontological meaning)—which would seem natural—or rather are only classifying categories with nominal value and purely "specular" in nature, that is, relating to considerations of "viewpoint."

He envisions two sets, the unmanifest and the manifested. "Non-manifestation contains both what we may call the unmanifestable, that is, the possibilities of non-manifestation, and the manifestable, that is, the possibilities of manifestation insofar as they are not manifested."[110] That is clear, but things get complicated when it comes to Being. Being is "the principle of manifestation" (this is admissible, even if we can see in it infinitely more than what is seen here by Guénon); and, the metaphysician continues, "*at the same time*" it includes within itself "all the possibilities of manifestation... *but only insofar as they are actually manifested.* Outside of being are, therefore, all the rest, that is, all the possibilities of non-manifestation, as well as the possibilities of manifestation themselves insofar as they are in the unmanifested state; and included among these is Being itself," since, as a principle, it cannot come forward.[111] This sentence is obscure. "Outside of Being," says Guénon, are the possibilities of non-manifestation that "include" Being itself, since, as a principle, it is not manifestable. Therefore Being is somehow outside of itself, it is excluded from its own

---

109 Guénon clearly affirms the contingency of manifestation in chapter 17 of his book, but this is a contingency of principle which does not affect the *esse* of the created.
110 *Multiple States of the Being*, 21. The manifestable, in its unmanifest state, is what Guénon calls "pure possibilities," carefully distinguished from the possibilities of non-manifestation: ibid., 88.
111 Ibid., 20.

possibility. And that is not all. A little further on, we read that "the manifestation obviously contains only the totality of the possibilities of manifestation insofar as they are manifested."[112] This is self-evident, but we are somewhat perplexed to realize that what is said now about the manifestation is exactly the same as what was said about Being a few lines earlier, namely that it "includes the possibilities of manifestation *only insofar as they are actually manifested*," even though Being itself is included in the unmanifestable. It would be understandable if we were told that unmanifested Being contains within itself the possibilities of manifestation insofar as not manifested, as is ever the case for the "Possibles." But, however incomprehensible, that is not what Guénon says. There are undoubtedly deep mysteries here, but despite his legendary clarity, Guénon hardly helps us glimpse them. The totalizing logic he uses seems to conceal some contradiction.

This is why we are inclined to assume that the categories Guénon uses are rather points of view, perspectives, ways of looking at things without ontological bearing, classificatory instances; in short, pertain to the specular mode. This would explain how the same set of possibles can belong to two different classes depending on whether one considers it from one point of view or the other. Thus, for example, we have the manifestable: when it does not manifest itself, it belongs to the non-manifested, and when it manifests, it belongs to manifestation. This is exactly what Guénon says, as we just saw. We will then ask two questions. First, what are we saying when we say that the manifestable, insofar as unmanifested, belongs to the unmanifested? Nothing; this is sheer tautology and redundancy: the unmanifested belongs to the unmanifested. Second, if this interpretation, in terms of point of view, is correct, it follows that these are the very same entities (i.e., possibilities of manifestation) that are being considered either as manifested or as unmanifested: the point of view does not change their nature. Should we therefore admit that the two *states* of the manifestable about which Guénon is speaking (a state of manifestation and a state of non-manifestation) differ

---

112 Ibid., 21.

only according to the point of view from which we consider them? But is this consistent with what he said previously, namely that the belonging of a possible to the manifested or to the non-manifest was solely a function of its nature? And, with this mention of nature, we leave behind the specular or "perspectival" interpretation to return to an ontological one. Now, since it is the nature of the possible that determines its membership in a set, should we not conclude that, to belong to the set of the unmanifested, the possibilities of manifestation must be, by nature, possibilities of non-manifestation?

We have not pursued this line of questioning—at the risk of tiring even the most indulgent reader—for the pleasure of raising objections, but to put a finger on the extreme difficulty of a presentation that sheds light only sparingly.

Many of the difficulties raised here would have been less, it seems, if Guénon had used less mathematical and more philosophical language, for example if he had better taken into account the meaning of the concept of possibility and reduced the importance of classification into manifestable and unmanifestable (but he was surely forced to do so for lack of a firm doctrine of *creation*). For, that there is an unmanifested state of the possibilities of manifestation, this is obvious and implied in the simple notion of *possibles*, which, in the state of possibles, exist only in God. And that is enough, without it being necessary to deploy the complicated, and sometimes acrobatic, apparatus of all these sets which, at the same time, both include and exclude each other. In truth, the possibilities of manifestation, as possibilities, are always unmanifested.

The same goes for Being, at least such as Guénon views it and which is basically only an ontocosmological reduction of the *esse* of St. Thomas, but which actually corresponds to a certain aspect of things; the paradox we have pointed out would be mitigated by positing this "Being" as an intermediary, an "isthmus" between the Uncreated and the created, as the polarization or principial punctualization of the Uncreated with a view to the existence of all things. Unmanifested qua principle, It confers its ontological mark on all existing things qua existentiator, which therefore belong to It and, in a certain way, are comprised within It. We can see why Guénon attributes to his "Being" only the manifestables insofar as they manifest. In some respects, the Guénonian Being is only the Being *of* manifestation, for the manifestables, insofar as they are manifested, are no longer manifestable but *manifested*. And the transcendence of Being, so often affirmed by Guénon, seems to fade into specular ideality from one point of view, from one aspect. According to him, the distinctions we make between Non-Being and Being, the unmanifested and the manifested, "far from being irreducible, exist only from the very relative point of view through which they are established, and... they acquire this contingent existence, the only existence of which they are capable, solely in the measure in which we ourselves bestow it by our conception."[113] Some will contend perhaps that we are talking about ideality, or even idealism here, and will object that, for a relative and contingent being, the point of view from which these distinctions are made is no less real, since it is precisely that of the human being that we are. Of course. Yet to be able to take this "point of view" into consideration, it is already necessary to make a distinction between the unmanifested and the manifested states of the human being that we are, therefore to be already subject to the illusion for which, we are told, the human point of view is responsible. In short, this is either a vicious circle, or a *regressus ad indefinitum*.

We could even address these matters in another way. Where is Guénon when he describes the distinction between degrees of reality and their supreme non-distinction? Does he have at his disposal an observatory (a "point of view") that would enable him to see both from the point of view of the human being and from the point of view of Non-Being? So, is there a super-point of view, that of Guénon, from which we encompass both the relative and the Absolute? Yes, a reader may be subconsciously persuaded. Sitting in his armchair, *The Multiple States of the Being* in hand, he contemplates in spirit both the Absolute from the point of view from which all distinctions are abolished, and the relative human one from which they are made. As for the reader, he has forgotten that this was itself

---

113 Ibid., 65.

only one point of view; this point of view is truly nowhere to be found and enjoys an all-seeing privilege to which, however, as a human being, Guénon has forbidden him access. In summary, just as there is no catalog to contain all the catalogs, likewise there is no whole for all the wholes.[114]

It is true that the all-seeing point of view, which embraces both the manifested and the unmanifested, might be based on what Guénon says about "descending realization."[115] According to A. K. Coomaraswamy, cited by Guénon, "one has not reached the end of the road until one knows *Atma* as Manifested and Unmanifested." It is therefore necessary to know *Atma* not only in itself, but also as it "radiates" into manifestation. In other words—and this is "descending realization"—it is necessary to realize "*Atma* embodied in the worlds." This teaching is all the more admissible in its principle as it does not seem unrelated to what Christ teaches in St. Matthew (6:33): "Seek first the Kingdom of God and his justice, and all these things shall be added unto you," which can be interpreted metaphysically as "Seek first the Absolute—and the relative will be given to you in addition." In a certain manner, the word of Christ is more synthetic than Coomaraswamy's commentary on the *Katha Upanishad*: it grasps things another way. The *Vedanta* seemingly teaches that, beyond the knowledge of *Atma* in itself, of the One as such, there is the knowledge of *Atma* present in things, "embodied" and "radiant": we know first the manifested manifold, next we ascend to unmanifested *Atma*, finally we descend back to the manifested while discerning the presence of *Atma* radiating in manifestation. Christ, more radically, tells us: this multiple, this relative, this world of creatures you think you know and own, but which you also experience as ever fleeing and escaping from you, it will only be *given* to you from the knowledge of the One-Absolute, only if you enter the Kingdom of the Father who contains within Himself all things, all relativity; it will be given to you in the manner of a grace, of an addition of knowledge, inasmuch as the truth is—and this

---

114 Cf. *The Crisis of Religious Symbolism*, 330–41.
115 "Ascending and descending realization," chap. 32 of *Initiation and Spiritual Realization* (Ghent, NY: Sophia Perennis, 2001), 167–79.

is in our eyes a fundamental metaphysical axiom—that only the More, and the infinite Beyond-More, "can do" the least.

However that may be, and now returning to the text of Guénon, it is clear that the notion of "descending realization" towards the manifested is difficult to reconcile with the affirmations concerning the nullity of the manifested compared to the unmanifested. While we might read in *The Multiple States of the Being*: "one must never lose sight of the fact that... from the standpoint of the Infinite the entirety of manifestation is strictly nil,"[116] we now learn that, far from being abolished from the point of view of the Supreme Self, the manifested, for the one who wants to go to the end of the way, must be known by descent into its own truth.

Correlatively hard to reconcile are the declarations on the non-existence, with regard to Non-Being, of the *specular* distinction between manifested and non-manifested. Far from being a mere optical effect, linked only to the human point of view, this distinction remains, since there is a descent, even for the one who has attained the knowledge of the Supreme Self, even though the manifested to which he must now return assumes from that point another meaning. Guénon was well aware of this discrepancy, which he tried to mitigate, but in a rather embarrassed manner, by declaring "one cannot say finally that the manifested is strictly negligible."[117]

What about God then?

The notion of the possibility of non-manifestation therefore offers formidable difficulties for thought; so far we have only touched on a few.

However, according to Guénon, we are able to conceive of them. For example, we "can conceive of that possibility which is the void, or any other possibility of the same order," such as silence, darkness, or the metaphysical zero (the four unmanifestables mentioned by Guénon); but we cannot conceive of them "in distinctive mode."[118] Indeed, with the unmanifes-

---

116 Page 72.
117 *Initiation and Spiritual Realization*, 169.
118 *Multiple States of the Being*, 24.

tables, we are at the level of Non-Being, that is, of the Supreme *Brahma* (*Parabrahma*), who Guénon and the Vedanta teach is *nirvishesha*, "beyond all distinctions."[119] However, the very way in which Guénon speaks of them implies their differentiation and therefore their distinction: these are, he says, so many "aspects" of Non-Being, "each being one of the possibilities that it contains."[120]

In fact, if we read the text carefully, we realize that the non-manifestable is only conceivable from the manifestable. Guénon explains, in a remarkable way, the relationship that speech maintains with silence, and concludes: "The relationship that is thus established between (non-manifested) silence and (manifested) speech shows how it is possible to conceive of possibilities of non-manifestation that correspond by analogical transposition to certain possibilities of manifestation, without our claiming in any way, even here, to introduce into Non-Being an actual distinction."[121] In fact, the formula "by analogical transposition" is disconcerting at first glance: a transposition is usually effected from the bottom up; here it seems to be the reverse: by analogical transposition the non-manifestable that is silence would correspond to the manifestation which is speech. Unless the formula (but the construction is then less natural) refers to "certain possibilities of manifestation," which would be metaphysically more understandable. In this case, it would be the possible (manifestable) "speech" which, analogically transposed, would correspond to the possible (non-manifestable) "silence." It seems that this was Guénon's thought, despite the ambiguity of its formulation: "speech," he states, "is nothing but silence expressed," which is quite correct, but silence "is also something more (and even infinitely more)"; in other words, silence is not only "the spoken word unexpressed," but also "the inexpressible."[122]

---

119 *Man and His Becoming according to Vedanta*, 1974, 26. Shankara, *Prolégomènes au Védânta*, I, 5th section, § 12, and 6th section, § 11; trans. Louis Renou (Paris: Adrien Maisonneuve, 1951), 55, 69.
120 *Multiple States of the Being*, 24.
121 Ibid., 24-25.
122 Ibid., 24.

We agree. However, what does this mean? Do we come to understand what a possibility of non-manifestation is? Should we use such a notion to account for what is "the inexpressible"? That the inexpressible *might* be expressed by speech is a truism. But here we have something more interesting: is the possibility "speech" expressed by manifested speech? Certainly not. Every manifested word is only a distant and deficient image, an echo, of uncreated speech, of the speech-essence. The proof is that this essential and principial Speech is the divine Word, Speech in the Principle that, *as such*, cannot be manifested ("No one has seen God at any time," John 1:18), but that, by that very fact, is, in the order of nature, the source of innumerable manifestations of itself, at the same time that, in the order of grace, it is "pronounced," indirectly "at sundry times and in diverse manners" (Heb. 1:1), and, directly, in Christic form.

This is then the "speech" possibility—and that is true for all the possibles—which, as such, is inexpressible. It is the manifestable in its entirety which, as such, in its state of a simple "possible," of a Divine Idea, is non-manifested. In short, the possibilities of manifestation, qua possibilities, are as unmanifestable as the Guénonian unmanifestable.[123] That which is manifested, that which we see in our world, are not these possibilities, but the creatures for which these possibilities are the divine exemplars. We are entitled to conclude that all possibles, whether they are pure possibles or relative possibles, are creatables, either forever uncreated or exemplars of creatures. God being an infinity of possibility, he is, by that very fact, an infinity of creatability.

But then a rather dizzying question arises: does it not follow, since in God everything is God, that the divine essence is posited, in principle, as infinitely creatable? Here we have a "catastrophic" consequence, which by itself alone would be enough to wreck the entire process we followed in the school of Christian theology: God, by definition, is uncreatable, or else he is not God. Should we therefore, in spite of everything,

---

123 In this sense, Guénon's possibilities of non-manifestation are comparable to the pure possibles of Scholasticism—Chenique's thesis—which is basically legitimate. But Guénon would have surely rejected it.

come back to Guénon's radically uncreatables, which themselves have at least the merit of preserving the transcendence of the supreme Principle? We do not think so, for here is the essential reason: it is precisely because it is *infinitely participable* that the divine essence remains *infinitely transcendent* to any participation, which is by definition always finite; we could say, in purely metaphysical terms, that absolute transcendence strictly implies infinite immanence. Besides, as we have seen, if there were possibles in God imparticible *by nature*, it would be illogical to also invoke the finitude of creation to account for their existence: the question, for these imparticipables, should not even be posited. In other words, God has no need for the theologian or metaphysician to preserve his transcendence; if we might dare to say, transcendence risks nothing. The infinite Good is infinitely diffusive of itself, or again, as St. John says, God is love, and by that very fact he infinitely overflows all his outpourings of love. So there is no contradiction in theological doctrine, provided one goes right to the end of its course and that we envision it in its radicality. It does not shut in on itself the concept of God, isolating it in its own reserved realm forbidden to any creature. To the contrary, it opens it infinitely to the totality of creation that, by that very fact, finds itself integrally included and transcended there. The divine essence, thus considered in its infinite Ipseity, is not the metaphysical "place" where all creation is obliterated, where all manifestation is "strictly annulled,"[124] but the place where creation gains access to its true reality.[125]

---

[124] *Man and His Becoming according to the Vedanta*, 26.
[125] This major metaphysical point has been addressed in several of our books, notably *The Sense of the Supernatural*, trans. G. J. Champoux (Edinburgh: T & T Clark, 1998), 132–40, and *Penser l'analogie*, 96–109. Guénon has spoken very negatively at times on the subject of love. *Caritas* seems to have for him only a moral and social sense, emotional in nature. At best, he says, "it can be understood, as do the Arabs, in the sense of 'cosmic charity'" (and, we will add, certain Christian theologians); but ultimately, "its sentimental and affective character is manifest; and the word love that you annex to it further confirms this impression" (to N. Maurice-Denis, Feb. 16, 1919; M. F. James, *Ésotérisme et christianisme*, 191). He spoke more positively of love in his 1926 article, "Radiating Heart and Flaming Heart" (*Écrits pour Regnabit*, ed. P. L. Zoccatelli [Milan: Arche, 1999], 65–67), although this view is much attenuated

Conversely, one might wonder whether the Guénonian conception risks, not in his declared intentions, but by his—very surprising indeed—expository style, conveying a kind of obliteration of the divine Principle. Certainly, the few references to the doctrines of India found in *The Multiple States of the Being* can persuade the reader that the subject matter of this book is what the major sacred traditions of mankind speak about, and therefore, basically, about God. This is, however, a predetermined—by mental habits of "religious" (origin)—reading of a work that does not ever, so to speak, mention the word "God"; or, when it does, the author finds it necessary to apologize, and to clarify that he is expressing himself in "theological terms...only to facilitate comparison with the customary points of view of Western thought."[126] But whoever truly enters into this metaphysical perspective has to renounce these habits and cease translating spontaneously, and as if unconsciously, terms like Infinity, universal Possibility, Non-Being, and Being into theological language, that is, as terms designating a unique reality called God and the metaphysical concepts for which they are simply expressing different aspects. In short, we must cease giving these names a divine referent. Guénon does not speak *of* Someone, of the One who the Catholic religion calls God, and who, in any case, transcends every mode of expression, of that Someone who subsists outside all language, the preeminent Other of all language through whom we leave behind all discourse. Guénon speaks to us about *states of being*. What being, we ask? Nowhere does he ask this question, nowhere does he answer it. Guénonian discourse is without referent, or rather is self-referential, not only in the sense in which Guénon often cites his own works, but in the much more radical sense in which it is established in itself by itself, in the sense that for itself it is its own basis: there is no "outside" to this book. Is the being about which he speaks man, is it God, is it any being whatsoever? It is all of these at once, indifferently, and "man"

---

in the second version of the article for *Études Traditionnelles*, June–July 1946 (*Symbols of Sacred Science*, 403).

126 *The Multiple States of the Being*, 94, fn 13.

himself is moreover only one state among an indefinite number of other states, such as "God," and to the exact extent that it might be useful to give a meaning to this term, that is, assign it a referent. Moreover, to pose the question: what is this book about? is to leave the strict metaphysical perspective that he offers and therefore prove that we have not understood it. In short, Infinity, Possibility, Non-Being, and Being are only states of being, and only designate instances of the different degrees of being. They are not discrete entities having their own and transcendent contents; these are the various hierarchical categories of an "anonymous" real, and this is why these are basically only points of view.

Such is, we believe, the true meaning of the Guénonian approach when considered in its seldom perceived radicality. It requires, if we understand this correctly, a total uprooting of the reader's being, an integral and ontological "deconditioning," which causes it to lose all its bearings, all its foundations, its bedrock, all its existential *situs*, and plunges it, suspended from nothing, into the indefinite immensity of a reality without name or gravity, the universal spherical vortex.[127]

If the readers of Guénon had a clearer awareness of what is being proposed to them, no doubt they would be less readily admiring. For, in truth, such a "shift," such an ontological disorientation (and not just a cultural one), have something dizzying about it. The surface of Guénonian discourse, always serene and clear, is like the surface of still water—still, but concealing fearsome depths. In this regard, one might wonder about the role played by capital letters in his discourse. From a strictly linguistic point of view, infinite, possibility, non-being, being, existence, &c., are common names expressing simple concepts of a philosophical nature. To write them in this lower case way would more openly reveal the specular character of the Guénonian exposition as we have just described it, and therefore also the difficulties of assimilation that it presents for a Western understanding spontaneously inclined to "theologize" everything that goes beyond the domain of

---

127 Cf. René Guénon, *Symbolism of the Cross*, chap. 20, 101–3.

nature. In adorning these terms with a capital letter, Guénon transforms them into metaphysical "divinities," for which they become the proper name, thus conferring on them the reality of principial entities: if every name is a noun, the proper noun is superlatively so and *a fortiori* creates a noun out of whatever it designates. Hence what, in a philosophical discourse, would pass for a simple abstraction, can take on the appearance of a quasi-theological term and make it easier to accept. No deception is involved here—Guénon is sincere—but better to avoid any ambiguity: how does one invite Westerners to a sacred uplifting of the "words of the tribe," without clothing these words in the Western form of the sacred that is always more or less "god-ish" in nature? In other words, Guénon speaks indeed of metaphysics, but in "religious" language. On the one hand, in doing so, he induces his readers to forget that this is only a speculative discourse and suggests that these notions have a mysterious and transcendent background. On the other hand, because they are purely intellectual metaphysical notions, and therefore transparent and universal, he deems he has given proof of the superiority of a metaphysical viewpoint over a theological one, which will be nothing but the metaphysical viewpoint's reduction to a particular revelation.

This "god-ish" sacralization of metaphysical concepts[128] is strikingly indicated in the way Guénon presents the "subsumptive" capacity of the categories of Non-Being, Being, or universal Possibility. These categories intervene in a discourse where they play a very active role (they "include," they "exclude," they "determine," &c.) as true metaphysical deities. No doubt we must take into account the constraints imposed by syntax: whenever one or another of these categories is the subject of an action verb, we necessarily attribute to it the value of an

---

128 It not only concerns Western theology but also applies to Eastern mytho-theology: Infinity and Possibility, specifies Guénon, "these are Brahma and Shakti" (*The Multiple States of the Being*, 12, fn 13). Certainly. But what is interpreting what? Is it Infinity that is a proxy for *Brahma*, and Possibility for his *Shakti*, which are then only symbolic terms, or the reverse? Some will retort that this is the same reality. Yes, probably, but not quite: Brahma says something that Infinity does not say and that sets us more immediately in the presence of divine mystery.

agent and, therefore, of a real being, for, following the scholastic adage *actiones sunt supposititorum*, "actions are characteristic of supposits," that is, of "personal beings." We thus risk forgetting that they are only the designations of different degrees of reality, and that they do not exist as discrete entities. Even if Guénon is sometimes careful to speak, not of Being, but of "the degree of pure Being"[129]—which seems to indicate that "pure Being" denotes a determinate degree of reality—the ambiguity remains to the extent that the term "Being" is adorned with a capital letter, which confers upon it the denotative meaning of *a* being. If we add that this "Being" is elsewhere identified with "*Ishvara*," the Lord creator of the Hindu tradition,[130] which can be rendered "the least inaccurately" by "God,"[131] one will agree that there is enough here to make us waver and lean towards the "god-ish" interpretation, if we had not been warned that this would be a "false interpretation leading to the substitution of 'a being' for pure Being."[132]

Thus, and unless we are mistaken, the Guénonian account oscillates between a possible "god-ish" presentation and a purely metaphysical one where the various degrees designated have only a specular significance, that is, are only points of view, even though the fact of identifying them by capital letters and entrusting them with the role of active subjects leads us almost irresistibly to endow them with some sort of objective reality. However, in the final analysis, it is metaphysical specularity that carries the day, if we get to the bottom of the matter; and, by the same stroke, conversely, the solidarity that unites the ontological with the theological is confirmed. Basically, the Guénonian doctrine is a radical non-theism.

A metaphysics of knowledge.

One is surely tempted to ask: what justifies such a perspective? What is it based on? To which Guénonian purists will answer that this question does not have to be posed:

---

129 *Multiple States of the Being*, 4.
130 *Man and His Becoming according to Vedanta*, 100 and passim.
131 Ibid., 19. Note that in Sanskrit there is no capital letter.
132 Ibid., 24, fn 3.

this perspective is based on itself and by itself; so be it. It is however not forbidden to wonder, not about the basis of the doctrine, but about its meaning, were it only to come to a more accurate awareness of it. At the end of our analyses carried out so far, the answer seems clear: the Guénonian approach can be characterized, not as a metaphysics of being, but as a metaphysics of knowledge, that is, gnosis.

It is true that, in *The Multiple States of the Being*, Guénon divides up the many degrees of being in an apparently objective sense, distinguishing between different orders of entities. But he is also careful to point out, where applicable, that these degrees only exist as a function of point of view. Scalar ontology is thus gradually transformed little by little into a specular ontology, if one can still speak of ontology. In any case, this orientation becomes evident when it comes to the last chapters of the book, where Guénon expounds "The Realization of the Being through Knowledge" (chap. 15) and the relationship between "knowledge and consciousness" (chap. 16).

We spoke earlier about a shift, an ontological disorientation, to which specularity invited the knowing subject. Quite exactly, this means that it is necessary to renounce any referential relation, to free oneself from all ties (cf. the "delivered in life") thanks to which we can situate ourselves—and we always situate ourselves in relation to a certain order of reality. So here we are, suspended in the infinite void, without reference, without compass bearings, without determination. In our experience is there anything that corresponds, even remotely, to this state of absolute *untetheredness*? Certainly, at least in some respects: it is the act of knowledge, considered in itself as intellection. Every being in this world is located somewhere (and not only in the physical sense of the term). But, to the extent that knowledge is the common act of the knower and the known, in this act the subject is no longer in itself, since, in a certain manner, it becomes the object, and the object is no longer in itself since, in a certain manner, it is in the subject. And this miracle that is knowledge, all knowledge, is realized by the miracle of intelligence. Where is the intellect as such (and not in its empirical, cerebral or psychological conditioning)? It is "outside the world," and that is why it is universal. Intelligence is the non-subject, it is openness, emptiness, the gap that the Creator opens in the subject by blowing into his face the spiracle of life, the "nostril" through which the world, leaving its existential *situs*, can enter the order of knowledge and give birth to the intelligible. Therefore, if we cease considering knowledge in its transitivity, in the movement by which the subject passes to the object, and we envision it *in itself*, in its pure possibility, we can say that we experience "something" of the inherently non-situated, freed from any location, and non-referential. Or, more exactly, it is knowledge itself that becomes the sole reference point. It is no longer objective being that determines knowledge, it is knowledge that makes out of possible being a determinate being and that therefore understands and exceeds it. This is exactly what Guénon means when he speaks of "realization through knowledge." Perhaps we will be tempted to see in this formula only the designation of one mode of spiritual realization among others. But there is more. Guénon also means that what knowledge realizes is reality itself. In other words, the term "reality" truly makes sense only as a function of knowledge.

Quite significantly, this teaching is given at the end of *The Multiple States of the Being*, in the chapter "Knowledge and Consciousness."[133] "Knowing" and "being," says Guénon, "are the two faces of a single reality." Then he adds: "At this point we should clarify somewhat how the metaphysical identity of the possible and the real should be understood [this refers to the beginning of the book where the author announces (17, fn 7) that he will subsequently give a more precise meaning to the word 'real']. Since everything possible is realized by knowledge, this identity, taken universally, properly constitutes truth in itself, for the latter can be conceived precisely as the perfect adequation of knowledge to total Possibility." We must therefore, if we are to really enter into this doctrine, stop considering objective being, the object of knowing, as a reality preceding the act that becomes aware of it. Objective being

---

133 Page 82.

only gains access to the order of the real through the realizing agency of knowledge. Prior to this awareness, objective being, in all rigor, is only a possible. By "objective being" is meant, not only that which falls within the domain of Existence or Pure Being, but also that which pertains to Non-Being, it being admitted that "being" is in this case apprehended "in its analogical and symbolic sense,"[134] a remark frequently repeated under the pen of Guénon, "obliged" as he is "to retain this same term in such a case for want of a more adequate one, but we attribute to it only the purely analogical and symbolic meaning without which it would be quite impossible to speak in any way of these matters."[135]

And indeed we have to recognize that there can be a kind of lie or at least illusion in all metaphysical discourse with an ontological focus, to the extent that it deals with something of which we have no actual experience: we believe that we have attained to the very things themselves, when, with our words, we are only wielding concepts. For all that, does it follow that we are doomed to agnosticism? Of course not. It is even necessary to combat with the utmost energy any thesis that, when it comes to the metaphysical order, argues that we cannot attain to any truth. Quite the contrary, just the idea of an eternal, infinite, and almighty God communicates to our mind something of his reality. However, it must also be recognized that this knowledge, certain in its conclusions, does not procure for us an actual experience of its object, that is, does not set us directly in its presence. In short, in ordinary knowledge, the metaphysical object is not given in its very reality, even though it is aimed at with certainty through the mediation of the concept. This mediate and indirect knowledge ("darkly

---

134 *Multiple States of the Being*, 82.
135 Ibid., 4. Guénon obviously attributes this obligation to Western languages unsuited to the expression of metaphysical ideas. That does not seem to us to be a foregone conclusion. Every human language, when it speaks, speaks *about* something (this is its denotativity) and therefore sets it up as an *objective being* (*Histoire et théorie du symbole*, 133–49). Besides, is it not curious to see Guénon invoke the *purely* symbolic nature of a term, thus relieving it of its proper meaning, he who has taught us, to the contrary, that only symbolism would bestow on signs their true reality?

and in a mirror," says St. Paul, 1 Cor. 13:12) does not allow its object to be fully "realized," in the dual sense of this term: in English *to realize* means "to become aware," "to render account," and in French "to realize [*réaliser*]," means to "accomplish," "to make real and actual." This is then ordinary and mediate knowledge, once its nature is recognized, which of itself calls for a higher knowledge, for a sacred knowledge through which what was only glimpsed becomes actually and fully real, and which thereby confers on the word "reality" its true meaning.

However, the dependence of "reality" on knowledge should not, in principle, be interpreted in the sense of classical idealism. This does not in any case endow awareness, or knowledge, with an existentiating or even creative power. We do not start here with the knowing subject posited in its solitude, in the manner of Cartesianism (but was Descartes a Cartesian?), and its Kantian continuations. It is neither the subject which is primary (as in subjective idealism), or the object (as in realistic objectivism), it is knowledge "in itself," the actualizing saturation of both and which is the very place where reality stands.[136] In short, every discourse forgetful of itself as a discourse, or, if preferred, any thinking and intelligent subject, forgetful of itself inasmuch as cognitive aim, does not tell the whole truth about its object, and therefore is untrue when it holds, contradictorily, that it is positing this object in its absolute independence, whereas this position is actually dependent on it. But, on the other hand, this is not a pure illusion either. The ontological orientation of the cognitive aim is essential to it. Intelligence, as we have said many times, is the sense of being, which means that being only has meaning for the intelligence. We must therefore also take into account this deep-seated ontotropism of any intellectual act and account for it. This is what, according to Guénon, is accomplished in the advent of "reality" as the realization of being through knowledge, at least if we have understood his doctrine.

---

[136] We have tried to expand on this point in an article, "Connaissance et réalisation," published in *Connaissance des Religions*, vol. III, nums. 2-3 (Sept.-Dec, 1987): 13-26. Some analyses in this article no longer correspond to our current state of thinking.

This is, we believe, the justification for this doctrine. This is why he is entitled to speak, despite the expression's paradox, of the possibilities of non-manifestation. It is in any case, in our eyes, the only way to give it an acceptable meaning. In relation to what can such possibilities actually be said to be "possible"? Not in relation to their existence, precisely since their nature excludes this. Proceeding further, to the extent that the sum of these possibilities constitute the Non-manifestable, that is, what there is of the loftiest, of the truly supreme in the order of the principial Real, should not these so-called possibilities rather be referred to as *realities*? The only conceivable answer is that they are possible only with regard to their realization through knowledge — in other words, from a perspective where knowledge is everything, and everything is only possible, realizable, through knowledge. And this is why, in a theoretical presentation, these principial aspects of Non-Being should be designated as "possibilities," and not as realities, in order to indicate to the reader that he should not forget that what we are talking about will "become" reality in the true sense only through metaphysical realization. To ward off the "objectivist reification" of all discourse, and to introduce into the theoretical statement itself the presence of a need for realization: this, it seems to me, is the underlying reason that legitimizes the mode of expression adopted by Guénon.

This explains why, from the beginning of *The Multiple States of the Being*, Guénon speaks of the Infinite as "universal Possibility"; not mainly because the Infinite would be seen as that which can be all, but because the All is seen from the viewpoint of knowledge and as able to be realized through knowledge. To speak of universal Possibility is to speak implicitly about the realizing function of total knowledge; this is therefore to appoint knowledge, or, if preferred, gnosis or metaphysics, as the modeless mode through which integral Reality happens. This universal Possibility is not so with regard to its existentiation, but with regard to universal knowability, that is, equivalently, to the universalization of the cognitive intellect that is no longer anything but one with the infinity of its "contents."[137]

---

[137] *The Multiple States of the Being*, 65.

If we return now to Christian theology to attempt a comparison with Guénonian doctrine, one point is evident: all that Guénon says about knowledge "as such," corresponds exactly to what St. Thomas says about divine knowledge. Certainly, unlike the Guénonian non-manifestables, the pure possibles of theology (which will never be anything other than possible) are creatables. They are however perfectly real, but only in the knowledge that God has of them and from the vantage point of this knowledge, which theology quite explicitly designates as "knowledge of simple intelligence." On the other hand, along the lines of realizational knowledge, the possible objects of the knowledge of simple intelligence and the possible objects of the knowledge of vision alike do not pre-exist with the knowledge that God has of them, but they are strictly contemporaneous with the eternal act in which God knows them. Lastly, and we will stop here, the divine intellect, like the universal intellect of Guénon, is perfectly identical to its intelligible content and should not be distinguished from it.

The path of gnosis described by Guénon in *The Multiple States of the Being* is therefore a path disregarding all *a priori* distinctions between the knowledge of a God and that of a man. We repeat, this knowledge is not ascribed to a knowing determinate being (man or God), ontologically primary with respect to it and hence upon which its cognitive modality would depend. It is posited in itself, first relative to the multiplicity of states of anonymous being, which are so many realizing participations in its permanent actuality. This being is neither God or man; it can only be viewed under one or the other of these aspects. But knowledge itself is one, whatever the degrees considered, "degrees that change nothing of its essential nature"; the only distinction we can make here is the one there is "between immediate and mediate knowledge, that is, between effective knowledge and symbolic knowledge."[138]

And yet this somewhat extraordinary discourse is addressed to human beings. To render it humanly admissible, it is therefore necessary to appeal, despite everything, to man's experience

---

138 Ibid., 80; "effective" corresponding to "immediate," and "symbolic" to "mediate."

of knowledge, namely that this is an act of intelligence. However, to take into account the intellect (*buddhi*) as that which knows, requires some clarification. On the one hand, explains Guénon, it should not be confused with "understanding" and "reason," which only give access to "mediate and symbolic knowledge," and, on the other, it must be transposed beyond *buddhi* when it comes to universal and unconditioned knowledge, that is, knowledge no longer subject to any condition whatsoever, even "divine."[139]

But it is the human creature who exercises the act of knowledge.

We have striven to grasp Guénon's discourse in its logic and therefore prove it to be correct. One clearly sees that, for this, we must consider knowledge "in itself," and, in the case of man, intelligence "in itself." And surely it is true that intellection (the intelligence in action) is something universal and even unconditioned. We have explained this on many occasions: intelligence, in its own act of intellective grasp, is unconditional, or, if you like, uneducable and ungenerable. All conditioning, all education, presupposes the intellectual act: intelligence can learn everything, except how to "intelligize." We can improve, modify, disrupt, or enrich the conditions of its exercise, but not produce the exercise itself, which is, *sui generis* and in its essence, always identical to itself, whatever the forms it assumes. This is why the light of the intellect is a certain kind of participation in the divine light, or even, if you will,

---

139   Ibid., 82 with note 3: "Here the term 'intellect' is also transposed beyond Being, and thus all the more so beyond *Buddhi*." Note that in placing understanding (*Verstand* in German) on the side of discursive and conceptual knowledge, Guénon conforms to the Kantian usage of this term, whereas, in prior philosophy, understanding is synonymous with intellect and intelligence. This is the case in French from the twelfth century, as well as in German. Jacob Boehme always employed *Verstand* in the sense of intuitive and penetrating knowledge and contrasts it with reason (*Vernunft*); cf. Alexandre Koyré, *La philosophie de Jacob Boehme*, 3rd ed. (Paris: Vrin, 1979, 39–40, fn 4. The same meaning for Leibniz: "*understanding* corresponds to what among the Latins is called *intellectus*, and the exercise of this faculty is called *intellection*," *New Essays on Human Understanding*, II, 21, § 5; 3rd ed., trans. A. G. Langley (LaSalle, IL: Open Court, 1949), 178.

that in every intellectual act it is, as to its "depths," God who thinks and who knows. This means that, in its original source, intelligence is openness to the infinity of God. This should not be seen as an intellectualist one-upmanship, the exaltation of a metaphysics that knows no bounds. To the contrary, it is an obvious fact, and philosophy, as shown by the doctrine of Malebranche or even that of Ruyer, suffices to establish this.[140]

For all that, the fact remains: in its actual manifestations the intelligence is always clothed in a determinate form, although it remains informal in its essence. On the other hand, and this is the decisive point, it is always borne in being by the human person. Guénon considers knowledge in itself and intellect in itself as a quasi-separate reality and not subjectivized in a person. He sees the states of being only under the form of states of knowledge, or again of "points of view," what we have designated as a specular ontology. It all comes down to modalities of intellection, acts of knowledge. The human being, as such, is almost ignored. True, it will be objected that Guénon by no means forgets this. On the one hand *buddhi* is clearly for him a personal (although non-individual) faculty and, on the other, whenever it is necessary to account for the manifested / non-manifested distinction, he brings in considerations of the "human" state, taking care to specify that this state is that from which we must start (wise advice, moreover, although it teaches us nothing not already known and which, clearly, we could not help but pursue). But we will point out that taking into account the human state of being is not necessarily to take

---

[140] What we are saying here might, wrongly, bring to mind the thesis of the "unity of intellect" (which we would more correctly call: the unicity of the intellect). According to this thesis (attributed by the medievals to Averroes) the "possible intellect is one for all men"; it is not the man who thinks, it is the intellect (St. Thomas, *On the Unity of the Intellect, Against the Averroists*, §1, trans. B. H. Zedler [Milwaukee, WI: Marquette University Press, 1968], 21). Fought over by St. Bonaventure and St. Thomas, this thesis runs afoul of the objection from the miracle of Pentecost: the Holy Spirit, the single Light of the intelligence, divides into as many tongues of fire as there are people in the Upper Room, pneumatizing each intellect. We will just say, with St. Thomas: "The natural light bestowed upon the soul is God's enlightenment, whereby we are enlightened to see what pertains to natural knowledge" (*Summa Theologiae*, IaIIae Q. 109, a. 1, ad 2).

Gnosis and Gnosticism in René Guénon

into account the human being. To take into account a state is to consider something constituted by a set of determinations defining a *nature*; this is not to consider the person in his *esse*. Here, being is called in only as a minimal ontological condition required to constitute a specular instance. In short, in these multiple states of being, there is much more about "state" than about "being."[141]

In other words, the concept of specular ontology, with all the consequences that we have examined, rests upon a *de facto* reduction of the human being to the intellect. This reduction having been acquired, actually, in that case, a state of being can be identified with a mode of knowledge, and this mode of knowledge can, where appropriate, be considered as realizing the identity of the knowing being and the known object. Otherwise — and this is indeed the sense of Aristotle's doctrine always quoted inaccurately by Guénon[142] — knowledge can be regarded as the common act of the knower and the known (what it is in truth, and already at the simple level of sensory knowledge) only on the condition that precisely this common act be that of the intellect and the intelligible, and not

---

141 This remark does not mean that the human being on his path to God may not pass through different states. On the one hand (*Love and Truth*, 132–35), the person (the spiritual principle that forms the unity of the human being) must be seen as the ontological relation that connects us to God (and vice versa as the gaze of God upon us), in such a manner that the spiritual *way* which leads us to God is none other than the dynamic realization of this relation that crosses the hierarchy of the degrees of reality. On the other hand, we find, in Christian thought, teachings that go in this direction; Evagrius of Pontus writes: "by true prayer a monk becomes equal to the angels" (*On Prayer*, chap. 113), which Fr. Hausherr comments on as follows: "the name 'man' is no longer suitable for the contemplative (or gnostic) who has attained the angelic state" (*Les leçons d'un contemplatif* [Paris: Beauchesne, 1960], 143). However, it is the same being who passes through these different states (which Guénon confirms), a being present, as a man, in its effectual and unique *actuality* (which is not Guénon's thinking). To be man is not, for this being, to assume a transitory and contingent form while he exists simultaneously in a multiplicity of other states. It is to be "made in the image of God," and it is as such that he can gain access to the hierarchical states of creation, all the modes of which are virtually comprehended in him: the microcosm summarizes the macrocosm. Man is not just an individual, transient, and contingent form, but by his theo-morphism he gathers within himself and transcends the entire universe. "Man," said Pascal, "infinitely transcends man" (*Pensées*, 434 [New York: E. P. Dutton, 1958], 121).
142 *The Multiple States of the Being*, 77–78.

that of the being that intelligizes. This is because the intellect is not the being who intelligizes (but only a faculty of that being), because it can, in its act, be identified with what it intelligizes. Aristotle says exactly this: "in a manner [*pos*] the [intellective] soul is all existent things." But he clarifies: "It is not the stone which is in the [knowing] soul, but the form of the stone."[143] The intellect is that which, of the human being, is open to universal otherness because it is the possibility (it is in this sense that St. Thomas calls it "possible intellect"), in the human being, of being cognitively united with all things. In other words, specifies the Philosopher, in order to preclude any mistake: "It would be better not to say that the (intellectual) soul pities or learns or thinks, but that the man does so with the soul."[144] Now, this intellect, which does not exist alone, is necessarily in a state of dependency to the person bearing it in being. The same goes for the intellect as for the eye, and this comparison is very commonplace. It is not the eye that sees, it is the man endowed with sight. Certainly, the radiance of the light to which the eye is sensitive and without which there is no vision, is one, informal, universal, non-human, and always the same, whether the radiance of the sun or the stars. Certainly, once opened and well-positioned, the (healthy) eye cannot help but receive that light. But it is the man who opens his eye and positions it and renders it capable of being acted upon by light; and it is also in the man that the act of vision takes place, that is, of visual *knowledge*, and therefore that sight has access to existence. The same is true for the intellect, which has being only as a faculty of a real and existing being.

It does not seem possible then to reduce being (*esse*) to a degree of knowledge. Scalar ontology can be *interpreted* in specular terms, and one must even do so if one wants to achieve a true understanding of the hierarchy of beings according to the different degrees of reality to which each of them belongs: the onto-cosmological *situs* of a being should not be devoid of sufficient

---

[143] *On the Soul*, III, 8, 431b and 432a (Hicks trans. 145). As we have already pointed out, Guénon cites this text inaccurately (forgetting *pos*) in *Introduction to the Study of Hindu Doctrines*, 115, 199. See also: *Christ the Original Mystery*, 40–42.
[144] *On the Soul*, I, 4, 408b 12 (Hicks trans. 33).

reason, and corresponds to a certain state of knowledge. But, for all creatures, whether peripheral or central, being (*esse*) is something more fundamental, more radically determinative, than the mode of knowledge. We say: for all creatures, since it is precisely by their being (*esse*) that creatures are creatures. By their mode of knowledge, on the contrary, one might almost say that they belong to the uncreated, to the extent that all knowledge, from the humblest to the loftiest, from sensation to contemplation, is, in its depths, a revelation of the essence, like something participating in the divine, and consequently more or less open to the uncreated. It is in this sense that St. Thomas can declare that the agent intellect is as if a light derived from God (*quasi lumen derivatum a Deo*), which Étienne Gilson summarizes: "This intellectual light within us is nothing other than a participatory likeness of the uncreated light, and, since the uncreated light contains the eternal essences of all things, we can say, in a certain sense, that we know everything in the divine exemplars."[145] And likewise, Meister Eckhart can state that there is "a power [the intellect] in the soul... and if the whole soul were like it, she would be uncreated and uncreatable. But this is not so."[146] It is not then the way to knowledge that, *by itself*, can account for the determination of the degrees of the real, it is the *esse* of each creature that founds its belonging to a particular degree of the real, and, by way of consequence, determines its mode of knowledge. This is why, even though we know, as to the depths of the matter, in the uncreated light, we do not directly grasp the essences-archetypes *as such*, even if we incontestably have a kind of intuition about them. Our knowledge is at once principial and divine in its depths, and relative and indirect in its mode.

Principial and divine knowledge is possible to the very extent, as Guénon says, to which it is an "aspect of the Infinite,"[147] namely an aspect in which the Infinite is known. From this point of view, there is no other knowledge than the one by

---

[145] *Le Thomisme* (Paris: Vrin, 1942), 297; cf. St. Thomas, *Summa Theologiae* I, Q. 84, a. 5.
[146] Sermon 24; *The Complete Mystical Works of Meister Eckhart*, trans. M. O'C. Walshe (New York: Crossroad, 2009), 161.
[147] *The Multiple States of the Being*, 11.

which God knows himself as an infinity of possibility, and, consequently, all knowledge, be it human or angelic, is in its depths eternal, or, if one prefers, timeless. And this takes into account one difficulty that should not be passed over in silence: what about this event that is human knowledge *from the side of what is known*, in this case, from the side of the Divine Object? In what sense can That which is a pure act, and therefore immutable, *undergo* the event which constitutes for It the fact of being known? This event cannot affect it, certainly, but for all that one cannot maintain that it is perfectly indifferent or foreign to it, which would mean that this act of knowledge did not happen. This is why it does not seem possible to respond to this difficulty other than by admitting that God can *be known* only by Himself, and therefore that the event of angelic or human theognosy is not something that "happens to God," but that, in its depths, is an eternal event, which we would realize if we ceased thinking of the event as referring to a before and after, as entirely taken up in a temporal series, which is equivalent to having an event's oneness disappear into an indefinite multiplicity of a vanishing succession of moments. The *reality* of the noetic event can only be the lightning-flash, in an intellectual mirror, of the everlasting actuality of the knowledge that God has of Himself in His Word, this Word which is the place of the possibles and in which every noetic event takes place. And this is because in Him knowledge, gnosis, is eternally accomplished since it can be realized at every instant by each intelligence open in its light.

It goes for the human intellect as it does for spheres that are suddenly opened, grace seconding nature, to the Ocean of light in which they have always been immersed. In one flash they "become" what they were, crystalline spheres, twinkling stars, lights in the Light. Each time that a starry intelligence is born in this way within divine Knowledge, each time that an "event of gnosis" occurs, which is nothing more than a possibility of the Infinite itself, so too each time the Supreme Thearchy realizes the mystery of its new and eternal birth to Itself, so too "each time" the Father begets his Word, his only and beloved Son, in the unity of his Spirit.

But, divine in its depths, the knowledge that is ours is also human in its mode. And only the consideration of the created nature of the human being can take this "modalization" into account. However, to truly consider the human being in its state of being as a creature, actually and concretely, is not only to posit it, in passing and out of necessity, as one ontological instance among others, it is also to leave behind the speculative and finally enter into reality, that of our existential condition; and this is to break with a certain illusion of metaphysical discourse. For, make no mistake, it is quite rightly here that this illusion arises. Knowledge, all knowledge, is, in the spontaneity and immediacy of its act, essentializing in nature: this is its inherent aim. To the extent that metaphysical theory describes things "in themselves," *sub specie quadam aeternitatis*, it situates what it is speaking about in a prototypical sphere, and, at the time of reading and meditation, draws us out of the conditioned world, making us live among pure objects. This is why, even more than for any other domain of human existence, it is important to ballast the soaring flight of metaphysical speculation with the weight of being, by relating knowledge to the being of the knower who is there, on earth, and nowhere else, there where God caused him to be born, caused him to sally forth from nothingness. The need for this ontological ballasting is much less when it comes to working or engaging in an action, because then it is the being of the person who is on earth grappling with the being of things and who hardly risks forgetting this.

However, to take into account the being of the creature necessarily implies that we also take into account the divine being in its creative causation, that is, in its complete power to make being emerge out of nothingness. And here we have something about which the doctrine of manifestation says nothing. According to Guénon, the difference between "manifestation" and "creation" parallels the difference between esotericism and exotericism, or again between "the metaphysical point of view and the religious."[148] In other words, the doctrine of creation

---

[148] "Creation and Manifestation," reprinted in *Insights into Islamic Esotericism and Taoism*, trans. H. D. Fohr (Hillsdale, NY: Sophia Perennis, 2001), 44–51. This article contains some very surprising statements. Among other things,

is a reductive translation, for the use of the multitude, of the doctrine of manifestation. Without subscribing to this thesis, we ourselves have hitherto used one or the other of these terms as quasi-synonyms. We must now mark their difference, however, in a sense other than Guénon's. Yes, vulgar creationism can in some respects appear to justify such a judgment; but should not we say as much (and perhaps more correctly) about the notion of manifestation in the mind of the average Hindu? If to the contrary we take the doctrine of creation at its most serious level, we can see that, metaphysically, it is in no way inferior to that of manifestation and even, at least on one point, surpasses it in speculative fecundity. That this point seems to have escaped Guénon proves that the doctrine in question conceals sometimes unnoticed depths.

To speak of the realm of universal Existence as a "manifestation" is to say explicitly that this realm is the one that makes "manifest," or again that reveals, what was hidden in the Principle. But, since there is no sense in speaking of a manifestation that would not manifest itself to anyone, this is in fact to have the production of universal Existence viewed from the vantage point of the human being, as the one for whom there actually is manifestation. Is this anthropocentrism more metaphysical than creationist theocentrism? This is arguable. Besides, and it is mainly this consequence that we wanted to stress, the doctrine of manifestation envisions the relationship there is between the Principle and its cosmic effects as a relationship of continuity: what is revealed in the manifested is the essence (the possible or archetype) contained in the non-manifest.

Guénon explains that, from the point of view of creation, "something completely essential is lacking...the notion of possibility" (48). This is perhaps true for Islam, but entirely false for Christian theology, as evidenced by what we have just explained and about which Guénon was not ignorant. A second difference, Guénon points out, is that religion considers only the dependence of the manifested on the Principle (which is expressed by the Lord-servant relationship), while "from the metaphysical point of view, this dependence is at the same time a 'participation,'" which indicates "a link between the manifested and the non-manifested, which enables beings to pass beyond the relative condition inherent in manifestation. The religious point of view, by contrast, insists more on the nullity proper to manifested beings" (50). It is hard to find a greater and more incomprehensible disregard for Christian theology.

Far be it from us any thought of rejecting such a perspective, quite the contrary. Moreover, this is a matter of scriptural teaching: "For the invisible things of [God] from the *creation of the world are clearly seen*," says St. Paul, made visible by his works to those who have understanding, namely "his eternal power and Godhead" (Rom. 1:20). Next, what we have here, as we have recalled at length, is a formal teaching of the most standard theology concerning God as "infinity of possibility," to which one might add the texts of St. Thomas on "the uncreated being of creatures."[149] The viewpoint of creation therefore includes what is most metaphysical in that of manifestation. But it adds something not explicitly found there, which is the taking of being (*esse*) as such into consideration, being in its irreducible radicality, that is, as a *differential* from nothingness, as *esse ex nihilo*. For there is no other means of attaining the first intuition of being than to "grasp" it as not-non-existent, as "that which juts out from nothingness."[150] A consideration of the degrees of being is relative and secondary with respect to the intuition of the *esse*, for, even if manifestation in its totality is only an illusion, still this illusion must *be*. Now, the intuition of being is made possible, at least for a cultural community, only within the context of the *ex nihilo*. God is not only the one who makes a *particular* being manifest, making it pass from the non-manifested state to the manifested, He is the one who "bestows all being" on the creature: being is the ever-lasting gift of a sallying-forth-out-of-nothing: *esse* is, fundamentally, *ex nihilo*. This can be equally said of the divine Being, but then the *Nihil* assumes an entirely different meaning.[151] As we see, the doctrine of creation gives access to an intuition of truly metaphysical being. And perhaps Aristotle would have encountered less difficulty in the search for a "science of being as being,"[152] if he had had at his disposal the idea of creation *ex nihilo*.

---

149 *Summa Theologiae*, I, Q. 18, a. 4; cf. *Love and Truth*, 351–53.
150 *Penser l'analogie*, 76–80.
151 Ibid., 92 ff.
152 This is the definition of the object of what will be called "metaphysics" and which Aristotle calls "first philosophy": *Metaphysics*, III, 1, 1003a 21.

But to speak of being as a bestowal, a donation, is also to speak of a donor who is Being itself and "More Than Being," since precisely He alone can bestow it. But the donation of being out of nothingness (other than Being by itself) introduces a discontinuity between the created and the Uncreated, between the being given and the donor Being, an ontological discontinuity doubled by an eidetic continuity, that of the *eidos*, of the essence or Idea, manifested here-below, non-manifested "on high." This discontinuity *founds* the existential *situs* of the creature; it constitutes *that from which* only the creature can turn itself towards the Principle, that otherness which accounts for its orientation towards the Identity that far surpasses it, that accounts for its noetic and spiritual tension towards the transcendent Object, that otherness without which the very act of knowledge would be inconceivable. Clearly the doctrine of creation expresses the dependence of the created on the Uncreated. But this dependence, which moreover no true metaphysics should reject, is also and at first the effect of a *gift*. God does not give being to take it back: his gifts are without repentance. Being is truly given and, by this gift, the creature is established in its freedom. It is necessary to choose. Either the entire manifestation is a useless parenthesis, and we will never be able to explain why the Principle has caused it to issue from Itself for the sole purpose of having it return there, or else it has a true and irremissible reality.

The doctrine of creation, far from opposing the exercise of gnosis, that is, sacred knowledge, seems the only one suited to account for its possibility, because it introduces the element of otherness into the core of the spontaneously identifying and assimilative cognitive process, an element without which knowledge, a natural act of the intelligence, cannot give birth to the awareness of a need to exceed itself. While teaching the creature that its existential *situs*, from which it gazes towards the Principle, is well within the cognitive process (the being of the knower is not knowledge), this doctrine also teaches that the creature's ultimate Object is beyond its grasp. It therefore teaches it to be detached from itself, to open up the concepts (etymologically, the "graspings") with which it works. It teaches it to renounce its own constructions, the statements of its discourse, and to awaken to another way of knowing, a knowledge apart, separate, sacred, humanly *inchoative*, unfulfilled, dispossessed of itself, a knowledge that no longer belongs to itself because its content is beyond any conceptual mode and that awaits its completion in an inextinguishable hope and in faith; but a knowledge nevertheless, an intelligence that is experienced in its inmost depths, in its heart, as inexpressibly connatural with what it contemplates, in darkness, within itself.

APPENDIX I
About the episcopates of Jules Doinel and Palingenius
(cf. note 27, 143)

As a result of the present study, as published in Dossier H — René Guénon (Lausanne: L'Age d'Homme, 1984), Robert Amadou sent us a very kind letter (dated May 7, 1984), accompanied by the text of an article on "The consecration and death of Jules Doinel," the last chapter of a very informed study about the founder of the Gnostic Church, published in the magazine L'Autre Monde, from num. 60 (May 1982) to num. 67 (January 1983).

In Ésotérisme et christianisme autour de René Guénon, Marie-France James declares that Jules Doinel, according to "information provided by Robert Amadou, who had himself received it from Augustin Chaboseau," "was marked with the episcopal seal by a regular bishop of the Church of Utrecht and, besides, by three Cathar bishops" (81). It would follow that, according to the very criteria of the Church of Rome, Jules Doinel, and therefore Guénon-Palingenius, would have received a valid (albeit unlawful) episcopal consecration. The letter from Robert Amadou, an excerpt from which we are giving here, denies this allegation: "I had confided to M. F. James a dossier on Doinel. She did not know much about it and the main point on which she cites it is incorrect. Actually, I have never endorsed the legends in circulation on a ritual consecration of Doinel. I am even quite sure that such a consecration never took place. In particular, there is in the archives of the Old Catholic See of Utrecht a correspondence from Doinel that shows him anxious

GNOSTICS OF THE 19TH AND 20TH CENTURIES

to get closer to contemporary Jansenism, but confirms, if that were needed, that no organic link ever existed between the Old Catholic Church and the restorer of gnosis. As for the rumor spread about by Augustin Chaboseau, it was unfounded."

Clarifications:

(1) Augustin Chaboseau (1869–1946) was a member of the Hermetic Brotherhood of Luxor.

(2) The schismatic Church of Utrecht arose at the beginning of the eighteenth century, following the rejection by the Cathedral Chapter of the Bull *Unigenitus* (1712) condemning Jansenism. The episcopal seat having become vacant, this Chapter elected a Jansenist bishop who was validly consecrated by Mgr. Varlet, (suspensed) bishop of Babylon. This Church, which still exists today, therefore has the apostolic succession.

(3) The "Old Catholic" Church arose in 1870 from a rejection of the dogma of papal infallibility proclaimed by the First Vatican Council. A number of prelates, priests, and laity, mainly in Germany and Central Europe, which rejected this dogma, soon came together in the schismatic, so-called "Old Catholic" Church. When the question of validly ordaining a bishop and priests arose, this Church turned to the Church of Utrecht. In 1889, at the time of a "lesser council," these two Churches decided to merge. "To the resulting united group the name 'Old Catholics' was applied" (H. Daniel-Rops, *Our Brothers in Christ* [London & New York: Dent & Dutton, 1967], 448–49).

(4) In Catholic doctrine, a valid sacrament is one that communicates the grace it signifies; only those sacraments are valid in which the minister benefits, directly or by delegation, from the apostolic transmission of which only the bishops are custodians. Moreover, a licit sacrament is one that is administered with the authorization and according to the provisions of the hierarchical Church. An illicit sacrament (unauthorized by the Church) can be valid (grace is indeed communicated) if it is administered by a validly ordained minister. Any regular bishop may validly confer the episcopate, even without the Pope's agreement. Validity refers to the "hierarchy of order" (custodian of the grace of Christ); licitness refers to the "hierarchy of jurisdiction" (the Church-society, endowed with rules and laws).

APPENDIX II

Neo-Gnostic doctrines (cf. note 29, 144)

The doctrines of the "Universal Gnostic Church," founded by Jules Doinel (Valentinus II), were set forth by Albert de Pouvourville (under the name of T. Simon, the "T" indicating that he is a bishop) and Léon Champrenaud (T. Théophane) in *The Secret Teachings of Gnosis* (100 pages in quarto, published by Lucien Bodin in 1907, with *Imprimatur* and additions from T. Synesius, Patriarch of the Gnostic Church of France). This work, now republished by Archè-Milano, in its "Archives" collection, in 1999, sets out its doctrines in five chapters; some of these doctrines are found in Guénon's works. Thus, what we read in the first chapters of *The Multiples States of the Being* on Non-Being, total Possibility and Being is directly inspired, even to vocabulary, by what we read in chapter I, "Outer Darkness" from the book of Simon and Théophane, although the tone is somewhat different, and Guénon gives proof of a superior intellectual mastery.

As we know (cf. Jean-Pierre Laurant, *Matgioi, un aventurier taoïste* [Paris: Dervy-Livres, 1982]), Pouvourville was a Taoist initiate, and the theses set forth in *The Secret Teachings of Gnosis*, with reference to Valentinus's gnosis, are given as if coming from the distant East. This is surely why, with regard to Non-Being, Guénon asserts that this expression "is directly inspired by the terminology of the metaphysical doctrine of the Far East" (*The Multiple States of the Being*, 20–21), although given that the Chinese language has no vocabulary for "being" at its disposal (in contrast to Indo-European languages), we do not at all see how it could speak of "non-being." T. Simon actually employs this term (op. cit., 15), probably as a Western equivalent for the Chinese *wu*, which rightly means: "there is not," most often correlated to *you*: "there is" (Isabelle Robinet, *Lao Zi et le Tao* [Paris: Bayard, 1996], 239). This equivalence is perfectly admissible. What remains however is that the syntagma "non-being" comes from Greek philosophy, and not Chinese metaphysics, and is found in Christian Europe within the Dionysian tradition. Major information on this subject is to be found in our article "Du Non-Être et du Séraphin de l'âme," in *Connaissance des Religions*, num. 1, January–March 1985.

The importance Guénon attaches to *Secret Teachings* is also indicated by the explicit quotes he gives of them, thus in *The Symbolism of the Cross* (chap. 24, 116), a book in which, moreover, references to Matgioi are the most numerous. And let us not forget that Albert de Pouvourville is the only person Guénon has publicly designated as his master: "Our Master and collaborator Matgioi" (the review *La Gnose*, September–October 1910, 219).

Is this importance justified? Simon and Théophane's book is not devoid of interest and bears witness to appreciable intellectual standards. However, there are some oddities. For example, on page 48 a sentence by Pascal taken from the *Mystère de Jésus* is given as a saying of Christ addressed to the pagans (?). And again, on page 58 we learn that "according to the vigorous expression of the Areopagite," the "Virgin of Light" is called the "Great Whore." We have not found this expression in Dionysius! However, what is standard among certain Fathers of the Church, such as St. Jerome, is, with reference to the prophet Hosea, to designate the Church (the new Israel) as the Great Whore (*In Hosea*, preface; P. L., 25, 817–18). But, above all, an avowed anti-Judaism and anti-Christianity is exhibited: "Jehovah, the anthropomorphic god, who drives to a superhuman excess all human passions [is the] monstrous shadow that matter, intercepting the celestial Ray, lengthens...in our misguided cerebralness" (42). The pope is an "autocratic pontiff," source of the evils that overwhelm men (45). In short, "Jewish Jehovism is only the glorification of the Demiurge," and "modern Christianity [is] the reflux of the Buddhist ocean on a Western shore" (46), a formula whose historical significance is not obvious.

More positively, this gnosis adheres without reticence to science and progress, from which it expects much: "the terminal goal [of humanity] is the creation of the science of its future and its goal, in other words its *essential religious Dogma*" (37, italics in the original). Neo-Gnostics in particular trust science to soon prove the plurality of inhabited worlds. And we are somewhat surprised to see the young Guénon—he is twenty-five years old—subscribe (*Studies in Freemasonry and the Compagnonnage*, trans. Fohr, Bethell & Allen [Hillsdale, NY: Sophia Perennis, 2004], 7, fn 12) to the following statement (to which he is referring): "For here, too, Gnostic theory seems to have predicted modern discoveries; in fact, it admits, in its doctrine, the plurality of inhabited worlds (and consequently the multiplicity of simultaneous saving missions," 27). Further on, page 28, it is specified: "this has to do with various planets in the same system (our solar system for example)." On these planets, different living conditions make for humanities endowed with different and adapted organs: such conditions "turn these living beings into Martian, Jupiterian, Venusian, or Lunar men who have, with terrestrial men, parallels and analogies and also divergences and oppositions that will certainly be demarcated and determined scientifically, and unerringly, by future findings" (28).

This is what, in 1911, Palingenius seems to adhere to; in any case, these are some of the extravagances that he invites his readers to accept. However, since he affirms (cf. *Études sur la Franc-maçonnerie et le Compagnonnage* tome 1, 197) [153] that he never varied his teachings, are we not entitled to conclude that the mature Guénon still professes the same "certainties"? Finally, we will recall that these "bishops" and this "patriarch" boast of teaching a sole and universal gnosis, superior to all religions, thanks to which they can look down from the greatest height on "individualist doctrines and the Jehovist religions" (2). All of this is not without a great deal of pretension, to put it mildly.

---

153 Trans.—Passage in French edition only.

CHAPTER 7

Christian Dogma and Schuonian Gnosis[1]

INTRODUCTION
Exposé on the gnostico-critical thesis.

"Gnostic" or "gnosticizing" interpretations of Christian dogma are not lacking. The most illustrious example of this is provided by Hegelian philosophy, as we have shown. One might even go so far as to maintain, along with Alexandre Kojève, that Hegel is the preeminent "Christian" philosopher, since he has tended towards a single end: to *philosophically* account for the survival of Christianity in human thought. His interpretations are always offered as statements about the true meaning of the Christian faith's "exoteric" formulas. Such is also the case with Frithjof Schuon, for whom the "gnostic" label should not be disputed, he himself having expressly laid claim to it in several of his writings. However, we also encounter with him something not found among other gnostic thinkers, not to the same degree in any case. He is not content to develop a "metaphysical" (= "gnostic") interpretation of Christian dogmas—the Trinity "Father-Son-Holy Spirit" identified with the triad "Beyond Being-Being-Existence," for example[2]—but, getting right to the bottom of things, as is customary for him, at once and without distinction, he launches a frontal attack on this dogma in both its canonical formulations and its theological explanations. This gnostic critique of Christian dogmas and their theological understanding is chiefly set forth in the "Evidence and Mystery" chapter of a book significantly titled *Logic and Transcendence* (first published in 1970[3]), the major thesis of

---

1 Essentially, this chapter was written between Sept. 1973 and Jan. 1974, and eventually corrected in March 2006.
2 *Understanding Islam*, trans. D. M. Matheson (Baltimore MD: Penguin Books, 1972), 69–70.
3 Trans. P. N. Townsend (New York: Harper & Row, 1975).

Christian Dogma and Schuonian Gnosis

which is that, contrary to Christian dogmatism, which claims a right to the (apparent) illogicality of revelation in the name of its super-rational nature, it must be affirmed that human thought is able to logically account for the most transcendent data: "every formulation that is illogical for reasons of profundity can be reduced to logical formulations of a subtle and complex character."[4] But, to be able to display the true logic or revelation "without clashing with common sense,"[5] it must be shown on the one hand that Scripture, the source of revelation, in no way imposes the dogmatic formulations that the Church, chiefly the Catholic Church, imagines it finds there, and, on the other, that the philosophical concepts, by whose aid theology claims to clarify and justify them, are unworkable and contradictory.

The first reason invoked by this gnostico-critical endeavor—one of the most peculiar ever—is that the raison d'être for divine revelation is man: "religion addresses itself to man, and man is thought"; consequently, "no religion has ever imposed on the human mind, or ever could have imposed, an idea that logic was incapable of approaching in any way."[6] Yet this is what dogma claims to do in the name of "a mysterious right to absurdity" for transcendence,[7] when it obliges us to believe "that God is at the same time absolutely one and absolutely three,"[8] or that the utterance "this is my body" has "the meaning of a rigorous and massive physical equation."[9] Surely this physical equation is useful in "a climate of emotional totalitarianism," but "transubstantialism" is nevertheless a false understanding of what is, in reality, "an oriental ellipsis."[10] Besides, "if in truth the Eucharistic species have literally become the flesh and blood of Jesus, how much better off are we for this

---

4 *Logic and Transcendence*, 112.
5 Ibid.
6 Ibid., 92; this argument was used by the antitrinitarian Socinians.
7 Ibid., 91
8 Ibid., 96. Such a formulation is absent from the documents of the magisterium. Moreover, the Trinity is not the *addition* of three juxtaposed persons, but the 'multiplication' of three relative persons; now: $1 \times 1 \times 1 = 1$.
9 Ibid., 94.
10 Ibid., 95.

so to say 'magical' operation,"[11] when we have faith in their efficacy "in the context of Divine inherence"?[12]

As much might be said about "trinitarism," which is, in fact, the product of a "logic that is dogmatically coagulative and piously unilateral."[13] Truly, "the theology of the Trinity does not constitute an explicit and homogeneous revelation,"[14] the reason being that "dogmatism, or exoterism, is essentially a planimetry, not an integral geometry."[15] It is incapable of accounting for revelation's subtle and complex data. For example, it affirms the perfect equality of the Son with the Father; if this is so, "then the term [Son, which implies subordination] is ill-chosen, and a different one ought, out of pity, to have been proposed"[16] by Scripture. A "supernaturalization out of denominational bias or sentimentalist absurdity"[17] is manifested here.

One of the consequences of these criticisms is that, from the viewpoint of gnosis, many of the interpretations of the Trinity anathematized as heretical could have been accepted by a truly gnostic reading of Scripture. "It must be recognized that more than one heresy, or so-called heresy, was worthy of interest, and could have been made use of if the dogmatic point of view were not narrow by definition. The whole problem of Trinitarianism is that it was found necessary to make divergent realities fit into a formula that had to present them bluntly as being convergent, while dogmatic opportunism stifled at birth certain intermediate truths that are metaphysically indispensable."[18] Thus the modalism of the Sabellians was "rejected because of an inability to combine it with a complementary thesis."[19] The doctrine of Sabellius (third century), ostensibly favored by Schuon, considers the Father, Son, and Holy Spirit to be three modes (hence the modern label "modalism") of the

---

11 Ibid.
12 Ibid., 94.
13 Ibid., 96.
14 Ibid.
15 Ibid., 108.
16 Ibid., 102.
17 Ibid., 113.
18 Ibid., 105, fn 12.
19 Ibid., 97, fn 7; also *Form and Substance in the Religions*, trans. M. Perry and J. P. LaFouge (Bloomington IN: World Wisdom, 2002), 33.

Christian Dogma and Schuonian Gnosis

unique Substance-Person of God, and not distinct persons. This is the first great trinitarian heresy. Arianism is open to an analogous remark. Without a doubt it is wrong to completely deny Christ's divinity, "yet one has to acknowledge that there is in his doctrine a correct and profound intuition, though it is awkwardly formulated in terms typical of Semitic and creationist anthropomorphism. Instead of rejecting Arianism altogether, one could have appropriated its positive theological intention, that of divine Relativity, which is the prototype for cosmic limitation.... The Council of Nicaea marks, not the victory of truth as such, but the victory of the most important truth to the detriment of essential metaphysical nuances":[20] "Arianism is not an intrinsic heresy."[21]

Although we could multiply them at leisure, we will end our citations here. The gnostico-critical thesis is presented mainly as a series of rectifications of dogma. Instead of saying: one single God in three distinct persons, the Church, integrating Sabellius in this way, would have had to speak of a single Substance-Person according to three hypostatic modes; instead of the consubstantial Son, the Church, according to what was incontestable in the thesis of Arius, would have had to recognize the subordination of the Son to the Father; instead of imposing transubstantialism, the Church, sensitive to the just criticisms of Luther, would have had to rest content with a simple affirmation of the divine inherence in the eucharistic bread and wine. It should not be denied, in fact, as one Schuonian gnostic informed us, that dogmatic formulations risk "arousing the incredulity of many," and that they "constitute prisons limiting the intellectual horizons of theologians of good faith who have been induced at present, by a certain logic, to weaken the Christian message and even to fall into heresy." In any case, it must be admitted, along with Schuon, "that no theologian, no council, is Christ, so that theology is not the whole message of Christ, above all when, proceeding by choices between alternatives—and it has had to do this—it stands

---

20 *Form and Substance in the Religions*, 209-10.
21 *Christianity/Islam, Essays on Esoteric Ecumenicism*, trans. G. Polit (Bloomington IN: World Wisdom, 1985), 128.

in need of many nuances"; hence the need for the Schuonian message that "surpasses the alternativism of dogma."

Truth to tell, Frithjof Schuon could express himself more rudely, which by itself shows just how radically "gnostic" his critique is. Having remarked to him, in the course of a conversation, that the dogmatism he maltreated so vigorously was the work of councils that had received the assistance of the Holy Spirit, he promptly retorted: "Even the Holy Spirit cannot prevent an ass from braying!"

Preliminary observations on the foregoing theses.

Before showing, from a formal and general point of view, why the gnostico-critical thesis is not admissible in Christianity, we must go over some of the questions raised by Schuon so as to underscore the gaps in his information and therefore the weakness of his argument.

The first remark called for has to do with determining the "scientific" level of his discourse. At first sight, one has the impression that Schuon's analyses deal with a rather "vulgar" generally widespread form of the faith, the overall image of which is present in the minds of all those, whether believers or not, who have not studied history and theology. Under this petrified and simplistic form, in all honesty, many Schuonian criticisms seem justified. However, these same analyses equally take into account numerous ideas of a much more technical nature (hypostases, relations, species, substance, modes and modalism, &c.) that by far exceed the ordinary level of religious knowledge. Now, these two levels are constantly jumbled together, one lending its support to the other. How then are we to doubt the authority of an author who, making himself the standard-bearer of simple logic, is also capable of attacking the most erudite theological constructions, unknown to the majority of his readers, and showing their impotence to account for the absurdities—recognized by all—of ecclesial dogmatism?

Such a jumble, presented in a quick and peremptory style, does not fail however to plunge a specialist into great perplexity, above all when he realizes that this critique of dogma and theology is basically, on many points—right down to philosophical argumentation—along the same lines as the most radical "Christian" modernism. This is indeed astonishing on the part of a thinker who, in other respects, reproached Mgr. Lefebvre and his disciples for not going to the end of their trajectory, that is for rejecting the sedevacantism to which he himself subscribed.

That said, we shall come upon some historical data of positive theology questioned in *Logic and Transcendence*, in connection with which are seen not only the insufficiency of the alleged information but even misconceptions, at least when abiding by the letter of the Schuonian text.

The most flagrant error concerns the notion of transubstantiation. According to Schuon, this doctrine signifies that "the Eucharistic species have literally become the flesh and blood of Jesus."[22] This phrase betrays a surprising misunderstanding of a doctrine whose purpose, to the contrary, is to show why the eucharistic *species* (the bread and wine such as they appear) *are not*, either literally or otherwise, the body and blood, but indeed the species of bread and wine: our senses do not deceive us. What is changed is the substance (the basic ontological principle) of bread and wine. This substance that our intellect alone discerns has become, strictly speaking, not even body and blood, but the *substance* of Christ's body and blood. This is a conversion, a passage (trans-) from substance to substance (from basic reality to basic reality), while the species (made known to us by our senses) remain unchanged in their own reality: "There is no deception in this sacrament," St Thomas states, "for the accidents [another name for species] which are discerned by the senses are truly present. But the intellect, whose proper object is substance...is preserved by faith from deception."[23]

Certainly one could reject the ontological distinction of substance and accidents or species, and therefore transubstantiation, and proceed with a different analysis of the real. Still, it must be done with full knowledge of the facts and not by going astray (at least as to the literal formulations) over the most elementary significance of this doctrine.[24]

---

22 *Logic and Transcendence*, 95.
23 *Summa Theologiae*, Q. 75, a. 5, reply to obj. 2.
24 We unsuccessfully attempted to point out this inaccuracy to its author.

According to Schuon, "the particular logic" giving rise to the dogma of transubstantiation stemmed from "its natural presuppositions, which among the Romans have the characteristics of physical empiricism and juridicism, whence the tendency toward trenchant equations and simplistic and irreducible alternatives."[25]

A question: Does this explanation make the least sense where eucharistic dogma is involved? The concept of substance, utilized by eucharistic theology starting with the ninth century, is Greek in origin, just like all philosophy, and not Roman. True, before the end of the twelfth century, Aristotle's work, except for the treatises *On the Categories* and *On Interpretation*, was unknown. It is therefore without reference to his philosophy that the distinction between substance and accidents (which will be called "species," "sensible appearances") is developed. Nevertheless it is clearly Aristotle's (reworked) doctrine, attributed to a pseudo-Augustine, that is governing this theological thinking and not Roman juridicism. On the other hand, when the dogma was proclaimed by the Fourth Lateran Council in 1215, the Church had been already Roman for ten centuries. How is it possible that juridicism and physical empiricism, to which this Church was heir, had not led it to create this dogma (which Schuon interprets wrongly) in its twelve hundred years of existence? Such remote causes, which have taken so much time to produce their effect, have every chance of being only theoretical and quite approximate, even if they are supposed to be carried out in a "climate of emotional totalitarianism."[26]

To the juridicism and physical empiricism of the West's Roman mentality, Schuon opposes the Eastern mindset. The word of Christ, "an Oriental" ("This is my body"), is an "oriental ellipsis" that by no means implies the "rigorous and massive physical equation" of transubstantialism. So be it. But then how is it that, hearing Jesus proclaim: "the bread that I will give is my flesh, for the life of the world," the Jews, they themselves orientals, cannot understand this "oriental ellipsis"? For they

---

25 *Logic and Transcendence*, 94.
26 Ibid., 95.

do not understand: "How can this man give us his flesh to eat?" (John 6:51–53). The *oriental* significance of this simple equivalence "in the context of the divine inherence"[27] of bread and flesh seems to elude them. Were they already victims of Roman juridicism and physical empiricism?

Analogous difficulties could be raised in connection with the Trinity. Setting aside many points of Schuon's exposé, we will merely examine what he says on the notions of "relation" and "hypostasis," where there prove to be errors in interpretation and even metaphysical doctrine; we will come back later to the notion of "substantial modes" that Schuon reproaches theology for having ignored whereas it may be read in St Thomas Aquinas among others.

Theology, as is known,[28] has the persons of the Trinity consist in the relations that define them. The Father is not someone who, beside his personal reality, would engender the Son, but He is the divine Essence insofar as it engenders the Son; He is, then, nothing but the Father, a pure engendering of the Son, a pure (subsistent) relation of paternity: the relations (of paternity, filiation, spiration) irreducibly distinguish the persons without dividing the Essence (or Substance). For Schuon, that "amounts to saying that they are nothing, for a pure and simple relationship is nothing concrete."[29] One is somewhat surprised to see the criterion of the concrete interjected here, the metaphysical significance of which is not self-evident. One is even more surprised to see a metaphysician, claiming to follow Plato or Neoplatonism, constantly opposing the Platonic intellect to the exoterism of Roman dogmatism, to ignore that Plato effected what Plato himself calls "the parricide of Parmenides," that is, the rejection of a "reified" conception of being, by showing that being was not only identity of self with self, but also alterity, that is to say *relation*: "Among things that exist, some are always spoken of as being what they are just in themselves, others as being what

---

27 Ibid., 94.
28 For an extended treatment of the Trinity, and 'subsistent relations' in particular, see *Love and Truth*, 253–84.
29 *Logic and Transcendence*, 97.

they are with reference [in relation] to other things."[30] Only for Aristotle's philosophy, which is an ontology of individual substance, is relationship the feeblest of all beings, being the accident of an accident, and this connection is confirmed by a certain ontologizing slant to Schuonian metaphysics: hence his recourse to the "argument founded on substance."[31] Be that as it may, we will recall this response by St Thomas Aquinas: "Some have said that relation is not a reality, but only an idea. But this is plainly seen to be false from the very fact that things themselves have a mutual natural order and habitude."[32]

Clearly, it seems that Schuon, as a consequence of his ontologizing and substantialist views, thinks that a positively determined being cannot help but be a substance, that is a "something." The accusation of conceptual inflexibility he levels at dogma can be, with good reason, leveled in turn against his own perspective, which inhibits him from truly understanding Thomas's theology of the Trinity and appreciating its remarkable suppleness. For him, "every relation indicates a substance, otherwise it represents nothing positive."[33] Therefore the Father is not only seen as engendering the Son, but as also "something" in Himself, which risks leading one to tritheism.

Likewise, he misconstrues the *theological* significance of the notion of hypostasis. This term has a very complex history that we cannot retrace here.[34] In any case, it seems to retain for Schuon something of the significance it assumed for Plotinus, where he designates the ontological foundations of the various degrees of reality: Soul (of the world), Intellect, the One. In Christian theology, in the course of the third and fourth centuries, it ended up being used in another sense

---

30 *Sophist*, 255d; in Plato, *The Collected Dialogues*, trans. Cornford (Princeton, NJ: Princeton University Press, 1961), 1001. The expression "parricide of Parmenides" is to be found at 241d. On being as analogy, *cf. Penser l'analogie*, third and fourth parts.
31 *Logic and Transcendence*, 75–84. Plotinus, invoked by Schuon in support of his thesis, refutes at length Aristotle's opinion on relation as "the least real of all categories" (*Metaphysics*, 1088a22) and shows that it must be considered real: Sixth Ennead, I, 6–8; MacKenna and Page, 254–56.
32 *Summa theologiae*, I, Q. 13, a. 7.
33 *Logic and Transcendence*, 101.
34 We have done this in *Love and Truth*, 253–57.

(rightly or wrongly) as the equivalent of the Latin *persona*, the significance of which is itself rather remote from the modern anthropological meaning of "person." And, make no mistake, present-day theologians are perfectly aware of the difficulties presented by the concept of "person" in the formulation of trinitarian dogma.[35] We do not have here a debate, then, on the true nature of the hypostasis, but only a question about terminology and the history of vocabulary. One always has the right to criticize theology, including that of St. Thomas, but obviously provided that one is informed about the significance of the terms it uses and its speculative intentions.[36]

Now, as to subordinationism (the Son is subordinate to the Father, not His equal), the proof of which Schuon sees in the *scriptural* term "Son" and which theology would have misunderstood on behalf of an untenable egalitarianism, some observations are warranted. First of all, this equality is also taught by Scripture: "[Christ Jesus], being in the form of God, thought it not robbery to be equal with God [*isa theo*]: but emptied himself, taking the form of a servant" (Phil. 2:6–7); likewise in St John (10:30): "I and the Father are One," *One* being here a neuter word (*unum* in Latin) and not masculine as might be expected. But on the other hand Christ teaches: "the Father is greater than I" (John 14:28), which dogmatics and theology have fully taken into consideration. This "inferiority" of Christ's human nature is referred to rather frequently. But this is also understood with respect to the divine Person: "There are subordinationist expressions in nearly all of the Fathers... What

---

35 Cf. among others, B. de Margerie, *La Trinité chrétienne dans l'histoire* (Paris: Beauchesne, 1975), 288–301; likewise, P. Cormier, "Question de personne," *Communio* XXV, 5-6 (Sept-Dec. 1999).

36 This knowledge is less widespread than might be supposed. The famous *Vocabulaire philosophique* of Lalande declares that "Christian writers of the era of Plotinus apply ['hypostasis'] to the three divine persons insofar as they view them as substantially distinct" (427), which is a mistake: substantially the persons are precisely not distinct. This difficulty stems from the fact that originally *sub-stance* is the Latin translation of *hypo-stasis*. But in the course of the centuries-long development of trinitarian vocabulary, *substance* has been set aside to designate the very reality of the one God, while *hypostasis*, assuming the meaning of an 'active subsistence,' came to designate the fact that this divine Substance (or Essence) subsisted according to three determined modes of subsistence.

is more, a certain subordinationism is taught by dogma itself: the subordinationism of the Persons insofar as the Father is the *principle* of the other two."[37] Hence the conclusion: "A *personal* and purely relative dependence is therefore a dogma, an *essential* dependence is a heresy."[38] Lastly, we will cite the commentary of St Thomas on John 14:25 ("the Father is greater than I"): "One could also say, as Hilary does, that even according to the divine nature, the Father is greater than the Son, yet the Son is not inferior to the Father, but equal. For the Father is not greater than the Son in power, eternity, and greatness [*magnitudo*], but by the dignity of a grantor or source ... So, the Father is greater because he gives; but the Son is not inferior, but equal, because he receives all that the Father has."[39] The personal dependence of the eternal Word with respect to the Father[40] is defining, then, for an "orthodox subordinationism."[41]

At the end of his "Evidence and Mystery" chapter, Schuon concedes that the logic in the name of which he criticizes the theology of dogma is not everything: it is in reference to, he says, the "mathematical" aspects of things, not to their "'musical" aspects, but "this in no way signifies that logic is to be despised."[42] Fair enough. But how does this concern St. Thomas, who is mentioned several times? Has he ever despised logic, as Schuon's remark presumes? Quite the contrary, in the history of theology it is hard to find a doctor displaying a similar mastery of this *science* and putting it to a more constant use (which some even consider excessive). Schuon is probably not unaware of this. But what he seems to ignore is, precisely, that logic is also a science. What he is referring to is what might be called the human mind's natural logic, "so deeply embedded," says Auguste Comte, "in all

---

37 Mgr. Bartmann, *Précis de théologie dogmatique*, tome I (Mulhouse: Salvator, 1937), 210ff.
38 Ibid., 249.
39 *Commentary on the Gospel of Saint John*, trans. F. R. Larcher, O. P. (Albany, NY: Magi Books, 1998), 92.
40 Lebreton, *Histoire du dogme de la Trinité*, tome I (Paris: Beauchesne, 1927), 521–22.
41 *Dictionnaire critique de la théologie* (Paris: P. U. F., 2000), 1180.
42 *Log.*, 113.

ordinary languages,"[43] and not the scientific formalization of it developed by Aristotle. Is this formalization therefore to be more despised than natural logic? It is in any case much more rigorous, but also, it is true, less easily open to the metaphysical ramifications implicit to the exercise of reason.

We do not deny that Christian dogmatics, on its most "exoteric" level, displays some quite paradoxical forms that seem to clash with natural logic, or that these paradoxes are often justified in the name of the divine mystery's transcendence: this would be to deny the obvious facts. We only object to two things. First, these paradoxes at least have a positive consequence: they teach us *de facto* that "the thoughts" of God are as "high above [human] thoughts as the heavens are above the earth" (Isaiah 55:9), something that awakens us at once to the sense of mystery and an awareness of our lowliness, without speaking of the speculative uplifting to which they goad the intellect, preventing it from resting in rationally satisfying formulations—that also merits emphasis. Second, it is uncertain whether the "gnostic" keys procured by Schuon truly make us enter spiritually into the mystery of dogma. Additionally, subjected to the Schuonian treatment, dogmas come out unrecognizable, emptied of their Christian substance, and "logically digestible," and one might ask further if a treatment with such acrimony is not quite pleasing in nature to conceited minds, by justifying their protesting individualism, their hostility with respect to the Church, and their scorn for a haughtily ignored theology. In some ways the gnostico-critical thesis echoes Jean-Jacques Rousseau's famous declaration: "to tell me to subject my reason is to insult the giver of reason."[44]

Essentially, everything transpires for Schuon as if Christian revelation were reduced as a whole to a text, the book of the Gospels. This textual object is offered for perusal to a Church— a Church marked by Roman juridicism and physical empiricism, as well as by "Western alternativism"—which clumsily strives to provide a rigid and rationally absurd translation. A

---

43 *Système de politique positive*, tome II (Paris: G. Crès et Cie, 1912), 259.
44 *Emile*, trans. A. Bloom (New York: Basic Books, 1979), 300: "God...did not endow me with an understanding in order to forbid me its use."

gnostic chances by who, perceiving the same object, takes possession of it in turn, and provides a metaphysically acceptable (in his judgment) translation. But the gnostico-critical thesis forgets one fundamental and decisive point: the book of the Gospels is not a meteorite descended directly from heaven that could be arranged by anyone however they might like. This book is the product of a Tradition and therefore of a magisterial Church that is its custodian. This Tradition — oral in its beginnings — goes back to Christ by way of the Apostles, and the text is to be read in this Christic and apostolic light. Tradition, Church, Scripture: such is the tripod at the basis of revelation in Christianity. Now, all this elementary and *perfectly logical* data is absent from the Schuonian account.[45]

This is why, at end of count, we must make a case for how "thunderstruck" a Christian of tradition will be at the foregoing theses. Is there not something implausible in the attitude of someone who does not hesitate to place on the scales two thousand years of Christian tradition, twenty councils, two hundred Fathers and Doctors of the Church — and himself; who recommences this history as a function of his metaphysical intuitions, and makes himself the authorized interpreter of Christ's words; who concedes that dogmatic formulations have a right to exist for the sake of the Western mentality; who teaches not only a metaphysical transposition of dogma, but even a new formulation of the dogmatic definitions themselves out of his reading of Scripture; in short, someone who abolishes the work realized by the Church over two thousand years, with the help of the Holy Spirit, and who recovers it in a way inoffensive to the "gnostic" Christian? Do we not have here what is called a lack of a sense of proportion? At the very least, such an attitude seems to betray a misunderstanding about the nature of dogma with respect to revelation and theology. This is what we would like to examine now.[46]

---

[45] Schuon only became a Catholic at fourteen and was a practicing one for just a few years. His position might be summarized, at least in "Evidence and Mystery" and some other texts, by saying that what we have here is Lutheranism revised and corrected by the *Vedanta*.

[46] Additional note: We have but rarely dealt with those texts not directly concerned with gnosis that Schuon has devoted to Catholicism in *Christianity/*

ON THE NATURE OF DOGMA

The gnostico-critical thesis intends to situate itself from the outset, and by essence, beyond the revelations that make up the different religions at the very level of the *mysteria in divinis*. The particular revelations are so many providential forms of a supreme and eternal *Revelatio in divinis* which is identical, in Christianity, with the divine *Logos*. As for the theologies, they are situated not above but below the revelations, endeavoring to achieve a speculative awareness of them. We have, then, three orders here: the purely metaphysical order essentially identified with the divine *Logos*,[47] the order of revelation identified historically with sacred scripture, and the order of theology identified culturally with the common faith of a religion. The

---

Islam. They would be open to the same remarks: there is an identical mixture of precise information, chiefly in liturgical matters, and ignorance of ecclesial doctrine, without mentioning his often sharp tone. Concerned about defending the Lutheran position on the Mass (Luther denied that the liturgical action performed by the priest at the altar is a true and real sacrifice offered to God, in essence identical to Christ's sacrifice), Schuon writes that, "if the Mass were equal to the historical Sacrifice of Christ, it would become sacrilege due to its profanation by the more or less trivial manner of its usage." He agrees that it "coincides potentially with the event of Golgotha, and this potentiality, or this virtuality, can always give rise to an effective coincidence; but if the Mass had in itself the character of its prototype, at each Mass the earth would tremble and would be covered with darkness" (32). The appeal to such a consequence, incriminating for the Catholic thesis, is pointless. We do not see how this stops the Mass from being identical to, in an unbloody sacramental mode (this is the Council of Trent's formulation), the unique sacrifice of Calvary: does the "coincidence" (to use Schuon's language) of a sacred rite with its "prototype" imply a formal identity? If yes, then the rites of all religions have been condemned, for they affirm their basic identity with their prototype, but under the form of a rite. Besides, it is Christ Himself who affirms this identity when he institutes the eucharistic rite: "This is my body which is *given up for you*," "this cup is the new Covenant *in my blood which is shed for you*." In its proper and visible form, the Mass is not the memorial of Calvary, but of Holy Thursday. However, the sacrificial reality of the Last Supper having been completed on the Cross, the reality of the eucharistic rite likewise requires its essential identity with the unique sacrifice of Christ, as well as with the resurrection of Easter. For there is only one Sacrifice: if the Mass is a true sacrifice — which the liturgical prayers declare — it can only be so through its identity with the Good Friday Sacrifice, otherwise it would be reduced to it. As for speaking about a "potential coincidence," that is irrelevant: a sacramental rite is what it is or it is nothing.
47 But not in its inevitably dialectical and discursive language-based formulations.

gnostico-critical thesis considers only these three orders: God in Himself, God in what He says of Himself, God in what the *intellectus fidei* says of Him. In such a structure there is, properly speaking, no place for dogma. When the gnostico-critical thesis views the case of Christianity, it is led then to purely and simply confuse the dogmatic order with the theological. It sees dogmatics as a particular theology, with the difference that it is not the theology of an individual, but of a religion as a whole that interprets, in terms of its own limitations and those of its history, the Word of God. The gnostic can be led, then, to reject one or more of these interpretations, dogmatically established by the Magisterium, when they seem to sin much too seriously against gnosis. The case of Islam seems to confirm the validity of such a conception. There is God, then the Qu'ran, then the theologies, that of al-Ash'ari for example. Under these conditions, it is perfectly possible to criticize the Ash'arite theses while the Qu'ranic revelation is respected in both its letter and spirit, which the great metaphysicians of Islam realize. Such a critique in no way injures Islam itself, which essentially amounts to the Qu'ran as far as doctrine is concerned. Similarly, some think themselves able to criticize Thomism without injury to Christianity—which is altogether exact—or even a particular dogma defined by the Church… but here this is no longer possible, for Christian dogma, that is, the contents proclaimed by the Christian faith, is identical to Christianity itself.

This difference will be more obvious if we compare what Islam asks a young Muslim and Christianity a young Christian to believe. In the Islamic faith there is nothing that is not *explicitly* affirmed in the Qu'ran, and nothing that is not quite simple: there is one sole God, the creator, requiter, and master of all things who has entrusted his message of salvation to a Prophet in the book of the Qu'ran. To be saved, it is enough to do the will of God. Now consider the young Christian. It is not the Gospel that he should learn by heart, as the young Muslim does the Qu'ran, but the Catechism, which is itself an abbreviation of Christian doctrine (dogma) and which, in its essence (but not in its form), goes back to the beginning (the *Didache*). Moreover, whether one is a child or adult, to be Christian does not mean to hold to the Gospel, but to the *Credo*, at least as to faith. Now, there is almost nothing of what the *Credo* and Catechism teach to be found, as such, in the scriptures, apart from those verses concerning the birth, passion, death, and resurrection of Jesus Christ. One might even point out that the descent into Hades of the Apostles' Creed is non-scriptural in origin...[48] Everything else laid out within the trinitarian framework stems from apostolic Tradition. As for the contents of the message, it far surpasses the proofs of any natural theology, and is presented under the form of mysteries.

As we see, with the modest examples just recalled, Christian dogma is intimately united with Christianity; it is absolutely impossible to separate the two.[49] Contrary to Islam, Christianity is not a religion of a book, but the religion of a *Credo*, of a cult: the Eucharist. Since this Credo is not conveyed by a book, it can only be conveyed by a magisterial tradition, that is, in essence, by a Church. Certainly the transmission of Holy Scripture, namely: (1) the words of Christ, (2) His acts, (3) the theological commentaries (of apostolic origin), is an essential function of the magisterial tradition. But the magisterial tradition is prior, according to time, to Holy Scripture, since this is what has written Scripture, determined its canon, and commented on it. Scripture is read *in* Tradition and not Tradition in Scripture. What we have here is a fact, not an interpretation. Conversely, from the viewpoint of eternity, Christ's every word and deed transcend the whole Christian

---

48 Apart, that is, from Peter's elliptical reference to Christ's preaching to the "spirits that were in prison" (1 Peter 3:19) — Trans.

49 This is, moreover, a situation in conformity with the structure of Christianity: Christianity is trinitarian in its essence and "incarnational" in its existence. In other words, everything concerned with the essence of Christianity goes back to the Trinity and should be conceived of with the help of a trinitarian model; everything concerned with its existence goes back to the Incarnation and should be conceived of by the model of the Incarnation. Basically this distinction corresponds to the Greek distinction between "theology" and "economy." Dogma, in its historical and ecclesial form, makes up as it were the doctrinal *corpus* that the message of Christ has assumed and from which it is inseparable (until the eschatological Revelation).

Tradition. But this involves an inward and essential transcendence, affirmed outwardly when one speaks of the inexhaustible character of the word of God.

We are now able to define a first conclusion: a quaternary structure must be substituted for the ternary structure implied by the gnostico-critical thesis, at least as far as Christianity is concerned. Between scriptural Revelation and theology must be inserted the dogma that defines Christian faith, and that theology takes for its object. For such is indeed the conception all Christian theologians (both Orthodox and Catholic) have had of their discipline, which presupposes a very clear distinction between theology and dogma. To reject this dogmatics, as Christian metaphysicians are invited to do by the gnostico-critical thesis, is therefore something entirely different than rejecting certain Asharite theses. In the latter case one does not touch on the essence of Islam, in the former one strikes, in the name of what must be indeed called evangelism, at the very essence of Christianity, at least such as it actually exists.

Well and good. We allow for the existence of a dogma distinct from theology. But what of its essence? What is this dogmatics, this doctrinal tradition? Seeing that this dogmatics was, beyond any doubt, not entirely formulated at the death of the last apostle (which closes Christian revelation), seeing that there was a progressive development of dogma, in the light of what has been called virtual revelation, that is revelation (Tradition and Scripture) insofar as it discloses virtualities not yet perceived or proclaimed, we must indeed grant that dogmatic formulations comprise a "human margin" of theological interpretation, since they are not found as such in Scripture or existing magisterial texts. It is to this question that we would now like to respond.

Our thesis is the following: all the while recognizing that a hiatus exists between the intrinsic contents of Revelation—which, as we have said, is transcendent—and the contents of dogma, and this by virtue of the very nature of things, we think that the Church, in defining revealed data, has not sought to *interpret* it theologically, but to *formulate* it dogmatically. The difference between theology and dogmatics is therefore, for

Christian Dogma and Schuonian Gnosis

ourselves, the difference between interpretation and formulation, which are in a certain manner each other's opposite. Theology is *fides quaerens intellectum*; dogmatic formulation is *intellectus quaerens fidem*. What does Scripture say? That is the question to which the dogmatic definitions are responding. Or again: what is it that my intellect should believe? Now, once the revealed data is defined, theological understanding can seek to understand it, and the Church has never dogmatically canonized a single theology, in other words: several ways of understanding are possible.

An initial remark, that a Christian cannot reasonably ignore, is imperative: in this work of formulating revealed data, the Church is guided by the Holy Spirit. "It is expedient to you that I go," says Christ in St John (16:7-13), "for if I go not, the Paraclete will not come to you... But when he, the Spirit of truth, is come, he will teach you *all truth*." "No Council or theologian is Christ," asserts the gnostico-critical thesis, concluding that the revealed data might be defined otherwise. This puts little value in the promise of Christ and Pentecost: "The Paraclete... shall receive of mine and shall show it to you."

Leaving aside the case of the theologian juxtaposed here with that of the Councils, by virtue of the already denounced theology-dogma confusion, we simply maintain that all ecumenical councils have had the assistance of the Holy Spirit, including Vatican II which, without being dogmatic, contains no heresy. Without doubt it will be objected that the guarantee of the Holy Spirit can be merely negative (is this not rightly the case with Vatican II?), and that the Paraclete cannot "prevent an ass from braying." But the conciliar Fathers have not always been asses. And if anyone retorts that, in any case, the Holy Spirit, all the while assuring the infallibility or inerrancy of church dogma, cannot erase the limitations proper to Greco-Latin humanity, then we must be allowed to ask just what that means. For these limitations are either accidental or indeed essential. If they are essential and alter the very essence of the Christic message that the Holy Spirit wishes to reveal, then the fault for this is God's, who would have had to change this humanity, or reveal to it a much simpler message. If they are accidental, which is evidently the only logical conclusion, then they do not essentially alter the revealed data conveyed and, in speaking about these limitations, one is simply uttering a truism, namely, that all humanity is defined by certain cultural determinations, and that a Greco-Latin is not a Hindu. We must recognize and not forget this; we must not universalize the necessarily limiting determinations of a particular mentality, not idolize categories of thinking. But we do not see how any mentality is exempt from limitations to the extent that it enjoys a near-absolute primacy over all others, or at the very least the kind of primacy that might avoid all the heresies attributable to the dogmatic rigidity of the Greco-Latins. After all, neither the history of Hinduism nor that of Buddhism exhibit any such thing. And, speaking only of the latter, we can see that the complete negation of the *jivatma* was too "apophatic," too "koanic" to be assimilated doctrinally, since the late but orthodox schools have revived this notion under varied forms.[50] Perhaps Westerners smitten with the East have the tendency at times to underestimate the oppositions between the diverse Hindu or Buddhist schools. Surely, Truth transcends all forms, but it is in fact obvious that these diverse schools were not always cognizant of the relativity of their viewpoints and have identified these viewpoints purely and simply with the Truth. From this we conclude that the assistance of the Holy Spirit in the working out of ecclesial dogma is necessary and sufficient to guarantee the essential fullness of the *revelatum*. Formulated in this way, the *revelatum* is everything it ought to be so that every mind can, by its mediation, gain access to all Truth according to its capacity.

A second remark to be called for is that, in fact, the doctrinal Magisterium has never, properly and positively speaking, *defined the revelatum*. The doctrine of faith is first a nearly tacit consensus by which every Christian shares in a submission to apostolic authority. The Magisterium intervenes only when this consensus has been broken, and only with great reluctance will it intervene with a positive definition. "The tradition of

---

50 Cf. E. Conze, *Buddhism, Its Essence and Development*, 2nd ed. (Oxford: Bruno Cassirer, 1953), 168–70.

Christian Dogma and Schuonian Gnosis

the Church is to dogmatize only for the sake of efficaciously ruling out an error." "The Church does not define for the sake of defining," but only when that is necessary to safeguard the revealed deposit (*traditum*).[51] For the Spirit's assistance is only promised to it for the transmission of the *traditum*, and as a function of the latter (Matt. 18:20), not therefore with a view to crafting a theological synthesis, which, moreover, the Magisterium has never done.

Our third remark will lead us right to the question that concerns us. What is then the concrete and historical attitude of the Church with respect to the data revealed in Holy Scripture?

First, as we have said, the Church does not offer to explain revealed data, but to formulate it. It is sufficient—but indispensable—to study the history of dogma to realize this. Yes, this history is long and complex. It covers several centuries. It occupied thousands of minds in every region of Christianity. It is attested to in the enormous mass of manuscripts, some as yet poorly known. From this immense history one idea stands out and little by little irresistibly comes to the fore: the Church has always faithfully sought out what was *said* in Scripture as a function of what Tradition taught—not to interpret the meaning of the text but define it, such is its rule. And define it, as much as possible, *without exactly engaging in theological interpretation*. The Church has striven to set "the letter of the meaning," while carefully and quite explicitly avoiding anything that might be a properly philosophical and therefore theological affirmation. It has always kept to "the level of the *revelatum*," being guided solely—all the documents prove this—by the most literal possible significance of the *revelatum*, and, for disputed cases, leaving it to Tradition. If this distinction between dogmatic formulation and theological interpretation is rejected, the actual history of Christian dogma becomes unintelligible. The facts show a Church maintaining, through a forest of countless and intermingled theological perspectives, one and the same dogmatic line. Before such an abundance of possible interpretations, and without considering the assistance

---

51 Cf. Congar, *La Foi et la Théologie* (Paris: Desclée, 1957), 48.

of the Holy Spirit, one truly wonders how these men did not go mad and what was then the rule followed by the Church that permitted it to set dogma, all the while leaving the field open to interpretation. Was this some particular and secret theology? A needless hypothesis; the norm is openly provided by an unconditional and almost intemperate fidelity to the traditional *revelatum*. To take one rather appropriate image, we could compare the Church to a translator who has to translate a written text—the deeper meaning of which sometimes eludes him—into a foreign language. This is a relatively frequent case. Now, although a knowledge of the deeper meaning surely enables him to better establish the literal meaning, yet everyone knows that it is not altogether impossible to establish a good translation of a not totally understood text. The text here is Scripture. It is ever symbolic. The translation is the dogmatic formulation made necessary by Scripture's symbolic nature. The deeper meaning is, in principle, theology. We are saying the Church is content to establish a dogmatic translation of the scriptural *revelatum*, in obedience to Tradition. It is up to theologians to gain access to the deeper meaning. Undoubtedly, there are some disputed and undecided points, since the Orthodox and Catholic translations are not strictly identical; but these differences are actually quite minimal.

The historical references for our assertions are multiple and cover the whole history of what is called positive theology. Quite consciously and explicitly the doctrinal Magisterium avoids either terms, or the accepted meaning of terms, that are directly and exclusively derived from a philosophy or a specific theology. And so, for example, this is what transpired with the word *hypostasis*, which lost its philosophical meaning as "underlying and authentic reality" and came to designate exclusively the divine Person, even before the Christian West elaborated a philosophy of the person, a philosophy absent from Greek thought.[52] And this is how it was with the term

---

52 The Council of Chalcedon, which defined the union of two natures in a single hypostasis, was in 451. The first *philosophical* elaboration of the idea of hypostasis (in the sense of person) was the work of Leo of Byzantium in the first half of the sixth century.

transsubstantiatio, adopted by the Lateran Council in 1215, in use among Latin theologians since around 1130, and outside of any express reference to Aristotle, whose work was almost unknown at that time.[53] It is much the same for the term *species*, deliberately chosen by the Council of Trent to avoid the too Aristotelian *accident*.[54]

We will clarify this truly fundamental point in the following way. We would like the defenders of the gnostico-critical thesis to become clearly aware of the actual conditions implied by their assertions, and this is so for the objective history of dogma as much as for the subjective and "psychological" reality of its development. Objectively, if dogmatics is only a theology, then, since this dogmatic line has a near-absolute continuity seldom seen in the history of ideas, it is necessary for an explicitly conceived theology to have existed from the start, a theology to which Councils, Fathers, popes, and bishops have explicitly referred, so as to orient themselves in the midst of thousands of discussions, at times dizzyingly subtle, proposing thousands of apparently plausible theses on the meaning of the *revelatum*, and all this over the course of more then fifteen hundred years! What is this theology then, where is it? Frankly speaking, nowhere. What exists, at the beginning, is a "rule of faith" (*regula fidei*), not in the sense of a formal criterion, but of the normative content of the truth received from the apostles. This rule of truth (St Irenaeus), this doctrine—Origen puts its authority ahead of Scripture—comes from Christ who, Clement of Alexandria tells us, gave "the keys of gnosis" confiscated by the scribes (Luke 11:52) to Peter, James, and John.[55] But no explicit writings are to be found concerning this gnosis, this deep understanding of Christic revelation: the nature of a living gnosis is opposed to this; we only find some essential remarks about it in St John

---

53 Notice that—something the gnostico-critical thesis should take into account—Thomas Aquinas the Aristotelian seldom uses this term, however canonized, preferring *conversio* instead.

54 The majority of theologians at the Council of Trent who worked on drafting those texts concerned with the Eucharist were not Thomists.

55 This thesis has been developed in *Christ the Original Mystery*, 277–95.

and St Paul. It is not this, then, that guided the Magisterium in its task, and it could not refer to this "Christic theology" (Christ is the true *Theologos*) or give a decision in its name. Besides (Origen deplores this), the ecclesial authorities were not always in a position to have access to such a knowledge. But the essential points of this Christic gnosis have been set down in a formulary, the Creed, entrusted, if not to the intellect, at least to the memory of the Church, and this is what accounts for the Church's extraordinary dogmatic fidelity. What was going on in the heads of popes and bishops when making their dogmatic decisions? Surely, the assistance of the Holy Spirit has never gone so far as to whisper into the ears of the Christian magisterium those formulas suitable for infallibly defining the meaning of the *revelatum*. Let us picture these men as they truly were: humble or zealous, hesitant, indecisive, sometimes understanding almost nothing in the discussions of the theologians, for this is how they are seen by history.[56] These men carefully avoided committing the *revelatum* to a theological interpretation. With their all too human reasoning, they were ostensibly guided only by the Scripture-bearing apostolic Tradition, and they had no other care than to settle the meaning of this Scripture; not even to interpret it, but to *say* it as precisely as possible, so that anyone who wanted to understand it might know at least what must be understood.

But, some will say next, as faithful as the Church might have been to the meaning of the *revelatum*, and taking into account the inevitable "human margin" that no one will deny, was not the Church led to formulate dogma in terms of what might be called the risks of a particular humanity's misunderstanding and therefore for reasons of expediency? We will not set aside this hypothesis *a priori*, but we will simply ask: are there any identifiable relationships between these reasons of expediency and the actual contents of the dogmas? To account for dogmas by reasons of expediency is to implicitly become involved in establishing an intelligible relationship of one to the other, of a particular expediency to a particular dogmatic content. Is this simply possible? That the Magisterium took into account

---

56 Cf. Cayré, *Patrologie*, tome I (Paris: Desclée, 1938), 213.

the human receptacles it was addressing is certain, and even obvious. But the facts show that above all it took them into account negatively, in other words, the Church strove to fix those points of the *revelatum* at risk of being misunderstood on the one hand, and, on the other, in the very formulation of a particular dogma, strove to forestall any misconceptions about the portion of *revelatum* fixed in this way. We have here two different tasks. The first task proves that dogmatics does not cover the entire field of the *revelatum*; the second that a particular dogma does not exhaust the meaning of the portion of *revelatum* defined. What is primary in both cases is the *revelatum*, not the human receptacle. The Church's concern is not to have a particular portion of the *revelatum* understood, to have a particular humanity grasp one of the truths of faith, but to express this particular portion in such a way that certain errors with respect to it are averted.

On top of this, some have retorted that these errors were not such in themselves, but only with respect to a particular humanity. These errors, those of Sabellius for example, could be viewed to the contrary as gnostic perspectives, dangerous only for certain people, even if they are the majority, not for everyone. This is why some speak of "reasons of expediency." This rightly seems to make little sense.

Let us go over the idea implicit to the previous thesis that seems to endow the Magisterium with a kind of duplicity: the Church would see the metaphysical import of Sabellianism, but, in its wisdom, would prefer a less metaphysical formulation, one less apt to lead minds astray. But this is a duplicity incompatible with the nature of things. It would be better to say: the Church has set aside Sabellianism because it has not understood its metaphysical significance. But ultimately it comes down to this: the Church sets aside Sabellianism not because it is false, but because it is dangerous. To what dangers then are the faithful exposed? Or, more precisely, what truth of faith is being endangered among the faithful? Formulated in just this way, we realize that this question admits of no response. For we need to first *define* this faith in itself, and show next what it risked in being altered—because of the narrowness of mental bounds native to Greco-Latin humanity—by the speculative audacities of Sabellianism. Now the sole definition of "trinitarian" faith apt to be changed by Sabellius can only be one of the traditional dogmas, namely a single God in three distinct persons;[57] only that which is exhibited by a defined form can be spoken of as changed. Historically, this is clearly what happened: Sabellianism explicitly contends with the traditional faith, and therefore *presupposes* its existence. The same goes, as we are beginning to see, for the gnostico-critical thesis. But this thesis also says something else: it affirms that "trinitarism" is a by-product of the anti-Sabellian struggle, and therefore regards it as later in time. In this way it upholds two contradictory things: *both* that the traditional faith, independent of Sabellius, nevertheless ran a certain risk with him, *and* that the formulation of this faith can only be explained by an express intent to repudiate Sabellianism.[58] Cause and effect are thus confused. But, if Sabellian modalism had triumphed, it is not another theology that would have been transmitted, but another dogmatics. And today's gnostics would not have had to transpose any trinitarian dogma, for the very word Trinity would have disappeared from Christian vocabulary. Christianity as a whole would have been different, that is, it would not be Christianity, for there was no other definition for a religious *tradition* than the one designated by its historical existence. And, hence, the gnostico-critical thesis would not

---

57 This dogmatic utterance is not a *definition* of the Trinity's Essence; it does not tell us what the Trinity is in Itself. It is only nominal: it defines what the Church calls Trinity. Once again we see the difference between formulation and interpretation.

58 Sabellius, so it seems, did not distinguish between Essence (or Substance) and Person. For him there was only one Person because there was only one God. This single Person is in turn, and *temporarily*, Father, Son, and Spirit. These distinctions are purely modal, that is, a function of our point of view and without objective reality. There is no real distinction between Father and Son. Sabellius does not profess the patripassianism of his predecessors (it is not the Father who is incarnated and suffers), but the divine Person ceases being the Father when It is incarnated in Jesus Christ. Father, Son and Spirit are mere labels based on the different aspects of the divine work (creation, illumination, sanctification). The term "aspect" is not moreover condemnable in itself, since Tertullian employs it (*species*) to really distinguish the Persons in an attack against the modalists (cf. *Adversus Praxeam*, Chap. II).

even have been able to declare that "Christianity, &c." In short, this thesis seems contradictory because it is tantamount to rejecting its object. Why reproach a circle for not having the properties of a square?

This is not all. There is a last, yet to be envisaged possibility. We could in fact deem that the disjunction posed—either Sabellius or the Trinity—is too exclusive. The gnostico-critical thesis admits of a presupposition, namely: there is a *mysterium quid* for which the trinitarian dogma and Sabellian modalism are each a different interpretation; it is to this *mysterium quid* that the gnostic refers in order to criticize the dogmatic formulation. But take heed! This *mysterium quid* is necessarily a supposition able to be formulated, otherwise why criticize the dogmatic statement and reproach it for being too narrowly, too rigidly exclusive, for what there is of the "incontestable" in Sabellius? Hence, the gnostico-critical thesis necessarily supposes that such a (non-anti-Sabellian) statement is possible. But it is up to it to formulate. Let someone supply us, then, with a formulation of this *mysterium quid* such that it admits of both a trinitarian and Sabellian interpretation. But this is just what no one has done. *All* metaphysical propositions relative to this *mysterium quid*, to our knowledge, *start* with the dogmatic Christian formulation in order to propose a metaphysical interpretation of it. Therefore they presuppose it, even and above all if this is only to surpass it; for, we repeat, we are not ruling out that someone might seek to surpass the ordinary level of understanding a dogma, we are only denying the possibility of substituting another formulation for it. In the end, what the gnostico-critical thesis (and not the merely gnostic thesis) is engaged in, and about which it should be, we think, clearly aware, is a replacing of Christian dogma with a doctrinal formulation able to fill the following functions through two thousand years: to faithfully uphold the *traditum*, to dispel outright heresies, to integrate, through its "metaphysical fluidity," the antinomic viewpoints of apparent heresies (which are in reality gnostic breakthroughs) and lastly to clearly teach the ordinary faithful. Otherwise, if one cannot do better than thousands of Fathers and Doctors, twenty Councils, and two thousand years of dogmatics, all things considered, then in the name of what is the work accomplished being criticized?[59]

Let us concede for now that the gnostico-critical thesis is pertinent here, namely, that the dogmatic Magisterium, setting aside by expediency the gnostic breakthroughs of Sabellianism, decides to present Christian humanity with a more simple, more subtle, and less dangerous doctrine. And let us again suppose a foreigner, ignorant of all Christian history, is asked what he might expect on the part of a Church wishing to adapt itself to an audience of limited mentality, so as to avoid every error arising from overly subtle formulations. Surely he will reply that he would expect rather basic statements apt for satisfying an equally basic need for intelligibility and, at the same time, determining the essentials of the faith in a sufficient manner. Now this is not at all what happened. How surprised our foreign observer would be to learn that every Christian ought to believe, from the age of seven, that there is *one* sole God in *three* distinct Persons, that one of these Persons *is* true God and true man, that He is born of a Virgin, that He is dead *and* risen, that He has left us His Body under the form of a host that is bread as to its species, but *Corpus Christi* as to its substance. "These are hard sayings," he will think. "If this is what is called adapting dogma to a limited mentality for reasons of expediency, then what would we have if it had not been adapted and reasons of expediency played no role! I do not understand the attitude of this Church, for you are stating here five or six well-nigh unintelligible propositions.

---

59 We are not saying that the metaphysical caliber of a particular gnostic cannot be superior to a particular Greek or Latin Father. We are simply saying: let someone prove that it is possible to do better, *ponendis positis*. Note well: one might attempt to formalize in the following manner the reasoning just presented. The gnostico-critical thesis asserts that the (trinitarian) faith risked being altered by Sabellius, and that this is the reason why the trinitarian faith was dogmatically defined in the way it actually was. Let us call F1 the (trinitarian) faith and F2 the *trinitarian* faith. Let it be stated that F2 is, by definition, anti-Sabellian, which we will write as F2 (non-S). Now, *either* F2 is identical to F1—and therefore F1 is also non-S by definition, and therefore it has nothing to fear from S; *or else* F2 differs from F1—and in that case, let someone define F1 for us, that is, let someone tell us, with supporting texts, what the pre-Sabellian (can it be called trinitarian?) faith was.

These propositions so obviously and so directly conflict with the reason of all healthy-minded people that I am led to suspect this Church of having lost its common sense. Why, against all evidence, did it need to uphold such mysteries over the course of two thousand years? This is a truly a history of insanity. About what, then, were these Fathers and Councils thinking? To save them, does God require that men subscribe to these unbelievable propositions? This is untenable. Since your Scriptures speak of a Father, Son, and Holy Spirit who—all three—are God, it seems to me that the Sabellian doctrine would rightly provide an interpretation that does violence neither to the text of your Scriptures, nor to human reason. Why then reject it? For reasons of expediency, some have asserted. I do not see which ones, or what danger the defined faith was in since, precisely, it was yet to be defined. No, you see, there is in my opinion only a single possible explanation for such a situation. Since this doctrinal Magisterium has proven, in other respects, that it was not insane, I am led to suppose that, in declaring what it declared, it was not seeking to understand the mystery, that is to give it *an* interpretation, but only to settle what was said in the text, whatever interpretation might be given to this saying in other respects. The Magisterium seems in some manner constrained, obliged, to do what it does. Would that it might act otherwise, in transmitting the *traditum*, than by repeating what the apostolic Tradition has taught. I say *constrained* because it seems to me that perhaps it would have wanted to say something else. No, it was not Sabellius who put the Christian faith in jeopardy; quite the contrary, it was the Church's dogmatic definition. To impose on a collectivity the mysterious contradiction of a single God in three distinct Persons is to toy with trouble. Why be surprised, under these conditions, if this collectivity rejected the Christian faith by reason of the absurdity of some of its propositions? That did not occur. But, from the human standpoint, this was the only possible forecast."

Let us summarize this discussion. We have Scripture on the one hand, dogmatic formulations on the other, and lastly the Christians themselves. How is this Scripture presented?

As a revelation at once esoteric and exoteric. The mystery is neither hidden nor dispelled. A man introduces himself there as God (the Father and I are One; before Abraham was, I am) and is presented as such (St John, St Paul). This man, who is also God, reveals to us at the same time a Trinity in the One God (the Spirit who proceeds from the Father), presents bread as His Body (and the Jews do not understand), dies (a God who dies), rises, and ascends to heaven.

Now we will look at the dogmatic formulation. What does the Church do? It can conceal the message or adapt it. It does neither. Let us suppose for a moment that these are texts belonging to a Jewish spiritual school. All difficulties vanish. There is no longer any need for dogmatic formulation; we find ourselves in the presence of a quadruple account of a spiritual adventure, other examples of which seem to be offered by the sacred literature of other nations. It is up to each disciple to understand the master's teaching. But this spiritual way is found to establish a religion. From that time on the Master's heirs are occupied with defining the *revelatum* (barring the acceptance of a religion with a variable doctrine, which would be equivalent to a non-religion). What could they do? Not account for the *revelatum*, maintain a strict monotheism, make Christ simply a prophet, the Eucharist merely a symbol? That is exoterism. And from then on more heresies. Or else make of it a metaphysics by appealing to the Kabbalah, Neoplatonism, reducing the paradoxes of the *revelatum* and pretending to surpass them with a higher gnosis? That is esoterism. Nor are they mutually exclusive. Rational monotheism for the masses, gnostic supra-theism for the elite, or even—an extreme hypothesis!—supra-theism for everyone? The Church, as we see, could adopt none of these solutions. What remained was the only way possible: keep to the level of the *revelatum* while striving to formulate it according to the Tradition as exhibited in Scripture, and in such a way that the human margin of interpretation is reduced to a minimum. The result is that the paradoxes of Scripture are not eliminated or overcome; they are defined, fixed, and sanctioned in their frankly paradoxical character—otherwise known as a mystery.

Lastly, we will consider the third point: the Christians. Let us distinguish non-metaphysicians from metaphysicians. For the first, doctrinal truth as officially presented reveals, by its difficulty, the divine transcendence. As for the gnostics, they rejoice in the paradoxical nature of the dogmas, for they see therein the sole way to awaken the human intellect from its rational sleep, and call it forth to anagogical transcendence,[60] to a gnostic passing beyond. How could it be otherwise? If dogma presented no speculative hardship—and since there is, moreover, no initiatic organization to guard, in secret, the gnostic tradition—how could there be a possibility of actualizing gnosis, unless the truths to be believed were propounded in such a manner that they invite us, by that very fact and even though apophatically, to an anagogical ascension? And the gnostic rejoices to see that, confronted with Arius, Sabellius or Luther, the Church has resisted the temptation to a rational accommodation of dogma.

SOME POINTS OF DOGMATIC HISTORY

It seems that any assessment of the possibly gnostic scope of what the Magisterium calls heresy implies, besides the meaning of authentic gnosis, a good knowledge of the facts. Now this knowledge is long and hard to acquire. One should not rely on the assertions of a basic manual.[61] If one is unable to consult the texts themselves—made nearly impossible by their abundance—this question must be studied in the historians of dogma and theology. Simply reading a handbook of patrology (Cayré, for example) makes us aware of our ignorance. Then we must read Tixeront, Lebreton, Régnon, Congar, Daniélou, Lubac, Urs von Balthasar, Bouyer, &c., if we wish to gain some idea of what has occurred.

Since Sabellianism is under consideration, we will say a few words about it first. Historically, the modalist thesis makes its appearance around AD 180. Specialists call it "Monarchianism,"

---

60 This expression is borrowed from St Dionysius the Areopagite.
61 Such as the one by Abbé Berthier (*Abrégé de théologie dogmatique et morale* [Lyon & Paris: Vitte, 1927] 4th edition), referred to by Schuon in his correspondence. This quite formal presentation is as little historical as possible. The first edition dates from 1894.

because it asserts the existence of a single (*monos*) Principle (*arche*). This thesis explicitly presents itself as a negation of the Trinity, and not of Christ's divinity as with Arius. Monarchianism is therefore a reaction against an already quite precise, although unformulated, trinitarian faith. "If Christ is God," declares Noetus the first monarchian, "he is surely the Father: otherwise he would not be God. And, if Christ has suffered, God has suffered [patripassianism], for he is one."[62] Noetus, who held a high position, appeared several times before a conciliar tribunal. He ended up being condemned (around AD 200) not in the name of theology (almost non-existent at that time), but of the traditional faith.

Before speaking of Sabellius, Praxeas—spoken of by Tertullian—should be mentioned. He is equally a modalist, known at Rome. He achieved great success with the crowds, who shouted "*Tenemus monarchiam, monarchiam!*" everywhere, a rallying cry meaning: a single God! The names Father and Son do not distinguish persons. They are merely conventions. The name 'Word' is a *flatus vocis, vox et sonus oris,* "a breathing of the voice, the voice and sound of the mouth," Praxeas declared.[63] He is then a nominalist. It is the Father who was incarnated and who descended into the womb of the Virgin. Praxeas is unknown to Hyppolitus, but his testimony agrees with Tertullian's in affirming that all these doctrines bear the mark of the simple and uncultured. Conversely, Hyppolitus and Tertullian show themselves at times more concerned for erudition than for the traditional faith. The Magisterium will not follow them on this terrain. Hyppolitus moreover will become schismatic, and Tertullian will fall into the Montanist heresy.

At this point Sabellius makes his appearance rather suddenly. Arriving perhaps at Rome from Libya, he becomes Noetus's disciple but refines his teacher's doctrine, and imbues it with such luster that it will henceforth bear his name. We are in fact poorly informed about this doctrine. Perhaps the doctrine of Sabellius was less 'heretical' than some of his later disciples made it. In any case, despite the relentless efforts of

---

62 St Hyppolitus, *Against Noetus*, 2, P. G., tome X, col. 805.
63 Tertullian, *Adversus Praxeam*, chapter 7.

Hyppolitus who, in his hatred of Sabellius, almost came to affirm three Gods (tritheism), Pope Zephyrinus refused to condemn Sabellius, and yet there are no grounds for accusing this holy pope of modalism. But, as we have stated, the Magisterium refuses to enter into theological quarrels. It was the successor of Zephyrinus, Callistus, who condemned Sabellianism, but also Hyppolitus, accused of ditheism (around AD 220).

If we cross from Rome to the East, we find that modalism was not unknown there. Origen refutes it implicitly (*De Principiis*, I, Praef. 4), and teaches that in God the Son is distinct from the Father (*De Oratione*, 15; *Contra Celsum*, VIII, 12). Origen was not a second-rate gnostic. One of Origen's disciples, Dionysius of Alexandria (dead about AD 264), rose up in turn against the Sabellianism that had spread to the East from Rome. But Dionysius of Alexandria in his turn, like Hyppolitus, exaggerated the distinction of Persons so that his adversaries accused him of tritheism. Pope Dionysius of Rome, before whom the quarrel was submitted, replied as always by recalling the traditional faith in a famous text: "For [Sabellius] blasphemes when he says that the Son himself is the Father and the reverse...[but neither must we, by an opposite error,] divide and separate the monarchy into three principles" (about AD 260).[64]

In the end, then, what is the Sabellian thesis? This is how it is defined around the fourth century by some knowledgeable disciples:

"God, the simple and indivisible monad, is a single person: He is called *uiopator*, Father-Son; but insofar as He created the world, He assumes the name Word. The Word is God the *uiopator* manifesting Himself through creation. This manifestation lasts as long as the world and means that the Word-aspect is permanently within God. Now to this world, created in this way, the monad reveals Itself in the Old Testament as lawgiver, this is the Father; in the New Testament as redeemer by the incarnation: this is the Son; and as sanctifier of souls: this is the Holy Spirit. But these three successive states of

---

64 Denzinger, *Sources of Catholic Dogma*, trans. R. J. Deferrari (Fitzwilliam NH: Loreto, 1955), 23.

the Monad do not constitute three distinct persons; they are only three aspects, three virtualities, three modalities, and as if three names of the same hypostasis."[65]

As we see, this thesis identifies the Person with the Essence. Not only does it deny the Trinity, but it even makes it impossible for any metaphysical transposition of a trinitarian dogma that grasps, in the relative Trinity of Persons in the bosom of the divine Essence, the immanence of a Supreme Relativity *in divinis*.

But is the traditional faith recalled by the popes indeed that of the Apostles? It is impossible to prove this entirely. However, and among hundreds of important testimonies, we will simply mention that of St Irenaeus. Irenaeus of Lyon lived at the end of the second century. He knew many presbyters, the disciples of the Apostles, and in particular St Polycarp, the last witness of the apostolic age and direct disciple of St John! Was there a Christian gnosis superior to that of St John? "Numerous disciples crowded around Polycarp to collect from his lips the last living echo of the apostolic age," relates tradition (Cayré, tome I, 72). St Irenaeus has then, by himself, collected the teaching of the beloved disciple, and moreover recounts, in his *Against the Heresies*, several words of St John himself. Now the trinitarian teaching of St Irenaeus, which does not utilize the term Trinity, is strictly in conformity with traditional dogma: the distinction of Persons, the perfect divinity of each, but possessed of different titles, for only the Father possesses divinity of Himself, being its source. Is this Asiatic, who acknowledges being not much of a rhetorician, to be qualified as having the same mental limitations as Origen the Greek, or St Augustine the African?

It is true that the word "person" is not in Scripture. The gnostico-critical thesis sees a certain limitation of revealed truth in the application of this concept to the Father, Son and Holy Spirit. But historically the opposite is true. The idea of person—unknown to Greek and Latin thought—is purely religious in origin. It was elaborated and defined exclusively to designate the three poles of the divine Essence, and thus to

---

[65] St. Epiphanius, *Panarion*, P. G., tome XLI, col. 1052-1061.

formulate trinitarian dogma. It is therefore hard to see this as the result of a limitation peculiar to the Greco-Latin mentality. Only beginning in about the sixth century do we see the dogmatics of the person (= hypostasis) be transformed into a metaphysics at first christological, but then progressively applied to human beings. Moreover the most standard theology sees in this a purely analogical term. To best appreciate the notion of person in theology, we must keep from reading into it those "personalist" connotations conferred on it by modern philosophy since Descartes, which it would not have for an Augustine, who makes use of the term only reluctantly and for lack of a better. What remains is that this theology, from Augustine to Thomas, is based in part on a metaphysics of relation so important that experts, like Gilson,[66] have seen in it the chief problem of medieval philosophy. And just as we must refrain from interpreting the term hypostasis in a Plotinian sense (thus to speak of a "hypostatic person" makes no sense in Christian language, since "hypostasis" is the Greek equivalent for "person" in Latin), we also must refrain from seeing subsistent relation as an "abstraction."

Now is the time to return to the notion of "substantial mode," that any gnostically inspired theology would have known how to develop, whereas Roman dogmatism would have confined itself to the "either persons or modes" alternative: if divine persons are modes, they are no longer persons.[67] Quite to the contrary, thinks Schuon, "a hypostasis is a substantial mode of the unique Substance, or it is nothing."[68] But this reproach is baseless. It is Sabellian modalism that is a prisoner to the alternative: either "mode" or "hypostasis," which is not traditional dogma. For heretical modalism the modes "Father," "Son," and "Holy Spirit' cannot be "persons"; they are mere labels, extrinsic to God: in God there is only Substance. For Catholic theology, to the contrary, the modes also have their own proper and subsistent reality; it is in this sense that

---

66 *History of Christian Philosophy in the Middle Ages* (New York: Random House, 1955), 270–71.
67 *Logic and Transcendence*, 103, note 1.
68 Ibid., 101.

it speaks of "substantial modes." In the quite representative *Dictionnaire de Théologie Catholique*, Father A. Michel puts it this way: "the Church Fathers recall that, in God, paternity and sonship indicate substantial modes which, all while being in contrast to each other, are distinguished from substance" by a "virtual" distinction, that is based objectively in the "virtualities of substance".[69] In this way does theology, by itself, account for what is right about the theses of modalism (a term which is, after all, rather recent). We find this 'orthodox modalism' in the writings of the great theologians. St Bonaventure sees the person as a *modus essendi respectivus*, a "mode of being proper" to each hypostasis.[70] Similarly, St Thomas speaks of "the way (*modus*) whereby God is in God as the known in the knower" and of "the way (*modum*) in which God is in God as the beloved is in the lover."[71] Even more clearly, he designates the person as "an incommunicable mode of existence" (*modus existendi incommunicabiliter*).[72] And the reactions of Byzantine theologians are, after all, revealing: they see in Latin theology, at least since St Augustine, either implicitly[73] or explicitly,[74] a form of modalism and Sabellianism.

As for the Eucharist, one advocate for the gnostico-critical thesis has asserted, to justify the Schuonian position, that the Church "had adopted an overly formalist and almost materialistic conception of the Real Presence, alienating in this way people of good faith." But, as we have shown, the "adopted" conception is in no way "almost materialistic." It is even meant to avert such an idea. Substance is not a material but a metaphysical reality, including the substance of the Body of Christ, a reality invisible in itself (and not only in the eucharistic bread), distinguished by the intellect alone.

---

69 Tome XIII, col. 2148.
70 *De Trinitate*, III, 2; cf. B. de Margerie, *La Trinité chrétienne dans l'histoire* (Paris: Beauchesne, 1974), 291, n 47.
71 *Compendium of Theology*, First Treatise on Faith, chap. 46; trans. C. Vollert (St. Louis & London: B. Herder Book Co., 1947), 41.
72 *Summa Theologiae*, I, Q. 30, a. 4, ad 2.
73 Paul Evdokimov, *L'Orthodoxie* (Neuchâtel: Delachaux et Nestlé, 1965), 136.
74 John Meyendorff, *A Study of Gregory Palamas*, trans. G. Lawrence, 2nd ed. (Crestwood, NY: St. Vladimir's Seminary Press, 1974), 228-29.

One commentary by St Thomas expresses it this way: "the dimensive quantity of Christ's body is in this sacrament, not according to its proper manner (namely, that the whole is in the whole, and the individual parts in individual parts), but after the manner of substance, whose nature is for the whole to be in the whole, and the whole in every part."[75] It is much more the non-theological presentation of the Eucharist that has caused problems. In this respect Orthodox doctrine, far from correcting the Catholic, outdoes it by positing a total *metabole* (a conversion) (substance plus accidents)! We readily acknowledge that many priests are rather poor theologians. But no one is prohibited from going to the sources. Twenty years ago we read that one priest, dazzled by scientific progress, proposed that the molecules and atoms of consecrated bread be analyzed so to experimentally ascertain the transformation! He had not understood that substance is not identical to atoms, but that it is the metaphysical principle of their physical reality.

THE DOGMATIC CAVERN OF GNOSIS

Up to this point we have avoided, as much as possible, dealing with the question in depth, keeping to the purely formal level. This is because the gnostico-critical thesis is refutable only if we keep in mind the difference in form (the formal object of the scholastics) between theological interpretation and dogmatic formulation. However we can say something basic about the question in light of the foregoing analyses. If the metaphysical transpositions of the Trinity indicated by Schuon in *Logic and Transcendence* are taken as models, we cannot help but be struck by a change in language (today one would say semantics) when going from dogmatics to metaphysics: not only are the words not the same, they do not even belong to the same tone, they are not even of the same nature. On one side we hear of Father, Son, and Spirit, of God and Persons (or Hypostases), and on the other Beyond-Being, Being, Existence, or Sat-Chit-Ananda, or the Absolute and Relativity. Bluntly put, we have on one side a religious language, on the other a philosophical one. Now, this philosophical language makes use

---

75 *Summa theologiae*, IIIa, Q. 76, a. 4, ad 1.

of strictly human concepts, while religion strives to make use of the language of revelation, that is to say of Scripture (setting aside the term Person, Hypostasis in Greek).[76] Clearly, and of course no one is claiming otherwise, dogma could not make use of philosophical language. This language is at once too human in its form, and too universal in its content. In metaphysics there is as if a negation, or rather an *a priori* ignorance of Revelation, and therefore of religion, which is always single.

We see then that the anagogic ascension is not achieved by a certain "rupture" with the plane of dogmatic formulations. But this "rupture" is interior. It cannot consist in a critique of Christian formulations for which metaphysical formulations, whatever they might be, are substituted. Why criticize this religious language, why in this connection speak of a "logic that is dogmatically coagulative and piously unilateral," of a "literalistic and quasi-mathematical interpretation of certain words in the Scriptures"? Taking into account the nature of the scriptural *revelatum* (the God-Man, identical to and different from God the Father) and the mentality of every collectivity, was it possible to do otherwise? The dogmatic formulation can for all that serve quite well as the basis for a metaphysical transposition, as exemplified by the Immaculate Conception [*l'Immaculée Conception*], seen as the Immaculate Conception [*la Conception Immaculée*] that God has of himself.

Once again it must be asked, however, if the magisterial definition of the Trinity, which arises, we are told, from a "logic ... determined by the necessity of adapting the mystery to a mentality more volitive than contemplative"[77] and constrained to "make divergent realities fit into a formula which had to present them bluntly as being convergent,"[78] it must be asked, we say, if this definition was not the most suitable one for safeguarding the possibility of a gnostic breakthrough to the Deity, or purely metaphysical Reality. We have shown this, and the facts indisputably prove it: Sabellianism (the

---

76 There is indeed a scriptural warrant for the term hypostasis in the Epistle to the Hebrews (1:3), but in that verse it means substance and not person.
77 *Logic and Transcendence*, 96.
78 Ibid., 105.

Christian Dogma and Schuonian Gnosis

good intentions of which are not being questioned, nor even perhaps, but we have never known anything about this, its metaphysical competence) leads to a rationalizing adaptation of the mystery. In any case, under its known form, it presents itself as a return to exoteric monotheism, introducing either change into God or nominalism into dogma. Before any assertion about the narrowness of dogma that must be "broken open" with the help of gnosis, it would be well to recognize that trinitarian dogma has already "broken open" exoteric monotheism. For us this is not an interpretation but a statement of fact. The trinitarian fact (we are not saying the theology of the Trinity) breaks at the first with natural theism's spontaneous tendency to reify. In any case, we do not see how Christianity, by accepting the Sabellian or Arian theses, as satisfying as they might be for human reason, could avoid degenerating into a kind of liberal Protestantism.

These remarks lead us to formulate, as clearly as we can, the question of the connections between dogma and gnosis. To do this we need to distinguish between a sacred metaphysics derived from gnosis and a natural theology, or theodicy,[79] derived from simple reason. There is at once continuity and discontinuity between the two: formal continuity, spiritual discontinuity. In appearance the same terms are used on both sides: being, one, absolute, relative, cause, &c. It is also the same intelligence, the same logic being exercised here and there, however simply discursive and dialectical in one case, or intuitive and transcendent in the other. And let us not forget that transcendent logic aims at fulfilling the needs of discursive logic in such a way that there is already, on the level of simple philosophy, a desire for an all-encompassing intelligibility, a "requisite" metaphysics. But, whereas the concepts of ordinary logic are truly the term (the end) of

---

79 The term theodicy, formed from *theos*, God, and *dike*, justice, was created by Leibniz (1710) to designate a philosophical doctrine seeking to justify God in the face of the problem of evil in the world. In the nineteenth century, by a normal evolution, it had come to designate, in the academic curricula of philosophy courses, as well as in the handbooks of scholastic philosophy, everything derived from natural theology, also called "rational theology": the knowledge of God that reason can attain by itself, independent of revelation.

the mental act that is thinking about them, in metaphysics they become mental symbols with a view to contemplation. However, by virtue of this formal continuity, metaphysics can also fall back into the "conceptual," gnosis can be reduced to theodicy, and even—for theodicy remains a speculation both valid and ordered to the true—into pseudo-gnosis, as shown by the examples of Hegelianism and Teilhardism. Dogmatics is situated *a priori* outside this blueprint. It is a "specifying" of Revelation that is not at first of a "speculative" truth but of a "sacred" truth. If the distinguishing mark of the intellect is to liken itself to everything it knows, to dissolve it in its own light, as for dogma, it presents truths having the nature of facts, irreducible and nearly "insoluble" crystallizations which seem to proclaim from the outset: "God's thoughts are not your thoughts."

The example of the great Christian gnostics is significant in this respect. Whether Clement of Alexandria, Origen, Evagrius of Pontus, Dionysius the Areopagite, Maximus the Confessor, Symeon the New Theologian, Meister Eckhart, or Nicholas of Cusa, none of them has ever experienced the least need to break the dogmas to accede to gnosis. This is a finding with something to think about. Quite remarkably, the most "excessive" of all these gnostics, Meister Eckhart, not only proposes no change to any Christian dogma, but even utilizes these dogmas as such, in their most traditional formulation, to make of them as if the fundamental axes of his gnosis. None of the charges against him in the 1329 bull of condemnation are concerned with a single sacred dogma. But, and this confirms our theory, they concern theology, and even theodicy or philosophy, they concern anthropology and cosmology. That Eckhart has broken, in part, with ordinary theology is certain. But his dogmatics differs in no way from that of every Christian. We readily acknowledge that Christian theology, in its search to understand the *revelatum*, draws its inspiration from a philosophy and a theodicy that can limit its speculative scope. St Thomas Aquinas remarks, at the beginning of *Contra Gentiles*, that we must distinguish between the truths known only by revelation, and the truths that reason can attain to naturally.

God, he adds, nevertheless wants to reveal to us naturally knowable truths because of the weakness of our intellect. Now these naturally accessible truths, such as the existence of an all-powerful God, first cause of the world and of beings, the existence of the soul, &c., these truths belong in fact to the order of theodicy, and—something remarkable—are rarely the object of a dogmatic proclamation strictly speaking. They truly form part of the Christian faith, and theology has commented on them extensively, but the Church has not always thought it necessary to dogmatize about them. Now the Eckhartian critique is brought to bear precisely upon these points; that is because everything comes down to the problems of the relationships between the Uncreated and the created, Being and beings. But this is also because this part of the Christian faith, the part concerned with the dogma of creation *ex nihilo*, is the most burdened with theological speculation, the part where revealed theology is the most necessarily tied to natural theology; hence the truths of this order chiefly concern something about which we have a natural understanding: the world. These are no longer exactly what we have called *sacred* truths, but philosophical or metaphysical truths: they have not been formulated as such either in Scripture or in any explicit fashion. We read about creation *ex nihilo* only in 2 Maccabees (7:28), a Greek text. Cosmology and anthropology are never set out for their own sake. When they are the object of a declaration by the Magisterium, they are therefore in part dependent on concepts foreign to revelation and, for that reason, revisable at least to a certain extent.

Eckhart ostensibly rejects a solidly "exoteric" conception of theodicy and anthropology. But he does not reject, does not even criticize any of dogma's sacred truths: the Trinity, the Incarnation, and the Eucharist are for him what they are for every Christian. What then are these dogma-mysteries for the gnostic? They are metaphysical "loci." In these mysteries the intellect of the gnostic *establishes* itself as if in a dwelling-place, and from there it endlessly contemplates the divine light, and tastes a joy at once fervent and serene. Such is the sight offered by the noble lineage of Christian gnostics, this and no other.

It is well known that for the Greeks *all* theology comes back to the contemplation of the Trinity. "The state of the intellect [that is, the state of pure intellection] is an intelligible high peak similar to the color of Heaven, upon which during the time of prayer the light of the Holy Trinity is resplendent."[80] And this light, as Evagrius of Pontus teaches, is the light of a perfectly divested intellect: "The naked intellect is consumed in the vision of itself and which [for that reason] is found deserving of communing in the contemplation of the Holy Trinity."[81] The gnostic Christian does not approach the dogmatic mystery then with the demands of a restless and suspicious reason: he would have himself established within, he would have himself, according to a contemplative expression, "dwell in the caverns of dogma." For anyone who remains without, dogma presents only the rough, harsh and disconcerting surface of its crust. But for anyone who passes inside this same mystery, into identity with its dogmatic structure, it becomes an ocean of inexhaustible light. True, breaking through the crust and entry into the cavern cannot be accomplished without reason's renunciation of its own light: "Superessential and more than divine and more than good Trinity, Thou who presidest over divine Christian wisdom... lead us... up to the highest summit of the mystic Scriptures, there where the simple, absolute and incorruptible mysteries of theology are revealed in the more than luminous Darkness of Silence;... this Darkness... which fills with splendors more beautiful than beauty the intellects *that know how to close their eyes.*"[82] The gnostic breakthrough of the dogmatic crust is the work of the Holy Spirit: "By His divine breath-like spiration, the Holy Spirit elevates the soul sublimely and informs her and makes her capable of breathing in God the same spiration of love that the Father breathes in the Son and the Son in the Father, which is the Holy Spirit Himself, Who in the Father and the Son breathes out to her in this transformation... for the soul united and transformed

---

80 Evagrius of Pontus, *Skemmata* 4; cf. Irénée Hausherr, S. J., *Les leçons d'un contemplatif (Le Traité de l'Oraison d'Évagre le Pontique)* (Paris: Beauchesne, 1960), 146.
81 Ibid. [Trans.—*Kephalia*, Third Century, 6.]
82 St Dionysius the Areopagite, *Œuvres*, 177 (Gandillac trans.).

in God breathes out in God to God the very divine spiration which God—she being transformed in Him—breathes out in Himself to her."[83]

As we see, Christian gnosis blossoms perfectly and without any limitations of any kind from inside trinitarian dogma. When the intellect becomes truly Christian, when it ceases disputing, with the help of its own logical instruments, the analytical formulation of dogma, when it renounces comparing the mystery with the categories of "universal metaphysics," then, radiating from the core of dogma, either muted or dazzling, a light shines into the mind, a light that can be translated into no other language than the Christian one. But this is precisely where we touch on the crux of the problem.

We have come to an impasse here. All statements of the gnostico-critical thesis basically have one and the same object in mind: to expose and attempt to lessen the "scandal" that Christian dogma is to "universal metaphysics." This is why it is important for this thesis to establish, on the one hand, the rights of the God-created human intelligence, which divine revelation should not deny since this intelligence is its raison d'être, and on the other to show that Scripture allows for another interpretation completely in harmony with "universal metaphysics." For all that we have a sense, but we claim no expertise in this respect, that neither Hinduism or Islam, in their doctrines, runs so clearly counter to "universal metaphysics" as Christian dogma does. This is because, and most particularly with trinitarian dogma, dogma seems to affirm a kind of theological "contingency." God is "just like that" and not otherwise: Father, Son, and Holy Spirit. Now metaphysics excludes whatever seems contingent, and chiefly on the supreme level, the divine level. Or rather it clearly allows for a supreme but undefined contingency, that of Supreme Maya. In Christianity this contingency itself seems fixed, determined by the trinitarian structure. As we know, metaphysics is manifested, at least in the mirror of the human intellect,

---

[83] St John of the Cross, *The Spiritual Canticle*, 39, 3; *Collected Works of St. John of the Cross*, trans. K. Kavanaugh and O. Rodriguez (Washington, DC: ICS Publications, 1973), 558.

as undertaking a universal and endless translation, concepts being only temporary mental crystallizations: there is no set metaphysical vocabulary, or one superior to another. Metaphysics is ever seeking what a particular word "means," that is, not to go from one particular religious language to another, but, by never stopping for any language, to gain access to an intuitive knowledge of the intelligible realities themselves, of the *mysteria in divinis*.

Now, if we ask a typically metaphysical question: "Father, Son, and Holy Spirit—what does that mean?" (in other words, what do they symbolize?), we notice that dogma, strictly speaking, does not answer this question, because it has nothing to say about it: Father, Son, and Holy Spirit do not symbolize anything; the Father is simply the Father, and so it is for the other Persons. From the gnostic point of view, which is more or less always Platonic in style, there is here a serious deficiency in intelligibility. To grasp the meaning of a term is always, in fact, to intuit or aim at intuiting an essence. When we say "Father," we are either speaking of the essence "paternity" along with everything that this includes, or saying nothing. The gnostico-critical method does not move beyond this alternative. It reproaches dogmatic theology for speaking of a "Father" abstractly reduced to the relation of paternity alone, a paternity that is only a relation, a paternity devoid of all those connotations attached to the "father image." But it does not see that the object of the working out of trinitarian dogma should not be to speculate on "father" symbolism. Such speculation is by no means forbidden, far from it! It is already present in the Prologue of St John, and will be formulated with the help of analogies offered by knowledge, identified with the Word, and love-will, identified with the Holy Spirit, among other possible analogies. But, to be faithful to revelation—the absolute rule for any theological work—it has to start with revealed data, and this data has to be first formed and defined. Such is the ceaselessly reactualized object of dogmatic *theology*: to grasp the trinitarian mystery, as revealed by Christ Himself, in its *pure logic*; not to "understand the Trinity," but to conceive of its possibility, that is to say its non-contradiction, with respect to the demands of the understanding, so that it does not buckle under the weight of such a mystery. And this is what the theology of St Thomas Aquinas achieves.

Does the Schuonian gnosis achieve this? When it identifies, for example, the Father with the Absolute, the Son with Being, and the Spirit with Existence, we might consider this interpretation not devoid of interest, just like other comparisons with other ternaries, neoplatonic ones in particular: in that case we are in the realm of interpretation. But it is not possible to rediscover the dogmatic formulation starting with its metaphysical interpretation, nor to substitute one for the other. As such, this interpretation does violence to the letter of the dogma as well as its spirit. To the letter, because it replaces the Persons with metaphysical concepts; to the spirit, because the dogma sees in the three Persons the ultimate intra-divine determinations, whereas the "metaphysical" sees only symbols open to a higher interpretation which the Magisterium, for reasons of expedience, has had to present as definitive truths.

Clearly, it seems that, with respect to the "universal (Guénono-Schuonian) metaphysics," all religious doctrines, where the principial divine is involved, can be reduced to the distinction of the Absolute and the Relative *in divinis*, of the Infinite and universal Possibility, of the supreme *Brahman* and its *Shakti*, of the *adh Dhat* (Essence) and the *Sifat* (the divine Qualities), without too much difficulty, without running counter to the formulations of the different orthodoxies, of all religious doctrines—except the Christian. Islam or Hinduism will be interpreted by delving into the mystery of the divine without encountering, on the part of the traditional form, any other opposition than that of a possible misunderstanding. But, in Christianity, the interior depth of the divine is dogmatized. The metaphysical interpretation is as it were "out-distanced," and that in such a way that it enters quite uneasily into the conceptual frameworks of "metaphysics." Guénon, who has said very little on this subject, was most likely aware of this when he noted, at the beginning of *The Great Triad* while reviewing the different ternaries of traditional symbolism, that it does not seem possible to include the Christian Trinity among them.

Must Christian dogma be abandoned then by separating the Scriptures from this dogmatics, and by interpreting them according to the demands of "universal metaphysics"? We think we have shown this to be impossible. Examined objectively, all the positive data of Tradition and Scripture—and first of all the (grammatically surprising) end of Matthew: "baptize in the *Name* [in the singular] of the Father *and* of the Son *and* of the Holy Spirit"—oblige us to admit that the trinitary doctrine comes directly from Christ. To criticize this is therefore to reject the teaching of the Word, to accuse Him of mental planimetry and of not having understood what He had as a mission to reveal, or, in any case, accuse Him of having taught it to apostles (chosen by Him!) incapable of understanding it, but the true significance of which is identified by a gnostic two thousand years later. Altogether too many absurdities. In this case must we renounce metaphysics? Yes and no: yes in appearance, no in reality. As we have seen, the Christian gnostic is at ease with dogma. Far from being an obstacle, it is offered as the support for a deepening and liberating contemplation. Certainly, for that to happen, it is necessary to accept a style proper to this mystical theology, to welcome it within itself, with its own semantics, in the specificity of its Christian identity, that is, without in any way seeking to refer itself, in understanding what is involved, to possible analogies with other sacred perspectives. It is necessary to delve into its own language, listen to it in silence, let it say what it has to say, without seeking to translate it into another language. In short—why hide it?—only a Christian can truly understand Christianity; assuredly not in one of its more or less peripheral elements (symbols or spiritual methods), but in what is essential. Each religion has thus a heart, an interiority impenetrable from without, which is its raison d'être, a secret between it and God, which eludes the jurisdiction of all metaphysics. To the objections of "universal metaphysics," the Christian can only respond: come and see! For him the mysteries are not the object of a metaphysically inquisitorial glance; they are only objects for contemplation. He contemplates the mystery just as the Church propounds it, and in silence, peace, patience and *love*, little by little—to mention just what every Christian is in a position to do—the mystery speaks and enlightens. That which our soul is taught enables us to discourse indefinitely, for it is inexhaustible. And when we compare these discourses to those of the universal metaphysics, we see that we lack for nothing, that in its own way our doctrine, experienced to its very core, says nothing less and says it all. We rediscover, then, in the distinction between Essence-Godhead and the relativity of Persons (which are subsistent relations), a distinction taught by the most standard theology, a distinction analogous to *Brahman nirguna*[84] and its *Shakti, Maha-Maya*. This Relativity *in divinis*, this *Immaculate Conception* (cf. "I am the Immaculate Conception"), is also the more than luminous Darkness of St. Dionysius. Now, how do we posit a real distinction between the relative Trinity and the absolute Essence without dividing God from God, and without transforming by the same stroke the Absolute into a kind of principial thing, since it would be in opposition to whatever would not be Itself, that is, without reducing it to the ontological level? This distinction is therefore a function of our intelligence. But that a distinction is *secundum rationem*, or virtual, does not mean that it is arbitrary or merely abstract; quite the contrary, it means that it has a *fundamentum in re*, in the virtualities of the thing itself, which can be designated in God as an infinity of possibility.[85] The viewpoint of knowledge is in this way integrated *in divinis* as a kind of synthetic witness to Creation.

What we have been invited to is to contemplate the Trinity as a whole, in its "sacred contingency," to let ourselves be seized by the unsetting brightness that it radiates and that ends up by illuminating all things.

---

84 *Nirguna* or *nirvishesha* signifies: non-qualified. Likewise, St. Thomas says that, in a certain manner, God has no essence (in the sense of a determination).
85 Two kinds of distinction "according to reason" are envisaged in Scholasticism. One, from "reason reasoning," is nominal (between "man" and "rational animal"). The other, from "reason reasoned," is based on virtualities formally distinct, although not existing separately in the being considered ("philosopher" and "Frenchman" in Malebranche).

CONCLUSION
Metaphysical Concepts and Dogmatic Revelation

What emerges from these analyses is that a metaphysics, the one formulated by Schuonian gnosis, cannot be the true universal language into which Christianity's particular dogmatics might be adequately translated. Not that the claim to universality of this gnosis is illegitimate. Quite the contrary, metaphysical language is necessarily universal, not surely in its vocabulary and syntax, nor even in its concepts, which are always in some respects the product of a specific culture, but as a philosophical language wielding concepts. By its nature, in fact, a concept is formally universal, having been abstracted from all particular existence. This calls for an added remark appropriate for metaphysical concepts such as being, possibility, existence, essence, &c. These concepts are not obtained out of an abstraction from the sensible. The mind elaborates them out of a knowledge both intuitive and inexpressible, and formulates them into "mental words" apt for inserting into a discursive meditation. They are then endowed, in addition to their own concept-nature, with a new universality, but this time intentional, as to what marks them as metaphysical, this is the aim of a reality itself universal. But this is only an aim for our consciousness through the mode of mental signs, not a face to face encounter with the metaphysical realities themselves. A metaphysical concept is of course a contemplation, a seeing, and this contemplative aim transcends its nature as mere concept: its contents surpass its form (in this it is precisely a sign). But what is present to our consciousness is the conceptual form, the mental sign, or rather it is actually the metaphysical reality itself, but under the form of a concept, that is, of a reflection in our thinking.

Now, it is important not to take the reflection for the model. That is unlikely to occur with "physical" concepts, because the object they make known is present in its sensible reality which, in a certain manner, blots out our thought of it. On the other hand, we are made aware of metaphysical realities, in an *express* fashion, only under the form of concepts. Almost inevitably the concept becomes then the object itself. Thought handles metaphysical concepts as if they were things, and this so much the more easily when whatever overflows and transcends them—reality itself, their ontological dayspring—is experienced by thought as something that eludes its grasp. Now, to work, thought needs to close concepts upon themselves, or momentarily forget that they do not altogether belong to it. This forgetfulness is exemplarily realized in formal logic (this is its legitimate function), as well as in strongly systematized philosophies, that is, each time the syntactic relationships between concepts prevail over their contents. But this can be equally realized in another fashion by the divinization of their form. This is at times the impression given by a reading of Schuon: metaphysical concepts as such are treated as veritable revelations, if not even as divinities; hence the poetico-mystical bearing of his metaphysical discourse. And that seems a clear hallmark of his gnosis. Once, having asked him if this might not run the risk of elevating concepts into idols, he replied without a pause: "But these are idols, and it is necessary to adore them!"

The previous reflections enable us to understand what is true in this astonishing reply. They also enable us to challenge what is unacceptable—obviously taking into account its provocative character—for to neglect this major fact that conditions our knowledge is impossible: we certainly see metaphysical realities and their light reaches the eye of our intelligence, *but from afar*. We cannot adore the vision that we have of them.[86]

This is where the relationship with revealed dogma comes in. It is this, in fact, which, by being formally conveyed as a message come from God, reveals to us at the same time the hither side of knowledge and gives us an awareness of its limitation. Knowledge by itself, in its pure act, cannot give us an experience of this limitation, any more, as Ruyer says, than the eye can see the edge of its vision. And it is indeed true that the light of our intelligence is, as such, a participation in the infinite light of God: "our every thought begins with God," Ruyer has

---

86 Schuon himself affirms: "There is a longstanding illusion that consists in wanting to approach the Absolute by the aid of the mind, as if there were not a measureless discontinuity between the most refined concept and Reality" (*Spiritual Perspectives and Human Facts*, trans. M. Perry, J.-P. Lafouge and J. S. Cutsinger [Bloomington, IN: World Wisdom, 2007], 135).

also stated. But this involves a participation or a reflection. How would we know if our intellectual gaze met with any obstacle — even more if, in the name of gnosis, all "dogmatic obstacles" are set aside, with the transparent horizon of its own speculation being substituted for them? Dogma alone is able to awaken the intellect from its noetic unconsciousness, because it alone offers a *metaphysical* object expressly "come from elsewhere," and which, by that very fact, *situates* the intelligent being, the cognitive subject, "here below." To deny the transcendence of dogma with respect to metaphysical intellection, such as it actually exists in the human being, is to make less obvious this being's awareness of its ignorance.[87]

The gnostico-critical thesis, a remarkable thesis as we have stated, has the rare merit of bringing fully to light the incompatibility of dogmatic logic with the logic of Schuonian gnosis, an incompatibility that is, most often, passed over in silence, anxious as some are to stress the "profound agreements," contrary to what its author has expressed in a most incontestable manner. Schuon is the only one to have done so, and done so with exceptional vigor.[88]

Are we then, as Christian readers, invited to choose?

Schuon would surely reply that this does not involve a choice: either the reasons for his critique are understood and by that very fact one is freed from a dogmatic prison, or else they are not understood, and then the freedom required for every choice is unavailable. We certainly agree, but not for the same reasons. If, for the Christian, it would not be a true choice, this is quite simply because to choose Schuon's gnosis is to renounce Christianity. But how can we do otherwise than "stand fast and hold the traditions, which [we] have learned, whether by word or by writing" (2 Thess. 2:15) until the end of the world?

---

[87] True, in religions without dogma, we encounter other "strategies" appropriate to safeguard against the possible *hubris* of the intellect; for example, in Islam, the well-known formula that often concludes doctrinal statements: "But God is more knowing."

[88] This is why we must confess not understanding the attitude of those — the Christian commentators on Schuon's work — who deem it in complete agreement with the dogmas of the Greek as well as the Catholic Church. Do these commentators, whose theological competence does not seem paltry, do justice to the thought of Frithjof Schuon, at least as disclosed in the texts cited?

THIRD PART

Concerning Christian Gnosis According to its Essence

(A PHILOSOPHICAL ESSAY)

CHAPTER 8

Memoir on Gnosis

HISTORY OF AN ENCOUNTER

When I began, in *La charité profanée* [*The Desecration of Charity*], to use the term gnosis, I had not the least idea about the discussions that the introduction of this term, yet understood in an orthodox sense, was going to arouse, nor the attacks to which I would be exposed. These attacks took a more decisive turn when I was invited to participate in the conference "Pagan Culture, Europe and Christianity," organized by the Saint Pius X University Institute, on April 19, 1980. I was invited to speak about gnosis, hence the title of my talk: "Christian Gnosis and Anti-Christian Gnosis" (published in the conference's proceedings).[1]

My intention was not to present myself as a "gnostic," or as a specialist in gnosticism, which I am not. Moreover, with the suspect connotation attached to the term gnosis, I was not inclined to claim it, and the interest that I afforded certain authors (such as Guénon and Schuon), for whom gnosis is understood in a good way, was not enough to alleviate all my hesitations. In fact I had no taste for the little I knew of the gnostic doctrines of Valentinus, Basilides, or Marcion, and their dramatic and complicated mythology. I was even (and still am) convinced that it is best to keep a wary eye out for the dangers of a certain gnostic trend of mind, which can manifest itself in the most diverse intellectual approaches. Difficult to define, this gnostic—or rather gnosticizing—tendency seems characterized by the more or less conscious conviction that there must be a secret (or reserved) knowledge able to establish us in a true intimacy with reality, even the most transcendent reality. For such knowledge, paradoxes and mysteries will only be apparent, and any sacred revelation, gnostically understood, will only be a symbolic crystallization of truths, truths the

---

1 *Vu de Haut* (Broût-Vernet: Editions Fideliter, 1981), 9–21.

intellect, by itself, is able to grasp as obvious. This—Hegelian philosophy is a good example[2]—constitutes in my eyes an excess, a *hubris*: its possibility is excluded for man here below, although its desire is inscribed, by nature, in any cognitive process, scientific as well as philosophical: knowledge is always the hope of a union with being.

However, it may happen that this hope, imagining itself on the way to realization, goes to extremes and convinces itself that, possessing *the* "Gnosis," it no longer needs to learn about reality such as the world would have us know it or as the grace of God reveals it.

Perhaps matters would have rested there, if, when I was working on my first book, I had not discovered, in volume two of Jacques Chevalier's *Histoire de la pensée* [*History of Thought*]—devoted to *Christian thought*[3]—the existence of Dom Jacques Dupont's thesis, *Gnosis. Religious Knowledge in the Epistles of Saint Paul.*[4] Reading this study convinced me of one thing: the term gnosis, which I thought stricken with infamy, was, with St. Paul, a resumption of the Greek-language Jewish tradition: he had chosen it as a specific designation for knowledge of God, a delightful and illuminating knowledge through which faith enters into its own depth and is engendered within us as the sense of God. I then realized that this term was also employed by several translators of the Greek Fathers, according to a perfectly orthodox intention, without their feeling always required to justify their choice. This necessarily meant that, for these scholars, such a transcription imposed itself, that there was no other solution, and that especially the translation of *gnosis* by "science" or "knowledge," was not wrong, of course, but insufficient to indicate the "technical" meaning as understood by Christian authors. So I too could use it.

---

2 To obtain my Diploma of Higher Studies in the History of Philosophy, at the request of my teacher, Robert Derathé, I composed a hundred page "memoir" on *Religion in Hegel's "Phenomenology of the Spirit"* (1954).
3 Paris: Flammarion, 1956; the note concerning Dom J. Dupont is on page 741.
4 *Gnôsis. La connaissance religieuse dans les épîtres de saint Paul* (Louvain and Paris: Nauwelaerts and Gabalda, 1949), 604 pages; reissued in 1960.

LATINS HAVE IGNORED THE TERM "GNOSIS"

Gnose as the transcription of "gnosis" is therefore accepted today in French. Current dictionaries consider this noun as belonging to the vocabulary of the history of religions and theology; this is indisputable. This usage raises, however, a rather disconcerting problem for which one hardly discerns the solution and which lexicographers seem to overlook. The French vocabulary of theology derives, in its near totality, from medieval Latin: until the sixteenth century, theology was hardly expressed otherwise than in Latin (like philosophy). This theological Latin is itself the heir of Roman Latin (both classical and vernacular) and of Christian Latin, scriptural Latin in particular. Now, the Latin language, whether Christian or not, is ignorant of any direct transcription of *gnosis* (which is not the case with all Greek terms). The old Latin versions (second century) of the Old Testament (made from the Greek of the Septuagint) and the New Testament (originally Greek), like the later version (end of the fourth-beginning of the fifth century) by St. Jerome, always translate *gnosis* by *scientia* (sometimes by *cognitio*).[5] Under these conditions, one would expect that French-speaking theology, following the Vulgate and the medieval tradition, would also speak of "science" or "connaissance" [knowledge], which, at least from the seventeenth century, is not always the case.

That said, even if *gnosis* (unless I am mistaken) is never transliterated into Latin, it is not the same for *gnostikoi*, the "gnostics" (heretics), rendered by *gnostici* (plural of a nonexistent *gnosticus?*), which we read for example in St. Isidore of Seville, or for *gnostike* (feminine of *gnostikos*, implied: *dunamis*), literally the "gnostic," transcribed into Latin by *gnostice* (genitive *gnostices*) and found in Fulgentius in the sense of a "faculty of knowing," "understanding."[6]

---

5 There are twenty-nine occurrences of *gnosis* in the New Testament: Luke 1:17, 11:52; Rom. 2:20, 11:33, 15:14; 1 Cor. 1:5, 8:1 (2 times), 8:7, 8:10, 8:11, 12:8, 13:2, 13:8, 14:6; 2 Cor. 2:14, 4:6, 8:7, 10:5, 11:6; Eph. 3:19; Phil. 3:8; Col. 2:3; 1 Tim. 6:20; 1 Pet. 3:7; 2 Pet. 1:5, 1:6, 3:18. Twenty-three uses in Paul, four in Peter, two in Luke. In 2 Cor. 2:14, it is translated by *notitia*, and in 2 Pet. 3:18, by *cognitio*; everywhere else it is rendered by *scientia*.

6 Isidore of Seville (560–636), the "last of the Fathers of the Western Church": *Etymologiae*, 8, 5, 6. The *Etymologies* are a vast encyclopedia. Fulgentius (between

CONCERNING CHRISTIAN GNOSIS ACCORDING TO ITS ESSENCE

The term *gnostike* is interesting insofar as Plato himself makes use of it, implying *episteme*, "knowledge," or *dunamis*, "faculty," "power." Thus, he distinguishes between (*episteme*) *gnostike*, "gnostic (knowledge)" and (*episteme*) *praktike*, "practical (knowledge)."[7] As for the (*dunamis*) *gnostike* of Greek philosophy, we find it again in certain medieval writers, especially in John Scotus Eriugena, under the Latin translation of *virtus gnostica*, "virtue" signifying "strength," "capacity," "power." Moreover, it does not have then only the meaning of a capacity for theoretical knowledge, such as natural reason. The *virtus gnostica* or "cognitive capacity" can also designate the infinite and supereminent power of the knowledge proper to God: "God made [these primordial causes] in the beginning [i.e., in the Principle; cf. footnote 9 below] as being kinds of foundations and principles of all the natures that are from Him, and He comprehends these causes in His supereminent and infinite gnostic power (*supereminent infinita sua gnostica virtute*)."[8] Can such a *virtus gnostica* be applied to human beings? A text from Book III of the *Periphyseon* seems to suggest this. Wondering how it is possible for there to be an "eternal creation" (which is assumed by the Eriugenian interpretation of the first verse of Genesis[9]), the master teaches his disciple (the *Periphyseon* is a dialogue between *Nutritor*, "master wet-nurse," and *Alumnus*, "suckling child") that it is impossible for a man to answer this question. *Alumnus* recognizes this: "No rational or intellectual creature can know the manner of the creation of things in the Word since it is revealed to the gnostic power [*gnosticae virtuti*] alone,"[10] which seems to imply that there is a higher mode of knowledge, characterized specifically as "gnostic," a mode capable, as St. Paul says, of "searching the deep things of God"

---

the fourth and fifth centuries, an African scholar): *Mythologiarum libri*. III, 10. cf. *Gaffiot* s.v.
7   *Politics*, 258e.
8   *On the Division of Nature (Periphyseon)*, Book II, 553A; trans. I. P. Sheldon-Williams and J. O'Meara (Montreal / Washington: Bellarmin / Dumbarton Oaks, 1987), 154.
9   "*In Principio creavit Deus*": "In the Principle (= the Word), God created"; cf. our book: *Un homme, une femme au paradis*, Ad Solem, Geneva, 2007, chap. VI.
10 Op. cit., III, 670B; Sheldon-Williams-O'Meara translation, 294.

Memoir on Gnosis

(1 Cor. 2:10). But such a "cognitive virtue" is supernatural and requires the reception of the Holy Spirit.

What about *gnosis* now? We know that the learned Irish monk John Scotus translated Dionysius the Areopagite from Greek into Latin. As was said above, and as Hilduin, the previous translator of Dionysius, had done twenty-five years earlier, *gnosis* is always rendered as *scientia*.[11]

There must therefore be a reason: strictly speaking, the Latin West, both ancient and medieval, was completely ignorant of a heresy—deemed to be major, if not even *the* heresy par excellence—which would have been called "gnosis," or, to remain within the lineage of Latin languages, which would have been called "science," "knowledge." We find no trace of it in the two greatest theologians of the Middle Ages, St. Thomas Aquinas and St. Bonaventure. On the other hand, there was indeed one category of heretic about whom almost nothing is known outside of what St. John of Damascus tells us,[12] and whom he calls the *Gnosimachi*, that is, "those who fight gnosis," a kind of radical fideist who rejected every endeavor of scriptural interpretation and theological elaboration of the faith. To abide by the letter of historically formulated condemnations relating to gnosis, the only one recorded in the history of the Church concerns opponents of gnosis!

Must we wait then for an era better-informed about cultural specificities, more sensitive to the historical singularity of movements of thought, more devoted to philology; in short, is it necessary to wait for the Renaissance and the centuries that followed for an awareness to dawn of the very particular character offered by the "knowledge" type of movement designated by the Greek *gnosis*, and that would surely be indicated by the appearance of the word "gnosis" in the French or even European lexicon? The answer to this question is not easy. Investigation, especially with regard to the foreign domain, would require quite extensive research. We will therefore confine ourselves to the French domain, or nearly so, and even keep

---

11 See the examples given by René Roques in *Libres sentiers vers l'érigénisme* (Roma: Edizione dell'Ateneo, 1975), 109.
12 *Book of Heresies*, 88; P. G., vol. 94, col. 757.

CONCERNING CHRISTIAN GNOSIS ACCORDING TO ITS ESSENCE

to what the most reputable dictionaries can teach us on this topic. Finally, last but not least, the investigation that follows will deal exclusively with "gnosis" understood as a religious or philosophical doctrine. So we will leave aside the almost obsolete use of the adjective "gnostic" for collectively referring to engraved stones, cameos with animal figures, amulets, lead tablets, fragments of papyrus bearing mysterious inscriptions: names of deities, exorcisms, spells, "kabbalistic" formulas, &c. These objects, usually of Egyptian origin, were called "gnostic" in the sixteenth century, probably because they had some kinship with numerical speculation or onomatic features found in the texts labeled as Gnostic by Christian heresiologists who have passed them on to us. This meaning has not completely disappeared from scientific publications, but is not reported by the dictionaries.

"GNOSE" IS ABSENT FROM FRENCH DICTIONARIES BEFORE 1840

The *Dictionnaire de l'ancienne langue française du IXème au XVème siècle* (1880) by Frédéric Godefroy does not have the word, no more than the *Dictionnaire de la langue française du XVIème siècle* (1950) by Edmond Huguet. Also ignoring it is that monument of erudition which is the *Dictionnaire de l'ancien langage françois depuis son origine jusqu'au siècle de Louis XIV* (written in the second half of the eighteenth century, but remaining unpublished until the end of the nineteenth) by J. B. La Curne de Sainte-Palaye. The *Dictionnaire universel* (1690) by Antoine Furetière, the *Dictionnaire françois* (1706) by Pierre Richelet and the *Dictionnaire critique de la langue française* (1787) by Father Jean-François Féraud, offer not one instance of the term. These dictionaries are language dictionaries, they record usage. One conclusion emerges: the term *gnose* [gnosis] is unknown to the French language, in its ordinary use, at least until the end of the eighteenth century.

Is this likewise the case for the encyclopedias? One might be tempted to believe it when one observes that, if I am not mistaken, the *Encyclopédie* of Diderot and d'Alembert (1777), in its "Gnostiques" article (which substantially reiterates the *Dictionnaire de Trévoux*), makes no mention of it. The same silence from Pierre Bayle in his *Dictionnaire historique et critique* (1697).

However, this silence is not universal. Although none of the encyclopedias consulted includes an article on "gnosis" before the nineteenth century, we come across the term, proof of its use, in articles on the Gnostics. So this involves a scholarly use, in works that pride themselves on their erudition. The *Grand dictionnaire historique*, known as "de Moreri" (1st edition 1675), in its considerably enlarged edition of 1740, writes in the "Gnostiques" article (tome IV, page 299): "Gnostics are not a particular sect, but a name taken by the first heretics; because they boasted of having extraordinary knowledge and enlightenment, which they called *gnoses*." The plural term becomes singular in the famous *Dictionnaire universel français et latin vulgairement appelé Dictionnaire de Trévoux*.[13] In the article "Gnosimaques" (tome III, col. 821), we read: "By *gnose* one commonly understands knowledge [Fr. = *science*], and the interpreters of St. John Damascene (the only one to speak of these heretics) translate the word in this way. I think it has a more particular meaning; in the early centuries of the Church it meant, or nearly so, what we call spirituality." The relevance and correctness of this assessment is admirable. In any case, this testimony proves that the term was in use among specialists, translators of the Church Fathers, and historians of Christian dogmatics.[14] And if many render *gnosis* by "gnose" and not by "knowledge" [Fr. = *science*], this is because they are well aware that this word does not have the very general meaning of "knowledge" or "science," but, as the (anonymous) editor of the article wrote, "a more particular meaning," that he correctly identifies as "spirituality." Similarly, we find the word "gnose" in the "Gnostics" article from Rev. Nicolas-Sylvestre Bergier's *Dictionnaire de théologie* (1789), which was regularly reissued and enlarged throughout

---

13 The town of Trévoux was famous for the printing press that the Duke of Maine, son of Louis XIV, had created there. This is why the town was entrusted with printing the famous dictionary, written by a group of Jesuits in Paris; hence the name *Dictionary of Trévoux* (1st edition: 1704, 3 vol.; last: 1771, 8 vols.). The present reference is to the 4th edition, in 5 vols., of 1743.

14 The seventeenth century produced considerable works in this field. Notice that Dom Calmet's *Dictionnaire de la Bible* (2nd ed., 1783) includes an article on "Gnostics" (tome II, 580–81), but speaks of knowledge [Fr. = *science*] and not of gnosis.

the nineteenth century.[15] Translating St. Paul (1 Tim. 6:20), he notes that the Apostle asks us to "shun worldly novelties and everything that opposes a knowledge falsely called *Gnose.*" He thus translates the single word *gnosis* both by "knowledge" and by "gnosis."[16]

UNTIL THE NINETEENTH CENTURY, "GNOSIS" WAS CATHOLIC

This use of the word "gnose" is not only a mark of specialized and scholarly works. It is also found under the pen of two of the seventeenth century's greatest writers, namely Bossuet and Fénelon. This is moreover what modern and contemporary language dictionaries point out. Émile Littré's *Dictionnaire de la langue française* (latest edition during the author's lifetime: 1877), in the article "gnose," gives a quote from Bossuet, taken from the *Tradition des nouvelles mystiques*: "They wanted to introduce a false gnosis in place of the true." The same information and reference to the same work of Bossuet is in the *Trésor de la langue française* (1971–1994), edited by Paul Imbs: "1697, Nouveaux Mystiques, III, 1"; the *Dictionnaire historique de la langue française* (1998), edited by Alain Rey, confirms date and attribution. It is necessary, however, to observe that the *Tradition des nouveaux mystiques* is a posthumous work by Bossuet, published only in 1753. It could not have played a role then in the circulation of the term "gnose." On the other hand, if *Tradition des nouveaux mystiques* was indeed composed around 1697 or a little before, it constitutes, it seems, a response to a handwritten work by Fénelon that Fénelon had submitted for Bossuet to read, its exact title *Le Gnostique de saint Clément d'Alexandrie*, a work in which Fénelon makes extensive use of the word "gnose." This work remained unpublished[17] (Bossuet

---

15 *Encyclopédie méthodique: Théologie*, Panckouck, 1789, tome II, 100. Panckouck, with reference to Diderot's *Encyclopédie*, undertook in 1781 the production of a huge *Encyclopédie méthodique* (it will eventually number 166 vols.), which, unlike Diderot's alphabetical order, is a collection of dictionaries each dealing with a subject. Bergier wanted to rectify and complete the religious articles of Diderot's *Encyclopédie*; 1st ed., 3 vols., 1789–1790; 2nd ed., 8 vols., 1789–1792.
16 On Abbé Bergier, whose work is important, read the work by Didier Masseau, *Les ennemis des philosophes. L'antiphilosophie au temps des Lumières* (Paris: Albin Michel, 2000), 237 ff., and 348 ff.
17 But its title is cited in the correspondence of Fr. La Combe, a disciple, by Madame Guyon.

refuted it without naming it) until 1930, the publication date, by Father Dudon, of the handwritten copy he had discovered in the Saint-Sulpice Seminary library; the publication is preceded by a long, historical, very "anti-Fénelonian" introduction.[18] This text was probably written in 1694. It is therefore to him that one can trace the first written attestations of the term *gnose* taken in a positive sense. What is certain, in any case, is that Fénelon greatly contributed to spreading its use in conversations within certain groups. We find an echo of this usage spoken of in the *Memoirs* of Saint-Simon (which began in 1694), an echo reported by Littré in his *Dictionnaire* under the article "gnose": speaking of the "small flock which was, at the court of Louis XIV, under Fénelon's direction," Saint-Simon names "Madame de Mortemart, afterwards Duchess of Béthune, that great soul of *gnosis* and best friends with the Archbishop of Cambrai."

The first conclusion to emerge from this (very incomplete) brief history is that the use of the term in the French language gradually tends to spread, from the end of the seventeenth century and during the eighteenth century, to become recognized, more or less officially, in the nineteenth century (the *Dictionnaire de l'Académie* records its existence in 1878). Thus the *Dictionnaire universel des Hérésies, des Erreurs et des Schismes* by Father M. T. Guyot, the first edition of which is in 1847, informs us that "the word *gnose*, from which is derived the word *gnostiques*, *illumined ones*, signifies a knowledge superior to common beliefs." And further he specifies: "the sectarians disguised their theft and the foreign origin of their theology under the name 'gnose,' *gnosis*, a word by which the apostles had designated the knowledge of Religion."[19] However, there

---

18 *Le Gnostique de saint Clément d'Alexandrie*. Unpublished pamphlet by Fénelon, published with an introduction by Father Paul Dudon, of the Company of Jesus (Paris: Gabriel Beauchesne, 1930). The review *La Place Royale*, in its num. 37, published Fénelon's text in 1996 without the introduction or the notes from Father Dudon, who had provided all references to the works of Clement of Alexandria according to the edition of Migne's *Patrologia*. A more recent edition was published under the title *La Tradition secrète des mystiques*, edited and introduced by Dominique and Murielle Tronc (Paris-Orbey: Arfuyen, 2006).
19 *Dictionnaire des Hérésies*, Publication de la Société Saint-Victor, XCV, 189 and 191.

is still some reluctance or hesitation. For example, Jean Cohen, translator of a posthumous work by J. A. Moehler, *Patrologie ou Histoire littéraire des trois premiers siècles de l'Église chrétienne*, published in 1843, in the chapter devoted to Clement of Alexandria, gives the following version of the German original: "The notion of Christian philosophy... is based on faith in divine revelation, the true foundation of salvation: welcoming within itself the various spiritual powers, it traverses knowledge (*episteme*) and thus arrives at *gnosis*, which is immutable knowledge and the contemplation of all things, in their origin, within God."[20] In the rest of the text, the same Greek term is used, but this time without italics, speaking of "Christian gnosis" or "Catholic gnosis" distinct from that of the heretics. Obviously, only the transliteration from Greek into French seems to him likely to safeguard the specificity of meaning, especially since German, like English, kept the Greek word directly transcribed as "gnosis."

The second important remark is decisive. In all the uses we have been able to identify between the fifteenth century and the beginning of the nineteenth century, the word "gnose" has, in French, a perfectly orthodox meaning. Here is the solid and indisputable fact, and if the orthodoxy of a Fénelon seems doubtful to some, then let us read Bossuet whose doctrinal rectitude in matters of dogma (at least for dogmatics as defined in his time) will satisfy the most demanding. The gnosis of Saint Clement, he writes, "is the 'knowledge of salvation' of which the scriptures speak; the 'knowledge' of which Saint Paul speaks, the 'knowledge of the Lord' foretold by Isaiah that would fill all the earth in the time of the Messiah. The gnostic is therefore nothing but a Christian worthy of the name, who has turned the Christian life into habit;[21] it is, in other words, this spiritual and intelligent man, who is light in Our Lord, this infallibly contemplative Christian.... I do not see that we must understand any other nicety, or, under the name of gnosis, any other mystery than the great mystery of Christianity, well-known by faith, and of course by the perfect,

---

20 Debécourt, Libraire-Éditeur, 1843, second tome, 32.
21 That is, "in habitu," in an acquired and permanent disposition.

because of the gift of understanding, sincerely practiced and turned into habit."[22]

The semantic situation of the term was then, for four hundred years, the exact opposite of what it is today, where gnosis is seen as heresy with a capital "H": it is the "eternal gnosis" that the Dominicans H. Cornélis and A. Léonard describe in the book that bears this title, and which is, moreover, one of the best written on the subject[23]; or again, it is *La Gnose universelle*, title of one of Étienne Couvert's four works devoted to denouncing this sprawling heresy.[24]

THE SCRIPTURAL DIGNITY OF GNOSIS

The attitude, so firm and so constant, for so many centuries of Christian thought, is easy to understand and is based on one major and decisive reason: it is the authority of Sacred Scripture that categorically forbids the identification of "gnosis" with a heresy, St. Paul having spoken of a "gnosis falsely called" (1 Tim. 6:20), in Greek: "[the objections] of a pseudonymous gnosis (*tes pseudonumou gnoseos*)," or even, if you like, "pseudo-gnosis." It is the *name* of "gnosis" that is involved here, and only true disciples of Christ have the right to claim this name, adversaries and heretics cannot claim "knowledge"; if they do—and they do since St. Paul warns us against them—they are impostors, usurpers. And usurpers of what? Of a name. If this name, that of gnosis, meant nothing other than "knowledge" in the most general sense, it would be difficult to understand why St. Paul takes issue with the lying use of the word, and not rather with

---

22 *Tradition des nouveaux mystiques*, chap. III, sect. I; Dudon, op. cit., 25. Étienne Couvert, in *La gnose contre la foi* (Chiré-en-Montreuil: Editions de Chiré, 1989), 183, invokes Bossuet's testimony against gnosis. The text that he cites, without giving a reference, is taken from the *Tradition des nouveaux mystiques*, chap. XVI, sect. 8 (Dudon, op. cit., 139). We grant that, in its expression, Bossuet's position with regard to gnosis shows a certain reserve, but, in this case, the text quoted by Etienne Couvert is not directed against (orthodox) gnosis, it is directed against the (Fénelonian) claim that it is a secret teaching. On this question of secrecy, one can read *Christ the Original Mystery*, 277–95.
23 *La gnose éternelle* (Paris: Árthème Fayard, 1959).
24 *De la gnose à l'oecuménisme* (1983), *La gnose contre la foi* (1989), *La gnose universelle* (1993), *La gnose en question* (2002), all published by Éditions de Chiré (Chiré-en-Montreuil).

the heretical idea of *what* it designates. Why does he not simply warn Timothy against "false knowledge"? No one will deny that the Pauline Epistles contain many warnings, and, even more, many polemical texts. St. Paul is an ardent warrior and he himself recommends that we put on the armor and weapons of the Christian knight. Now, the adversary that must be fought, the error from which one must be preserved, the heresy which must be conquered are always directly targeted in their own reality, always, except once, in the case of gnosis, where what is targeted is the usurpation of a name: what is being denounced is a pseudonymy. And this is so true that the *pseudonymos* of the Epistle to Timothy (6:20) is a *hapax* in the entire New Testament: it is only mentioned in this one place. This says something about the worth that St. Paul attaches to the term *gnosis*.

And that is not all. The term "gnosis" is used here absolutely. St. Paul does not frame gnosis with a modifier, as he does on other actually not very numerous occasions (2 Cor. 4:6; 10:5, where he speaks of the *gnosis tou Théou*, the "knowledge of God"; and Phil. 3:8), but he only makes mention of *the* "gnosis," which implies, either that this is knowledge par excellence, or else— one not excluding the other—a specific term, coded in some fashion, and which, for St. Paul as for the recipients of his letter has a precise and immediately identifiable meaning.[25] This is the major reason why it is not expedient to translate *gnosis* by "knowledge," because the meaning in French [Trans.— and English] is somewhat indeterminate. No doubt the translation "gnosis" entails serious drawbacks, given its current connotation: nowadays it risks entangling the interpretation of the text in a supersaturated problematic. Besides, no French translation of St. Paul has made that decision. And yet, is there another? What misinterpretations are we not exposed to when translating *gnosis* by "knowledge," as the French [and English] versions usually do! At best, one is liable to be misunderstood. And

---

25 "Once again," writes J. Dupont of 1 Tim. 6:20, "the term *gnosis* without any determining object, answers to the precise and pointed use made of it by Doctors of the Law" (op. cit., 255). "Doctor of the Law" is the usual translation of *nomodidaskalos*; today's specialists render it as "nomodidaskalos" in order to retain its technical character: someone expert in the revelation of Moses, the Torah.

this is the most frequent case: the modern reader, when he meets the term knowledge under the pen of St. Paul, easily sees that this knowledge has nothing to do with Einstein or Heisenberg, but as to what the Apostle is speaking about, that he does not know—except by reading demanding and often quite lengthy works—and finally becomes uninterested in the matter without further misgivings. This is the least detrimental, especially since there is, in any case, truly no satisfactory solution, as generally happens with translation problems. This is why a few scholars, including Jacques Dupont, to avoid both "knowledge" (too neutral) and "gnose" (too connotative) have resigned themselves to transliterating the Greek in the form of *gnosis*, which is a stopgap measure. This notwithstanding, we will grant that it was legitimate, in accordance with such a long tradition, to keep the word "gnose" with the orthodox meaning to which it unquestionably has a right, by virtue of the most imposing authority, that of Scripture.

What is quite astonishing, however, is that this scriptural datum carries no weight for those who have set themselves up as the most fastidious and intractable guardians of dogmatic orthodoxy. They do not hesitate to break with a two-thousand-year-old tradition of respect for terms and modes of expression in Holy Scripture, a respect which, in the second century, led St. Irenaeus of Lyon to write, not an *Against Gnosis*, like some recent more or less competent writers, but a *Denunciation and refutation of the "gnosis with lying a name"*—for such is the true title of this vast work that, from earliest times, we have become accustomed to designating under the title of *Adversus Haereses* (Against the Heresies). By renouncing the Pauline terminology, one concedes a first victory to those we claim to fight, one abandons to them this beautiful name of gnosis that the Greek-language Jewish tradition had bequeathed to the first Christian generation, one allows this sacred treasure to be stolen, this word sanctified twenty times by the great St. Paul, and perhaps even by Christ the Lord (Luke 11:52), one surrenders it into hands of counterfeiters, and then one lays blame for this on those who strive to despoil them of this stolen bounty that is rightfully ours!

CONCERNING CHRISTIAN GNOSIS ACCORDING TO ITS ESSENCE

For that is the truth, and the most serious studies have definitively established this: the notion of *gnosis* and the use of the term as inherited by St. Paul are of Jewish origin. I will not undertake to provide proof after the work of Father Spicq, Dom Jacques Dupont, Father Louis Bouyer, and a few others: so many scholars of indisputable authority. I will content myself with making a few comments.

FROM PAGAN GNOSIS TO JUDEO-CHRISTIAN GNOSIS

The word is incontestably Greek, and we must start with the Greek if we want to understand why the Jewish translators of the Hebrew Bible adopted it. Gnosis means "knowledge," this much is settled, or even "science," which is also expressed as *episteme* in Greek. One might conclude that *episteme* and *gnosis* are synonyms; and this is actually sometimes the case, but not always. In the example given above (*Politics*, 258e), Plato distinguishes two kinds of *episteme*: "the practical" (*he praktike*), that is, what relates to action (*praxis*), and "the gnostic" (*he gnostike*). If we translate *gnosis* with "science," we must translate *gnostike* (its adjective in the feminine) by "scientific," and therefore *he episteme gnostike* by "scientific science," which is redundant. We could obviously render *gnostike* by "theoretical," according to the classic opposition of theory and practice. But this opposition is somewhat misleading unless one gives "theory" the meaning of the Greek *theoria*, "contemplation." For this is indeed what is involved here, not certainly in all cases (the lexicon of Plato is not systematic), but in major occurrences, particularly with regard to knowledge of the Good, that is, of the supreme and unconditioned Principle, the divine source of essences and beings: "That which communicates the truth to the knowable (*gignoskoménoïs*) and to the knower (*gignoskonti*) the power of knowing, declares that this is the Form of the Good. Being cause of knowledge (*episteme*) and truth, you must conceive it as knowable (*gignoskomenen*). Yet however beautiful they both are, gnosis (*gnosis*) and truth, if you judge that there is something still more beautiful than these, you will judge rightly on that" (*Republic*, 508e).

We must therefore reject Father Bouyer's assertions on this subject, who states: "In classical Hellenic culture, it is not *gnosis* or *gnomai* which are used for a specifically philosophical knowledge, but always *episteme* and *epistamai*. Philo was the first to use in this sense the vocabulary which will be that of gnosis... among the Greeks, who are not themselves dependent on biblical language, *gnosis* and *gnomai* only designate sensory knowledge, without any reference to some notion, either philosophical or theological."[26] These rather peremptory assertions are in fact far from the truth, as shown by the few examples cited. And perhaps it could be argued that the "gnostic science" of which Plato speaks does not exclude a certain revelation—intellectual in nature—as seen in the previous text, where it is the Form of the Good that communicates gnosis and therefore according to which gnosis "is received." But anyway, what is beyond doubt is that we do not find in Greek literature, the use of *gnosis* taken absolutely with a properly technical sense ("gnosis") prior to the appearance of the Septuagint Bible. And if we cannot find the word used in this way, this is because the thing itself is not there either.

Greek-speaking Judaism therefore used the noun *gnosis* to translate the Hebrew *dahat* (knowledge), and the verb *gignoskein* to translate *iadah* (to know), conferring on these words a specific meaning—although not exclusive: not all uses of these words in the Bible are "gnostic." This meaning is on the whole that of "knowledge of God," that is, of his Word, of his Will, of his Activity in human history. That such a meaning is unknown to the Greeks is less astonishing than it seems: for a Greek there is precisely no *gnosis tou Theou*, "knowledge of God." "The divine images, linked to names or given form by the attributes, belong to the cultic technology, not to theology;

---

26 Louis Bouyer, *Gnôsis. La connaissance de Dieu dans l'Écriture* (Paris: Cerf, 1988), 158–59. Many other texts of Plato than those advanced here could be cited: cf. Édouard des Places, S. J., *Lexique de la langue philosophique et religieuse de Platon* (Paris: Belles Lettres, 1964), tome I, 114. We regret not being able to agree on all points with such a significant author, one of the greatest theologians of our time. His legitimate desire to restore Christianity to its Hebrew roots, against the nineteenth-century historians who saw in it the product of a Hellenization of Jewish tradition, no doubt led him to be content with cursory inquiries in certain areas.

they fulfill a practical function; but have no cognitive value.... The Greeks did not develop a theology; we must not create in their place what their wisdom has always rejected."[27] On the contrary, the Jews were aware of having received a revelation from God: God made himself known, he is not only a power, he is also a Being entering into a relationship of love with his people, communicating his Name and teaching them his Law.

From this fundamental religious intuition there developed, not a true theology in the sense that this term will receive with Christianity, but a "culture of gnosis" between the third and first centuries BC in Hellenistic Judaism. This culture assumed three main forms, ones that identify themselves expressly by means of the term gnosis. One of these forms, the work of the rabbinical school, is of a "legal" nature (in the broad sense): gnosis is the knowledge of the Law or *Torah*; hence the name *nomodidaskales* given to its proponents, that is, in Greek, "teacher (*didaskalos*) of the Law (*nomos*)," against whom St. Paul contends (I Tim. 1:7). Another form considers gnosis as a charisma, a gift given by God to interpret Scripture and to know

---

27 J. Rudhardt, *Notions fondamentales de la Pensée religieuses et Actes constitutifs du Culte dans la Grèce classique*, 2nd ed. (Paris: Picard, 1992), 107 and 111. Is this conclusion in contradiction with what Plato tells us about knowledge of the Good? Answering this question would lead us too far from our current topic. In the strict sense of the term (a doctrinal elaboration of revelation) there is no Platonic theology, because there is, in Plato's concrete experience, no manifestation of the *Logos* of the *Theos*. The transcendence of the Good is such that it belies any Word. But, as Victor Goldschmidt shows (*Platonisme et pensée contemporaine* [Paris: Aubier, 1970], 41–47), Plato's thought is fundamentally and entirely religious: "It is impossible to distinguish between scholar and believer in the dialectician: the Forms, the Values he studies do not allow him at any time to remain 'neutral' to the very extent that the Good endows them with being what they are. Knowledge of the Good is 'the perfect initiation.' But this initiation is for the beyond: it is posited as a requirement. The Good illuminates all dialectical research; it is no one's direct goal." "Neither the vision of God or theology are at the disposal or even within the reach of mankind." On the metaphysico-mystical significance of Plato's philosophy, see *Penser l'analogie*, 135–214. Indeed, there is the monumental work of Proclus entitled *Platonic Theology* (6 volumes in the Saffrey-Westerink edition [Paris: Belles Lettres, 1968–1997]). But it is about "theology in the Platonic sense of the word, namely a discourse on the divine and the gods, what Proclus often calls a 'mystagogy'" (tome I, lxi). Werner Jaeger asserts the same in *À la naissance de la théologie. Essai sur les Présocratiques*, 1947, trans. from German (Paris: Cerf, 1966), 8: "the ancient world [was] totally unaware of a *supernatural theology*."

Memoir on Gnosis

how to draw from it rules for living. The Prophets possess in an eminent way the charism of gnosis, and St. Paul takes up this tradition when he distinguishes "speaking in tongues" (glossolalia) from "speaking either by revelation or by gnosis, or by prophesying, or by teaching" (1 Cor. 14:6). Finally, the term gnosis is found in what is called "Jewish apocalyptic," a designation that encompasses an important spiritual current, producer of a vast literature of "revelations" (this is the meaning of the word "apocalypse") flourishing in the first century BC and into the time of Christ. The Apocalypse of St. John illustrates perfectly, but in Christian mode, the nature of this current that brings into play a very complex angelology. Knowledge of Jewish apocalyptic was greatly enriched, if not turned upside down, by the discovery of the Qumran texts. Not that this intertestamentary literature calls into question traditional data received by the Christian faith—lovers of sensationalism, in this regard, will be disappointed—but because it reveals so many things about the spiritual currents at the time of Christ and at the time of the New Testament writings, which in turn has altered the ideas we had until then about these writings.

These three forms of Jewish gnosis, clearly identified by Jacques Dupont, constitute the traditional basis of Pauline gnosis. They define the cultural climate in which St. Paul develops his thought and provides him with the elements of his vocabulary (both ideas and words). So there is no direct borrowing here from pagan philosophy or mysticism. However, as Fr. Bouyer points out in his article devoted to Dom Dupont's study,[28] on the one hand these three forms of Jewish gnosis are in reality often closely linked ("clearly there was partial confusion rather than opposition between apocalyptic and rabbinic circles"), and, on the other hand, the "apocalypticists" as well as the *nomodidaskalos* are heirs to a very ancient Jewish mysticism, well before the first century BC, the existence of which cannot be questioned and without which many Pauline texts remain unintelligible.[29]

---

28 "Saint Paul et les origines de la gnose," *Revue des sciences religieuses*, University of Strasbourg (January 1951): 70–75.

29 The existence of a large body of oral traditions dating back at least to Moses (the unwritten Torah that God gave to Moses along with the written

That said, Pauline doctrine confers on Jewish gnosis a truly transcendent metaphysical depth and spiritual breadth. But there is no need to stress here what I have already addressed elsewhere.[30]

From these few remarks we can see how much the vision that nineteenth-century historians had of gnosis differs from the one presented by today's historians. "The word gnosis," explains Simone Pétrement, "used to mean, as we know, a Christian heresy, the oldest of heresies, a form of Christianity that already appears somewhat in the time of the apostles, but which is developed and becomes known with a certain precision only in the second century."[31] Now here is what Fr. Adelin Rousseau explains in the introduction to his translation in a volume of *Against the Heresies* of St. Irenaeus of Lyon: "During the first two centuries, the term 'gnosis' (= 'knowledge') was commonly used by Christian authors to denote a deep religious knowledge having to do with the loftiest mysteries of the faith, especially that of the mystery of the salvation of the world through the Cross of Christ."[32] This is why Louis Bouyer is entirely justified in writing, in his article "Gnôsis: le sens orthodoxe de l'expression jusqu'aux Pères": "Clement and Origen, far from creating 'gnosis' with orthodox intent, received it from the Church. We can understand what they did only if we start with this fundamental given."[33] Father Th. Camelot best sums up the conclusions of current research when he

---

Torah of which it is the explanation) is beyond dispute. The portion of these traditions relating to civil legislation and liturgical rules was compiled and written in Galilee around AD 200 by Judah ha-Nasi under the name of *Mishna* ("repetition," "second" law or *deuterosis* in Greek). Some esoteric and mystical teachings were preserved, at the same time, in the *Tossephta* ("supplement" to the *Mishna*) and other fragmentary collections. These compiled traditions are the first written traces of what will be called, in the thirteenth century, *Kabbalah* ("Tradition"). These esoterico-mystical currents constitute one of the elements of the cultural environment within which the Christian Scriptures were written: cf. *Christ, the Original Mystery*, 239–48. On the origin of the Aramaic *kabbalah*, cf. J.-M. Mathieu, *Le Nom de Gloire. Essai sur la Kabale* (Méolans-Revel: DésIris, 1992), 183–200.

30 *Christ the Original Mystery*, Chap. 8.
31 *Le dualisme chez Platon, les gnostiques et les manichéens* (Paris: P. U. F., 1947), 132.
32 Paris: Cerf, 1984, 9.
33 *Journal of Theological Studies*, IV (1953): 188–203.

states: "It is during the Hellenistic period that the words *gnosis* and *gignoskein* and their derivatives acquire a meaning properly and usually religious.... this phenomenon is due to the influence of the biblical tradition of the Septuagint and is set in the context of the Jewish, especially Alexandrian, apologetics of the diaspora. There was neither the creation of a previously non-existent terminology, or a pure and simple borrowing from everyday language or philosophical traditions, but the adapting, specifying, and enriching of materials already widely used and reinterpreted as part of a supernatural epistemology. From a rational type of knowledge inquiring into the existence and nature of God, one has passed over to a knowledge of faith."[34]

THREE REASONS TO BE SILENT

Obviously, I would like to have some of my works found in the lineage of this orthodox gnosis. But should we respond to the attacks and suspicions that have targeted my work for over twenty-five years? Should we argue and dispute about each of the points in question? Several considerations have dissuaded me until now.

The first is the pointlessness of such an undertaking. Reading under the authorship of Christian Lagrave that "Jean Borella" is a "Guénonian who needs no introduction,"[35] I conclude that I cannot escape the label attached to me, even though I have explained, in a book of over four hundred pages, just what my "Guénonism" was.[36] All my statements will be suspect and my remarks accused of duplicity. The "Gnostic" that I am supposed to be disguises his true thinking, declaring like Descartes: "when entering this theater of the world where until now I have only been a spectator, I move forward masked (*larvatus prodeo*)."[37]

---

34 *Dictionnaire de Spiritualité*, tome VI, article "Gnose et gnosticisme."
35 "La thèse du complot face à la critique," *Lecture et Tradition*, num. 324, February 2004, 32 (this was a response to the criticisms that Paul Sernine, in his book *La paille et le sycomore* [Paris: Servir, 2003], developed against Etienne Couvert's theses).
36 *Ésotérisme guénonien et mystère chrétien* (Lausanne: L'Age d'Homme, 1997). The English translation bears the title: *Christ the Original Mystery: Esoterism and the Mystical Way, with Special Reference to the Works of René Guénon*.
37 "Préambules"; *OEuvres philosophiques de Descartes* (Paris: Garnier Frères, 1962), tome I, 45.

CONCERNING CHRISTIAN GNOSIS ACCORDING TO ITS ESSENCE

My corrections will be just so much dissembling, as were the denials of Priscillianists who, as St. Augustine tells us, were authorized to perjure themselves publicly rather than reveal the secrets of the sect: "*jura, perjura, secretum prodere noli,*" that is to say: "swear, perjure yourself, do not reveal the secret."[38]

Why be surprised at this? The hunt for gnostics is a gratifying activity. It automatically confers on those who take it up a patent of orthodoxy and shrewdness. No disguise can fool such hunters. And yet their task is harsh and difficult: on the one hand, gnosis is almost indefinable in itself, assuming the most diverse and unexpected forms; on the other, it creeps in everywhere. In short, it is said to be "universal and eternal," which is no small feat. Hiding under a very innocent exterior, it presents all the more danger as the vast majority of the Christian people have never heard of it, and are unaware of the most insidious and terrible threat that has ever loomed over their faith.

What discernment, fruit of the firmest *sensus catholicus*, is needed to detect such a deadly poison, to thwart the tricks of the poisoners and finally unmask them! Will we ever be able to pay our debt to these heroes of intelligence, these benefactors of the faith?

Against these certainties, what can the gnostic do when finally chased out from behind his "good apostle" veneer? His protests would be only hypocrisy; should he beat his breast in repentance, he would still be suspected of slyly reaching for the poisonous weapon within his bosom, hidden there for the infesting of the faithful. Let him stand aside then and fall silent, and may God have mercy on his soul!

I had nothing to say in reply to my accusers, whose remarks, moreover, could only surprise me for a moment, but which, on reflection and given their origin, seemed hardly avoidable.

A second reason dissuaded me from intervening in the debate and responding to the charges against me. This reason,

---

38 *De haeresibus*, 70; J. Tixeront, *Histoire des dogmes*, tome II (Paris: Lecoffre, 1909), 239. The doctrine of Priscillian, bishop of Avila (340–385), seems to be a mix of several heresies, a certain Manichean gnosticism for one. Its interpretation is much debated today. Despite the efforts of St. Martin of Tours, he was beheaded for the "crime of black magic." He was the first bishop formally convicted of heresy by the secular arm.

or rather set of reasons, continues to be valid and prevents me from answering all the complaints issued in my regard. In a nutshell, this is a matter of competence. It is not enough to write many books on gnosis to earn the title of historian and scholar. On this account, many more or less occultist writers of the nineteenth or twentieth centuries, who have written extensively on this subject, should be regarded as expert references, which they are not. It is also necessary to have studied this question in the original texts, and therefore to know some rare languages, such as Coptic and Syriac, besides Hebrew, Greek, and Latin, not to mention modern languages: German, English, Spanish, Italian, &c., in which these texts have been edited and translated. To the mastery of these languages must be added knowledge of historical, religious, and theological, or even ethnological data, without which the reading of the texts remains a dead letter. Such studies require considerable time, uncommon intellectual qualities, and availability of tools of the trade that cannot be found in all libraries. This is why the nonspecialist—which is what I am—cannot do otherwise than rely on the work of scholars; not that one has to surrender all critical thinking in the face of their interpretations and conclusions, but because there is no means of acquiring knowledge on any historical question whatsoever except by finding out about it from those who have studied it.

Now, one must admit, this is an obligation that one generally prefers to ignore, especially in those subjects where major issues of faith are involved. What interests us is being able to judge and pass sentence with the backing of that science alone whose conclusions matter to us. Science, here, is instrumentalized: one asks it to provide us with ammunition to crush the opponent in a trial decided beforehand; the rest, the long inquests which precede the conclusions, are rather boring. And if conclusions are wanting, which often happens in such complex matters, then science itself is no longer of any interest at all.

Such an attitude is not to be blamed in any case. In comparison with scholars, the majority of the Christian faithful have neither the time nor the means to learn so as to come to a decision. And yet on many occasions our life experiences demand that we pronounce on what we know poorly or not at all. There is no other solution than to rely on the decisions of the Magisterium, that is, Church authorities. It is no longer the same when one proposes to write a book, and a book on gnosis, a subject that is today, in the unanimous opinion of specialists, one of the most embroiled in the history of religions. Previously an appendix-chapter to the history of Christianity, reserved for the uncommon researcher, gnosis has become, over the past thirty years, a "crossroads" for multiple works, and "the intersection is threatening to become congested. Adjacent to the traditional routes of patristics, of the history of ideas, and of the history of the Church, a whole network of new paths has appeared, arteries and crossings, tracks and paths, even corridors and cul-de-sacs, with names like: papyrology, codicology, oriental linguistics, and just plain linguistics, paleography, history of research, history of texts, comparative philosophy and religion, museology, sociology, semantics, and psychoanalysis."[39]

Faced with such a situation, and on the part of anyone who undertakes to deal with such a subject, one is therefore entitled to expect that care be taken to become informed, albeit succinctly, of the current state of research. Clearly, one is often quite wide of the mark. Among the denouncers of the "gnostic tumor," everything transpires as if the urgency and gravity of the danger authorized hasty allusions and quick conjectures, the end justifying the means.

Does this mean, however, that recognized scholars are alone authorized to write on gnosis? Certainly not. And first, being a resolute supporter of the freedom of expression (things being what they are today), I would not prohibit (with what power?) anyone saying what they want to on the subject of their choice — obviously along with its risks and perils. But this is not what is essential. What is really decisive here is that we cannot subject theological or metaphysical truth to the dictatorship of history, a purveyor of more or less certain facts, the meaning of which necessarily depends on the idea one has of their nature. This idea is obviously formed from

---

39 Michel Tardieu and Jean-Daniel Dubois, *Introduction à la littérature gnostique*, tome I, 7–8.

the data provided by the historical study of the phenomena considered. But how does anyone know that these phenomena arise from gnosis and will inform us what it is in its concrete forms, if I do not have at my disposal a preliminary concept which will allow me precisely to take into consideration such cultural phenomena to the exclusion of all others and identify them as manifestations revealing the essence of gnosis? But I am "spinning my wheels." Only history reveals to me that there is something called "gnosis," and yet this cultural form will remain a dead letter if nothing corresponds to it in my conceptual universe, which means: if gnosis does not correspond for me to a possibility, that is, to an essence.

Here one has a glimpse into the complexity of the problem I am addressing at this moment, a complexity such that it has dissuaded me thus far, even more than the two previously mentioned reasons, from answering my detractors: not only is such a response *a priori* made futile by the deep-seated nature of their prejudices, not only would it demand from me countless rectifications and restatements of the problem's scientific data, but again, failing to address the issue of gnosis in itself and for itself, for want of having tried to develop a real concept (and not just a description based on some data more or less understood), that is, for want of asking oneself how it was speculatively possible that someone might be a "gnostic," my detractors use, in order to accuse me of it, such a confused and contradictory notion that any denial would fall short: one cannot refute a cloud. In fact, the only specific thing in all of this is the name *gnosis*; as for its content and definition, they vary according to the needs of the prosecution: nominalism is certainly not on my side.

GNOSES AND GNOSTICISM

In a brief book called *Les heresies de la gnose du Professor Jean Borella* (preface by Bishop Bernard Tissier de Mallerais), Father Basilio Meramo asserts that, in my opinion, not only is man in the likeness of God, "but he is even God himself."[40] Obviously I have never written or thought any such thing, which

---

40 Editions Les Amis de Saint François de Sales, Sion, 1996.

is as ridiculous as it is false. But my heresy is explained: it is simply gnosis, because "gnosis does not differentiate between *a being created in the image and likeness of God* and *a being who is the image and likeness of God.*"[41] Only, there is this: it is not especially gnosis that unites the two formulations, it is Scripture.[42] In the *Book of Wisdom* (2:23), it is said that God made man "to the image of his own likeness": *eikona tes idias idiotetos*, literally: "image of his own peculiar quality." The absence of the preposition "in" before "image" is also found in St. Paul who declares (1 Cor. 11:7): "Man is the image and glory of God." Finally, as for asserting the divine character of man, again Scripture provides the least questionable evidence of this. Psalm 8, verse 6, praises the Lord for having made the man "a little lower than an Elohim." Then Psalm 82:6 places this word in the mouth of God: "I have said: you are of the Elohim, you are all the sons of Elyon [the Most High]"; a word taken up again by Christ who quotes it and confirms it: "Scripture calls Gods those to whom the word of God came—and the Scripture cannot be broken" (John 10:34-35). And we could still cite the curious verses from the book of Exodus (21:6 and 22:8) where the judge, the one who must settle disputes and pronounce judgments, is called "God," without further specification.

By no means is this about impressing the Word of God into the service of "gnosis," but only to point out that, if these teachings are read by my detractors as obviously foreign to everything they call "gnosis," why should similar statements, from my pen, be interpreted as proof of my heresy, unless

---

41 I do not know on the evidence of which text Father Moramo attributes such confusion to (heretical) gnosis. In the "Gospel of Thomas" (which is not a Gospel), we read: "Adam came from great power and wealth, and he was not worthy of you; for if he had been worthy, he would not have known death." (85; H. C. Puech, *En quête de la gnose*, tome 2 [Paris: Gallimard, 1978], 23). This *logion* is without parallel in the canonical gospels. And Puech's remark (ibid., 198-99): "Moreover, we have to recognize the small place held here by 'adamology.'" This *logion* 85 poses some problems, but it is clear that it places Adam, made however in the image of God, below Christ's disciples, in accordance with Pauline theology that distinguishes the first "psychic" Adam from the second "pneumatic" Adam.

42 This theme is developed in *Un homme, une femme au paradis* (Genève: Ad Solem, 2008).

Memoir on Gnosis

by virtue of prejudice? And this prejudice is itself only the product of a refusal, the refusal to consider gnosis in itself and to ask oneself about its essence. Gnosis is thus identified with the descriptions that historiography gives us from various religious schools of the early Christian centuries and confined to a nomenclature of theses, many of which are clearly heterodox from the Christian point of view. However, I do not recognize any of these heretical theses, and everything I have written is aimed at combating them. Bishop L. Duchesne, in his *Histoire ancienne de l'Église*, thus summarizes the basic points common to all schools qualified as gnostic by heresiology:

- "Nature and law, whether Mosaic or natural, are the work of spirits inferior to God the Father, the supreme and true God.
- "It was in Jesus Christ that this supreme God was manifested.
- "The true Christian can and must free himself from the creating and law-giving powers to draw closer to God the Father."[43]

Never having experienced the slightest inclination, even remotely, for the first and third of these theses (the second is perfectly orthodox), and again: never having suspected — until reading about them in the writings of gnosticism — that they could have sprung up in someone's mind, I cannot begin to comprehend how they were attributed to me, unless by the single token of the word "gnosis," which I certainly had employed, but by making clear in what sense I was using it, namely that of St. Clement of Alexandria and the Greek Fathers. Of this orthodox gnosis, the same historian writes: "Clement of Alexandria strives to promote, under the name of true gnosis — *alethine gnosis* — complete Christianity. His endeavor has nothing but the name in common with the 'gnosis' whose failure we have recounted."[44]

This is why, I repeat, the inquiries about the nature of gnosis are inevitable, inquiries which, for an answer, will not be satisfied with a positivist reduction to the data of historiography,

---

43 Tome I (Paris: Fontemoing, 1906), c. XI, 153–54.
44 Reprinted in the *Dictionnaire Apologétique de la Foi Catholique*, ed. A. d'Alès (Paris: Gabriel Beauchesne, 1924), tome II, col. 312.

like Binet and Simon, inventors of the first intelligence test, who answered those who asked: but what is intelligence? "It is what our test measures."

In their *Introduction à la littérature gnostique*, Michel Tardieu and Jean-Daniel Dubois confine themselves to a purely historical, that is to say descriptive, point of view, and by no means do I dispute the legitimacy of this approach, since it is a handbook "intended for students and researchers," intended to be "useful and practical."

They are thus led to distinguish eight senses, from the "epistemological" gnosis of a Plato in the fourth century BC, right up to the "esoteric" gnosis of a Ruyer, or the "psychological" gnosis of a Jonas. Some of these eight senses are obviously linked by relationships of direct kinship.[45]

For her part, Madeleine Scopello, a specialist in gnostic and apocryphal texts (Coptic, Greek, Latin) from the end of Antiquity, distinguishes only two senses: "By gnosticism, we designate a movement of thought centered around the notion of knowledge (*gnosis*) which developed in the second and third century of our era within the Roman Empire. By 'gnosis', on the other hand, we designate universal tendencies of thought which find a common denominator in the notion of knowledge. Manichaeism, mandeism, and the kabbalah can be considered as forms of gnosis."[46] In reality, these specialists, like most historians who have studied this question, more or less agree, and Madeleine Scopello is only recapitulating the distinction between gnosticism and gnosis as adopted by the whole of the scientific community at the Messina Symposium in 1966.[47] In the classification of Tardieu and Dubois, gnosticism corresponds to what they call the "obvious sense," while the term gnosis may be applied to all the other senses. In short, gnosticism represents a well-characterized and relatively

---

45 *Introduction à la littérature gnostique*, table on page 22.
46 "Courants gnostiques," in *Histoire du christianisme*," ed. J. M. Mayeur, Ch. and L. Petri, M. Vénard, vol. 1, *Le Nouveau Peuple (des origines à 250)* (Paris: Desclée, 1990), 332; by the same author: *Les Gnostiques* (Paris: Cerf, 1991).
47 *Le Origine dello Gnosticismo — The Origins of Gnosticism*, Colloquium of Messina, April 13-18, 1966, Texts and Discussions, edited by Ugo Bianchi, in "Supplements to Numen," tome XII, Leiden, 1967, xxiii.

Memoir on Gnosis

identifiable religious phenomenon—even if the questions posed by its origin, its deep nature, as well as the variety of its historical forms and ritual and social practices, are far from being resolved—while gnosis is a label attached to very disparate realities in the name of a presumed rather than verified unity of nature. It is to the point that Tardieu and Dubois judge "hasty" or "not very rigorous" the use made of this term by Gershom Scholem in connection with the kabbalah, or by Massignon and Corbin in connection with sufism.[48]

This distinction between a historically fairly well-defined gnosticism and a multifaceted gnosis with problematic unity— a distinction mentioned in previous chapters—has been contested. It is seen as a convenient way of conferring a patent of orthodoxy by standing apart from recognized heretics. But this is not true; this distinction is made in the most blatant manner. This is in no way a trick or an evasion. Besides, one does not see what interest the most diverse and ideologically disparate historians would have had in unanimously agreeing on such a distinction if it did not correspond to the evidence, even if a particular form of gnosis may present some features in common with a particular form of gnosticism which obviously does not possess a monolithic unity. Still, everyone can recognize for themselves the difference between gnosis and gnosticism. To do this it is enough to become acquainted, for example, with the general statement on gnosticism offered by Jean Doresse in the *Histoire des Religions* from the Pléiade encyclopedia,[49] which is a very comprehensive presentation and of great clarity despite the complexity of the subject; it is enough to find that it offers very little in common with the "Princeton gnosis" spoken of by Ruyer, no more, besides, than with the perspective that I have outlined in some of my texts and am trying to further clarify in the present work. Simone Pétrement, who strives to come to the defense of gnosticism in her work entitled significantly *Le Dieu séparé*, confirms, as if there were any need for it, the distinction in question: the "new gnosis," she writes, "which, according to Ruyer, was developed among

---

48 *Introduction à la littérature gnostique*, 33.
49 Vol. 2, 1972, 360-423.

certain scientists at Princeton, indeed seems to be the very opposite of Gnosticism."[50] And she shows without difficulty how the Ruyerian semi-pantheism and his rejection of any Savior of the Christic type is in contradiction with gnosticism's separated God and the theme of the "Savior saved."[51] Finally, what advantage would my "simulated orthodoxy" have found in pointing out a distinction which would surely have spared me from any declared heresy, but which would also affiliate me with all manner of non-Christian gnosis?

Today, the distinction between gnosis and gnosticism is no longer just a matter for historians of religions. It is taken up and confirmed by the highest authorities of the Catholic Church, which is only just. The Congregation for the Doctrine of the Faith, in a document of October 15, 1989 entitled *Letter to the Bishops of the Catholic Church on some aspects of Christian meditation*, at num. 8, contrasts gnosis, "an illumination or superior knowledge of the Spirit," which therefore is "not a good proper to the soul, but... a gift," to a "pseudo-gnosis" that is a "deviation"

---

50 Paris: Cerf, 1984, 41. This very scholarly book supports, rightly it seems, the thesis of the "Christian origin" of Gnosticism; the decisive argument being: we know of no well-defined gnosticist text prior to Christianity—which does not exclude Greek, Oriental, or Egyptian influences. That said, in New Testament matters Simone Pétrement, we repeat, adopts the positions of the most modernist exegesis for reasons that also appear as little disqualifying as are, in her eyes, the reasons of those historians to whom she is opposed.

51 The myth of the "Savior saved" is told in the "Hymn of the Pearl," preserved in the *Acts of Thomas*. The King's Son is sent to Egypt to look for a pearl guarded by a serpent in the midst of the sea. Having lost any memory of his mission on account of having eaten the food offered him by the Egyptians, he receives a letter from his parents that, having become speech then light, reminds him of his saving task and guides him towards it: *Acts of Thomas*, "Hymn of the Pearl," 108–13 (verses 1 to 105); *Écrits apocryphes chrétiens*, ed. François Bovon and Pierre Geoltrain, text translated, edited and annotated by Paul-Hubert Poirier and Yves Tissot, vol. 1 (Paris: Gallimard, 1997), 1418–25. The *Acts of Thomas*, of Syriac origin, is one of the most important New Testament apocrypha (150 pages in the "Pléiade" edition); it contains praise poems of great beauty. We also find the theme of the "savior saved" in the *Gospel according to Philip* (codex II, 3): "Jesus... was begotten anew. He [who was] once [anointed] was anointed anew. He who was redeemed in turn redeemed others" (*Nag Hammadi Library*, 152). In *L'Archange empourpré* (a collection of 15 mystical treatises of Sohrawardî), Henry Corbin compared *The Recital of Occidental Exile* to the *Hymn of the Pearl* from the eighth treatise (Paris: A. Fayard, 1976), 267–87.

from it. It is the first time a document of the ecclesial magisterium uses the term "pseudo-gnosis," distinguishing it from gnosis which is a progression "in the knowledge and witness of the mysteries of the faith by the intimate sense of spiritual realities...experience[d]" (num. 21).[52]

Regarding these "memoirs of gnosis," there is no longer anything essential to add. Having been implicated personally from various directions, I had to speak in the first person and speak, as objectively as possible, about the history of my mind, its philosophical history—meaning, a history in which events, apart from life's encounters, are most often tied to readings, as well as to discoveries or awareness gained through meditation. In the course of this history, two points have remained unchanged: faith in Catholic doctrine and fidelity to certain metaphysical demands of my thought.

---

52 Quoted from PierLuigi Zoccatelli, *Hermétisme et emblématique du Christ dans la vie et l'oeuvre de Louis Charbonneau-Lassay (1871–1946)* (Milan: Arché Edidit, 1996), 108–9. The author points out, in the same sense, a statement by Mgr Giuseppe Casale: "Gnosis [is] a desire, a request; pseudo-gnosis or 'gnosticism' [is] an answer, and a false answer" ("I cattolici e la sfida dei nuovi movimenti magici," in C. E. S. N. U. R., *Il ritorno della magia* [Milano: Àncora, 1992], 147).

CHAPTER 9

Concerning the Concept of Gnosis According to its Formal Unity

THE DISTINCTION BETWEEN GNOSIS AND GNOSticism is therefore something recognized. But in the name of what are we justified in giving the name gnosis to currents of thought or spiritual, philosophical and religious movements, as diverse as Masonry, occultism, Ruyerism, alchemy, Pythagorean, Evagrian or Clementine theology, New Age, the rantings of the *Da Vinci Code*, Guénonian metaphysics, &c.? What unity of meaning do we perceive under such terminological scattering? We cannot answer all aspects of such a question. If this unity exists—which we are inclined not to reject *a priori*—it can be only relative, even analogical and very difficult to define. For our part, we propose to see here, as we have suggested on several occasions, a certain *virtuality* of knowledge, not solely of a particular knowledge, but of knowledge as such. All knowledge is a desire for the apprehension of being, the hope for an encounter with what is. In sensory knowledge, this desiring dimension is somehow masked, obscured, eclipsed beneath the object's excess of presence. Reality occupies consciousness and makes it forget the desire that bore it along towards things. Sensory reality is what is more than present, what absorbs and exceeds our cognitive expectations, and which, by that very fact, if we reflect on it, evades and resists us. On the contrary, when we turn to non-sensory realities: ideas, feelings, scientific laws, mathematical entities, cultural representations, philosophical notions, &c., these intelligible objects give themselves to us only under the mode of what-is-not-there, as the goal always at a distance from our cognitive aim and only this aim, this intentionality, exists for us. The object seen makes the eye forget who sees; the object thought gives birth to a thinking with self-consciousness. Having given birth to its own consciousness, knowledge discovers itself as a cognitive capacity, and therefore as a "place" or "environment" for the hoped-for revelation of being. All speculative knowledge is therefore oriented and carried along by the native conviction that this knowledge has the power to open itself to a perception of the being that it aspires to, certainly not to create it *ex nihilo* (this would be the illusion of a certain idealism), but to receive it as its proper object. This contemplative capacity (and therefore this need for contemplativity) is inherent to the very nature of knowledge and cannot but determine the spontaneous consciousness it has of itself when it is in action. In other words, in all cognitive activity there is a *gnostic* dimension, the conviction of a possible encounter between intelligence and being, in short a kind of mystical faith in intellective power. Obviously, this mystical faith is never more lively than with philosophical thought. In this regard, we must recognize that every philosophy contains in its depths a gnostic intention or hope, precisely to the extent that, of all the intellectual approaches, it is the one most devoid of sensorially given objects. The scientific approach, in the natural sciences, remains tied to the sensory, the point of departure and outcome of its abstractive operations: it is infra-gnostic. The mathematical approach, which treats every mathematical entity as a structure of relationships (or which at least strives to do this) is in some fashion ultra-gnostic: it realizes the unity of being and knowledge, but of a being objectively reduced to knowledge which, while constructing this knowledge, forgets itself therein. It proposes an ideal of perfect knowledge, while freeing itself from its relationship with the cognitive subject. Mathematical abstraction is as if detached from the process that gives it birth: mathematical being seems freed from the project that engendered it, it exists for itself as a pure being of reason, unconnected to any raison d'être whatsoever. It no longer has meaning for human subjectivity, absorbing within itself and for itself all its intelligibility: a being (almost) devoid of being, because (almost) devoid of mystery.

CONCERNING CHRISTIAN GNOSIS ACCORDING TO ITS ESSENCE

To the contrary, the philosophical object, that is, what anyone who sets out on the philosophical path desires and hopes to know, retains its ontological mystery, namely the irreducibly mysterious character of veritable being, that whereby it is given to thought as coming from transcendent depths. With regard to the philosopher who inquires and hopes for an answer, the philosophical object (being, essence, freedom, necessity, causality, truth, &c.) presents itself with a kind of quasi-empirical consistency, a kind of intrinsic reality, analogous to that of an object of the sensory world; we expect that a careful and patient examination of this reality will reveal its nature to us little by little, at least partially. Just as sensory observation discloses something of the object observed, likewise philosophical meditation is naturally based on the conviction that a prolonged intellectual observation of its speculative object will *apprehend* (were it even by reminiscence) something about it. Otherwise, we do not truly see what might induce anyone to become involved in an endeavor aimed at knowing something that does not seem *directly given* in any manner. But at the same time, on the philosophical path, the object *to be seen*, where presence and absence combine, never obscures the intellectual gaze; quite the contrary, it activates lively awareness of it. The cognitive subject, in proportion to the inquiry (which is just as well a purification and a transformation of the gaze itself), gives birth more and more clearly to its own truth and desires more and more ardently an intelligible being which makes sense *for itself*, which is the non-abolishing fulfillment of its gnostic faith.

Can this fulfillment happen? Can this gnostic faith's prayer be answered? The history of thought shows in any case that its realization is extremely difficult and problematic. Philosophical hope discovers, at the cost of many disappointments, that it will never be quite fulfilled here below. And as we know, out of this metaphysical disenchantment, Kant has created the principle of his whole philosophy, which is a critique of our power to know: human understanding is sheer conceptual construction *activity*, and there is no passivity in it, that is, no receptive capacity with respect to an intelligible object, which would allow us to know this object; in short: we have no intellectual intuition,

Concerning the Concept of Gnosis According to its Formal Unity

but only a sensory intuition (perception through the senses). From this point of view, Kantian philosophy is the most a-gnostic of all philosophies; or rather presents itself as the most rational formulation of principles for every agnosticism: Kant or the prolegomena to any future philosophy that would wish to present itself as a-gnostic. We have shown elsewhere[1] why criticist radicalism had to be rejected. Here we have a strange intellectual blindness in a prodigiously gifted speculative genius, but one who did not see that intelligence should see only that it does not see if, precisely, it had not seen. To write the *Critique of Pure Reason*, that is, to perceive the limits of our cognitive power, the intellect must by itself surpass these limits and may be intelligibly *affected* by this intelligible object that is knowledge. We say the intellect, one might just as well speak of reason: both are different modalities of the same spirit. Certainly, as St. Paul teaches, "we now see through a mirror enigmatically, *per speculum in aenigmate*" (1 Cor. 13:18), but we see. The intellect is a mirror, it only captures reflections, images, and these in an obscure manner (*in aenigmate*), but it truly receives these obscure images, otherwise there is no knowledge, and *not even sensory knowledge* would be given to us. In other words, reason is potentially more than reasoning, the intelligence is potentially more than intellection.

It is this more, this "gnostic surplus" that is manifested in what is called the gnoses, and which is incited to manifest each time the object proposed to the intelligence belongs to the supersensible order. The gnostic reactions elicited by such proposals may be of a very diverse nature and relate to very different objects. But it seems one can deem there is gnosis whenever intelligence is induced to continue its knowledge-effort beyond whatever it has experienced naturally, that is, each time it seeks to intimately fathom what it is thinking, to be united with it in complete intelligibility. This can be the case with the supersensible realities of being, essence, world, substance, causality, the true, the one, the beautiful, &c. This is also the case with those divinely revealed realities that are the Trinitarian mystery and the mystery of the

---

[1] *The Crisis of Religious Symbolism*, 350–56.

redemptive incarnation of Jesus Christ, the difference being that the intelligence discovers within itself the presence of metaphysical realities, like transcendentals and universals in whose presence it can do nothing but acquiesce (unless one blinds oneself, as often happens in modern philosophy), while sacred realities are given from the outside (*ex auditu*), in the manner of sensory realities, but from a supersensible outside, or rather a supersensible beyond. This is why religion, even more than metaphysics, is able to awaken the gnostic desire, which, in the consciousness it possesses of itself and of its strength, can be led to lose sight of the conditions for its exercise. It is then that gnosis becomes heterodox.

With respect to philosophical knowledge, the conditions that govern the exercise of gnosis are those of the human mode of all knowledge. The intellect, in its essence, has something of the more than human, but it is the person who knows: we only perceive essences through the mediation of concepts and beings of nature, therefore by the mode of signs. It is indeed the light of the essence that comes to us and is collected by the mirror of the intellect, a supersensual and superconceptual light, but we only know it "negatively" in some fashion, only as the *beyond* of every sensory or mental sign. And this is already a true miracle, a true knowledge, which communicates to us a certainty "invincible to all scepticism," as Pascal says,[2] but a certainty blinding by excess of light: this is what we called the "semantic experience," as certain as it is hardly sayable and whose certifying force—as Descartes has clearly seen—is inseparable from its actuality. This is why, as human beings, we feel the need for assuring ourselves retrospectively about this certainty—an indirect assurance—by subjecting it to and testing it with the control of reason, which is effected only by relating metaphysical certainties to each other, that is, by their being brought into discourse: reason, or logic, is necessarily about relationship, but it only works with the data of the metaphysical intelligence or the sensory intuition. Such are the two poles of human certainty: intrinsic certainty of the intuition of essences, but essences which remain transcendent

---

[2] *Pensées* (New York: E. P. Dutton, 1958), num. 395, 107.

to the properly human exercise of knowledge; extrinsic certainty, on the other hand, by a verification of their discursive coherence. Even so, logic itself (or the formalization of the rules according to which reason works) obeys first principles (identity, noncontradiction, excluded middle, &c.), which are of an intrinsic, direct and infallible certainty: they are known by themselves and look to both metaphysical knowledge and logical regulation. As regulators, they are immanent and connatural to intelligence, but considered in themselves (identity in itself = the One; noncontradiction in itself = infinite and meontological possibility), they extenuate the intelligence and retain their mysterious transcendence.

As long as philosophical gnosis remains conscious of the essentially relative and revisable nature of its formulations, it remains legitimate. By its gnostic intention it eludes rationalist reduction and *prepares* the mind for mystical contemplation, by conferring on the concepts it utilizes a spiritual vibration that prolongs them towards the essences of which they are the reflection and opens them to the Light from above. It seems that one encounters such a philosophical gnosis, for example, in the third metaphysical Meditation of Descartes, on the idea of infinity, or in certain books by Father Auguste Gratry.[3]

Obviously, the risk is great, under the impetus of this gnosis, to attribute to these concepts the value of a divine revelation (in the active sense of the term) and to make of them direct and "personal" manifestations of the Holy Spirit. The re-enchantment of metaphysics can go as far as idolatry. One then introduces into the speculative gaze an attitude of an adoration aesthetic in nature, as if, before these ideas, we were in the presence of so many gods. And one goes astray.

However, we are far from denying that the intellectual contemplation of metaphysical ideas is, in some respects, aesthetic in nature; we have even, on the contrary, stressed the necessity for this.[4] To contemplate is always "to see," even with the eyes of the mind, which implies that, whenever ideas are involved,

---

[3] Cf. for example *Philosophie. Logique*, tome 2 (Paris: C. Douniol / J. Lecoffre, 1858) and *La Philosophie du Credo* (Paris: C. Douniol / J. Lecoffre, 1864) — Trans.
[4] Cf. *supra*, 292–3.

CONCERNING CHRISTIAN GNOSIS ACCORDING TO ITS ESSENCE

we recognize a kind of "sensory presence" (*aisthesis* means "sensation"). For want of this intellectual sensitivity (under the pretext of pure rationality), for want of acknowledging (Kant), at the secret heart of thinking activity, this intellective *passivity* or receptivity, we are prohibited from truly entering "into metaphysics," and we reduce the mystery of being to the conditions of its mental expression. Yes, in their primal source, metaphysical ideas are icons of the Holy Spirit. But it goes for these intellectual icons as it does for painted icons. According to the decisions of the Seventh Ecumenical Council (Second Council of Nicaea, 787), we are "to kiss and to render honorable adoration (*prokynesis*) to them, not however to grant true worship (*latria*) according to our faith, which is proper to the divine nature alone."[5]

This is why Schuon's (provocative?) statement that we reported at the end of chapter 7[6] ("yes, the metaphysical concepts are idols and we must adore them") is inadmissible. Let no one object that this "staggering" statement concerns transcendent realities whose concepts are mental signs, because worship of the divine Absolute, of Infinite Being, of the Supreme Good, clearly does not pose any problem for the believer: it is even unconditionally required; therefore it can only involve, as it happens, the conceptual forms themselves, considered separately, and not their content, which is not being called into question.

However, not only should these conceptual forms not be the object of a *precept* of worship, which is *due*, in the proper sense, only to divine Reality, but in addition they are not in themselves susceptible to homage: in short, they are not ontologically adorable. For, just as painted icons are so painted with materials, colors and forms borrowed from earthly substances, although the model is not made by human hands (it is "acheiropoieta"), so intellectual icons are indeed painted by the Holy Spirit (at least faith, and a deepening reflection, persuade us, since we have no direct awareness of this), but it is by means of those elements and forms—individual and cultural—according to which all thinking activity operates.

---

5 Denzinger, *Sources of Catholic Dogma*, 302, page 121.
6 Cf. *supra*, 257.

This is why these metaphysical intellections have a natural character, and, strictly speaking, should not constitute, as Schuon argues, a subjective revelation, the revelation itself being seen as an objective intellection; if this chiasmus corresponded to factual truth, revelation, objective intellection, would lose its obscurity, its supernatural "strangeness," coming from Heaven, and intellection, subjective revelation, would render revelation useless. But well we know that what revelation announces "does not enter into the heart of man" (1 Cor. 2:9). We must therefore distinguish, among intellectual forms with transcendent content, those which are imposed by revelation (the notions of "trinity" or "incarnation," for example), and those that come under the speculative grammar of all metaphysics. Only the first have, insofar as they are conceptual mediations, something of the sacred, their divine origin being expressly signified. They are therefore also expressly supernatural and may be the subject of a kind of worship—what theology designates as a worship of relative latria (such as that addressed to the cross of Christ or to his humanity)—because these conceptual signs are positively and visibly connected to the reality towards which they lead, just as the flesh of Christ is eminently so to his divine person.

But the same is not true of metaphysical concepts whose divine origin, in our ordinary experience of them, is merely implied and does not present itself as such. They cannot therefore justify by themselves an attitude of adoration, and, hence, if one persists in demanding it, this attitude will above all express the human subject's own will to project onto his intellectual productions the individual iridescence of a sacralization, a "revelation for oneself" which risks shutting up the human being in a fantasized metaphysics. Surely metaphysical concepts emanate from the Logos "which enlightens every man," and are formed in the understanding by the Holy Spirit; it is, moreover, the ineffaceable honor of Descartes to have shown, through a long meditation, that the idea of infinity within us could only be the mark of the divine Artisan on his work. But, exhibiting a kind of connaturality with intelligence, which is naturally "supernatural," these truths should not wrest the intelligent being from itself, should not save it, they do not introduce a saving rupture into the being of the knower. Now, the commandment to worship, taken literally, does not express, on the part of God who imposes it on us ("only one God shall you adore") a jealous care for safeguarding his transcendence, but the desire to save us. It is not for his sake that God asks us to worship him, it is for ours, because only this attitude and this act of adoration *initiates* us, causes us to enter the path of salvation, that is, teaches us to place ourselves in the presence of God. It is not the intelligence that ought to be saved—in a certain manner, being a light as if derived from God (*lumen quasi derivatum a Deo*, says St. Thomas), it is already saved—it is the human being. And the human person can only be saved by existentially turning toward Salvation, by "violently" wresting himself from a certain empire of the world, not that it is bad in itself, but it is for human beings insofar as they are not at liberty to assume its omnipresence: we must first seek the kingdom of God and his justice, before the "rest," the kingdom of the world, be given "in addition." The *act* of worship establishes such a rupture. From the outset and concretely it situates our existence in the presence of God, turning us towards him, he whom we neither see nor imagine, but whom we recognize by faith as the Absolute which infinitely surpasses all vision and all knowledge.

We understand that here we need to retain a distinction between the order of metaphysical knowledge and that of revelation, not as to the reality of what is involved with either one, but as to the human approaches implied. Whether we are speaking of the Absolute, of God, of the supreme Principle, or of the Infinite, we are speaking of the same Reality, whether one is Abraham, Isaac, Jacob, or Descartes, Leibniz, Malebranche: there is only one sole God (we are leaving aside here the distinction, a little too hackneyed, between God and Godhead). And that is why, moreover, the God of the intelligence being in himself the God of faith, the metaphysician can be naturally drawn to cast the gaze of faith on his Ideas, to confer a religious value on his concepts. Likewise, conversely, religious faith can be drawn to treat the *revelatum* as a metaphysical object, as an "intelligible form" of the same nature as those whose presence faith finds in its understanding and whose transcendent root is not always perceived. In both cases we are dealing with an inauthentic gnosis, and this is the source of gnosticism (faith parodied in metaphysical mythologies) as well as of philosophical gnosis that endows metaphysical or cosmological—even anthropological—themes with a kind of sacred value: metaphysical mythology in the first case, mythological metaphysics in the second.

It seems that the "religious" thought of Father Teilhard de Chardin, in some respects, illustrates this second case quite well. This is not gnosticism in the historical sense of the term, and the orthodoxy of his faith should not be doubted. But this is unquestionably a philosophical, or rather a deviated gnosis. It is not warped in everything it says, nor in all its demands: on the contrary, it is even perfectly legitimate, if not extremely urgent, to seek to endow Christian thought with a cosmology open in its depths to the revelation of Christ. But this gnosis is warped, on the one hand, by its distraught adherence to evolutionism (which is by no means a scientific theory, but an explanatory myth), and, on the other, by the poetic-mystical atmosphere in which his anthropo-cosmological speculations are steeped. The gnostic excess of this doctrine is betrayed by the sentimental religiosity with which all the concepts that he utilizes are invested: everything is in the vision, nothing, or almost nothing, in the thing seen. In this sense, Etienne Gilson is perfectly right to qualify Teilhardian thought as gnosis: "Whoever," he writes, "has followed the history of Christian thought finds himself in a known country. Teilhardian theology is one more Christian gnosis." But reservations are advanced in the text that follows: "and," Gilson continues, "like all gnoses from Marcion to the present day, this is a *theology fiction*. We rediscover here all the traditional characteristics of the genre: a cosmic perspective on all issues or perhaps rather a perspective of cosmogenesis, a morality of cosmogenesis, a vision of cosmogenesis."[7] This text harbors many surprises regarding any similarity between Teilhard and Marcion, who actually differ

---

7 *Les tribulations de Sophie* (Paris: Vrin, 1967), 68.

on all accounts. And first, the relationship of the Marcionite doctrine—which is indeed a *theology fiction*—to Gnosticism, in the opinion of the best specialists, is a problem. Absent in particular from Marcion's work—known only from his adversaries—is that metaphysical mythology so characteristic of Gnosticism: his speech is simple and "reasonable." Next and most importantly, about which there is no doubt, is the radical miscosmism that animates all his thought. Matter is inherently evil and the source of evil. It is the work of the God of the Old Testament, a secondary God, just but cruel and insensitive. We ought to escape from this creation, from this poorly made world, and we can do so thanks to Christ whom the supreme God, the good God, has sent to save us. He has come into the world, but has assumed evil flesh only in appearance: Marcion is basically a docetist.[8] We are surely at the antipodes with Teilhard's thought, which could almost be described as a cosmolatry, "almost" because the world is created by God, not with a view to its present state, but with a view to its Christic transfiguration, a transfiguration which is that of "Holy Matter," the unique fabric of cosmic reality, Matter-Spirit in constant creative and unifying transformation. We are indeed close to pantheism, which Teilhard was not far from recognizing in himself, but a rectified pantheism, which does not exclude God's transcendence: "'The world is still being created, and it is Christ who is reaching his fulfillment in it.' When I had heard and understood that saying, I looked around and I saw, as though in an ecstasy, that through all nature I was immersed in God."[9] Moreover, Teilhard by no means has the feeling of moving forward in a known country: "How is it, then, that as I look around me, still dazzled from what I have seen, I find that I am almost the only person of

---

[8] Cf. E. Amann, the "Marcion" article, *Dictionnaire de Théologie Catholique*, tome IX, col. 2020; more recently: the brief notice by B. Aland, "Marcion-Marcionism," in the *Dictionnaire Encyclopédique du Christianisme Ancien*, tome 2 (Paris: Cerf, 1990), 1541-43. Docetism, from a Greek verb *dokein*, which means "to seem," "to appear," is a heresy which maintains that Christ had only put on the appearance of a body, that he was not a "true man."

[9] "Cosmic Life," *Writings in Time of War*, trans. R. Hague (New York & Evanston: Harper & Row, 1968), 60; on Teilhard's avowed "pantheism," cf. ibid., 15-16.

my kind, the only one to have *seen*? And so I cannot, when asked, quote a single author, a single work, that gives a clearly expressed description of the wonderful 'Diaphany' that has transfigured everything for me."[10]

Finally, the idea of a cosmogenesis does not seem necessarily tied to gnosticism. Before dismissing it under a derogatory label, we should first recognize that it simply expresses the truth, certainly not in the strict Teilhardian sense, distorted by an omnipresent evolutionism which constitutes a real "epistemological

---

10 "The Christic" (March 1955), in *The Heart of Matter*, trans. R. Hague (San Diego, New York, London: Harcourt Brace, 1978), 100. The "diaphany" designates the property that Matter has (according to Teilhard) of allowing the Spirit to radiate. The work of Father Teilhard has aroused disproportionate enthusiasm, and, it must be admitted, through his visionary lyricism it can only foster this kind of enthusiasm, and even delusions. He intends to present to believers a "theology" reconciled, in its essence, with science. But this is at the cost of a certain ignorance of *both* theology *and* science, which is not to be reduced to geology and paleontology: unless we are mistaken, Teilhardian cosmology totally ignores *the most important modern-day scientific revolution*, that of quantum physics; but this revolution makes the very notion of matter vanish. Father Teilhard seems to be always telling us: "Christians, do not be afraid of matter, it is good, full of life and spirit." But what about this matter itself as revealed to us by science? Teilhard says nothing about it, and yet he is contemporary to quantum theory and the unresolved crisis (the "drama of quanta," writes Louis de Broglie in his preface to the book by J. L. Andrade e Silva and G. Lochak: *Quanta, grains et champs* [Paris: Hachette, 1969], 9), that this theory introduces into our idea of reality (cf. Wolfgang Smith: *The Quantum Enigma. Finding the Hidden Key* [Peru, IL: Sherwood Sugden, 1995]). All the daring, all the much-vaunted novelties of Teilhardian thought refer to nineteenth-century physics (if only to combat its ideologically materialist repercussions), a physics almost completely obsolete, and officially so since 1927 (the Fifth Solvay Congress, which formalizes the renunciation of the realism of physical theories). As for the sources of his all-embracing and somewhat obsessive evolutionism, they date back at least to 1859 (Darwin, *The Origin of Species*), if not even to 1809 (Lamarck, *Zoological Philosophy*). The Teilhardian endeavor, this must be strongly emphasized against many of its detractors, corresponds to an objective and urgent need: to develop a cosmology in accord with Revelation. But the solution, as proposed, is hardly acceptable: it is neither philosophy nor science. Teilhard metaphorizes more than he thinks, and it is often the images that think for him, and in a very systematic manner. There remains, in addition to the legitimate intention of this enterprise, the enchantment of a style of thinking and writing, inseparably. François Chenique, in "Le Cas Teilhard" (chapter 17 of *Sagesse chrétienne et mystique orientale* [Paris: Dervy, 1995], 344–66), provides some biographic clarifications and advances some original hypotheses. This presentation benefited—this is in part its interest—from the advice of Father Pierre Leroy (a Jesuit scholar, disciple and friend of Teilhard) whom F. Chenique had consulted.

obstacle," but in the sense that, in its basic reality, the world is "genetic," or as Ruyer says, "embryogenetic": everything in the world is "making itself," without it being necessary to assume that this genesis, or rather *these* geneses in innumerable multiplicity, are subject to a law of evolution which would bend their development towards an Omega point. There is something of reality making itself in every being and for every being. The advent of new species is a fact; a causal continuity between species can only be a theory which does not, moreover, recognize the importance of the "vertical" causality exerted by the subtle and trans-spatial world on its corporeal manifestations, not to mention any causality semantic in nature.

Marcionite gnosis is anti-cosmic, Teilhardian gnosis is cosmolatrous. What they have in common, if this is the case, cannot therefore pertain to their respective doctrinal contents, as everything is in opposition, but only to a certain cognitive attitude. If, moreover, the term *theology fiction* is well-applied to Marcion, it is much less applicable to Teilhard, who, in matters of fundamental theology, as Father de Lubac has shown, hardly strays from traditional doctrine, about which he has basically little to say; above all he has produced a *cosmology fiction*, it being understood, of course, that the second is not without repercussions on the first. But one like the other makes its concepts identical to revelations. Breaking free from Church doctrine, that is, from the faith of the Apostles, Marcion set himself up as the founding interpreter of Scripture in the name of the demands of his understanding. Likewise Teilhard, rejecting the principles of traditional cosmology, set himself up as the prophet of a new vision of the world and man in the name of the demands of an all-embracing evolutionism known through a kind of quasi-pantheistic revelation. Herein lies, we think, the gnostic deviation, which is a deviation, or a perversion, of the gnostic dimension inherent to the very activity of any metempirical knowledge.[11] One might see here

---

[11] We use *metempirical* in the sense that this term designates, not what exceeds all possible experience — for there is an experience of what is semantic, an experience of the intelligible — but what is not provided by the senses. This is why we could classify the world among the non-sensory realities. The

simply an excess of confidence in the products of his own thinking; it would not be wrong, but certainly insufficient, since one would designate by that nothing but what is called "intellectual pride," which is present in many thinkers (and a few others) who are by no means gnostics; they may even be altogether a-gnostic. What is specific to the gnostic process is its "religious" character. In the eyes of the gnostic intellect (whether orthodox or deviant), intellectual forms are imbued with sacred value, clothed with a numinous aura endowing them with the mysterious presence of a near-revelation. Which explains why the "false" Gnostic may have no awareness of this pride and perceive himself, to the contrary, as quite humble before the splendor of the truths he thinks he perceives.[12]

These are not then, we think, the elements of a doctrine that enable it to be identified as a gnosis, whether orthodox or deviant, since these elements may differ considerably from one

---

world is actually never *seen*. We see things and beings. But the idea that these sensory realities are part of an objectively existing whole and posited in its own order only corresponds to a judgment of the intelligence and is by no means given in perception. After all, it seems that the "idea" of a *world*-ly and objective permanence of reality is absent from animal knowledge.

12 Guénon disdainfully rejects the idea of intellectual pride, on the pretext that it would be contradictory. Pride, a feeling of the individual order, cannot be associated with the intellect, which is of a supra-individual order (*Initiation and Spiritual Realization*, chap. 15). Surely the intellect, as such, is no stranger to the "pride-humility" opposition. But it is not the intellect that, of itself, exercises the intellectual act; it is the human being in whom the intellectual faculty is present, and who can take pride from what it is given to perceive. As St. Thomas Aquinas observes, the intellectual power is not the *subject* of pride, but it can be the cause. And he sees as proof of this the fact that the angels, intellectual creatures, also knew pride (*Summa Theologiae*, II-II, Q. 162, a. 3). Moreover, for Guénon, humility is as individual and sentimental, as hardly spiritual and metaphysical, as is its opposite pride (ibid., 80). Therefore, to follow Guénon, we should conclude that the Word Incarnate, declaring "I am meek and humble of heart" (Matt. 11:29), only testifies to the sentimental limitations of his individuality. And likewise, when the Theotokos sings: God "has regarded the humility of his handmaid," and again: "He has scattered the proud in the conceit of their heart," and again: "He has lifted up the humble" (Luke 1:46–52). Of course, Guénon was perhaps not thinking of this evangelical humility when he wrote this study; but just how could he not have thought about it? We can also see in Guénon's attitude, to his defense, a reaction against a pious and intentionally anti-intellectual "humilitarism"—quite widespread in his time—but which is the caricature of true humility, and which infringes upon the legitimate demands of the intelligence no less than on its dignity.

doctrine to another, or may even be completely opposed. Consequently, and to the extent that the qualification of gnosis can be legitimately attributed to whatever it is that one attributes it to, it seems necessary to situate its positive unity in a certain mental form, a cognitive attitude — which we have attempted to describe — rather than in this or that thesis. This conclusion is not original. It is found more or less in a remarkable study by Albert Franz on the gnosis of the German philosopher Schelling. The question he examines is whether Schelling's philosophy can be called gnosis, whereas its author strongly condemned ancient gnosticism — after having observed that "the concept of gnosis... has been until now hardly able to be systematically determined."[13] His philosophy deems itself able to say, with certain precautions, that it is "a kind of neognosis insofar as it claims, like gnosis, to be a knowledge of 'last things,' of the metaphysical relationships of God to the world, of the primal reasons for being; like the gnostics, this knowledge is not nourished by simple reason but equally [by Myth] and Revelation."[14]

---

13 "Gnose et Métaphysique dans la dernière philosophie de Schelling," translated from German to French by Nathalie Depraz, in the collection published under her editorship and that of Jean-François Marquet: *La gnose, une question philosophique. Pour une phénoménologie de l'invisible* (Paris: Cerf, 2000), 169.
14 Ibid., 173.

CHAPTER 10

How Gnosis Arrives at Knowledge

THE IDEA OF GNOSIS IS THAT OF AN INTRINsically sacred knowledge, that is, sacred by virtue of its own nature and not only by virtue of the (religious or divine) object that would particularize it as such. Although this nature is revealed to itself only at the moment when the cognitive power attentively sets its sights on a metempirical object, it is in fact inherent to any act of knowledge, even the most elementary sensory knowledge, but then it is in a non-conscious mode. This means that gnosis is everywhere, or that knowledge is fundamentally gnostic, as surprising as this statement might seem, and even though we are unaware of it most of the time or refuse to admit it. This is so because adamic knowledge was so and because, however altered by original sin, it retains in its depths the memory of its native openness to the native being of things. Adamic gnosis is the sacramental act by which the world and man are born to knowledge of themselves, that is, are in some manner "saved," or rather escape from their possible "ontic" reduction, from their factuality, and are connected to their essence. For man, marked by original sin, this sacral form of knowledge is found in the eyes of the child discovering the world, or in the eyes of the poet and the artist communing with the immanent creativity of things, each of which is like a miraculous surge out of nothingness. It is also rediscovered among those who are not expressly and literally poets, during certain graced moments, and more generally, in the all but forgotten memory of our first meeting with things.

It is not then the presence of gnosis, the sacred dimension of all knowledge, that must be explained, but indeed rather its absence, since, in its profound and full reality, knowledge is always sacred. But it is not so in all its actual modalities.

CONCERNING CHRISTIAN GNOSIS ACCORDING TO ITS ESSENCE

This is why it is necessary to distinguish between "gnosis" and "knowledge," just as the secular regimen of the cognitive process imposes it on us. As we will see, it is precisely starting from this secular regimen which, since original sin, has become ours, that we will have some chance to understand how gnosis can come about in knowledge, how knowledge can become gnostic. In so doing, we will no longer be gaining access just to the formal unity of gnosis, but to its essential unity, insofar as that is possible.

The first point to consider therefore concerns the disappearance of the gnostic quality of knowledge, at the very least its absorption, repression, and reduction to unconscious latency. More important indeed than Freud's psychic unconscious is the pneumatic (or spiritual) unconsciousness of gnosis and its burial in the sleep of the mind. This occultation can be related to original sin to the extent that gnosis is identical to adamic knowledge. It is not lost in the sense that it would have been destroyed, but it is forgotten, or even denied, and is no longer present and active in the cognitive operations of the human being; *it is waiting to be awakened.*

An objection might be raised here. If, as we claim, the gnostic quality forms part of the essence of knowledge, should not its erasure and reduction to a latent state lead to the disappearance of knowledge itself? We have in fact already answered this objection; but some clarifications will be useful.

Formally, what constitutes the cognitive process is the act by which the intellect grasps its object. As such, the intellect, in the act of intellection, is universal, but with a somewhat negative universality, that is, insofar as it is neither properly human, angelic, or even "divine," except in the sense that God is considered precisely as the transcendent integral of all beings and therefore as the One in whom and by whom everything truly and positively has access to universality, for, in God, everything is God. The universality of the intellect is easily observed in the example of what for us represents the very type of pure truth, namely mathematical truth: two plus two is four for a human, as well as for an angel and for God; this truth does not rightly belong to anyone. But this in no way means there is, numerically, only one intellect for all men, an "Averroist" thesis strongly combatted by St. Albert the Great, St. Bonaventure, and St. Thomas Aquinas,[1] and contrary to the evidence. As we have repeatedly recalled, following Aristotle, it is not, in the concrete sense of the term, the intellect that exercises the act of knowledge, it is a human being (through his intellect); and a human being is not his intellect. The intellect is, in each person, his receptivity to divine light, and this receptivity, opened by God in the face of Adam by the "spiracle of life," is necessarily specific to each human being.[2] This intellect is dependent on the human subject, who remains master of his orientation towards the uncreated light.

There is therefore in man, and first of all in Adam, something deeper and more radical than the intellect—which is moreover neither "in the depths" nor "on the surface." This is one's ontological person, one's very being as a creature whose free will is, at the anthropological level, the most direct expression; because, before being an intellect, the human being is a creature, and this "creaturehood" is what is most profound in him, that from which everything else is exercised. Man is not an intellectual being, like the angels; he is a person-being, not the image of this or that aspect, of this or that divine possibility, like the angels, but of God as such, of God considered outside of every quality and every attribute, in its unnamable reality. Here we have the reason why God could become man and not angel, and why also the mystery of this person who is the human creature is impenetrable and will ever be so, except in the eyes of God, unknown to all creation, even to the highest of the angels, a unique and incommunicable gaze, and which constitutes *by this very fact* the absolutely

---

[1] St. Thomas d'Aquin, *Contre Averroès*, introduction, translation and notes by Alain de Libera (Paris: Flammarion, 1994).

[2] On the spiracle of life (*spiraculum vitae*), cf. *Love and Truth*, 182–94. There is a major scriptural basis for this doctrine, and that is the event of Pentecost. The Holy Spirit manifests in the form of fire that is divided "like tongues, and one came upon each of them" (Acts 2:3). This personalization of the descent of the Spirit presupposes the reality of the person who receives it and the presence, in each of the recipients, of an intellect that this descent comes to pneumatize; cf. ibid., 163–66.

transcendent and absolutely unspeakable uniqueness of the person. In other words, the uniqueness of the person can be ontologically founded only by and in the unique gaze of the divine One on a particular individual, an *ontonoetic* relation that constitutes the very being of the person. For the *knowledge* that God has of such a human creature is precisely this creature's *being*, and the person realizes his being by ascending along this "pre-existing" ontonoetic relation until the moment when it "will truly know as also [it] *has been truly known*": the spiritual future thus coinciding with the ontological past. The human person becomes what it is (1 Cor. 13:12).

But this is equally why adamic knowledge must be a gnosis, that is to say a sacred knowledge. Strictly speaking, this sacredness of adamic knowledge does not depend on the cognitive act as such; it depends on the free orientation of the person of Adam towards the object of his *desire*, towards this beyond of the world and of himself, which gives itself to him, not in the form of a nature, but in the form of a command. Although Adam's mind grasps natures (each name that Adam gives to creatures designates their true nature), Adam does not, however, find in these creatures "any help like himself" (Gen. 2:20). This disappointment reveals, in the adamic intellect, the presence of a desire, of an expectation, unsatisfied by any cosmic presentation: the orientation towards a Self that transcends all nature and all quality, which he experiences within himself as a lack and a need, because therein lies the mystery of his person, which will be revealed to him only by meeting the woman, "bone of my bones and flesh of my flesh," the mediator of the discovery of the path towards the surpassing of all nature, towards what can only be called the supernatural. This desire for the supernatural comes from well within the intellect, from its ontological root—but it is within him that it speaks—and this is why he aims beyond and introduces into himself the disquiet of a transcendence. This disquiet and anxiety might vanish or be suffocated beneath the over-presence of things, yet knowledge remains; it may even *seem* more limpid and serene: it acquiesces to all nature, it is completely naturalized, everything is *just so*, without why, without distance, without perspective, without reason, eternally just so; and the mystery of the subject is absorbed into the intelligible transparency of the object. But, although the intellect can forget itself in grasping an object, it is not the same for the human being, who, at the very moment of his discovery of the world, does not recognize himself as similar to anything in the world and ontologically has an experience of distance and otherness, like an absence. This is why the intellect is not only brimming and saturated with natures, but it is also transfixed by a desire for supernature.

It will be understood that we are referring here to the famous *desiderium naturale* spoken of by St. Thomas and which has given rise to so many theological debates in the last century around Fr. de Lubac's book: *The Supernatural*.[3]

When it comes to this natural desire for the supernatural, however, there has been much more debate about nature than about desire. But one is no less important than the other. It is the desire for an infinite supernature that introduces into knowledge the tension towards a transcendence and confers on it its sacred quality, i.e., that makes of it a gnosis. This tension is not that of the intellect itself as a simple cognitive function, but that of a creature who intelligizes, and which is called love. What Augustine says of our heart also applies to Adam's: "you have made us for Yourself, O Lord, and our hearts are restless until they rest in You."[4] So there is no radical difference between gnosis and the sense of the supernatural by which the intellect is oriented towards the transcendence of God. We will put it this way: gnosis is the sense of the supernatural applied to knowledge.

The dependence of cognitive sacredness with respect to the person of the knowing subject does not mean that this sense of the supernatural is not virtually inherent to the nature of

---

3 *Surnaturel—Études historiques* (Paris: Aubier, 1946), 498 pages. A new edition, with Greek and Latin quotations translated, was published by Desclée de Brouwer in 1991, 634 pages. St. Thomas speaks of the intellect's natural desire to see God in *On the Truth of the Catholic Faith (Summa contra Gentiles)*, Book 3, Part 1, 57, 4 (Garden City, NJ: Image Books, 1957), 192. See also my book, *The Sense of the Supernatural*.
4 *Confessions*, Book 1, 1.

the intellect; this is the reason why St. Thomas speaks rightly about a *natural* desire, that is, a desire specific to the nature of the intellect. It is in and by itself that the intellect is, *in reality*, a desire for God. But for the intellect to know this and posit this as such, for it to be aware of its desiring nature, it is necessary that it discover itself as the act of a human subject, and as a spiritual act, that is, of a nature of which the world of bodily beings, whether living or not, offers no example. It is therefore necessary that the intellect cease to be invisible to itself and indistinguishable from the intelligized object, that the mystery of its being and the ontological taking root of its "orientation towards" is revealed to it. One might say, since the intellect is the mirror where the light of the Word, which "enlightens every man" as St. John says, is received, that the intellectual mirror must be reflected back on itself somehow—realized by the discovery of that which is similar to it—and thereby become aware that there can be no reception of light if *it itself* does not include a dark side, an ontological, unknowable below, from which only it can turn itself towards the light.

In other words, the meaning of transcendence, that is, the meaning of a "beyond" correlates with an experience of a "this side" of things. Knowledge, from a strictly phenomenological vantage point, as a pure appearing to intellective (or sensorial) transparency, establishes us in a perfect immanence of ourselves with things, and, vice versa, of things with our intellect, resulting in a kind of forgetting or unconsciousness of the tension between a "beneath" of appearances (*subjectum* means "that which is put under") and an object, which is "beyond" appearing, the non-appearing from which it comes "in front of" (ob-) us. That knowledge is gnostic which knows itself to be knowledge, which grasps itself as a glance proceeding from below to the beyond, and which therefore finds itself, in its subjective ontological root as well as in its objective and transcendent end, in a way "foreign" to the immanence that constitutes it. Only through this can knowledge, escaping its phenomenological reduction, be called *salvific* and sacred: salvific because there is someone who must be saved (the case with fallen man) or at least called to a superior state (the case with Adam in paradise); sacral because "separate," according to the etymological meaning of the term "sacred" which indicates something that has been withdrawn from its natural domain and inserted into a divine order, that which defines a truly transcendent Object.

It is therefore the awareness of this side of things that makes the transcendent spring up and sally forth, and, conversely, it is the awareness of the transcendent, that is, of what surpasses *us*, that reveals *us* to ourselves as *that which* is surpassed and that must be surpassed. In such a case, oriented and dynamized by this tension that traverses it, knowledge becomes true gnosis.

This orientation and dynamization are the work of grace, at work already with Adam, who is not only the impersonal intellective mirror in which creation is known and named, but who is also a person who must himself be known and named. That requires the "objectification" of the adamic unconsciousness (Adam plunged into a mysterious sleep) and the fashioning of the woman as a helper similar to himself. It also requires that whatever is known in the intellective mirror, whatever is the object of knowledge, be traversed and surpassed, that is, be seen as a symbol, as the presentification of a Beyond that speaks to Adam himself and not only to his intelligence, and that calls him towards Itself.

But grace is efficaciously given only to someone who agrees to receive it. Adam's discovery that there is a dark side to the mirror, that is, the awareness of the foreignness of his being in relation to the intellectual light that he receives in it, is also an awareness of his freedom, and therefore of his ability to refuse to obey the commandment imposed on him. The revelation to Adam that his being is a being of desire is clearly given to him as a grace, but this grace will become effective and bear fruit only on condition that it be put to the use required by its finality. It is given to him to turn *himself* towards What surpasses him: the function of the mirror is to collect the light that comes from on high. This illumination is saving (or uplifting) only on condition of the being receiving it becoming consciously involved, of there being an *active* reception, in other words: on condition that this reception results from an act of the receiving subject, that it results from the voluntary orientation of the subject towards the light. It is not given to him so that the receiving subject turn towards himself and strive to seize upon himself, but given to him precisely so that, having recognized himself as subject, he can actively ignore himself, and no longer passively do so as with cognitive unawareness. In short, it is given to him so that he might understand that, *being* the "image of God," this being will become its own act, will actively realize the truth of its nature, only if it turns towards the One whose image is reflected in it; otherwise the image disappears, or rather it cannot fulfill its likeness, since, having turned towards itself, this being displays, to the emanation of the divine light within it, its dark side, that is, its egoic being, reduced to itself and no longer a servant of divine immanence. Having "turned" in this way, the adamic being will then seek its own image, the reflection of itself on the surface of things and beings, a Narcissus indefinitely sinking into the fleeting depths.

Such is the paradox of self-discovery: Adam finds himself in order to give himself to the One of whom he is the symbol, to open himself to the transcendence that traverses and uplifts him, to forget himself in the light which is his origin and his end.

CHAPTER 11

Gnosis Lost or Agnostic Knowledge

GNOSIS IS THE GRACE OF A DESIRE FOR transcendence informing and galvanizing knowledge. When this grace is lost, when it is withdrawn from the fallen Adam, only knowledge in its natural, or rather less than natural, exercise remains because, for fallen man, a vertical being, there is no purely and exclusively natural state (except in the abstract): he either ascends or descends. But finally, and because it is not possible to express ourselves otherwise, we will speak by convention of a neutral state of knowledge, the state we ordinarily experience. We will not attempt to describe it, it would be irrelevant, especially as it is dealt with in most works of philosophy. We will be content to remark that this postedenic state is that of a knowledge that is rightly a-gnostic, or which claims to be such, and the perfect realization of which is science. It is defined as objective insofar as, on the one hand, it excludes (or disimplicates) the subject's being from the cognitive process (or reduces it to the state of an epistemic subject), and, on the other hand, ends up being the object (reduced to its scientific determinations). Agnostic knowledge therefore proceeds with a dual exclusion-reduction of the world's being as well as man's. Or again: the epistemic subject, like the epistemic object, is what remains of man and the world with respect to science in the Galilean sense of the term.[1]

Is this neutral state a stable one? From the standpoint of agnostic science, an affirmative is required. Agnosticism is even the condition required to reach a stable state of knowledge, whereas, to the contrary, gnostic concerns — metaphysical with

---

[1] We are referring here to the notion of "epistemic closure of the concept" formulated in our *Histoire et théorie du symbole*, 101–12.

the being-object and mystical with the being-subject—can only disturb and destabilize the cognitive process. It is at least one widely shared belief that the pure form of the cognitive process constitutes an absolute without which no truth is possible, and whose ideal type, for us humans, is provided by mathematical knowledge. And that seems indisputable. In other words, the grace of gnosis withdrawing from the cognitive process leaves this process unchanged in its own nature—this is what St. Thomas Aquinas teaches.[2] However, this state of pure nature is a theoretical and abstract state, real without any doubt, but with the reality of a physical law whose rigorous mathematical formulation adapts to few variations in concrete physical reality: such as the ellipse that the Earth's orbit traces around the sun. Likewise for Adam, and in general for everything concerning the relationships of nature and grace. Outside of grace, nature cannot subsist without being altered and degraded, although it cannot disappear entirely: man cannot cease being a man, even at his most contemptible, and never comes to the end of his fall. Conversely, grace cannot operate without nature. An extrinsicist conception of grace is as artificial as an abstract conception of pure nature. It is in its very nature that nature is open to grace and calls for it.

This is why agnostic knowledge, as to its concrete effectuation, is less than knowledge and cannot completely adapt its existence to its essence: it fails to be itself. The double epistemic reduction is never perfect: neither the being of the knowing subject, nor that of the known object can be entirely excluded. Hence the disturbances and crises stirred up by scientific knowledge, with quantum physics being a prime witness. This is not a conflict between opposing theories or the discovery of a still poorly understood region of reality

---

[2] That which is proper to the nature of Adam, such as intelligence or will, cannot be lost by sin, since this constitutes human nature as such; otherwise the postlapsarian Adam would no longer be a man. But this nature is weakened in its operations: *Summa Theologiae* II-II, Q. 85, a. 1 and 2. Against Luther, the Council of Trent decrees: "If anyone shall say that after the sin of Adam man's free will was lost and destroyed, or that it is a thing in name only, indeed a title without a reality, a fiction, moreover, brought into the Church by Satan: let him be anathema"; Session VI, canon 5; Denzinger, *The Sources of Catholic Dogma*, 815, 258.

(although all this could also be taken into account); this is a crisis relating to the cognitive process itself, as established and practiced since Galileo (to be brief).

In other words, a dissatisfaction in the cognitive process itself cannot fail to emerge on the side of the known object as well as on that of the knowing subject. This dissatisfaction obviously does not date from today. What is specific to the current crisis of scientific knowledge—a crisis that has lasted for about a century and does not seem anywhere close to being resolved—is that it appeared at the core of the scientific approach itself, a science having attained, or so it thought, to a full and exclusive self-possession and that no longer needed to ask the philosopher-class about anything. In fact, the philosophers in fashion, such as Heidegger, Sartre, Foucault, or Derrida, completely "ignore" in their philosophical works, that is, in their thinking activity, the upheavals introduced by physics into our conception of corporeal reality, so that today it is the physicists who pose the most challenging metaphysical questions.[3] But the incompleteness of the cognitive process, in the exercise of its neutral and agnostic state, has long been highlighted by philosophers, at least certain ones, with Plato foremost among them. His doctrine of knowledge, which distinguishes between the discursive manipulation of concepts (*dianoia*, mathematical knowledge) and intellectual intuition (*noesis*, the vision of Ideas), introduces precisely the tension of a transcendence into the cognitive process, the tension required by any quest for Intelligibles within the purview of knowledge, Intelligibles which are rather aimed at by the intellect than grasped in all their reality; Mallarmé has admirably summed this up in his famous line: "Glory of long desire, Ideas."[4] It is with Aristotle

---

3 Heidegger knew about those doubts cast on physical reality ensuing from quantum theory. He read Planck and Heisenberg; for example: "Science and Meditation" (1953) in *Essais et conférences* (Paris: Gallimard, TEL, 1980), 67–68. But the problems posed to thinking by quantum reality played no part in his own thinking about reality. He declares, moreover, "science does not think" (*What is Called Thinking?* [New York, London: Harper & Row, 1972], 26). Now, as it happens, science does think, in the Heideggerian sense, insofar as the real it strives to inspect becomes properly unthinkable.

4 "Prose pour Des Esseintes," *Poèmes* (Paris: Gallimard, 1952), 80. On Plato's gnoseology, see *Penser l'analogie*, 134–214.

CONCERNING CHRISTIAN GNOSIS ACCORDING TO ITS ESSENCE

that the sufficiency of neutral knowledge, at least insofar as that is possible, makes its appearance. For, although it is true that the dominant intention of Aristotle is to constitute the theory of an entirely natural knowledge (there are only natures or intelligible forms immanent in things), nevertheless he was led to posit with God, the motionless mover, a Form of forms transcendent to the whole order of nature.[5] What remains is that Aristotelianism proceeds in the direction of an agnostic science, while Platonism favors an approach through gnosis, with all the excesses and deviations that this might entail. This postulation about a gnostic form of knowledge is found again in Nicolas of Cusa, Pascal (the "knowledge of the heart"), and Spinoza (the "third kind of knowledge").

But this dissatisfaction does not only arise in philosophy, in the effort to reopen, if possible, science to its gnostic dimension. It is also manifested, and more easily, in the approach of artists and poets, most often contrary to a science decidedly identified with its neutral form, and given up to its rationalist closure. No need to insist on this hackneyed theme: only the poet sees, the scholar is blind—this is quite far from the truth. Victor Hugo may declare: "under the real world, there is an ideal world, which shows itself, dazzling the eyes of those that serious meditation has accustomed to seeing in things more than things... poetry is not in the form of the ideas themselves. Poetry is everything there is of the inmost in everything."[6] But this idea of poetry as a mystical knowledge, which we find as well in Rimbaud, Breton, or Saint-John Perse, transforms art into religion and, beyond the successes of genius, nourishes the most stubborn illusions, taking simple psychic impressions for spiritual states.

---

5 "It is difficult," writes Robin, "to both deny and maintain the transcendence of forms... how are we to join to Nature a supernatural principle without which there would be neither Nature nor Thought?"; *Aristote* (Paris: P. U. F., 1944), 205.
6 Preface to *Odes et Ballades*, 1821, *OEuvres Complètes*, Jean Massin's chronological edition, tome II, 5. On this point, see *The Crisis of Religious Symbolism*, 234–45.

CHAPTER 12

The Art of Gnosis is Taught by Transcendence

THAT A NEED FOR GNOSIS MANIFESTS ITSELF, under quite diverse forms, within the neutral regimen of knowledge, appears certain. Obviously, the "epistemologically correct" objections of rationalist thought, which sees in this need only a resurgence of a prelogical and infantile mentality, will have to be set aside. Previous analyses, in any case, should leave no doubt as to its legitimacy in principle. The entire question then consists in asking under what conditions this need, legitimate in principle, may in fact be so, and therefore really be satisfied. If we could answer this question, we would be in possession of a criterion making it possible to distinguish between pseudo-gnosis and the real one. Moreover, it is quite remarkable that St. Paul has spoken of "gnosis falsely so called" (a *pseudonymous* gnosis, 1 Tim. 6:20), and not simply of a "false gnosis." Perhaps one should not assign a disproportionate importance to this semantic datum. However, a false gnosis could be a gnosis mistaken about its object, while a pseudo-gnosis is knowledge (a cognitive process) which deceitfully gives itself out as what it is not, insofar as it is true that authentic gnosis is first of all a quality of the cognitive process before being the showing forth of an object. Or at least we thought we might characterize it in this way.

The gnostic quality of adamic knowledge is a grace, that is, a gift from God. Of this grace Adam has the greatest need insofar as the inherent perfection of the cognitive process is for him at the highest degree, with things offering themselves to him in total transparency. At this degree, the risk for immanence and a "fencing in" is therefore also at its highest. What more could Adam desire? Paradise is a garden of delights where all desire is fulfilled, where the harmony and union of knowing and known are at their peak, and where, therefore, the cognitive process may experience the strongest temptation to close in on itself. Never has humanity run a more extreme risk than in paradise (and this is precisely what happened), the risk of fulfilling and fulfilled knowledge, of a satisfied knowledge, oblivious to transcendence. The condition of fallen man is, in this respect, much more favorable, with its heartbreaking imperfection being so visible: everything revives in him the need and hope for a salvation and something beyond ones own existence. On the contrary, everything in paradise plunged Adam into an enchantment filled to overflowing with beauty, everything that is except the prohibition about tasting the fruit of the Tree of the knowledge of good and evil.

The transgression of the ban—original sin—is therefore a sin of knowledge, a sin of gnosis if one prefers, and that alone would suffice to show the major importance of the theme we are studying. But from this we can only deduce that gnosis is a sin. In reality, the fault of Eve and Adam is a sin *against* gnosis, against true knowledge, that is, against knowledge which, *whatever its degree of perfection*, is aware of its incompleteness, its limitation and the transcendent "beyond" of its authentic fulfillment. This incompleteness and this limitation are signified to the First-Formed by the prohibition imposed on the Tree of the knowledge of good and evil, the tree whose fruit makes known not only what there is of good in creatures, but also what there *can* be of evil in them, namely their finiteness. Not that finitude is by itself an evil. It is, as such, inseparable from the created good, since it is the very condition for the existence of this good. It is then, in a way, invisible and redeemed by the positivity of the created good. Moreover, true gnosis knows this finitude, but implicitly in the very knowledge of the created good and of its perfection, a knowledge [Fr. = *connaissance*] of praise and gratitude [Fr. = *reconnaissance*] for the glory of the Creator. This gnosis agrees to "ignore" this finitude as an object to be known for itself, because this finitude is God's secret, creation's secret. Far from positing it in itself, it assents to this finitude as to that which enables any creature, and first the human creature, to ascend

The Art of Gnosis is Taught by Transcendence

towards its Principle. Conversely, the pseudo-gnosis to which Satan invites Eve is knowledge that wants to grasp finitude for itself and as such, to grasp it, that is, seize and possess it (the eating of the forbidden fruit). This is a knowledge which closes in upon itself and thereby closes the object upon itself (the prototype of the epistemic closure of the concept), whereas true gnosis keeps itself open and keeps its object open towards that which surpasses the known as well as the knower. This is why the cognitive drama that was original sin could not but constitute the major event in human history before the coming of Christ. The truth is that the knowledge of created being's finitude can actually be realized only by the grace of its transcendence: it is the opening towards its transcendent beyond that reveals the world to us as a completed totality.[1] It is therefore in reality the gnostic quality of an adamic noetics that, alone, could enable him to access the plenitude promised by the knowledge of things: it is on the condition of seeking first the kingdom of heaven that the kingdom of earth is given to Adam.

Quite convincingly, what we have here is an obvious philosophical truth. The limit that circumscribes the finitude of every creature is, in itself, elusive: one is either inside the creature and one has not yet reached its "edge," or one surpasses it and is outside of it. This is the paradox of the limit: as the limit *of* the creature, it pertains to the being of the creature, it *is*; but precisely insofar as it is the limit, it marks the "place" where the creature ceases to be, it means that the creature is not there. The limit is and it is not. To know the limit, or the finitude of the finite, is to understand that the finite is precisely finite [Fr. = *fini*, i.e., finished, completed], that its being is a being surpassed, and this is therefore necessarily to go beyond: the finite only comes to an end and attains

---

[1] Cf. *The Crisis of Religious Symbolism*, 106–10. As for its being, the world is complete. The infinity of cosmic space is only an indefinitude, something whose end cannot be reached *spatially*: there is no "edge" to space. Space cannot limit space, and the end of space, since it is its end, is necessarily "outside" space, just as the end of time is "outside" time. The logic here is compelling, and the imagination must admit defeat. Space is finite, but not spatially. Moreover, the least thought is "outside" space and therefore in this respect a "limit."

its completeness there where it comes to an end and ends with its own surpassing.[2] This is exactly what the last word of Christ on the cross means; the fulfillment of the creature within Him is the effacing of the creature: "Jesus therefore, when he had taken the vinegar, said: It is accomplished. And bowing his head, he gave up the Spirit" (John 19:30). "It is accomplished" is a rendering of the Greek *tetelestai*, which implies that the *telos* is attained, the end realizes its fullness, *es ist vollbracht*.

Conversely, the sin of Adam and Eve—and first of all their error, from which obedience would have preserved them—is to succumb, under the persuasion of Satan, to the promise of fullness heralded by the sight of the forbidden fruit, both "beautiful to see and good to eat." This fruit, which is that of the knowledge of good-and-evil, is the knowledge of the finite as simply finite, and not of the finite as finite *through* that which exceeds and transcends it, that is, basically through the Infinite to which the finite refers as to its cause and principle. The finite is given to the knowledge of Adam, creation is offered to him, not so that he might stop there, but so that in some manner he might forget this finitude, or rather, so that in forgetting it he fulfills it, he "realizes" it by pursuing it to its eternal and infinite Possibility. To this extent, for this

---

2 This is why Descartes is perfectly right to argue, against his objectors, that "in some way I have in me the notion of the infinite earlier than the finite—to wit, the notion of God before that of myself" (*Meditations on First Philosophy*, Meditation III, § 23; Haldane translation). The infinite is not the product of the negation of the finite, except in appearance, since to conceive of the finite is to trace a limit, and since any limitation is conceived of and can be brought about only within an unlimited something, and therefore since the finitude of all things only has meaning in relation to a primary and absolute infinitude. There is a properly philosophical explanation of this doctrine in *The Crisis of Religious Symbolism*, 341–46 and 358–73. Hence it also follows that only the infinite "knows" the finite, in other words, that God alone knows the creaturehood of the creature, and not the creature itself, which never coincides with its own ontological limitation. As we have stated on many occasions (but who has understood what this means?), only the absolute Sur-Plus can do the least. And that is why only God can save the creature, being at once below and beyond its finitude: what we call the "gnosis of Good Friday." God somehow passes under the creature, being lower than the lowest, to lift it up to what is higher than the highest. The relative is incapable of itself, only the Absolute is capable of the relative; cf. *Love and Truth*, 397–400.

The Art of Gnosis is Taught by Transcendence

condition, finitude is good ("God *saw* that it was good"), the finitude of the created is a good since, without it, it would not be and since being is good. If in fact the created were not finite, it would not have being qua created: this finitude is therefore integral to its perfection, that is, to its being achieved and its completeness.[3] But just as in and through the gaze of God the goodness of the finite is revealed, so in and through the gaze of the transgressor Adam, finitude is revealed and actualized as evil, that is, as indefinite. By fixing his sight on the fruit of the forbidden tree, by eating it, that is, by knowing it and by assimilating it, Adam would know the finitude of the created in and through the created itself, and no longer by surpassing it towards what terminates and completes it, towards the beyond that realizes it, but by delving into finitude as such. Now, as we have repeated in many ways, the finiteness of the finite (which limits it) cannot be reached on the very plane of the finite, since only the Infinite "knows" the finite. This is how Adam entangles himself in the indefinite, the unfinished, the inexhaustible, the imperfectible, the "without-hope" of achieving, the evil-of-the-good, not absolute evil which does not exist since it would be devoid of any ontological positivity. Indeed it is the object itself that, by its *inaccessible* finitude, then becomes as if a "beyond" of

---

[3] We have wrongly implied in some of our books that the finitude inherent to creation was the source of evil in the world, or that, God alone being perfect, creation was necessarily imperfect: hence the evil. This doctrine, broadly developed by a few authors, does not seem, as such, reconcilable with biblical revelation. Creation is perfect, not with an absolute perfection—which belongs only to God—but with a relative perfection, *secundum quid*; it is perfect according to the finite nature that is its own (according to its "form," St. Thomas would say), it being out of the question that the work of God could be imperfect: God does everything he does well. The thesis that we reject comes down to saying that creation, not being the Creator, necessarily includes evil, since "God alone is good" (Luke 18:19). But, not only does such a formulation risk leading us back (against its very intention?) to the gnosticist conception of an evil world produced by an evil creator, it also tends to confer on evil, which it seems to make an inevitable component of the created, the consistency of a substantial reality. Evil is certainly bound up with finitude, not as its necessary consequence, but as its negative possibility, the possibility that introduces original sin when Adam illusorily denies, and, on its own plane, the finitude of the created.

knowledge, presenting itself to one's intelligence as an illusory transcendence, the appearance of a transcendence in the depths of the cosmic horizon.

The situation imposed by original sin on gnosis is paradoxical. Fallen man has surely retained the need for transcendence; in some respects, this need is even heightened, since, in paradise, what threatened Adam was rather the temptation of immanence: Heaven, it has been said, touches the earth there. In other words, the theophanic power of paradisal creation was such that it could make Adam forget that it was not God. One would be entitled to speak here of a risk of pantheism. And was it not to a temptation of this nature that Eve actually succumbed when, believing the serpent, she gave credence to the deifying virtue of the eating of an earthly substance? We also find, it seems, in the various pantheisms, something like a nostalgia for a paradisal state, and therefore a rejection, more or less explicit, of the dogma of original sin; this is also the case with certain gnostic currents.

The temptation of pantheistic immanence was forestalled, in paradise—and the transcendence of the divine sphere was thus indicated and signified to Adam—by the prohibition of a fruit that was in appearance indistinguishable from permitted fruits. The ban therefore teaches two things to Adam: negatively, he does not know everything, God is more learned; positively and by this very fact the *almost* perfect knowledge of creation must be surpassed towards a beyond to which it now knows that it gives access only to the extent of its own obliteration. Heaven and earth really tell of the glory of God; adamic cosmology is revealed to be truly operative theology— here is gnosis—but this is on condition that Adam first have faith in the Divine Word, and not in the light of his own knowledge. Such is the strength, such also the limit of the first gnosis, before Adam's disobedience.

With the fall, things change in some respects. The earthly descends, or, what amounts to the same thing, the celestial ascends back to heaven. However, at its core, creation retains the whole of its theophanic truth, but the spiritual gaze of man is no longer able to perceive it directly, or to realize it effectively. Theology can no longer find its point of departure in a transcended cosmology.

This is why, after the fall, so that the latent need for gnosis might find a way to be actualized according to the truth of his nature, the bestowal of a truly transcendent object is required for the knowledge of fallen man. Such an object constitutes by itself a paradox: insofar as it is given, it is present and immanent to human intelligence; but it can be the actualizer of an authentically transcendent aim only insofar as it is absent, out of reach. This paradox is most exactly realized by the object of faith, in other words by the revelation of truly supernatural divine realities, and therefore by the revelation of a religion, that is, of truths to be believed, of rites to observe, acts and behaviors to accomplish. The universe of religion, with all its elements, then plays a role for fallen man, the very role that the paradisal world played for primordial man. This religious universe must be kept and cultivated. As in paradise, the sacred forms that populate this universe are full of grace and full of God, the Lord is with them, and the fruit of the womb of this virginal land, this fruit of the Tree of Life, can now be eaten: it is the living bread that came down from Heaven.

It is therefore now necessary to specify and complete the previous descriptions. So far we have considered gnosis as a mode, or, better yet, as a *state* of knowledge; which it most assuredly is: here we have, one might say, subjective or spiritual gnosis. But there is also an objective or metaphysical gnosis that we will now discuss.

CHAPTER 13

Gnosis is also an Objectively Stateable Knowledge

THE ARTICLES OF FAITH OF THE CREED—AND already the dogmas of Hebraic revelation—sometimes received the name of gnosis. These are true supernatural objects. Transcendent by their origin and immanent by the effect of divine grace, they provide to subjective gnosis the possibility of being exercised under the guarantee of revealed truth.

This identification of faith with gnosis might be surprising. How is it possible to consider all the baptized who have accepted the Creed and who profess it as so many bearers of gnosis? This by no means corresponds to the idea one might have of orthodox gnosis from what St. Paul has to say about it ("not all have gnosis," 1 Cor. 8:7) or from Clement of Alexandria, who speaks of a secret tradition. Besides, the very content of the *Creed* seems to have nothing gnostic about it, since it consists essentially in the stating of a certain number of sacred facts relating to the life of Christ. These objections are not lacking in vigor. Remember, however, as we have recalled in the first two chapters of this book,[1] the transmission of the Creed was concealed, during the first centuries, by the discipline of the arcane, which may not be unrelated to the mysterious nature of the truths enunciated. The objection we are discussing therefore results, not from factual evidence, as is thought, but from the loss of the mysterial (or esoteric) meaning, which profanes and trivializes the declarations of the rule of truth.

On the other hand, if we must grant that objective faith (the dogmatic statements) cannot be purely and simply identified with gnosis (otherwise there would be no more need to

---

[1] This question is dealt with more fully in *Christ the Original Mystery*, 239–314.

Gnosis is also an Objectively Stateable Knowledge

speak of "gnosis"), we must also take into consideration two things. The first is that the *Creed*, whatever the text retained, already represents a doctrinal development, a "form," a "rule of truth," that goes beyond the pure and simple scriptural data: trinitarian theology, christology (incarnation and redemption), pneumatology, ecclesiology, and lastly eschatology—all these explain in speculative terms what is given in Scripture only in terms of historical facts or symbols. The *Creed* in itself is already a gnosis of revelation whose source can only be Christ, then the Holy Spirit, the pentecostal Light of the *revelatum* in the minds of the apostles. The second thing to consider is that these objective statements of faith, including all that Christ did and said and to which the apostles were witnesses (whom we know, we ourselves, through the Gospels) were welcomed into the memory, but also into the intelligence of the witnesses. Now, except in the borderline case of the most radical fideism, this intelligence cannot but strive to grasp this intelligibly, as much as possible. Such a grasping, which the intelligence performs using its own means, necessarily requires ways of understanding that cannot be qualified other than as metaphysical, meaning that this term embraces the knowledge of universal principles as well as anthropology and cosmology (including angelology). To this science, St. Paul and Clement of Alexandria give the name of gnosis, and perhaps it is this science that Christ designates when he speaks in Luke (11:52) of "the key of gnosis," which we should probably understand in the sense that gnosis is a key which opens the mysteries of faith (and not only in the sense that this would involve an opening to gnosis). It is about this gnosis and its forms that we would now like to speak.

Thus specified, and in its first form, metaphysical gnosis (in the broad sense) is adamic in origin. It is identical to the language of Adam that itself results from an encounter of the primordial human intellect with paradisal creation. It was then that the universal forms of his cognitive apprehension of reality were actualized in his intelligence. The synthetically ordered totality of these intellectual forms, considered apart from the realities of which they are the cognitive apprehension, constitutes what we can call the metaphysical memory of humanity, and that others will call *philosophia perennis*. Obviously, its transmission through millennia and according to the Babelian dispersal of human dialects will be accompanied by loss and alterations. Formally universal in principle, like the intelligence for which it is the proper language, metaphysics is, in fact, only transmitted with the help of particular but not easy to discern cultural concretions.[2]

Hebrew thought (the implicit or explicit "theology" conveyed by Jewish culture) is one of these concretions: it results from the application of adamic memory to the understanding of the Abrahamic-Mosaic revelation. The Jew Jesus is immersed in this culture and, as for what Catholic theologians call "acquired knowledge," it is given form by culture, not in the sense that the Jewish culture of his time would teach him something he would not already know about God, but in the sense that this culture imprints its own form on mental representations by which Scripture *speaks*. Beatific knowledge (the vision of God) and infused knowledge (possessed by angels) are in a perfect state in the soul of Christ. But Christ also learns how to speak Aramaic, how to speak and read Hebrew, each new knowledge being illuminated and certified, as to the mode of acquisition, even to its ultimate depths, by the constant light of infused knowledge.[3] Such is the conceptual grammar that is necessarily formed in the mind of Jesus, to which it is necessary to partially add the one conveyed by the Greek language then quite present in Palestine and with which he was in contact. It is therefore this speculative grammar that Christ had at his disposal to teach the new Revelation that he brought to

---

[2] This theme of a metaphysical tradition adamic in origin is studied in *Aux sources bibliques de la métaphysique* (Paris: L'Harmattan, 2015), 121–41. As for its universal nature, let us recall this teaching of St. Thomas: "The intellect of man is in potentiality to all intelligible things," *Summa theologiae*, III, Q. 9, a. 3.
[3] Some, relying on John 7:15: "How does this man know letters, having never learned?" argue that Jesus could not read: e.g., Jacqueline Genot-Bismuth, *Un homme nommé Salut. Genèse d'une "hérésie" à Jérusalem* (Paris: F.-X. de Guibert, 1995), 164. This is not what the text says, but only that Jesus had not attended a rabbinical school. He knew how to read. St. Luke confirms this: "on the sabbath day, in the Synagogue, he rose up to read" (4:16). According to Tradition, it was Mary who taught him how to read.

Gnosis is also an Objectively Stateable Knowledge

the world. But use transforms the instrument according to the requirements of the object to which it is applied. Hebrew gnosis, the categories of understanding equally available to the apostles to whom the Christ spoke in private, "indoors," in a direct and explicit way, and no longer only in parables, are insufficient for receiving his message intellectually: one does not put new wine in old wineskins. It is therefore necessary that a third form of gnosis, after the adamic and the Hebrew, be constituted, this time Christic, that is, "neoadamic" (the gnosis of the new Adam), directed chiefly, no longer just to thoughts of creation and the Creator, of the Bridegroom of the chosen people, but to thoughts of supernatural realities, about the mystery of God in Himself, in his Trinitarian interiority and in his redemptive incarnation, matters about which Jewish messianism had not the least notion. Elementary as we might suppose it, this metaphysical grammar could not but have existed because it is connatural to the activity of all human thought, whether implicitly or explicitly, depending on the degree of perfection and self-awareness of this thinking. Concerning Christ, this thought of the message to be revealed *in human terms* necessarily reaches its highest degree of self-awareness: Jesus is not an ecstatic utterer of words he does not understand. He knows what he is saying, knowing what has a bearing not only on the content of the message, on its truth, but also on its modalities of expression and their raison d'être; because, as St. Paul says, "if I pray in a tongue, my spirit (*pneuma*) prays, but my intellect (*nous*) is unfruitful," that is why "I will pray with the intellect also" (1 Cor. 14:14–15). But attention is rightly most often drawn to the genius of Jesus the Teacher, the "Proverbist," which transcends all categories of teaching and bursts into parables; this is not what we shall consider. We will focus on something less apparent, more mental and philosophical in nature, if you will, but just as necessary. For Christ had to endow those of the apostles intellectually qualified to receive it with something analogous to a "general theory of human and divine realities," as required by the revelation for which he was both message and messenger. To pronounce dogmas without providing the means to intellectually grasp their meaning, without providing the intellect with the means to relatively but essentially understand them, is to act in vain. And Hebraic gnosis, with which certain apostles were endowed by cultural training, would not allow for this: what was required was what St. Paul calls significantly a "renewal of the intellect" (Rom. 12:2). How was this new gnosis formed in the human soul of Christ? Nobody knows. His education had, if we dare say, benefited from the lights of the Eternal Word and the illuminating flux of the Spirit. The fact remains that, being man, Christ also produced the requisite mental forms, not only based on the transcendent illumination of the Word and Pneuma, but also based on Jewish (and Greek) cultural data that were reworked and transformed, "renewed" in a supra-adamic state, a state no longer primordial, but *principial*. Now, concerning the production of these mental forms (and not their content, which is none other than the revelation of the Kingdom of God in its mysteries), the role of the divine illuminating flux must undoubtedly be seen as that of a guarantee conferring supreme authority on these forms.

In other words, and without claiming in any way to fathom the secret of relationships, in the person of the Son, between his divine and human natures, we believe that the divine illuminating influx into his human soul did not go so far as to dictate to Christ the conceptual and language-based forms of his message, but that these forms were the human work of Christ speaking to men, yet working by the power of the Holy Spirit, for the Spirit is always and everywhere the One who unites the unformedness of the essence with the form of existence.[4] It is by the Holy Spirit that the prophets speak, that the Truth of God becomes speech, and that the Word becomes flesh.

Such is, we think, the gnosis that Christ, according to several testimonies, communicated to a few chosen apostles; at the very least this is an aspect of that to which the term gnosis has been applied. In general, historians and patrologists have hardly dwelled on the assertions of Clement of

---

4 Cf. *Love and Truth*, 363–64.

Alexandria, and some other Fathers, concerning the reserved teaching of gnosis by Christ to Peter, James and John (then Paul). Basically, many hardly believe in the historical reality of such a transmission, contrary however to the most certain testimonies, as shown, in particular, by Cardinal Daniélou: belief in the existence of a teaching of Christ set aside for a few apostles is more or less universal during the first three centuries.[5] We also find it in St. Irenaeus of Lyon, Tertullian and Origen, as well as Clement. But it is true that the nature of this gnosis remains something hard to define. As it is apparently something other than the faith summarized in the articles of the *Creed*, some suppose that it might consist of anthropo-cosmological doctrines, relating in particular to angels, to the different Heavens where they reside, how to relate to them and to receive help and revelations; this is called "Jewish apocalyptic" (*apocalypsis* means in Greek "revelation"), a set of doctrines quite widespread at the time of Christ, although esoteric in nature. This is Daniélou's thesis. This identification, which is based on some irrefutable data, has the merit of highlighting the importance of Judeo-Christian esotericism in the first and second centuries. But this identification is far from corresponding to all the descriptions of gnosis given by Clement. It is in fact predetermined by the idea that gnosis can only consist in a set of "secret doctrines" superimposed on the teaching of the common doctrine.

That the term gnosis was applied to the designation of these doctrines is certain. But it would be hard to understand if Clement of Alexandria had used—with a clear Christian conscience—only this meaning when St. Paul had warned against

---

[5] "The Secret Traditions of the Apostles," *Eranos Jahrbuch* 31 (1962): 199–215. The distinction between an exoteric teaching and an esoteric one can be seen in all the philosophical schools of antiquity, in particular in Plato and Aristotle. This is about adapting the levels of teaching to the intellectual capacities of listeners, not to hide inflammatory, subversive, or immoral doctrines, as is so readily imagined today. Thus Aristotle's *Metaphysics* was part of the esoteric writings, which is justified, given the extreme difficulty of this text: one does not enter into philosophy by simply wishing to do so. Note that, according to Gospel data, Christ dispensed a teaching on three levels: to the crowds (in parables), to the Twelve (the proclamation of kerygma), and lastly to Peter, James and John: Sr. Jeanne d'Arc, *Les Évangiles—Jean*, v; cf. *supra*, 42, fn 24.

a certain "angelic theurgy" in several of his epistles.[6] And it would be even less understandable that the disciple of Christ that Clement was might have believed that the loftiest and most reserved teachings of his Master concerned doctrines of a certain interest, but in any case of a cosmological nature, and therefore inferior. "It is clear," writes Daniélou, "... that this is something other than official tradition, contained in the rule of faith, the Creed."[7] No, it is not clear at all and does not correspond to all "definitions" of gnosis we read in Clement. True, these items of information are quite disconcerting, and we must surely give up reducing Clementine gnosis to a single sense. But it seems that some texts would become clearer if one adopts the solution we are advancing, namely that, at least in one sense, gnosis designates a "conceptual grammar," metaphysical in nature, required for thinking about the revelation of the Gospel and which Christ had formed in his human soul in order to make intelligibly admissible the teaching of the faith's doctrine. For we must never forget that this involves, in Clement, a teaching *received* from Christ, which is certainly distinct from the truths of the rule of faith, but which is also inseparable from it and which is governed by this rule: "for gnosis is received from Christ when, placing ourselves in the School of the Church, we hear Christ himself comment on Scripture."[8] There is then the object of faith *and* the understanding of this object: "Prophecy [= Scripture] is foreknowledge [pre-*gnosis*] and knowledge [*gnosis*] is the understanding [*noesis*] of prophecy."[9] It makes possible an assimilation of the divine truths of faith through the intellect.[10] That is why Clement brings this gnosis closer to Greek philosophy, which, however, for lack of the Christic revelation, fails to realize its "desire for wisdom" (the etymological meaning of the Greek *philosophia*):

---

[6] This thesis was discussed in greater depth in *Christ the Original Mystery*, 242–48.
[7] "The Secret Traditions of the Apostles," 200; we are simplifying Daniélou's thesis, but without, we hope, betraying it.
[8] *Strom.* VI, 134, 4.
[9] *Strom.* II, 54, 1; *Stromateis Books 1–3*, trans. J. Ferguson (Washington, DC: Catholic University of America, 1991), 195.
[10] *Strom.* V, 114, 1.

Gnosis is also an Objectively Stateable Knowledge

Gnosis is in a way wisdom: indeed, it is a knowledge [*episteme*] and a firm and sure comprehension of present, future, and past realities, transmitted and revealed by the Son of God. Consequently, if contemplation is the goal pursued by the wise man, anyone who still devotes himself to philosophy [= one who is still "desirous of wisdom"], no matter how much he presses on towards divine knowledge, will not attain it unless the prophetic word is explained by instruction, an instruction through which he learns the realities that are, will be, and have been, by also learning *how* they are, will be, and were.[11]

Gnosis is therefore an *instruction* bearing on present realities: the universe as it is; future realities: the "new Heavens and the new earth" of the eschatological transfiguration of the world; and on past realities: the creation of the world. It enables us to learn not only what there is, what there will be, what there has been of such realities (taught by the prophetic word, Holy Scripture, and Christic revelation), but also *what* these realities are, will be, and were. Gnosis is therefore the key that opens human intelligence to a firm and sure understanding of the *nature* of the realities whose existence we learn of from Mosaic and Christic revelation, this key that the *nomodidaskaloi*, the doctors of the Law, that is, the "scholars of the Torah," those who received in deposit the gnosis of the unwritten Torah, the masters of Hebrew esotericism, have possessed in vain. Since "they have not *entered*" into this gnosis, they have closed themselves to its "initiation," and those who wanted to enter, those who wanted to be *initiated*, they have hindered (Luke 11:52).[12] Finally, that this gnosis, in its development, is a human work (but of a humanity which is that of Christ) intended for men, is this not what Clement suggests when he

---

[11] *Strom.* VI, 61, 162; we are quoting from the translation of Mgr. Patrick Descourtieux, *Les Stromates VI* (Paris: Cerf, 1999), 185, modified by inserting elements from the Daniélou translation.

[12] Curiously, Louis Bouyer writes in *Gnôsis. La connaissance de Dieu dans l'Écriture*: "although they do not use the noun, the synoptics have applied the verb *gnomai* to the mystery of God," 158. This is not correct. Luke writes: *ten kleida tes gnoseos*, "the key to knowledge" (11:52).

writes that "gnosis is a kind of perfecting of man as man"?[13]

Let us stress one last feature: this gnosis, which Clement tells us pertains to what we call "metaphysics,"[14] can be summarized in a few words and should not be thought of as a vast treatise on philosophy. It seems that proof of this is found written in the prologue to the Gospel of St. John, which indeed contains the whole metaphysics of revelation, that is, the intellectual keys to the Christian *revelatum*. These keys to gnosis were given by Christ. St. John tells us: "the only-begotten Son, [God] who is in the bosom of the Father, that One was made the interpreter (*exegesato*)" of "God [whom] no one has ever seen" (1:18). He does not tell us that he has made known his existence, for in fact God was known before Christ, but he has "done the exegesis" for us, he has "explained," "expounded," "made comprehensible" for us—so many terms which are indeed the senses of the verb *exegeomai*, literally: "to lead out of" (constructed here without additional direct or indirect object). Through the mediation of Christ, the Inaccessible God was "led out of" the divine realm and made accessible to the human mind. Or again, and complementarily, Christ has "initiated us into God"[15] and should even be translated: Christ *is* the initiation into God, he *is* hermeneut and hermeneutics. We believe in any case that the usage of *Logos* to designate the Son, a usage which it is not forbidden to think comes from Christ himself, attests to this metaphysical reading of

---

13 *Strom.* VII, 55, 1; *Miscellanies Book VII*, trans. F. J. A. Hort & J. B. Mayor (London & New York: Macmillan & Co., 1902), 97.

14 *Strom.* I, 28, 176; Ferguson trans., 152. Here Clement pairs "epopty," the summit of the "really great mysteries," with the "metaphysics" of Aristotle.

15 This construction is found in certain manuscripts and among certain Church Fathers; it might even be translated: "God, no one has ever seen him, except the only Son; in the Father's bosom, it is he who has led" (Boismard, *St. John's Prologue*, trans. Carisbrooke Dominicans [Westminster, MD: Newman Press, 1957], 67. Fr. Spicq (*Lexique théologique du Nouveau Testament* [Paris: Cerf, 1991], 531–33) shows that the meaning is that of interpreting, being the hermeneut. This is not about "bestowing a revelation," but about "narrating, explaining, describing." Father de la Potterie (*La Vérité dans saint Jean*, Analecta Biblica 73 [Rome: Biblical Institute Press, 1977], tome I, 213–28) devotes a lengthy study to *exegesato*. He judges Boismard's construction ill-supported and "forced." However, he admits the meaning of "revelation," but taken absolutely: "the only Son was himself the revelation."

Gnosis is also an Objectively Stateable Knowledge

the Christic *revelatum*. By this reading, the believer is made capable of an intellective assimilation of the mysteries of the Kingdom. If one seeks to know what might be the central concept of Christian gnosis, it is here, St. John is teaching it to us: it is that of the Word made flesh.

In short, the qualification of gnosis in the objective sense of the term has been legitimately applied to two inseparable aspects, the second of which is governed by the first. Objective gnosis is first of all revealed truths (the *revelatum*): they make known the sacred realities of the religious universe. Bossuet goes no further than this meaning, and this is the meaning St. Paul has in mind when he writes: you Jews "possess in the Law (Torah) the very expression of gnosis" (Rom. 2:20). On the other hand, objective gnosis is also the set of metaphysical (and anthropo-cosmological) truths with the help of which the *revelatum* can be thought about, what one might call, in view of its function as an instrument, a metaphysical *organon*. Such an *organon* is present in the Jewish tradition. We perhaps find mention of it in Luke, when Christ accuses the *nomodidaskalos* of having "taken away the key of gnosis," therefore the keys of knowledge that would enable entry into an understanding of revelation, and assuredly in St. Paul: Rom. 15:14; 1 Cor. 1:5, 8:1, 8:10–11, 12:8, 13:3, &c.

It is also present, and since its beginnings, in Christian tradition. Without this metaphysical *organon*, neither the theology of St. Paul nor that of St. John are explicable. This is evidenced first and foremost by the use of *Logos* to designate the Son of God, a use that perhaps goes back to a "secret" teaching of Jesus Christ himself. However that may be, and regardless of the countless questions and debates raised by the introduction of this term, two indisputable facts remain: on the one hand the text has us read it *ex abrupto*, without preparation or explanation, as a known designation of the second person of the Trinity; on the other, it is a Greek word. Now, at the time when St. John wrote his gospel (the end of the first century?), and without denying anything of its taking root in the biblical tradition, *Logos* is important to him, seeing that it is taken absolutely (without complement), a "Hellenistic" constellation of philosophical ideas that St. John could not entirely ignore. It is the signature to the major pact that Christian theology, at its *scriptural* birth, contracts with Greek intellectuality for all the rest of its history.

CHAPTER 14

How Gnosis Changes into Gnosticism

We NOW HAVE AT OUR DISPOSAL A criterion that should allow us to distinguish between true (objective) gnosis and pseudo-gnosis. That gnosis is orthodox whose content is given by revelation: the objects thus proposed to knowledge are both present by grace and absent by transcendence. They offer the intelligence a real possibility of welcoming them and surpassing their formal limitation towards their transcendent root. For the basic structure of subjective gnosis remains, in a fallen state, what it was in the state of innocence: it is still a sacred knowledge, that is, knowledge that aims at surpassing the immediate given towards that which, of a divine nature, is mediatized. Just as in the earthly paradise adamic knowledge is only truly sacred if it passes through the objects of its world to their creating source, so the knowledge that the fallen man grasps of the objects of his religious world is truly gnostic only on condition of opening them and extending them towards the divine realities that they presentify. This is what Christ teaches in St. John (14:6–9): "Whoever has seen me has seen the Father," and (11–12): "the Father is in me *because* I am going to the Father." Christ is the pre-eminent sacred "Object," perfect divine immanence, "God with us" (*Emmanuel*), because he leads to the Father, because he is going to the Father, not only by the event of his death, resurrection, and ascension into Heaven, but also by the permanent actuality of his filial essence: it is in his very nature that Christ is timelessly the Passover of God, the passage and the ferryman to *El Elyon*, the Most High, the Transcendent. We must look to the Son, not only to see the Father, but again, to see the Son in his truth; we must see the Father in him and go through him to himself, because he is the way. This is also

CONCERNING CHRISTIAN GNOSIS ACCORDING TO ITS ESSENCE

what St. Paul teaches when he informs us that the letter kills and the Spirit quickens. This is why we named this *spiritual* gnosis, because it is the effect in us of the grace of the Spirit. That which opens the revealed form to its divine nature—that form in which the divine has been enclosed by the operation of the Holy Spirit—is the gaze of a pneumatized intelligence. But that means every glance of faith is not necessarily a glance of gnosis. In itself faith contains all gnosis, but in us, in our act of faith, it can stop at the revealing form: literalism, fideism, and fundamentalism are related. St. Thomas warned against this reduction to form: "the act of the believer," he said, "does not terminate in a proposition, but in a thing" (*actus credentis non terminatur ad enuntiabile sed ad rem*).[1] As we have seen, it is Adam's and Eve's mistake in paradise to put their faith in the shape of a creature and stop there. However, there is a difference between original sin and religious literalism: the forbidden fruit belongs to the order of nature, while the object of faith belongs to the order of the supernatural. In paradise, it is nature, the whole of creation, that is revelatory—subject to obedience to the divine commandment (paradise is earthly). In the state of the fall, creation certainly retains its revelatory capacity for the intelligence: "since the creation of the world, what of God we do not see is made visible, being understood by the things that are made, even his eternal power and Godhead," says St. Paul (Rom. 1:20). However, this "natural" revelation no longer has, by itself, any saving efficacy. Something more is needed, a revelation of the divine as such. The work of grace that constitutes the basis of a religion is greater than that of the creation of the world. Thus, the simple clinging by faith to the letter of received truths is already in itself a grace and ushers us into the order of grace; this would not be a sin as was Eve's clinging to the deifying virtue of a simple earthly fruit (what was deifying was precisely not to eat, to acquiesce to the ban, and therefore to recognize this fruit as separate, reserved for God, "sacred").

This fruit was not, in fact, bad in itself; it was for mankind that its consumption was fatal. Why? As the fruit of the Tree

---

[1] *Summa theologiae*, II-II, Q. 1, a. 2, ad 2.

of the knowledge of good and evil, it symbolizes the knowledge of the ontological finitude of the created. This Tree is planted in the center of paradise, like the Tree of Life with which it is only one. If we represent paradise by a circular plane, the Tree of Life corresponds to the upper vertical axis, perpendicular to this circular plane at its center, which is the starting point of its horizontal extension; this axis is the Tree of Life, but insofar as it is traversed by man, a vertical being, *from the bottom up*, therefore insofar as Adam is turned towards the divine Source from which all life emanates, and therefore insofar as he "ignores" the plane of existence that bears it. Adam looks either up, or in front of himself, not below. Only God, the Creator, can look up and down (direction of the creating ray), since he is higher than the highest and lower than the lowest: only the Most "can do" the least. But the center of the Edenic circle, the origin of its horizontal expansion, is also the "place" of its end, the point where it is terminated, since it is actually the point where the creating ray has halted: metaphysically, only That which is without origin is endless, while for every creature its origin is also its end. Thus the central axis or Tree of Life of Paradise is also the Tree of good-and-evil as it is traversed by man from top to bottom, that is, insofar as Adam wants to know, of this realizing knowledge specific to primordial man, finitude from its own plane of existence. And he knows it, not as such—which is impossible—but as that which alters and corrupts being or the good, as if the evil-of-the-good. This descending route, which therefore wants to usurp the mode of vision that belongs only to God and under whose light alone is revealed the goodness of creatures ("God *saw* that it was good") is sometimes represented by a serpent whose coils twine as it descends around the trunk of the Tree of Life with its head downward. Adam will henceforth know this "ground" of his existence: bent over it, he must earn his bread by the sweat that falls from his brow.[2]

If now, after this brief look at the logic of the biblical account, we return to considerations of the supernatural order, we see that the situation has partially changed.

---

2 Cf. *Love and Truth*, 144–48.

CONCERNING CHRISTIAN GNOSIS ACCORDING TO ITS ESSENCE

The fruits of revelation are not restricted: they are given to all and good to eat, at least for all those who are part of this new paradise that is the universe of religion. However the same necessity remains. The strict, literalist, and formalist observance of this incomplete revelation that is the Mosaic Law (Torah) can be a cause of one's downfall: "For as many," says St. Paul, "as are of the works of the law are under a curse" (Gal. 3:10); and in fact it is not the Mosaic law that justifies, it is faith. And Christ himself makes this clear: "The words that I have spoken to you are spirit and life" (John 6:66), that is to say: do not stop at the words spoken (*rhemata*) — however definitive they might be as indicated by the verb in the perfect: *lelaleka*, "I have spoken"—but perceive the spirit that is in them and open yourselves to the life they contain in abundance. Gnosis is therefore everyone's duty; it consists, according to the formula of St. Paul, to go "from faith to faith," *ex fide in fidem*: "justice (that is, the way of sanctification) is revealed in the Gospel [the message of Christ] starting from faith to go towards faith" (Rom. 1:17), from formal faith to faith-life.

"The Church," writes St. Irenaeus of Lyons, "has been planted as a paradise in this world; therefore says the Spirit of God, 'Thou may freely eat from every tree of the garden,' [Gen. 2:16] that is, eat from every Scripture of the Lord; but you shall not eat with an uplifted mind, nor have any contact with the gnosis of the heretics. For these men do profess that they have themselves the knowledge of good and evil; and they set their own impious minds above the God who has created them."[3]

This brings us to the heart of the debate, and the point is delicate. Moreover, how would it not be so? If the heretical gnosis has had such importance in the history of Christianity, if it could seduce so many of the most intelligent minds and produce so many works on such an ambitious metaphysical and spiritual level, this is because it corresponds, or appears to correspond, to the deepest and highest aims of the religious soul. Gnosticism has evolved, it is true, and gradually indulged in constructions of disconcerting complexity. But the themes

---

3 *Against the Heresies. Demonstration and Refutation of Gnosis with the Lying Name*, V, 20, 2; Fr. trans. A. Rousseau (Paris: Cerf, 1984), 628.

developed by the first known heresies, that of Marcion (if he is a gnostic at all), or that of Valentinus, retain a relative simplicity. If it were only the disorderly productions of an unbridled Eastern imagination, it is hard to understand why these heresies were so successful. The intention that drives the cognitive process of gnosticism is therefore much the same as that which presides over true gnosis, and one might say much the same for all other kinds of gnosis.

Should we conclude, with regard to its subjective form, that gnosis is one and differs only according to various objects that give it its specificity? Does it follow then that by itself, as simply a mode of knowledge, gnosis is neither heterodox nor orthodox, but only becomes so through its object? In many ways—but not all—it is surely necessary to answer yes. There is a gnostic postulation, a desire for gnosis, in all intelligence. And it is in the nature of this desire to include a possibility of excess. Gnosis is excessive or rather "exceeding," to the very extent that it is an orientation towards the sacred, since only that which is divine is by definition transcendent to the world. The language here must be clear. It is not by accident, it is by essence that gnosis is bound up with religion. And although it is fashionable, among opponents of gnosis, to mock the pretension of its views and denounce its lack of moderation, how can we not but realize that this aspiration to the highest knowledge is inseparable from the nobility of the human spirit, that it is the indelible mark of this spirit? "Earnestly desire the best gifts," says St. Paul (1 Cor. 12:31).

It is therefore not in itself that we must look for the principle of the deviation of gnosis, but in a certain relation with its object. After careful consideration, it is obvious that the constraint incurred by knowledge when an object is given to it, whatever the nature of this giving, is the mark of its ontological limitation. In its act the intellect is universal, but not in its existential *situs*, since it needs to go from potency to act. It is therefore not the creator of its object:[4] its object

---

[4] Contrary to what Kant thinks (*Critique of Pure Reason*, § 17, trans. P. Guyer & A. W. Wood [Cambridge: Cambridge University Press, 1998], 249–50), the notion of an intuitive (human) intellect in no way implies that it is the

always precedes it, and, in this respect, any knowledge includes a point of ignorance identical to the very being of the intelligent subject. This is why St. Paul declares that partial and obscure gnosis will give way to total and perfect gnosis only when "I shall truly know (*epignosomai*) even as I have been truly known (*epegnosthen*)" (1 Cor. 13:12). Gnosis becomes epignosis (true knowledge, from the Greek *epignosis*) only if the knowing I is truly known, that is, only if it is truly identified with the knowledge that God has of it from all eternity: future knowledge ("I shall know") is identical to timeless knowledge ("I have been known"). It is knowledge "face to face," where we know in the face of God the knowledge that God has of our face (*prosopon*).[5] For gnosis, to become aware that it is, in terms of its actuation, dependent on its object is inevitably to become aware that it is the act of a subject, because there is only an object for a subject. This dependence is imposed on gnosis as a condition of its current state, and teaches it that it is not pure gnosis, that it is not, by itself, pure knowledge. In other words, by this it learns that there is for it, *a priori*, something not-currently-knowable and that, whatever the feeling it has about its own transparency, there is, within its own process, something like an obscure background. Where is this not-currently-knowable, how do we identify *a priori* the object that conceals it? Knowledge does not know it, no more than the eye can see the edge of its own vision, since, by definition, all that is object for it—even itself as a knowing subject—appears to it as known, and therefore as knowable (even if this is just an appearance).

Having understood this, the knowing subject is right to submit to that which is more knowing than itself. To submit is to obey the authority of a superior. If gnosis obeys the divine order, this is not because it intellectually recognizes its truth: if indeed this were the case, it would have no need for

---

creator of its object, which is only true for the divine Intellect. Kant uses this as an argument to deny the existence of such an intellect. We must rather conclude that, even though intelligible, the object of the intellect still conceals an (ontological) obscurity.
5 Cf. *Love and Truth*, 253–55.

an order to comply with what the order dictated. We do not need an order to admit that two plus two is four, and it is not the intelligence that first obeys, it is the will. Certainly, insofar as it is the sense of being, receptivity to reality, intelligence can be described (analogically) as sheer obedience to what is. But this "obedience" is only one with its being: one should speak in that case of passive obedience. On the other hand, if obeying implies the possibility of saying no, in short, if it is a true *act* of submission, active obedience, then it amounts to free will. In this case, the function of intelligence will be limited to authorizing the will to comply, to authorize this to the extent that, qua intelligence, it knows itself powerless to recognize the divine nature and saving power of a *particular* created form. Intelligence is surely capable of attaining metaphysical objects and acquiring some knowledge of them. It is also capable of grasping the ontological and symbolic relation that sensible realities maintain with metaphysical realities, by a process of analogy that reascends from the terrestrial to celestial, but it is incapable of following the reverse path for that which, moreover, no longer stems from the order of the nature of things (whether physical or metaphysical), but from the order of grace, that is, from God's saving initiative. By itself, the intellect cannot have any sure knowledge that a particular sensible form (speech, man, animal, vegetable, mineral) is "full of grace" and invested with divine authority, however numerous and pressing might be the reasons for believing it. And yet, for us, nothing should be more necessary. For it is not enough to apprehend that our gnosis is not all-knowing and, thereby, become inclined to seek elsewhere than in ourselves for the transcendent knowledge that will keep us from losing ourselves (unless one would resign oneself to despair); we still have to know who to turn to, who to listen to, who to obey. Nothing in the world can decide for us the choice of this authority—that is, nothing except our will. This is called an act of faith, and that is why this act is a grace, a pure gift from God: it is ours and yet does not come from us, it is a secret between God and our being that we cannot fathom intellectually, we can only carry out, although we can see here, in hindsight, a kind of mysterious instinct for the supernatural. God gives this grace of faith to all who are open to its reception. But nothing can replace the act by which we give ourselves to it.

The subject, here, is therefore necessarily thrown back on his freedom, the very freedom that allows Eve to put her faith in the serpentine word rather than the divine word. For freedom is only the other side of a commitment. And that this is a commitment of a "gnostic" nature is evident from the text of Scripture: what Eve, then Adam, desires is deifying manducation-knowledge, which is the very definition of gnosis. Certainly all the fruits of paradise are good to eat-know and possess in themselves this spiritual virtue, all except one that the human creature cannot recognize by its appearance, but only on the faith of divine prohibition. And that is why one can at once maintain, on the one hand, that Adam's sin is to halt his cognitive gaze at the creature, thus confining it to its contingency and its finitude, instead of transiting it towards what truly ends it, and, on the other hand, that this same gaze, this same cognitive intention, is gnostic in nature, that is, is ever aspiring to deifying knowledge: if you eat of this fruit, "you will be like gods." Man cannot do otherwise than to want and seek God: all knowledge is desire for the divine Being. But Eve deceives herself. She thinks she knows what in reality she does not know and what she has no means of knowing that she does not know, none, except obedience to the divine word. To believe that one knows what in reality one does not know, such is the pseudo-gnosis, which is in some manner the reverse of learned ignorance.

Now, by committing oneself to pseudo-gnosis, one shuts oneself out from true gnosis, one loses the grace of saving gnosis. Gnosticism illustrates precisely this reversal. We mean here gnosticism in the sense that this term, of English origin, was used by nineteenth-century historians to designate a set of more or less Christian religious currents of the first three centuries, currents of a "sectarian" nature, which themselves were designated by the names of their founders: Bardesanes, Valentinus, Carpocrates, Basilides, &c., to whom we can add

How Gnosis Changes into Gnosticism

Marcion, with whom, however, we do not encounter those mythologico-metaphysical speculations of classical gnosticism.

This sectarian gnosis[6] is characterized, in particular, by the rejection of Mosaic revelation, that is, of the Torah. Again, we need to be clear: what is rejected is not so much the reality of that which is encountered in the First Testament, as its saving value. Everything said about the creation of the world, original sin, and the history of mankind did take place, but it is not [for the gnostics] the work of the supreme and truly good God. The Testament of Moses is not lying about the facts, as the state of the world that his God created shows only too well; he is lying about the nature of this God, in reality a simple Demiurge, devoid of kindness for his creatures. It is not he who can save man and lead him to deification. In short, in the eyes of gnosticism, it is the Old Testament gnosis that is a pseudo-gnosis. We are in somewhat of an analogous situation, but in the reverse direction, to that of Eve before the Tree of knowledge of good-and-evil. The fruit of this Tree seems beautiful and good to her while the word of God informs her that its eating is fatal. The Serpent's argument rejects neither the existence of this Tree nor any other, but he denies the truthfulness of the divine Word, to which he opposes his own. Eve has no way of being sure of the divine truthfulness beforehand: she can only accept it in faith, or believe the serpentine word. In the same way the Christian stands before revelation's Book just as Eve stood before the fruit. That is why St. Irenaeus says that the Church, which brings this Book-Fruit to us, is a paradise planted by God, which means that this Fruit-Book is beautiful to see and good to eat. Opposed to this is the discourse of gnosticism, which does not deny the reality of its content, but which challenges its saving power: the gnosis of this revelation is not the true gnosis, and the wickedness of the world attests to the wickedness of its creator. One clearly

---

6 Certain authors, René Guénon in particular, have derived "sect" and "sectarian" from the Latin *secare*, "to cut": "Etymologically, whoever says 'sect' necessarily says scission or division" (*Perspectives on Initiation*, 69). As appealing as it is, this etymology is false: the Latin *secta*, "way of life," derives from *sequi*, "to follow," both literally and figuratively.

sees here that the qualification attributed to gnosis (whether true or false) is a function of the object to which it applies, and that the determination of this object is a matter of faith in the word that entrusts it to us, that conveys it even down to us, i.e., basically, a question of faith in Tradition. This is why St. Irenaeus speaks of the pride of the heretical gnosis which "casts its thoughts above God the Creator."[7] Pride does not consist so much in "wanting to know too much," as is sometimes said, but rather in claiming to know more than God, or, at least, more than what we deem to be God's Word. Now, how can we know that this indeed has to do with his Word? How can Irenaeus know that he is right to put his trust in the *theological* truth of the first Testament, not only as to the reality of what is being said, but as to its spiritual fullness and its deifying power? How can he know that Scripture speaks not only of the world's creation and humanity's history, but also and above all of the true God himself, and the Covenant he has made with men? To these questions, only one answer is possible. We bestow our faith on the word of the apostles, witnesses of Christ, and on that of the Church that faithfully guards it. Everything comes down then to verifying this fidelity. And this is the main point of Irenaeus, because, in the final analysis, there is no other. And that is most reasonable. One can obviously study gnosticism's mythological-metaphysical constructions in themselves and, to refute them, subject them to a philosophical criticism. But this criticism can be itself the subject of counter-criticism, stressing in particular that the aforesaid constructions are perhaps not understood in their true meanings. And this counter-criticism does not seem completely baseless. When we read for example what St. Irenaeus and St. Hippolytus tell us, in a contradictory manner moreover, about the thought of Basilides,[8] we have the feeling

---

7 *Against the Heresies*, II, 25, 4.
8 Basilides lived and taught in Alexandria in the second century. According to him, his doctrine dated back to a secret tradition from the apostle Matthias. Cf. Hippolytus, *Elenchos* (Rebuttal), VII, 20; Irenaeus, *Adv. Haer.*, I, 24, 3-7; Clement of Alexandria, *Strom.* II, 113, 3 to 114, 1 &c. Also: Dictionnaire de Théologie Catholique VI, 1444-46; Dictionnaire du Christianisme Ancien (Paris: Cerf, 1990), I, 355.

of seeing fragments of doctrines there (thus the supreme God is qualified as "non-being," *ouk on*) which, restored to a Platonic context, could acquire coherence and meaning. This is true.[9] What remains, however, is that all schools of gnosticism have rejected the theological truth of the Old Testament and the most basic teachings of the Christian faith. And so, if the term Christian has an identity, it can be attributed only to the rule of faith transmitted by the Church and of the continuity of which everyone can be assured without difficulty.

True gnosis is therefore that which finds its spiritual and deifying nourishment in the Tree of Ecclesial Tradition planted by the Holy Spirit. And that is why the pseudo-gnosis that rejects the fruits of this Tree is obliged to create a "garden" piecemeal, at once mythological and metaphysical. Devoid of revealed sacred forms, it borrows the themes of its religious universe from the various philosophical or mythological currents of its time: Greek, Jewish, Egyptian, Near Eastern, &c., and transforms them into characters and actors of a cosmogonic drama, after having transformed biblical figures conversely into simple allegories, endowing these abstractions with a sacred aura, suitable for providing indispensable numinous objects.

---

[9] Simone Pétrement dedicated her life to the rehabilitation of gnosticism. Her intent was to show that it is more truly Christian than people imagine. For her, the Cross of Christ truly separates God from the world. This interpretation seems to betray a rather dizzying misunderstanding of the revelation of Christ. As already pointed out, she places a surprising confidence in certain conclusions of modern exegesis whose results are less certain than she thinks, not to mention a quite harsh and one-sided reading of the texts of John or Paul. The trees of her abundant erudition hide from her the forest of the Christian message.

CHAPTER 15

Death and Resurrection of the Gnostic Intellect

BASICALLY, GNOSTICISM PROCEEDS FROM A fusion, or rather confusion, between the two aspects of objective gnosis that we distinguished in Chapter 13, namely: the *revelatum*, especially under the form of its dogmatic elaboration (the rule of faith), on the one hand, and, on the other, what can be called the metaphysical *organon* underlying this elaboration. Now, this metaphysical *organon* truly deserves the title of gnosis only if ordained to the intelligible reception of the revealed object. This is the classic doctrine, within the medieval purview, of theology as *fides quaerens intellectum*, faith in search of its understanding. And, since the work of intelligence is called philosophy in the Middle Ages, it follows that one ought to call philosophy the "handmaid of theology," but it is in the sense, as Étienne Gilson has pointed out, wherein philosophy "serves" theology to actualize itself as a science. This does not involve an inferiorization of the philosophical act: just because mathematical disciplines serve to express the laws of physics, does it follow that they are placed in a state of inferiority compared to the science that uses them? In reality, theology is philosophy as it strives to think about the *revelatum*.

However, we should be clear: the case of metaphysics is not in all respects comparable to that of mathematics. Certainly an instrument is all the more useful when it is in itself more perfect, and therefore the metaphysical *organon* will serve all the better for the intelligible reception of the faith, since this reception will be free and autonomous in its own exercise. But metaphysics, as a speculative act, has the peculiarity of recognizing by itself that the object of its cognitive aim remains transcendent to it as to its being. What the intellect grasps is the specific form of its mode of grasping. That is something Kantian criticism also says when it declares that the metaphysical Ideas of the world, the self, and God are only the objectification of the need for a unity of reason; a unity of exterior phenomena: the world; a unity of interior phenomena: the self; a unity of all things: God. This need for unity *regulates* the functioning of the reason, and therefore these Ideas have a regulatory use, but reason cannot contemplate them in themselves, cannot use them *speculatively*: the Ideas of reason do not make us *know* anything, says Kant, we can only *think* them, and they only reveal to thought the functioning of thought.

But this is not true. The shape of our intellective aim is not a projection of subjective conditioning, because then we would have no means of perceiving them. Either the intellect *is* openness to being, or else there is no intellect. But to maintain that there is no intellect, in other words that the intellect *is* not, is only possible provided that "to be" and "not to be" has *meaning* for the one who states this proposition, which implies that he has this faculty of intelligible receptivity which is precisely called "intellect." The philosopher has no choice: as a man, whether we like it or not, whether we know it or not, we are condemned or dedicated to intellectual receptivity. To reduce the act of understanding to a conditioned functioning makes sense only if it is something other than that: an intellectual seeing. The intellect does not produce this sense, it receives it from its object or, again, it perceives it, and no intelligence in the world can logically argue the contrary, although most of modern philosophy, even most of theology, is committed to the Kantian path of the negation of intellectual intuition. The form of intellectual aim is specified by the object it aims at, it is therefore a mode determined by *participation* in this object (towards which the third degree of abstraction directs us), it truly causes us to know something about this object, insofar as it is informed by this aim.

However, the intellect also knows that it does not attain, in its full reality, the metaphysical object from which it nevertheless receives the specification of its intentional aim. It only attains it under a certain mode, not as such. Metaphysics aims at what is loftiest and the horizon it envisions is open to infinity: as for the object of its aim, there is no "beyond" with metaphysics, not even the *revelatum*. But, to the very extent that it is only a target, insofar as it knows itself to be passively informed and oriented by its object, where it is somehow subject to the object's determining law, *experiencing that it cannot think otherwise about the object about which it is thinking*, it intuits itself as being thought by "something" that it does not think in full, and which, as such, eludes it.

This is why, by itself, it is inclined to turn towards revelation, by itself because it is in expectation of the revelation of being from which it gathers within itself an intentional annunciation. A sense and desire of being, the intelligence lives in the hope of an unveiling; intellectual attention, as Malebranche has approximately stated, is the natural prayer of the soul. By that, the metaphysical intelligence is called from within to respond to what religious revelation offers, all the more strongly when this revelation presents itself as the very embodiment of Truth become finally visible, finally unveiled. But the passage from metaphysical aim to commitment of faith shifts the intelligence from light to darkness: it is world- and situation-changing. The metaphysical object was in the light only because of its remoteness. Now that it is in front of us, now that we can touch it in faith, our gaze fails and we lose knowledge: we must close our eyes, we must no longer know anything.

There is then, at the entry into faith, a *sacrificium intellectus*. The intellect must renounce its own light, as much as possible: blessed "are the intellects that know how to shut their eyes,"[1] wrote Dionysius the Areopagite, for entry into unknowing is a veritable knowing. But even if the intelligence must die with Christ, it must also be resurrected with him. This is precisely the sacrifice that pseudo-gnosis refuses to accomplish. And we are no longer speaking here solely about historically defined gnosticism. Surely, as we have seen, historical gnosticism includes a metaphysical dimension. One can even consider it as tending essentially to allegorize metaphysical themes under a mythological parodying of religious elements, borrowed

---

[1] *The Mystical Theology* I, 997B.

Death and Resurrection of the Gnostic Intellect

especially from Christianity. In so doing, and to the very extent that it wants to be in conflict with the traditional Church, opposing its own revelations to those of the common faith, it situates itself entirely within a religious climate. The question of knowing then how it viewed the relationship of philosophy to religion is difficult to characterize. In its philosophy, gnosticism was very eclectic, although most of the themes it utilized dovetail with a very diffuse Platonism prevalent everywhere at that time. But its primary concern was not of a speculative nature: it was religious, and we might even say that metaphysics is there from the outset subordinated to "revelation." However, this subordination is not experienced as a sacrifice of the intellect, because philosophical speculation is never posited by the "gnostics" autonomously within its own system. This is, moreover, what Plotinus reproaches them for: they do not speak as true philosophers.[2]

---

2 *Enneads*, II, 9, 6, 45–50; 2nd ed., trans. S. MacKenna (London: Faber & Faber, 1956), 137–38. This Ennead is commonly titled "Against the Gnostics," or "To the Gnostics" (*Pros tous Gnostikous*). This is the title given it by Porphyry in the first (chronological) list of Plotinus's works in his *Life of Plotinus* (5, 33). In the second (systematic) list, the Ennead is titled: *Against those who say that the Demiurge of the World is wicked and the world is evil* (24, 56–57), which highlights its content and focuses directly on the misocosmism of the gnostics and their condemnation of the Creator-God. Some have wondered if Plotinus was not also targeting Christians, confused by him with the gnostics. Marginal indications conveyed in three manuscripts affirm this; we read for example: "Porphyry speaks of 'gnostics' by designating us Christians," or: "Because Christians are said to have 'gnosis'" (Richard Dufour, *Treatise 33* [Paris: Garnier Flammarion, 2005], 237). In fact, Valentinian and Sethian gnostics, therefore (heretical) Christians, attended the teachings of Plotinus. Father Festugière (*La Révélation d'Hermès Trismégiste*, new ed. [Paris: Belles Lettres, 1986], tome III, 59, fn 3) doubts that these gnostics were Christians, at least not orthodox Christians. But was Plotinus able to distinguish between orthodox and heretic? It is certainly not the same for his disciple Porphyry (*Life of Plotinus*, 16), who wrote the most anti-Christian work of antiquity (*Against the Christians*, 15 books partly lost). For Simone Pétrement, the influence that gnosticism might have exerted for a time on Plotinus should be taken into account, probably through Numenius of Apamea, whom Plotinus read and who made a distinction between the supreme God and the Demiurge (*Le Dieu séparé*, 26, fn 37, which refers to the works of H. C. Puech, R. Harder, E. R. Dodds, G. Quispel, J. Zander, &c.). The study of gnostic manuscripts discovered at Nag Hammadi, as H. C. Puech had foreseen ("Plotinus and the Gnostics," 1957, *En quête de la gnose*, tome 1 [Paris: Gallimard, 1978], p 94) and clarified in an *Appendix* (ibid.,

CONCERNING CHRISTIAN GNOSIS ACCORDING TO ITS ESSENCE

We would like to turn now to recent forms of speculative gnosis that are situated from the first outside any relationship, whether conflictual or otherwise, with the faith of the Church. Surely they are not unaware of all religion, since they are deemed the finally luminous truth of what religions express obscurely. But their starting point is not that of a historically recognized revelation, it is that of an intellectual illumination placed, *a priori*, above revelations. Anxious about legitimacy despite everything else, these forms of gnosis claim derivation from the primordial science that is actuated in Adam under the effect of the presentation of the world. That was when, as we have repeatedly emphasized, the first metaphysics and cosmology were developed that will be transmitted, after the fall, to the sons of Adam and will constitute the basis for that *philosophia perennis* whose presence can be seen everywhere in humanity. It is this, as we have seen, that will necessarily prove useful — following the changes that it will subsequently undergo — for the intelligible acceptance of this "new world's" presentation, a presentation that is itself a divine revelation. However, and this is what some of these recent forms seem to ignore, to the very extent that revelation is the presentation of a "new world" to human intelligence, to be received, it requires new modes of cognitive apprehension, as the progressive development of Christian theology proves, for, as Christ declares: "They do not put new wine into old wineskins, or else the wineskins break, the wine is spilled, and the wineskins are ruined. But they put new wine into new wineskins! And both are preserved" (Matt. 9:17). Thus, the *philosophia perennis*, for all that in the new doctrine refers to the ancient world, remains the *organon* of intelligible reception: the notion of a transcendent, eternal, and almighty God, and the notion of creation (Rom. 1:20). But this *adamica philosophia* should agree with a *philosophia christiana* that develops new concepts: trinity, incarnation, redemption, eucharist, sacraments, &c. Surely it develops

---

113), makes it possible to find, in treatises of a Valentino-Sethian nature, a portion of the technical vocabulary used by Plotinus, and with which he was therefore acquainted.

them using the elements provided by primal metaphysics, since there are no others, but by transforming and supernaturalizing them: thus for the notion of "consubstantial" implemented at the Council of Nicaea, or that of "person" distinguished from "nature" in the Council of Chalcedon.[3] In either case, whether *adamica* or *christiana*, the *philosophia* remains "secondary," or "reactive," since it arises from the object's initial action, whether natural or supernatural, on the human intellect. And we have sufficiently shown that herein lies knowledge's ontological limitation for there to be any need to come back to this. We speak of ontological limitation, that is, as to the being of the knowing intellect, to the extent that, to be itself, the intellect depends on its actuation through its object. However, in itself, the intellect is potentially universal. It can in principle think everything, but on condition that something is given to it to consider; not that it is the thing given that confers on the intellect its actuality — which would make no sense, the thing communicating only its form — but because it gives the intellect the opportunity to manifest the continual actuality of its intellective nature (the agent intellect).

We conclude, before analyzing one last time some of these modern speculative gnoses, that a true speculative gnosis will only be the one that remains conscious, as to its actuation, of its dependence on the gift of an object, a dependence which itself arises from the fact that all knowledge is the act of a being, and of a contingent being since it is situated in the world. There is no knowledge without an object having been first given to intelligence; but further, so that the desire for all knowledge which gnostically exceeds all that precedes it may be fulfilled, it is also necessary that the given object be withdrawn, at the same time that it gives itself, towards the transcendent assumption of itself, towards the reality of a "hinter-world" (no offense to Nietzsche) of which it is but the epiphany. This is only possible through the merciful descent of the *revelatum*. The revealed object, the sacred object — that

---

[3] We have called this the "theological heightening of concepts": *Christ the Original Mystery*, 117-21; on "consubstantial," cf. ibid., 112-16.

alone is what can elicit the sacral actualizing of knowledge. This means that the exercise, the effective implementation, of the metaphysical *organon*, accedes to gnosis only insofar as the conceptual objects upon which it is exercised are placed at the service of faith's realities.

CHAPTER 16

A Last Glance at the Guénonian-Schuonian Gnosis...

Our meditation on true gnosis has led us to this conclusion: speculative gnosis, or sacral metaphysics, is Marian in essence; she is only there to carry the *Logos* to the world, and for that alone. Mary "gathers," "ponders all these things" (*sumballein*), one with the others, "in her heart" (Luke 2:19) only because she is, and inasmuch as she is, "the handmaid of the Lord." Otherwise, the mystery of the Ave turns back into Eva's betrayal of trust.

But by virtue of the "situated" nature of speculative knowledge considered in itself, by virtue of the privilege of universality it enjoys (as it is for mathematical truth, which pertains *in its own right* neither to Heaven nor to the earth), the mind is drawn to give to statements of doctrinal gnosis the value of transcendent realities for which they are only the intellectual expression. Almost irresistibly, the adamic science, at least what will still subsist of it, becomes a kind of sacred object, an end in itself; it acquires a normative and paradigmatic character. We lose sight of the fact that concepts are sacred only by their service to the truths of the faith, and one can even go so far as to see here the icons of a revelation appropriate for the gnostic's intelligence: in doing so, one forgets that Mary, the prototype of the intellect, that is, of intelligible receptivity, is the Immaculate *Conception* only as the Mother of the Christ-Logos, insofar as she would have herself be servant to his manifestation in the flesh.

It is in the light of this conclusion that we would like to try, one last time, to identify the real meaning of the gnosis envisioned by Guénon and Schuon. This examination is justified insofar as no twentieth century work has asserted its claims in favor of gnosis more potently and more convincingly than the work of these two authors. True, as famous as they may be, these works, or at least Guénon's (for whose work alone, in fact, the question is posed) are still not accepted as on a par with the major intellectual productions of our time. The reason is probably due to the resolutely "sacred" and "traditional" nature of their speculative commitments, whereas the European and even American intelligentsia would rather be free of all metaphysical faith.[1]

In undertaking this final critical review, our intention—do we really need to stress this?—is not to denounce everything that these two authors were able to bring us. Both (from various points of view) have taken a most decisive step outside modernity and its anti-spiritual culture. Into a secularized world, which rejects all confessional, mainly Christian, discourse, into a world which is that of *the death of God*, they have introduced an extremely vigorous metaphysical language that has reopened a path to the sacred and the transcendent, and that has restored its nobility and its strength to the religious sphere. They were able to restore their cultural presence and their living meaning to the symbols and the doctrinal statements of the great spiritual traditions of humanity, striving to awaken in the depths of the modern soul the innate sense of the divine and its manifold forms, providing as needed the essential keys to their interpretation. And all of this is

---

[1] This silence is all the more remarkable, whether just in appearance or "official" in nature. Unofficially, and in reality, the work of Guénon—which is to be distinguished, by its very classical style, from Schuon's quite modern, even somewhat "baroque" style—has been known and even read very attentively by a considerable number of the most famous writers of the twentieth century. This is what Xavier Accart shows, in a monumental thesis of 1222 pages: *Guénon ou le renversement des clartés. Influence d'un métaphysicien sur la vie intellectuelle française (1920-1970)* (Paris: Archè, 2005), which lists almost all French authors (and sometimes foreigners) who are more or less "Guénonized": from Antonin Artaud to Raymond Queneau via André Gide, Georges Bataille, Henri Bosco, Max-Pol Fouchet, Mircea Eliade, René Daumal, Jean Paulhan, André Breton, Simone Weil, &c., the track record is dizzying. Hence the paradox: on the one hand, we "ignore" a work whose content disrupts the habits of European intellectuals, on the other hand everyone reads it covertly. We may wonder if this notoriety, as extensive as it is unacknowledged, does not have its raison d'être in the work itself, which combines with the impeccable (and somewhat solemn) academicism of his literary presentation, sometimes strange and, at its most extreme, quite fantastic, content.

presented, mainly with Guénon, in a climate of extreme intellectual rigor and traditional orthodoxy, that is, of strict ritual observance and condemnation, in practice, of all mingling of religious forms.

There is therefore no question of indicting these two authors—to whom, moreover, we owe a lot—but simply of highlighting certain items drawn from their works that often pass unnoticed, and that are nevertheless revealing, at least in some respects. This examination is, moreover, easier to carry out in Guénon's case than in Schuon's, for obvious reasons, reasons that stem from the formal clarity of Guénon's pronouncements.

Everyone will agree that Guénon's gnosis deems itself a faithful manifestation, on the intellectual level, of the primordial tradition, of primal doctrine, one that could be called the *metaphysica adamica*, the deposit of which is kept within Agarttha, and of which Guénon (thanks to what filiation?) is the transmitter for modern times. From this universal, integral, and immutable *metaphysica adamica*, Christian doctrine, at least that which is expressed in the Creed's rule of truth as in theology, is only a secondary adaptation and, to tell the truth, an exoterization limited to the religious form.

That being said, one realizes that it never occurs to Guénon to ask himself whether, perchance, the appearing of a new revelation, and such a one that nothing similar to it is found in the known history of religions,[2] does not entail the emergence of new ways of thinking. Either Guénon puts new wine in old wineskins, reducing for example the concept of incarnation to that of *avatara*, or else he is uninterested and makes nothing of it: to our knowledge, there is for him no "metaphysical" interpretation of the trinity, which is rather astonishing, since, in the purely theological order, it is the loftiest mystery of Christian doctrine. Basically, as harsh as this observation may be, it must be admitted that, in Guénon's eyes, God can teach

---

2 Guénon himself agrees with this, since he remarks (*The Great Triad*, 2nd ed., trans. H. D. Fohr [Hillsdale NY, Sophia Perennis, 2001], chap. 1) that the Trinity does not correspond to any known traditional ternary. Likewise, he points out that nowhere else is found the exact equivalent of the Christian sacraments (*Perspectives on Initiation*, trans. H. D. Fohr [Hillsdale NY: Sophia Perennis, 2001], 153).

a metaphysician nothing that he does not already know; as for what would lie outside his speculative field, for that which does not fit within the pre-established framework of his ideas, he has nothing to say.

We will now come to the sacralization of doctrinal terminology observed with him and revealed by some of his remarks. Of course, we know very well that, in principle, Guénon does not identify metaphysics with the forms of discourse that express it. He would no doubt subscribe to the axiom of St. Thomas: the intellectual act (of the metaphysician) is not ended with the statements (of his discourse) but with the realities they designate. For Guénon, what is essential is even inexpressible. His texts, however, contain some ambiguities. When he writes that "metaphysics affirms the fundamental identity of knowing and of being," we understand. But when he continues: "it not merely affirms it but realizes it as well,"[3] we are surprised: we have passed without saying so from metaphysics-theory to metaphysics-realization. Now, we do not really see how a reading, even the most rapturous, of a metaphysical text (Guénon's for example) where this identity is affirmed, would lead to its actual achievement. True, Guénon is careful to specify that basically being and knowing are one, and that one can speak of the object of metaphysics, which is therefore distinguished here from that about which it speaks, only in a "purely analogical way," invoking the role of intellectual intuition, as well as the incompleteness of Western metaphysics (Aristotle). That intellectual intuition realizes a certain identity between intellect and "intelligized" is certain, but that it realizes identity between being and knowing is excluded. On the other hand, that metaphysics is complete if it speaks of "realization," or incomplete if it does not speak of it, changes nothing in the matter: it is always about *speaking*, a discourse is still involved. The metaphysics treated in these pages is understood moreover in the sense of a theoretical presentation (he himself speaks of his "conceptions"), and thus derives from the order of language. Otherwise, we would no longer understand his remark about "European languages and especially the modern

---

[3] *Introduction to the Study of the Hindu Doctrines*, Part 2, chap. 10, 115.

ones, which seem particularly ill-adapted to the exposition of metaphysical truths,"[4] which in good logic ought to apply first to the language of Guénon himself.

Moreover, it cannot be denied that quite often Guénon judges the metaphysical or simply theological character of a doctrine, not according to its object, but according to the form of its statements, so that it is these statements that become as such the objects of Guénonian "gnosis"—perhaps not intentionally by the author, but in fact and for many of his readers. Thus Guénon offers an example to help us "understand" what he means by "the translation of metaphysical truths into theological language": "The immediate metaphysical truth 'Being is,' when expressed according to the religious or theological mode, gives rise to another proposition, namely that 'God exists'"; it would still be necessary, for these two propositions to be equivalent, to be able to "conceive God as Universal Being," on the one hand, and, on the other, to "identify existence with pure Being, which is metaphysically inexact."[5] Hardly anyone but Guénon doubts that theology rises even to the concept of Universal Being and distinguishes Pure Being from existence. But how does the proposition "Being is" pertain to this supreme and absolute knowledge, barely glimpsed by Aristotle, totally

---

[4] Ibid., 75.
[5] Ibid., 84. The identification of being and existence, a metaphysical error for Guénon, is nevertheless a fact in several sacred languages, including Sanskrit and Hebrew: "in the Hebrew language one does not distinguish between being and existence," according to Shlomo Pinès, "Dieu et l'Être selon Maïmonide. Exégèse d'Exode 3, 14 et doctrine annexe," in *Celui qui est. Interprétations juives et chrétiennes d'Exode 3.14* (Paris: Cerf, 1986), 15. This lack of distinction does not prevent Guénon from commenting metaphysically in "The Ontology of the Burning Bush" (*Symbolism of the Cross*, chap. 17) where he nowhere points out the polysemy of *Eheieh* (transcribed today under the form '*ehyeh* which is "the first person singular of the imperfect verb *hayah*," André Caquot, "Les énigmes d'un hémistiche biblique," in *Dieu et l'Être. Exégèse d'Exode 3.14 et de Coran 20, 11-24*, Études Augustiniennes, 1978, 17; *hayah* can mean "to be," including in the copulative sense, "to exist," "to live," &c.). Let us note in passing that Guénon (*Symbolism of the Cross*, 94) identifies *Eheieh* with *Ishwara* "which similarly contains in itself the ternary *Sacchitananda*." However, for our part, we know of no text confirming this relationship. Shankara, in his *Commentary on the Vedantasutras* (I, 1, 19) relates *Sacchitananda* to the supreme Brahma. In the *Crest-Jewel of Discrimination*, 263, he writes: "*Sacchitananda, Atma* which is infinite and unchanging is *Brahma*."

ignored by the moderns, and for which the theologumenon "God exists" would be only a diminished and even faulty equivalence? Would Robespierre, celebrating the cult of the Supreme Being, therefore be a greater metaphysician than St. Thomas Aquinas worshiping the God who is, who was, and who is to come? In itself, the proposition "Being is" pertains to philosophy and has nothing of the unknown about it. In scholastic philosophy, it proceeds from the third degree of abstraction, after physical, then mathematical abstraction, a degree that is rightly called: metaphysical abstraction.[6] Whether one accepts or rejects it, it remains a proposition that unites two terms: "Being" and "is" (this is a proposition called *de secundo adjacente*, because it adds only one term to the first term, while "God is infinite" is a proposition *de tertio adjacente*). As such, this proposal is thought. Its focus is clearly on an extramental reality, but, of this extramental reality (Pure Being), thought knows (almost) nothing. Therefore the proposition "Being is" belongs to the order of supreme knowledge not by itself and *by virtue of its form alone*, but by the depth of the speculative gaze that perceives in this form the transcendent reality towards which it beckons us. In short, we clearly do not understand why one of the formulas is advanced as highly metaphysical and the other is regarded as reductive and deficient. If the essential thing is inexpressible, why occupy oneself so captiously with formulations? And how can we forget that, for all readers of both Guénon and the theologians, the word God designates the absolute, eternal, and infinite Being, but what leads them to prefer a term borrowed from abstract philosophical thought? Is one not justified in saying that Guénon stops at words and concepts, since for him it is the terminology that decides the esoteric or exoteric nature of a proposition?

In some respects, the preference could be explained: to speak of Being, even with a capital letter, is noncommittal; one is in the order of concepts, which are indeed universal (in the

---

6 In physics one disregards the specific matter of such and such a body and retains only common sensible matter; in mathematics, one disregards sensible matter in general and retains only intelligible matter (number and extension); in metaphysics, one disregards all matter and considers being as being: St. Thomas, *Summa Theologiae*, I, Q. 85, a. 1, ad 2.

Middle Ages they were called "universals" and even, for some, "transcendentals"). And this is precisely because "being" is an abstract notion (as to its mode of signifying, not as to what it designates) that can be clothed in the prestigious intellectual garments with which Guénonian discourse adorns it. But there is something else regarding the notion of God. Not to mention the religious grounding it implies, the idea of God refers to the idea of a being who is *the* Being: "I am He who is,"[7] not to an abstraction. And this is because "He who is" is a being that actually gives rise to the idea of being. It is ontology that is the daughter of theology and not the other way around, as Guénon asserts, and this is also, we believe, Aristotle's thesis.[8] In other words, it is the theological formulation which, by the transcendence it suggests (God as the Being above all being) truly introduces one to the metaphysical order.

Finally, what remains to be asked is whether the formula "Being is" belongs to the domain of universal knowledge. We will obviously admit that what such an expression designates is indeed the first and absolute Reality. But its mode of designation, as for itself, and contrary to what Guénon asserts, is as culturally determined as the word "God," is just as contingent, and possibly more so. For, in fact, there is hardly anywhere but in the Indo-European languages, where its forms are extremely developed, that the verb "to be" has assumed such an importance and has become the subject of so much speculation. In Chinese, for example, such a formula would be impossible: "the Chinese," says Jacques Gernet, "did not have...a verb for existence, nothing that allows this notion of being or essence to be conveyed which is so conveniently expressed by the noun *ousia* or the neuter *to on*."[9] No doubt

---

7 According to the translation of the Septuagint. On the ontology and the meontology of the Burning Bush, in a somewhat different sense from that of Guénon in *The Symbolism of the Cross*, chap. 17, see *Penser l'analogie*, 89–117.
8 *Metaphysics*, VI, 1026a 30; Vrin, Tricot, 334 and *Penser l'analogie*, 61. That the vision of the Pure Being is first of all religious is confirmed, it seems to us, by Plato, Shankara, and Ibn 'Arabi.
9 *Chine et christianisme. Action et réaction* (Paris: NRF, 1982), 325. Let us recall that the translations of Father Wieger are very glossed, and that those of Matgioi to which Guénon sometimes refers are, in the opinion of a Guénonian sinologist such as Pierre Grison, useless.

Chinese uses other means to signify the same (?) idea, but not the same formula. Now, the whole line of argument rests on a discussion of formulas, from which Guénon draws truly exorbitant conclusions.

The demonstration is over. No doubt to be complete, it should include a history of the word "being" across the world's cultures, which far exceeds our capabilities. But it clearly seems that the major importance given to the notion of being (*esse*) in Western philosophy is tied to its relationship with the idea of God. Whether this idea came from Greek philosophy,[10] or whether it resulted from an influence of Mosaic revelation on Greek thought,[11] what remains is that this is the religious aim that has fashioned the meditation on being and conferred on it its supreme metaphysical significance. Devoid of this theological dimension, and reduced to itself, the notion of being can even become, for example in Heidegger, the principal deconstructor of metaphysics. In any case, to the minds of nearly everyone today, it possesses a quite impoverished content. The term being acquires a transcendent and vaguely sacred meaning only as a secular, neutral, and philosophically appropriate substitute for God: one then endows it, as does Guénon, with a capital letter. And so one becomes witness to this sacralization of the most abstract language so characteristic of Guénon's speculative gnosis.[12]

---

10 As G. J. de Vogel rightly argues, criticizing Étienne Gilson: "'Ego sum qui sum' et sa signification pour une philosophie chrétienne," in *Revue des sciences religieuses*, tome 35 (1961): 337–55.

11 This what Eusebius of Caesarea asserts (*Preparatio Evangelica*, XI, 10, 16), attributing the statement of Plutarch (*De E apud Delphos*, 17–20, 391F–393C, end of chap. 17): "we say to the god: 'Thou art,' rendering to him the appellation of 'being' as his true and unerring and solely appropriate name" to the revelation of God to Moses (Exodus 3:14): "*ego eimi ho on*," "I am Being," or "He who is" (*ho on* is composed of the masculine article *ho* and the masculine present participle *on* = "being," unlike Greek philosophy which uses the neuter noun: *to on*). This statement by Plutarch is perhaps the first attestation of the designation of God as (preeminent) Being.

12 In a letter to Jacques Masui, André Préau writes: "Guénon, someone both forceful and loving authority, has accustomed his readers to substitute a concern for conformity with a concern for the truth.... This is how Guénonism often assumes the appearance of a simple academic exercise" (Letter of January 23, 1954, in Xavier Accart, *René Guénon et le renversement des clartés*, 1010).

A Last Glance at the Guénonian-Schuonian Gnosis...

If we turn now to the work of Schuon, we will consider it in its general form (and no longer, as previously, on the specific point of its relation to Christian dogmatics). In order to likewise subject it to an examination, one observation is necessary: such an examination is quite difficult, since the work offers so few formal openings for discussion. It has neither the conceptual and terminological precision, the very marked coherence, nor the immutable impersonality of Guénon's discourse. Its indisputable logic is not discursive, or dialectical: it is imperious, expeditious, resolutely schematic, with an intentionally "fulgurating" simplicity. As for the tone of his presentations, it is inspired, dynamic, with a mingling of poetry and mysticism that aims at placing its readers in a situation of spiritual urgency and proximity to the divine, in the name of a decisive self-evidentness. Schuon excels in short sentences, short paragraphs, suggestive and elliptical evocations, rather than in long didactic developments.

In him we encounter, unlike the abstract and denuded style of Guénon, an "iridescence" of ideas that sometimes attains a certain beauty, but that risks making the apprehension of these ideas less easy in their speculative nakedness. In any case, it confers on his explanations a kind of sacrality, which contributes not a little to their undeniable seductiveness: one might speak here of an "aestheticization of metaphysical discourse." The mode of expression of Schuonian gnosis is thus akin to a prophetic style of religious literature and occasionally assumes something like the allure of a revelation.

The eminence of Schuonian gnosis, in the eyes of its messenger, does not therefore reside in the terminological perfection of its modes of expression. Schuon is moreover varied in his vocabulary, much less concerned with its paradigmatic fixity than with the internal force of his vision, a vision whose presence he wants to communicate. What is meant to transcend all religious forms is the very essence of gnosis, not precisely this or that metaphysical formula. However, although he has sometimes varied his terminology, Schuon has never varied the basis of his perspective, the one heralded by the title of his first work published in French, namely, gnosis, or quintessential and absolute esotericism, as the transcendent unity of religions. That is why he first gave it the name of *religio perennis*, then *sophia perennis*. It is indeed, he believes, a religion, or, more exactly, the religion of religions and the wisdom of wisdoms, the religion of the golden age, of the Universal Man, the religion for which his doctrine, both public and private, provides an explanation. Such is the place that Schuonian gnosis intends to occupy, the "supreme place" where it has always meant to situate itself. And that is also why this gnosis, in its general form, is essentially connected to religion as such and that it is therefore led, more than Guénonian doctrine, to take a position with regard to existing religions, and even—this is observed with respect to Christianity—to denounce their dogmatic crystallizations. Schuonian gnosis is thus inclined to break the traditional forms as much if not more than it integrates them ("whoever would have the kernel must break the shell," he liked to repeat). Much less sensitive than Guénon to the continuity of Tradition, a universal criterion of orthodoxy (he does not believe in the existence of the King of the World), he speaks in the name of an inspiration come directly from Heaven (as his spiritual function) and connatural, he thinks, with the pneumatic substance of his being.

If therefore we accept distinguishing in the legitimate notion of gnosis, such as we tried to formulate it, a doctrinal dimension, objective gnosis as enunciable metaphysics on the one hand, and, on the other, a spiritual dimension, subjective gnosis as a state of knowledge, it is clear—in simplifying it a little—that Guénon falls rather under the first (he is a *pundit*, a "teacher") and Schuon under the second (he is a *shaykh*, a "spiritual master"). As such, these two authors can be considered, in principle, major figures of gnosis, and teachings difficult to find elsewhere may be gathered from them, teachings that open sacred worlds to the intelligence. In sum, they have fulfilled, in many ways, for the modern world, the function of awakening gnosis, that gnosis buried in the sleep of the mind mentioned above.[13] But it it is not possible to

---

13 See chap. 10, 306.

embrace their trajectories and follow them to their ends, each of them having conferred on his perspective, along the lines particular to each, a mirage of absoluteness. The first trajectory leads us to the mythology of Agarttha, where the King of the World watches over the deposit of primordial Tradition, the *metaphysica adamica* allegedly superior to the doctrine of Christ; the second commits us to a kind of *religio metaphysica*, a transcendent unity of all religions and all revelations, where human individuality risks exalting itself beyond measure.

CHAPTER 17

...And at Some Others

WE NOW HAVE TO REVIEW, AFTER THIS last look at Guénon and Schuon, some of the contemporary authors who, in various ways, speak of gnosis, either to praise it, or to condemn it. None of them has presented it with a conception as decisive as that of the two previous authors.[1] However, a few words must be said about them to the extent that their works, being public, are involved in current debates on gnosis. Clearly we cannot be, for all that, exhaustive in this area. Our somewhat disparate book is not an academic work, let alone a systematic treatise. It takes in only a few stages of a long-pursued reflection intent on being both Christian and philosophical.

Gnosticism itself being at issue here, especially from what we learn from the manuscripts discovered in 1946 in Egypt at Nag Hammadi, we accept, for want of philological and historical competence, what the most serious science has told us about it: a wise precaution not always observed. We know in fact that one of Nag Hammadi's texts, the *Gospel of Thomas*—which besides, let us remember, is not a gospel, but

---

1 An exception should be made for the polytechnician Raymond Abellio who, outside the Guénonian School, wanted to develop a general theory of gnosis. He mainly rejects Guénon's exclusive reference to the Orient. He himself thinks he has found the model for pure intellectuality in the philosopher Husserl and the mathematician Hilbert. By way of meditation on the *I Ching* (and Kabbalah), these two thinkers led him to the discovery of *La Structure absolue* (Paris: Gallimard, 1965) in which is displayed an extraordinary ability to build a system dynamically integrating esoteric traditions (now "outdated"), with data from universal history, with the gnostic's spiritual development. Abellio also became involved in "subversive" political activities, then in the drafting of a powerful and original novelistic work. He seems to have been unable to free himself from a basic promethianism animated by a combinatorial intoxication never short on ingenuity and resolutely triumphant. It is hard to avoid the feeling that this prodigious machine is running on empty.

a simple collection of "words" (*logia* the plural of *logion*) — has elicited an immense literature, where the most erudite works mingle with the most specious and most tendentious esoteric speculations. Among the latter, we must mention the work of Émile Gillabert,[2] founder of the "Metanoia" association, which took this "gospel" as surety for its own doctrine. He sees it as the most direct witness to the authentic message of Christ, prior to the canonical gospels, which, under the nefarious influence of Paul, fabricated a Jesus who through his sacrifice is a suffering messiah and redeemer, whereas he was actually an initiate whose message is exclusively initiatory and unrelated to any saving exploit. Gillabert sees the proof of this thesis — apart from the works of modern exegesis, among others those of Boismard upon which he bestows the least critical reliance — in an accord between the Gospel of Thomas, as interpreted by him, and "eternal metaphysics," for which René Guénon provided the explanation: "traditional metaphysics, and it alone, provides the keys to the Gospel of Thomas"; this metaphysics "is found in René Guénon."[3] Thus Gillabert and his school are, among our contemporaries, the few to claim both gnosticism and Guénonian gnosis, which is quite astonishing when one recalls what Guénon thought of Alexandrian gnosticism.[4]

Despite its denials, it is clear that the School of Metanoia does not recognize the importance of historical data, especially Pauline theology, or even Eastern thought, and is not to be taken truly seriously, although some of its teachings are not devoid of interest.

However, when it comes to Nag Hammadi, broad historical scholarship does not constitute a guarantee of understanding. In this regard, we will note the case of Elaine Pagels, whose book *The Gnostic Gospels* has been translated into French (proof of its

---

[2] *Paul, le colosse aux pieds d'argile, Paroles de Jésus et pensée orientale, Jésus et la gnose, Judas, traître ou initié* (Paris: Dervy, 1974).

[3] Raymond Ollier, "Les grands thèmes métaphysiques de l'Évangile de Thomas," in *Question de*-53, a special issue on *La gnose éternelle — révélations sur un mystère*, edited by Émile Gillabert, July–September 1983, 89.

[4] Cf. supra, chap. 6, fn 53, 151.

importance) under the title: *Les évangiles secrets.*[5] This author, who held the chair of religion at Columbia University, a specialist in early Christianity and gnosis, speaks of Christ, Christians, spiritual currents, martyrs (despised by Marcus Aurelius who sees them as "morbid exhibitionists," and whom she considers "neurotic masochists"[6]) with an insensitivity, a mediocrity of views—ascribing to orthodox Christians only motives of the social or political order[7]—that leaves a strange and even a somewhat annoying impression. We can only endorse the comments by Gedaliahu Guy Stroumsa: "E. Pagels wonders why Irenaeus reacted so violently to the simple Valentinian 'modification' of monotheism.[8] Pagels' surprise might reflect a widely held attitude among modern intellectuals: a certain inability to actually take seriously, beyond all sociological determinism, religious ideas and their power in the ancient world."[9]

As we see once more, the philological and historical sciences will not suffice unless accompanied by a real understanding

---

5 The American edition of this work was published in 1979 by Random House; the French edition, translated by Tanguy Kenec'hdu, was published by Gallimard in 1982.
6 Op. cit., 81.
7 "[P]ersecution gave impetus to the formation of the organized church structure that developed by the end of the second century," ibid., 98.
8 Ibid., 33-34.
9 *Savoir et Salut* (Paris: Cerf, 1992), 180. This reproach is not valid for Jacques Lacarrière's book, *The Gnostics*, trans. N. Rootes, foreword Lawrence Durrell (New York: Dutton, 1977). This rather eccentric author wanted to write a plea in favor of gnosticism, past and future, the theses of which are brought together in a full-dress scholarly and literary meditation. But sadly, everything transpires against a backdrop of anti-Christian hatred ("the barefaced hypocrisy of Christian morality," 64) which betrays, under the romantic mask of a taste for decadence, a true spirit of gnosticism. Lacarrière thought it his duty to quote in his book this "staggering" thought by Raymond Abellio: "The death of a bee, assassinated by his queen, is charged with as much meaning as the massacres of Dachau" (page 6, quote from *Les yeux d'Ezéchiel sont ouverts*). But behind the provocation, no doubt intended to make us feel the audacity of gnostic "lucidity," there is only stupidity and lack of awareness, for the queen is not *free* to not kill the bee; in other words, this is by no means an assassination, but the accomplishment of a biological function as necessary and determined as digestive functions. The death of the bee is therefore endowed with infinitely more (biological) meaning than that of deportees in concentration camps, the horror of which plunges its roots into the depths of meaninglessness and the enigma of nihility's freedom.

of what is involved. In some respects, we find both science and understanding in Gershom Scholem, in what he calls "Jewish gnosis," a characterization whose potential relevance is disputed by Tardieu and Dubois.[10] However, he is content to use, for good or ill, a category from the history of religions without developing the concept further.[11]

Evidence of this alliance between knowledge and understanding is much clearer in the case of Henry Corbin, not only in terms of Iranian and Andalusian gnosis, but even for gnosis in general, since he has spoken of it often and aired his views on this subject extensively.[12] The following text is particularly significant in this respect:[13] "the concept of gnosis, on the part of both philosophers and historians who, by prejudice or lack of information, make of gnosis what it is not, that is to say on behalf of the so-called modern neo-gnostic cosmogonies," is subject to "many ambiguities.... Gnosis is neither an ideology, nor a theoretical knowledge in contrast to faith. Saving knowledge by itself, its very contents, speaks to faith. It is wisdom and it is faith, *Pistis Sophia*. It is not limited to the gnosticism of the first centuries: there is a Jewish gnosis, a Christian gnosis persisting throughout the centuries, an Islamic gnosis, a Buddhist gnosis. And above all, in no way does it merit an abusive use of the word 'nihilism' being made with respect to it. Rather, it is the antidote to it. For to reject this world with a view to another world towards which this one is the passage, this is not nihilism."[14] This definition, in a

---

10 *Introduction à la littérature gnostique*, 33.
11 Gershom Scholem, *La Kabbale. Une introduction. Origines, thèmes et biographies* (Paris: Gallimard, 1998), 69–89.
12 The *Cahier de l'Herne* devoted to Henry Corbin (1978) contains two important texts: one (23–37), "De Heidegger à Sohrawardî," is the transcription of an interview with Philippe Nemo, June 2, 1976, on France-Culture; the other, which follows (38–56), "*Post scriptum* biographique à un Entretien philosophique," dates from June 1978. These two texts, and many of Corbin's other books, contain explanations of his idea of gnosis.
13 Henry Corbin, born 1903, died October 7, 1978; the text quoted, of June 1978, thus represents the last state of his thinking.
14 Op. cit., 55. Of note is the allusion to "modern neo-gnostic cosmogonies" that seems to be aimed perhaps at Raymond Ruyer and *La gnose de Princeton*. A curious detail: we have in our possession a copy of *L'Archange empourpré*

way, can be in accord with the one we have proposed, particularly when Corbin asserts that gnosis is *Pistis Sophia*, literally "Faith-Wisdom."[15] However, the end of the paragraph points to a connection between gnosis and gnosticism that a reader of St. Paul cannot endorse. Certainly, for Corbin, gnosis is not reduced to gnosticism, but that gnosticism is an authentic form of gnosis, this we believe is profoundly inaccurate and objectively unsustainable. When, in addition, we read on the previous page that "centuries of theological, dogmatic, and peremptory certainties have confused the Supreme Cause of all the worlds, the Supreme Principle unknowable to man in his present condition, with the personal and personalized God," that, "secularized, these concepts have been converted into totalitarian ideologies," and that we should "rediscover *our* God versus the God of all systems," for "gnosis, whether that of a Valentinus, an Ibn'Arabî, or an Isaac Luria, has always been wary of this confusion between Supreme Cause and personal God,"[16] we understand that this perspective has, in reality, little to do with the one we have tried to stress here. When we read such remarks, we are led to ask: and where is Jesus Christ in all of

---

(Paris: Fayard, 1976) that Henry Corbin presented to Ruyer, with the following dedication: "to Professor Raymond Ruyer, in homage from an Iranian gnostic and his translator. In very cordial sympathy. Henry Corbin."

15 The *Pistis Sophia* is a Gnostic work in Coptic, translated from the original lost Greek, and possibly dating from the first half of the fourth century: cf. Tardieu and Dubois, op. cit., 80–81. An English translation by G. R. S. Mead first appeared in 1896 with a revised edition in 1921. It involves a dialogue between Jesus, Mary Magdalene, and the other disciples; its gnosis may be of Valentinian origin. It is the longest and least studied of Gnostic texts that have come down to us.

16 Ibid., 54. On Isaac Luria, one can read the article devoted to him by Scholem: *La Kabbalah*, 629–40; also, the study of Esther Starobinski-Saffron, "Exode 3,14 dans l'interprétation de Rabbi Isaac Luria et chez quelques maîtres hassidiques," in *Celui qui est—Interprétations juives et chrétiennes d'Exode 3.14* (Paris: Cerf, 1986), 207–16. One observation: to apply to the absolute and infinite principle, beyond (as is said) the "personal God," the name of Supreme Cause is, in metaphysics, a major error: the name of cause implies relation to an effect (the world) and cannot designate God in his absoluteness. Corbin's gnosis lacks rigor and proves to be less metaphysical than the dogmatic theology of Thomas Aquinas: "This name 'good' is the principal name of God insofar as He is a cause, but not absolutely, for existence considered absolutely comes before the idea of cause," *Summa Theologiae*, I, Q. 13, a. 11. "God was not 'Lord' until He had a creature subject to Himself," ibid., a. 7.

this? what does he tell us about God? what does he teach us about the "Supreme Cause of all the worlds"? about the Creator of Heaven and Earth? what theology, what idea of God does the *Pater Noster* prayer—which Christ taught us—imply? For having confused the person of the Father with the Supreme Cause, was not Jesus Christ only an exoteric theologian, has he "transgressed the imperative of apophatic theology?" has he "lost the sense of what are essentially theophanies and their necessity," he who was the pre-eminent theophany ("who has seen me has seen the Father," John 14:9)? This is a strange lack of awareness in a great scholar, no doubt animated by the best intentions, an ardent and loving soul, but who, for lack of gnosis, precisely, is incapable of grasping the deep unity of the dogmatic and the metaphysical. What he wants to suggest to his readers, if they consent, is that they are part of a "spiritual chivalry," of an informal Order, an Order of the Principial Temple, the "axis of an esoteric tradition prior even to the historical order of this name," that they can be members of what "Christian theosophists... have called the 'Inner Church.'" This spiritual chivalry is in "Quest for *its* God.... In Quest of a God who is neither Almighty nor the Great Judge, but the eternal lover, tormented, anguished, and disappointed, that the Jewish mystics intimately perceived in the person of Yahweh."[17] This is certainly something to flatter the vanity of many esoteric dreamers, although the pathos of a God who is an "eternal lover, tormented, anguished, and disappointed" may disconcert some: God is not in love, God is love, which is very different. As for the myth of the "inner Church," which others will call the "Church of John," as opposed to the "Church of Peter," this runs counter to the teaching of St. Paul, who reminds us that the Christ is not "divided" and a disciple of Christ does not have to say he is of Apollos, Peter, or Paul (1 Cor. 1:12). This surely does not mean that there is not, for some, a more interior understanding of the mysteries of the Kingdom revealed in Jesus Christ—an understanding to which, however, all Christians are invited. But one cannot form these Christians into a group, a category of beings endowed with

---

17 *Cahier de Herne: Henry Corbin*, 54.

a "nature" different from that of others (the "pneumatics" of Valentinian gnosticism, to be distinguished from the "psychics" and "hylics") and justifying the name "Church."[18] Whoever calls himself "gnostic" has lost gnosis.

It is most regrettable, we repeat, that Henry Corbin, in order to illustrate what is, in his eyes, the way of gnosis, mentions only the names of Eckhartshausen, Isaac Luria, and Ibn 'Arabi,[19] without speaking of Valentinian gnosticism, and that he has not dreamed of applying the word to Jesus Christ. Besides, however numerous and enthusiastic the mentions of gnosis might be in Corbin, it is clear that, unless I am mistaken (I have only a partial knowledge of his immense work), although he has provided suggestive descriptions of gnosis, he has not rigorously developed the concept. The notion, for him, remains vague: it is a connotative rather than a denotative term. This is not to say that such a development, necessarily philosophical in nature, would deliver up the secret and very reality of gnosis, which are of another order. And yet this alone, to the very extent that it is *attempted* on the basis of a theoretical analysis of the cognitive process, enables us to speculatively take into account its possibility and therefore its meaning.

We find with Robert Amadou, an eminent expert on Louis-Claude de Saint-Martin, an attempt to formulate a precise doctrine of gnosis (often critical with regard to Corbinian theses, particularly on the existence of a "metahistory"). "The gnosis of which I speak," he tells us, "and to which I dedicate myself and to which I invite others, is a knowing by no means exclusive of love, quite the contrary, which possesses in its perfection—gnosis is perfect knowledge—four principal

---

18 Cf. *Christ the Original Mystery*, 277–95, where these issues were dealt with as fully as possible. Henry Corbin himself points out the disadvantages of using the terms esotericism or gnosis: "The word 'esotericism' is, along with some others, a source of misunderstandings and no less serious reservations. We must employ the terms esotericism, gnosis, and theosophy, because we do not have any other terms to best translate the technical terms" (*En Islam iranien* [Paris: Gallimard, 1971], tome I, xiv). But we are unsure whether his use of it does not eventually promote this kind of confusion.
19 We are not disputing or endorsing, in the present work, recourse to the three mystics mentioned here. We only regret that Corbin did not take into account the teaching of the Incarnate *Logos*, or the theology implied.

features to specify it: it is religious, traditional, initiatory, and universal.... Of course, when I say that the gnosis is perfect knowledge, when I expressly state it, this has to do with gnosis in itself—God is the great Gnostic as he is the only Theologian—and not with one's apprehension of it, except at the end. But can this be attained during the earthly course of a human life? And permanently? And by how much?"[20] We would readily second these words, especially insofar as Amadou refers to Christian revelation as to that in which gnosis reaches its full reality. However he speaks in the name of a "Western Tradition" whose Christic message would be the properly divine component, but whose unity and identity seem quite problematic. Moreover, it often occurs to him to draw haphazard conclusions from his vast readings, for example when he deduces, from the discovery of a hitherto unknown letter from Clement of Alexandria, the existence "of a primitive Christian esotericism, with a secret gospel and particular rites, a particular baptism, in short, an initiation."[21] Not that we must reject any idea of a teaching on several levels

---

20 *Occident, Orient. Parcours d'une tradition* (Paris: Cariscript, 1987), 9.
21 Ibid., 131. This discovery, made in 1958, was published in 1973 by Morton Smith (*Clement of Alexandria and a Secret Gospel of Mark* [Cambridge, MA: Harvard University Press]). This letter appeared "at the end of a book printed in the seventeenth century, on the front and back of a blank page and on the front of a sheet used for binding" (*Écrits apocryphes chrétiens* [Paris: Pléiades, 1997], tome I, 59). The three handwritten pages (eighteenth-century writing) were photographed by Morton Smith. In 1980, the book (which was in the monastery of St. Sabas) was transferred to the library of the Patriarchate of Jerusalem, but the pages in question are no longer there: what has become of them is unknown (ibid., 60). Is this an ancient or modern fake? In any case, specialists have set aside "Morton Smith's provocative thesis 'that this gospel (a few fragments contained in Clement's supposed letter) would attest to the practice, through Christ, of a secret baptism. If we admit the authenticity, what remains is that Clement recognized a scriptural canon less strictly defined than ours—which is not new: Daniélou, *Gospel Message and Hellenistic Culture*, 455–58—but also that he rejected the interpretation that the Carpocratic gnostics gave of this unduly claimed secret gospel. 'Secret' is a translation of the Greek *mystikos*, which would be conveyed more exactly by 'mysterial.' The two extracts from the secret Mark cited by Clement are inserted, according to the indications Smith gives, in a canonical text which they hardly modify (Mark 10:32–46). Finally, the indications provided by Clement on the existence and destination of the two 'Marks' are of an uncertain interpretation, which everyone can ascertain for themselves" (ibid., 63–67).

from the origins of Christianity, and therefore of a certain esotericism, if one insists on this term; but, as established by the most reliable data, this esotericism did not include any proper rite other than the sacraments of Christian initiation (baptism, confirmation or chrismation, the Eucharist) or the transmission of an evangelical corpus entirely distinct from the canonical gospels: all initiationist mythology ought to be rejected here. For this reason, and a few others, we cannot consider Robert Amadou's theses other than as a curiosity: his views are often original and suggestive, but, we believe, very fragile and too steeped in occultism.

With Eric Voegelin, an original thinker and author of an important work highly regarded in the United States, we leave behind the world of "philognosticism" to approach that of anti-gnosis.[22] Taken quite amiss, the concept of gnosis finds with him an almost unlimited expansion, to the detriment of a very precise understanding. It is a historical category, designating an attitude recognizable in every time period, being expressed in very diverse philosophies and movements of thought, but communing in a certain vision of man and the world, of man as master and organizer of historical development, with Hitlerian and Stalinist totalitarianisms its direct manifestations. As we can see, this is the exact opposite of the thesis of Corbin, who saw on the contrary the source of totalitarian systems in the "anti-gnostic dogmatism" of the Roman Church. For Voegelin, the "movements deriving from Marx and Bakunin, the early activities of Lenin, Sorel's myth of violence, the intellectual movement of neo-positivism, the communist, fascist, and national-socialist revolutions" are thus part of the "gnostic movement."[23] Doubtless it is still possible to identify a "gnostic" component in many intellectual and ideological approaches, mainly in those rejecting empirical reality and doing violence to it in the name of what is believed to be the total truth.

---

22 Eric Voegelin (1901–1985) was born in Cologne. Fleeing the persecutions of the Gestapo, he went into exile in the United States in 1938 and continued the academic lectures he had given in Vienna. He was a philosopher and historian of political ideas and ideologies.

23 *Science, Politics and Gnosis*, trans. W. J. Fitzpatrick (Chicago: Regnery, 1968), 4.

... And at Some Others

But, to subscribe unreservedly to the assertion that "Marx is a speculative Gnostic,"[24] the notion of gnosis must be emptied of any relation to what Clement of Alexandria tells us about it. Voegelin does indeed quote a well-known text from Clement (otherwise translated in a rather obscure way): "gnosis is the knowledge of who we were and what we became, of where we were and whereinto we have been flung, of whereto we are hastening and wherefrom we are redeemed, of what birth is and what rebirth."[25] But this is actually a definition by Theodotus, a Valentinian gnostic, that Clement combatted, not his personal thesis.[26] This definition-description, reproduced many times, no doubt expresses the "existential anguish" of one who feels "thrown into the world," according to Heidegger's expression (who therefore also belongs to the gnostic movement) and who has questions about his destiny: from this cosmic dereliction, and the melancholy that accompanies it, has been formed (with Hans Jonas in particular) the major theme of gnosticism. However, this is a modern interpretation that seems to project upon some ancient expressions themes and feelings partly stemming from romanticism.[27] Francois Sagnard, the editor of *Extracts from Theodotus*, and one of the foremost experts on Valentinian gnosis, in his commentary on the just-quoted text, is right to point out: "all this [the cosmic pessimism of gnosticism] is, moreover, only a factitious drama, a tragicomedy, for the gnostic is assured of his 'salvation.'"[28] Voegelin's analyses are not lacking in strength or depth, and his thought, which

---

24 Ibid., 23.
25 Ibid., 10.
26 Clement made a collection of texts entitled: *Extracts from the works of Theodotus and of the so-called oriental school at the time of Valentinus*. Valentinus taught between AD 140 and 160. His disciples were divided as to whether the body of Jesus was of a *psychic* (Italic school: Heracleon and Ptolemaeus) or a *pneumatic* nature (Oriental school: Axionicos and Bardesanes). Theodotus, about whom we know nothing, probably belonged to the second. Some of the collection's extracts do not come from him. The work also contains texts by Clement. The specialists are more or less in agreement on what derives from Clement and what from the Valentinians. The quoted passage is drawn from extract 78 (Sagnard edition, Sources chrétiennes 23 [1970], 203, and 8–21).
27 But La Fontaine wrote: "... nothing / Is my sovereign good / So much as the dark pleasure of a melancholy heart."
28 Sources Chrétiennes 23, 203, fn 3.

is resolutely Christian, deserves attention.[29] But his views on universal history are so general that they always prove true for some aspect, without however clearly accounting for the very complex historical manifestations he would like to shed light on.

More interesting, from our point of view, is the collective work entitled: *La gnose, une question philosophique. Pour une phénoménologie de l'invisible*.[30] This collection testifies to a serious, attentive, and non-reductive openness (coming as it does from academic philosophy) on the question of gnosis: it is no longer seen as a history of religions category, but as "a possible representation of metaphysics," according to the excellent programmatic formula of Nathalie Depraz.[31] However we cannot follow her when she declares that this gnosis-metaphysics is foreign, despite some appearances, to the religious, theological, and "especially mystical" spheres,[32] except in considering the religious, theological, and mystical spheres as states and practices of a merely psychic nature.

For us, to the contrary, gnosis is intrinsically related to the religious, the theological, and the mystical, inasmuch as it is a sacred knowledge.[33] As we have striven to show, this

---

29 We would be less severe than Arthur Versluis in his article "Voegelin's Antignosticism and the Origin of Totalitarianism" (*Telos Review*, num. 124, [Summer 2002]: 173–82). He is right to reject the thesis of a gnosticist origin for totalitarianism, but what Voegelin brings out about Nietzsche is very penetrating.
30 Edited by Nathalie Depraz and J. F. Marquet (Paris: Cerf, 2000). In 2007 Cerf published a collection of articles by J. F. Marquet entitled: *Philosophie du secret. Études sur la gnose et la mystique chrétienne (XVème-XIXème siècle)*. Most of these are monographs on Paracelsus, Postel, Dorn, Boehme, Kircher, Jeanne Guyon, Swedenborg, Saint-Martin, Ballanche, Baader: learned, sometimes difficult, always vigorous studies. Note, however, unless I am mistaken, that none of the authors studied here, with the exception of Baader, used the term gnosis to describe their doctrine.
31 Op. cit., 11.
32 Ibid.
33 This is also what Michel Henry asserts when he declares: "We must recognize that Christianity is an Arch-gnosis.... In its words which are foreign to the truth of the world and which will not pass away when the world passes away, in its texts, which we have called initiatory, doesn't Christianity actually initiate us into the secret hidden since the origin of the world, into this great secret that we are?" *Incarnation. A Philosophy of Flesh*, trans. K. Hefty (Evanston IL: Northwestern University Press, 2015), 261.

...And at Some Others

knowledge is not sacred solely by its object, otherwise all discourse on God or the divine in general would be gnosis. It is sacred insofar as it is experienced, in full consciousness, as a separate knowledge, as a cognitive state different from ordinary knowledge, and which is, however, its fulfillment. For knowledge, which by nature is a relation to the otherness of being, gains access to its natural identity only by a supernatural tearing away from itself, only if it is dispossessed of self by the transcendence of the object revealed to it: under the effect of its grace, this knowledge dies and becomes what it is. Thus, far from being, at least in its beginnings, a state that would establish the knowing subject in a stable oneness with the known and possessed object, gnosis is the cognitive experience of entering into the radiance and attraction undergone from the object glimpsed. An experience of knowledge, of course — otherwise what is the point of talking about gnosis? — but also, or rather *by that very fact*, an experience of unknowing. And this is why there can be no real gnosis without love, because only love, which is "blind," can ultimately teach the intelligence to shut its eyes. In other words, when the intelligence finally understands that it must renounce keeping its eyes open because its gaze is the last obstacle to its union with the Object glimpsed, is it not love that ultimately bears it along in this traversing of the more than luminous Darkness where "God" seems to have abandoned it?

> "If I speak with the tongues of men
> And even those of the angels,
> But have not Love
> I am become as sounding brass
> Or a tinkling cymbal.
> And if I should have prophecy,
> And should know all mysteries
> And all gnosis,
> And if I should have all faith
> So that I could remove mountains,
> And have not Love,
> I am nothing."
>
> St. Paul, *First Epistle to the Corinthians*, 13:1–2

GENERAL CONCLUSION
Hymn to Holy Gnosis

AROUND 1436, IN CONSTANTINOPLE WHERE he had come to study Greek, a young Latin cleric, Thomas of Arezzo, discovered, at a fishmonger, "in a heap of wrapping paper," a manuscript which he bought "cheaply."[1] Eager to become a missionary among the Muslims with three Friars Minor, "to seek with them the palm of martyrdom," he gave this manuscript to Ivan Stojkovic (John of Ragusa), a learned man and future cardinal, who brought this document to Basel, where the famous humanist Johann Reuchlin, author among other works of *De Arte cabalistica*, was able to acquire it.[2] After his death in 1522, the manuscript came to the Alsatian Abbey of Marmoutier, then, around 1793, made its way into the Strasbourg municipal library, where it was destroyed, along with so many other treasures, on August 24, 1870 in the fire started by Prussian artillery bombardments. Fortunately, two Alsatian scholars, Cunitz in 1842, Reussen in 1861 (revising the Cunitz recension of the original), had made very neat copies, not to mention three other copies from the sixteenth century, one of which was used by Henri Estienne for the text's first edition (1592).

This manuscript contained twenty-two short works of various dates (from the second to the ninth century), for the most part apologetic in nature. The fifth is entitled: *Of the same (Saint Justin, philosopher and martyr) to Diognetus*. Henri Estienne, for the first edition, took the liberty of preceding this title with the mention of "Letter," but it is not a letter. The attribution

---

[1] *A Diognète*, introduction, critical edition, translation and commentary by Henri Irénée Marrou, Sources Chrétiennes 33 (Paris: Cerf, 1951). The passages in quotes refer to pages 6, 8, 238.
[2] *De Arte cabalistica*, the first systematic exposition of Kabbalah by a Christian (1517), was translated into French by François Secret, published by Aubier-Montaigne in 1973, and entitled: *La Kabbale (de arte cabalistica)*, and into English by Martin and Sarah Goodman, published by the University of Nebraska Press in 1983, and entitled: *On the Art of the Kabbalah. De Arte Cabalistica*.

Hymn to Holy Gnosis

to Justin does not stand. The dedicatee, a pagan of quality with questions, to which the tract is responding, might have been Claudios Diognetos, a Roman administrator stationed in Egypt around 200 (Marrou hypothesis). As for the author (about twenty names have been proposed), Marrou presumes—given the probable date of the text and its kinship to the *Protreptic* of Clement of Alexandria—that it could be Pantaenus, Clement's teacher, who had traveled to India and about whom Clement wrote: "He was the true Sicilian bee, culling out of the flowers from the meadow of prophets and apostles and generating in souls the pure honey of gnosis" (*Stromateis* I, 1, 11). *To Diognetus* contains, in any case, in its few pages, some of the most beautiful passages of Christian literature. We reproduce here the Epilogue (from XI, 6 to XII, 9), arranged in the form of a poem. This final exhortation, comments Marrou, "appears to be an orthodox reclaiming of the notion of gnosis, rescued from its potential deformations and integrated into the body of healthy theology...: our author is a Catholic 'gnostic' passionately attached to this marvelous word and to this ideal, anxious to wrench it away from the heretical gnostics, from the upholders of 'a gnosis that does not deserve the name,' *pseudonumou gnoseos*."[3]

> 6. Here the fear of the Law is sung,
> The grace of the Prophets recognized,
> Faith in the gospels strengthened,
> The Tradition of the Apostles preserved,
> And the grace of the Church exults.
>
> 7. Sadden not this grace
> And you will know the secrets
> That the Word reveals
> Through whomsoever he wishes,
> Whenever it pleases him.

---

[3] We have made only changes in detail to Marrou's translation, except in XII, 5 where we have adopted one of the possible translations pointed out on page 82, fn 3, but not retained. Finally, we have kept the word "gnosis" to translate *gnosis*, which Marrou translates as "knowledge," except in his Commentary (234-40), where he translates it as "gnosis."

8. All that the will of the Word commands us,
   Inspires us to lay open to you with zeal,
   We share it with you,
   Out of love for the revelation we have received.

XII, 1. Come closer,
   Lend a docile ear,
   And you will know all that God accords to those
   Who truly love him:
   They become a garden of delight;
   A tree laden with fruit, with vigorous sap,
   Grows in them,
   And they are adorned with the choicest fruits.

2. For this is the land where were planted
   The tree of gnosis and the tree of life,
   But it is not the tree of gnosis that kills,
   No,
   It is disobedience that kills.

3. For it is not without reason that it was written
   That God originally planted in the midst of the Garden
   The tree of gnosis and the tree of life,
   Showing us, in gnosis, the door of life.
   Those who did not know how to use it well,
   Were laid bare by the snake's imposture.

4. For there is no life without gnosis
   Nor sure gnosis without true life.
   This is why two trees were planted, one nigh to the other.

5. This meaning the Apostle had in mind when,
   Blaming the gnosis exercised
   Apart from the rule of truth that leads to life,
   He declares:
   "Gnosis puffs up, but love builds up."

6. For whoever thinks he knows something
    Without true gnosis,
    The very gnosis to which life bears witness,
    That one does not know anything:
    The serpent deceives him
    Because he has not loved life.
    But he in whom gnosis is accompanied by fear
    And who ardently seeks life,
    This one plants in the hope and the promise of fruits.

7. Let gnosis be united to your heart,
    Let the Word of truth received in you become life.

8. If this tree grows in you,
    If you desire its fruit,
    You will not stop harvesting
    What you want to receive from God,
    That which the serpent cannot assail
    Nor deceit infect.
    Eve is no longer seduced,
    But virgin she proclaims her faith.

9. Salvation is manifested,
    The Apostles are filled with understanding,
    The passover of the Lord advances,
    The times are fulfilled,
    The world is put in order
    The Word delights in the teaching of the saints;
    By Him the Father is glorified,
    To whom be glory forever and ever.
    Amen.

SCRIPTURE INDEX

OLD TESTAMENT

GENESIS
2:16 • 338
2:20 • 308

EXODUS
21:6 • 284
22:8 • 284

PSALMS
8:6 • 284
82:6 • 284

WISDOM
2:23 • 284

ISAIAH
55:9 • 221

2 MACCABEES
7:28 • 249

NEW TESTAMENT

MATTHEW
6:33 • 180
7:6 • 42
16:19 • 25
25:29 • 61
end • 254

MARK
10:32–46 • 371

LUKE
1:17 • 263
1:46–52 • 303
1:76–77 • 60
2:19 • 353
4:16 • 326
11:52 • 25, 60, 231, 263, 273, 331

JOHN
Prologue • 56, 58–59, 252
1:9 • 53
1:15 • 60
1:18 • 183, 332
3:13 • 78
3:29–30 • 60
4:22–23 • 9
4:22–24 • 24
4:23 • 42
6:51–53 • 217
6:66 • 338
7:15 • 326
10:34–35 • 284
11:11 • 61
14:6–9 • 335
14:9 • 369
14:11–12 • 335
14:28 • 219
14:25 • 220
16:7–13 • 227
17:3 • 7–8
19:30 • 320
20:31 • 8

ACTS
2:3 • 307

ROMANS
1:17 • 338
1:20 • 203, 336, 350
2:20 • 263, 333
11:17–24 • 31
11:33 • 263
12:2 • 328
15:13–14 • 25
15:14 • 263, 333

SCRIPTURE INDEX

1 CORINTHIANS
1 Cor. • 23
  1:5 • 263, 333
  1:12 • 369
  2:2 • 56
  2:9 • 297
  2:10 • 265
  2:15 • 43
  6:3 • 43
  6:12 • 43, 44
  8:1 • 43, 263, 333
  8:1–7 • 25
  8:2–3 • 39
  8:7 • 39, 263, 324
  8:10 • 263
  8:10–11 • 333
  8:11 • 263
  9:19–23 • 44
  11:7 • 284
  11:23 • 27
  12:8 • 263, 333
  12:31 • 339
  13:1–2 • 375
  13:2 • 263
  13:3 • 333
  13:8 • 263
  13:12 • 61, 192, 308, 340
  13:13 • 61
  13:18 • 293
  14:6 • 263
  14:6–19 • 28
  14:14–15 • 327
  15:8 • 26

2 CORINTHIANS
2 Cor. • 23
  2:14 • 263
  4:6 • 263, 272
  8:7 • 263
  10:5 • 263, 272
  11:6 • 263

GALATIANS
1:12 • 27
1:16 • 27
3:10 • 338

EPHESIANS
1:15–18 • 25
1:21 • 56
3:16–19 • 25
3:19 • 263

COLOSSIANS
Col. • 23
1:14 • 25
2:3 • 263
2:8 • 56

PHILIPPIANS
2:6–7 • 219
3:8 • 263, 272

2 THESSALONIANS
2:15 • 258

1 TIMOTHY
1 Tim. • 23, 41
  6:20 • 7, 38, 263, 268, 271,
      272, 317
  6:21 • 29

2 TIMOTHY
2 Tim. • 41

TITUS
Titus • 41

HEBREWS
1:1 • 183

1 PETER
3:7 • 24, 263

2 PETER
1:5 • 263
1:6 • 263
1:19 • 54
3:18 • 263

NAME INDEX

A
Abhinavagupta, 159
Abraham, 238, 298
Accart, X., 168, 354, 360
Adam, 284, 307-8, 311-12, 314, 317-18, 320-22, 325, 337, 350
Aland, B., 300
Albert the Great (Saint), 307
Alembert, J. Le Rond d', 266
Alès, A. d', 285
Allar, R., 67
Allen, M., 79, 134
Alquié, F., 96
Amadou, R., 143, 205, 370-72
Amboise, J. d', 96
Ambrose (Saint), 8, 55
Amelineau, E., 20
Amman, E., 300
Andrade e Silvia, J. L., 301
André, J., 129
Apion, 46
Apollonius of Tyana, 142
Apuleius, 46
Aristotle, xiii, 22, 73, 81, 153-56, 164, 173, 197-98, 203, 216, 218, 221, 231, 307, 315-16, 329, 332, 356-57, 359
Arius, 213, 239-40
Aspect, A., 129
Augustine (Saint), 53, 55, 156, 242-44, 280, 309
Augustus, 20
Averroes, 196, 307
Axionicos, 373

B
Baader, F. von, 64, 71, 109, 139, 374
Babelon, J., 94
Baker, J. A., 54
Bakunin, M. A., 372

Ballanche, P. S., 374
Bammate, N. D., 152
Bardesanes, 342, 373
Barnabas (Saint), 25, 54
Bartmann, B., 220
Basilides, 49, 108, 137, 261, 342, 344
Bataille, G., 44, 354
Bayle, P., 266
Bell, J. S., 129
Benz, E., 71, 140
Bergier, N. S., 267-68
Berthier, J., 239
Bethell, C., 134, 142
Bianchi, U., 286
Binet, A., 286
Bloch, E., 70-71
Bloom, A., 221
Boehme, J., 50, 73-74, 109, 139-40, 195, 374
Bohr, N., 106
Boismard, M.-E., 59, 332, 365
Bonaventure (Saint), 169-70, 196, 244, 265, 307
Bonino, S., 165, 169-72
Bosco, H., 354
Bossuet, J. B., 138, 268, 270-71, 333
Boulet, R., 168
Bousset, W., 4, 37, 137
Bouyer, L., 29, 239, 274-75, 277-78, 331
Bovon, F., 288
Brach, J.-P., 19
Breton, A., 96, 316, 354
Brinkmann, K., 50, 73
Broek, R. Van, 19
Broglie, L. De, 301
Brown, R. F., 85
Buddha, 115, 124, 140
Bultmann, R., 22, 24
Butler, S., 125

383

NAME INDEX

C
Cairns, H., 67
Callistus (Pope), 241
Calmet, A., 267
Camelot, Th., 278
Capra, F., 106
Caquot, A., 47, 357
Carmignac, J., 103
Carpocrates, 36, 342
Casey, R.P., 21
Cayré, F., 232, 239
Celsus, 28, 36, 47
Chaboseau, A., 205-6
Chacornac, P., 142, 144
Champoux, G.J., 8, 23, 41, 75, 184
Champrenaud, L., 143, 207
Charon, J.E., 14
Chenique, F., 58, 163, 165, 168, 171, 183, 301
Chevalier, J., 163, 262
Chomsky, N., 120
Cicero, 152
Clamer, A., 103
Clement of Alexandria, 7, 28, 31, 36, 39-41, 53-54, 57, 67, 136-38, 140, 231, 248, 269-70, 278, 285, 290, 324-25, 328-332, 344, 371, 373, 377
Cohen, J., 270
Comte, A., 112-13, 115, 220
Congar, Y., 229, 239
Conrad, A., 175
Conze, E., 228
Coomaraswamy, A.K., 159, 180
Corbin, H., 49, 287, 289, 367-70, 372
Cormier, Ph., 219
Cornélis, H., 19, 38, 271
Cornford, F.M., 218
Correggio, 92
Costa De Beauregard, O., 106, 129
Couvert, E., 271, 279
Creuzer, F., 98

Cunitz, E., 376
Cutsinger, J.S., 257

D
Dagognet, F., 113
Dahlstrom, D.O., 50, 73
Daniélou, J., 4, 54, 239, 329-31, 371
Daniel-Rops, 206
Dante, xiii
Darwin, Ch., 301
Daumal, R., 354
Davy, M.M., 94
Deferrari, 241
Deledalle, G., 114
Denis, M., 168
Depraz, N., 304, 374
Derathé, R., 262
Derrida, J., 315
Descartes, R., 49-50, 81, 155, 192, 243, 279, 294-95, 297-98, 320
Descourtieux, P., 331
Désilets, A., 134
D'Hondt, J., 72, 84
Diderot, D., 266, 268
Dietrich, L., 93
Di Giovanni, G., 70
Diognetus, 376-77
Dionysius of Alexandria, 241
Dionysius of Rome (Pope), 241
Dionysius the Areopagite, 29, 61, 136, 164, 208, 239, 248, 250, 255, 265, 348
Dodd, C.H., 8
Dodds, E.R., 349
Doinel, J., 142-43, 205, 207
Doresse, J., 4, 10, 19, 28, 35, 48
Dorn, G., 374
Dubois, J.-D., 19, 37, 49, 105, 110, 282, 286-87, 367-68
Duchesne, L., 285
Dudon, P., 40, 138, 269, 271
Dufour, R., 349

Name Index

Dupont, J., 7, 23–24, 43, 262, 272–74, 277
Durrell, L., 366
Dyde, S.W., 78

E

Eckhart (Meister), 53, 67, 70–71, 73–74, 99, 103, 139, 199, 248–49
Eckhartshausen, K. von, 370
Edlebi, A., 51
Einstein, A., 110, 116, 273
El Hallâj, 159
Eliade, M., 19, 65, 115, 354
Encausse, G., 143
Epiphanius (Saint), 36–37, 44–45, 242
Erb, P., 74
Espagnat, B. d', 106, 129–30
Evagrius of Pontus, 40, 65, 197, 248, 250
Evdokimov, P., 244
Eve, 10, 318–19, 322, 342–43

F

Fabre des Essarts, L., 143
Faivre, A., 19, 49
Fénelon, 39–40, 137–38, 268–70
Ferguson, J., 320, 332
Festugière, A.J., 4, 48, 349
Feuerbach, L., 71, 75
Fichte, J.G., 117
Fitzpatrick, W.J., 372
Flamand, E.C., 93
Flavius Josephus, 46–47
Fohr, H.D., 40, 46, 48, 79, 134, 143, 148, 201, 209, 355
Foucault, M., 315
Fouchet, M.P., 354
Franz, A., 304
Fulgentius, 263
Furetière, A., 266

G

Galileo, G., 81, 155, 315
Gandillac, M. de, 62, 82, 84, 152
Gaucelin, 154
Genot-Bismuth, J., 326
Genty, P., 143
Geoltrain, P., 288
Gernet, J., 359
Gex, M., 109
Gibelin, J., 82
Gide, A., 354
Gillabert, E., 38, 49, 365
Gillet, L., 93
Gilson, E., 132, 199, 243, 299, 346, 360
Godefroy, F., 266
Goethe, W., 140
Goldschmidt, V., 276
Goodman, M. & S., 376
Gratry, A., 295
Gregory of Nyssa (Saint), 29, 58
Gregory Palamas (Saint), 244
Grison, P., 359
Guénon, R., xi, xiii, 40, 45–48, 64, 78, 106, 134–209, 253, 261, 279, 290, 303, 343, 353–65
Guilbert, P., 103
Guilhabert de Castres, 142
Guthrie, W.K.C., 173
Guyer, P., 339
Guyon, J., 268, 374
Guyot, M.T., 269

H

Haarscher, G., 70
Hadot, P., xii, xiv
Hague, R., 300–301
Haldane, 320
Hamilton, E., 67
Hanegraaf, W.J., 19
Hani, J., 94
Harder, R., 349

NAME INDEX

Harl, M., 29
Harnack, A. von, 4, 20, 137
Hausherr, I., 197, 250
Hefty, K., 374
Hegel, G. F. W., 17, 49-51, 64-104, 109, 117, 140, 157, 210
Heidegger, M., 59, 315, 360, 367, 373
Heisenberg, W., 106, 117, 273, 315
Henry, M., 374
Heracleon, 373
Herrigel, E., 74
Hilbert, D., 364
Hilduin, 265
Hippolytus (Saint), 3, 20, 31, 344
Hirsch, C., 129
Hodgson, P.C., 85
Hort, F.J.A., 332
Hugo, V., 316
Huisman, D., 114
Hull, R.F.C., 74
Husserl, E., 364
Hyppolite, J., 69, 72, 96

I
Ibn Arabi, 67, 359, 370
Ibn Gabirol, 29
Imbs, P., 268
Irenaeus of Lyon (Saint), 3, 7, 20, 29, 31, 35-37, 39, 41, 142, 231, 242, 273, 278, 329, 338, 343-44, 366
Isaac, 298
Isidore of Seville (Saint), 263

J
Jacob, 298
Jaeger, W., 276
James, M.F., 135-36, 142-44, 184, 205
James (Saint), 42, 54, 67, 231, 329
Jeanne d'Arc (Sister), 42, 329
Jerome (Saint), 208, 263
John of Damascus (Saint), 7, 164, 265, 267

John of Ragusa, 376
John of the Cross (Saint), 59, 138, 251
John Scotus (Eriugena), 55, 264-65
John the Baptist (Saint), 59, 61
John the Evangelist (Saint), 25-26, 28-30, 36, 42, 54, 56, 58-60, 67, 184, 227, 231, 238, 242, 252, 277, 310, 329, 332-35, 345, 369
Jonas, H., xii, xiv, 20, 286, 373
Juda ha-Nasi, 278
Jung, C.G., 115
Justin (Saint), 3, 376-77

K
Kant, I., 84, 95, 157, 292-93, 296, 339-40, 347
Kaufholz, E., 71
Kavanaugh, K., 251
Kenec'dhu, T., 366
Kierkegaard, S., 99, 101
Kircher, A., 374
Kittel, G., 22
Klibansky, R., xiii
Knox, T.M., 71, 85
Kojève, A., 69, 95, 99-100, 210
Koyré, A., 68-69, 83, 195
Kuntzmann, R., 19

L
Lacarrière, J., 366
La Combe, F., 268
La Curne de Sainte-Palaye, J.B., 266
La Fontaine, J. De, 373
Lafouge, J.-P., 212, 257
Lagrave, Ch., 279
Lalande, A., 219
Lamarck, J.-B. de Monet de, 301
Lambert, D., 163
Lane, H.R., 96
Langley, A.G., 195
Lanza Del Vasto, 93
Lao-Tzu, 67

Larcher, F. R., 220
Larousse, P., 140
Larre, Cl., 67, 103
Laurant, J.-P., 142–44, 207
Lawrence, G., 244
Lebreton, J., 220, 239
Leeuw, G. Van Der, 127
Lefebvre, M., 215
Legros, R., 70
Leibniz, G. W., 106, 160, 173, 195, 247, 298
Leisegang, H., 19, 37, 107
Lemaigre, B. M., 99
Le Nain de Tillemont, S., 20
Le Nourry, D., 20
Léonard, A., 19, 38, 271
Leo of Byzantium, 230
Leroux, P., 146
Leroy, P., 301
Libera, A. de, 307
Lietzmann, H., 137
Lin-chi, 103
Lings, M., 151
Littré, É., 138, 268–69
Lochak, G., 301
Louis XIV, 138
Louis XVII, 136
Lubac, H. de, 239, 302, 309
Lukacs, G., 70
Luria, I., 368, 370
Luther, M., 213, 223, 239, 314

M

MacKenna, S., 218, 349
Maharshi (Ramana), 58
Malebranche, N., 196, 255, 298, 348
Mallarmé, S., 315
Mandouze, A., 55
Marcion, 10, 108, 137, 261, 299–300, 302, 339, 343
Marcus Aurelius, 366
Margerie, B. de, 219, 244
Marignac, P., 101

Maritain, J., 95
Marquet, J.-F., 304, 374
Marrou, H. I., 376–77
Martin of Tours (Saint), 280
Marx, K., 71, 81, 372–73
Masseau, D., 268
Massignon, L., 49, 287
Massin, J., 316
Massuet, R., 20
Masui, J., 366
Matgioï, see Pouvourville
Matheson, D. M., 93 210
Mathieu, J.-M., 278
Matter, J., 138
Matthias (Apostle), 344
Maurice-Denis Boulet, N., 135, 144, 167–68, 171–72, 184
Maximus the Confessor (Saint), 248
Mayeur, J. M., 286
Mayor, J. B., 332
Méhat, A., 36, 67
Meramo, B., 283
Merleau-Ponty, J., 116
Merleau-Ponty, M., 15
Meyendorf, J., 244
Meyer, M. W., 20
Michel, A., 244
Milhaud, G., 167
Mill, J. S., 112
Miller, A. V., 75
Moehler, J. A., 277
Molay, J. de, 143
Monod, J., 117
Moreri, L., 267
Moses, 7, 58, 98, 102–3, 124, 272, 277, 343, 360
Mosheim, J. L., 20

N

Nemo, Ph., 367
Nicholson, R. C., 134
Nicolas of Cusa, 70, 248, 316

NAME INDEX

Noetus, 240
Northbourne (Lord), 52
Numenius of Apamea, 349

O
Ollier, R., 365
O'Meara, J., 264
Origen, 7, 28, 36, 40, 47, 136, 231-32, 241-42, 248, 278, 329

P
Pagels, E., 365-66
Pallis, M., 93
Panckouck, C.J., 268
Panofsky, E., xiii
Pantaenus, 377
Papus, see Encausse
Paracelsus, 374
Parmenides, 217
Parmentier, M., 96
Pascal, B., 197, 208, 294, 316
Pasteur, L., 50
Paul (Saint), xi, 7, 24-27, 29-32, 34, 38-39, 41-45, 48, 54, 56-57, 61, 141, 166, 192, 203, 262, 264, 268, 271-74, 276-77, 284, 293, 317, 324-25, 327-29, 333, 336, 338-40, 368-69
Paulhan, J., 354
Pernoud, M. and R., 94
Perry, M., 212, 257
Peter (Apostle), 24, 42, 54, 67, 225, 231, 263, 329, 369
Pétrement, S., 5, 19, 29, 37, 41, 49, 105, 108-9, 278, 287-88, 345, 349
Petri, Ch. and L., 286
Philip (Apostle), 288
Philo of Alexandria, 23, 275
Piclin, M., 126
Pigeaud, J., xiii
Places, E. des, 275
Planck, M., 315

Plato, 9, 22, 58, 66, 79, 102, 150, 152-53, 156, 217, 264, 274-76, 286, 315, 329
Plotinus, 10, 218-19, 349-50
Plutarch, 46, 360
Poirier, Ph., 288
Polit, G., 163, 213
Polycarp (Saint), 36, 242
Pomar (Duchess of), 142
Porphyry, 349
Postel, G. de, 374
Potterie, I. de la, 332
Pouvourville, A. de, 143, 207-8
Praxeas, 240
Préau, A., 360
Priscillian, 280
Proclus, 276
Proctor, R., 94
Prodicos, 36
Prucker, E., 24
Ptolemaeus (Gnostic), 373
Puech, H.-C., xii, xiv, 4, 19-20, 35, 37, 137, 284, 349
Pythagoras, 152

Q
Queneau, R., 354
Quint, J., 71
Quispel, G., 37, 349

R
Raphael, 92-94
Raulet, G., 71
Régnon, Th. de, 239
Reitzenstein, R., 24, 137
Renou, L., 182
Reuchlin, J., 376
Reussen, E., 376
Rey, A., 268
Reynolds, B.R., 71
Reyor, J., 146
Richard, M.-D., 53
Richelet, P., 266

388

Name Index

Rimbaud, A., 316
Robespierre, M. de, 358
Robin, J., 47, 142, 144–45, 151
Robin, L., 316
Robinet, I., 207
Robinson, J.M., 20
Rodriguez, O., 251
Rolland, Ph., 41
Rootes, N., 366
Roquebert, M., 142
Roques, R., 265
Rosenkranz, K., 69
Rousseau, A., 35, 278, 338
Rousseau, J.-J., 221
Rudhardt, J., 276
Rumi (Jallaludin), 51, 100
Ruyer, R., xiv, 13–14, 16, 49–51, 64, 66, 105–33, 157, 196, 257, 286–88, 302, 367–68

S

Sabellius, 212–13, 233–37, 239, 240–41
Sade, D.A. de, 44
Saffrey, H.D., 276
Sagnard, F., 373
Saint-John Perse, 316
Saint-Martin, L.-Cl., 139, 370, 374
Saint-Simon (Duc de), 138, 269
Salome, 61
Sand, G., 146
Sanderson, J.B., 71, 99
Sartre, J.-P., 80, 111, 315
Saxl, F., xiii
Schaeder, H.H., 137
Schelling, F.W., 64, 117, 304
Scholem, G., 49, 287, 367–68
Schrödinger, E., 106, 117
Schuon, F., xiv, 52, 64, 78, 93, 141, 163–64, 166, 210–58, 261, 296–97, 353–55, 357, 359, 361–62, 364
Scopello, M., 286
Seaver, R., 96

Secret, F., 376
Sernine, P., 279
Serres, M., 113
Sertillanges, A.D., 41, 163, 168
Shankara, 58, 67, 146, 159, 182, 357, 359
Sheldon-Williams, I.P., 264
Shimony, A., 129
Sigaud, P.-M., xi
Simon, T., see Pouvourville
Simon Magus, 142
Sinaceur, A., 113
Smith, M., 371
Smith, W., 301
Sohrawardî, 288, 367
Speirs, E.B., 71, 99
Spicq, C., 274, 332
Spinoza, B., 76, 100, 175, 316
Starobinski-Safran, E., 368
Stewart, J.M., 85
Stroumsa, G.G., 19, 266
Swedenborg, E., 374
Symeon the New Theologian, 40, 248
Synesius, see Fabre des Essarts

T

Tacitus, 46
Tardieu, M., 19, 37, 45, 49, 105, 110, 282, 286–87, 367–68
Taveneaux, R., 139
Teilhard de Chardin, P., xiv, 107, 157, 299–302
Tertullian, 4, 46–47, 234, 240, 329
Teyssedre, B., 88
Theodotus, 373
Theophane, T., see Champrenaud
Theophrastus, xiii
Thibaut, G., 159
Thomas (Apostle), 34–35, 284, 288
Thomas Aquinas (Saint), 17, 53, 132, 156, 162–72, 175, 178, 194, 196, 198–99, 203, 215, 217–20,

389

231, 243–45, 248, 253, 255, 265, 298, 303, 307, 309–10, 314, 321, 326, 336, 356, 358, 368
Thomas of Arezzo, 376
Thackery (S.St.J.), 46
Thelwall, S., 46
Tissier de Mallerais, B., 283
Tissot, Y., 288
Tixeront, J., 239, 280
Townsend, P.N., 210
Trévoux (Dictionnaire de), 266–67
Tronc, D. and M., 269
Turner, J.E., 127
Twinch, C., 67

U
Urs von Balthasar, H., 239

V
Valentinus, 20, 35, 49, 137, 142, 207, 261, 339, 342, 368, 373
Varlet, D.M., 206
Varro, 8
Vax, L., xi

Vénard, L., 286
Versluis, A., 374
Voegelin, E., 372–74
Vollert, C., 244
Voltaire, 139

W
Wallace, W., 51, 72
Walshe, M.O'C., 71, 103
Watson, B., 104
Weil, S., 354
Westerink, L.G., 276
Whitehead, A.N., 125
Whorf, B.L., 120
Wieger, L., 359
Wood, A.W., 339
Wunenburger, J.J., xi

Z
Zander, J., 349
Zechariah, 45, 60
Zedler, B.H., 196
Zephyrinus (Pope), 241
Zoccatelli, P.L., 184, 289

www.ingramcontent.com/pod-product-compliance
Lightning Source LLC
Chambersburg PA
CBHW020217170426
43201CB00007B/242